D0556894

5 JUL 1978

AMERICAN ENCOUNTERS/GLOBAL INTERACTIONS
A series edited by Gilbert M. Joseph and Emily S. Rosenberg

This series aims to stimulate critical perspectives and fresh interpretive frameworks for scholarship on the history of the imposing global presence of the United States. Its primary concerns include the deployment and contestation of power, the construction and deconstruction of cultural and political borders, the fluid meanings of intercultural encounters, and the complex interplay between the global and the local. American Encounters seeks to strengthen dialogue and collaboration between historians of U.S. international relations and area studies specialists. The series encourages scholarship based on multiarchival historical research. At the same time, it supports a recognition of the representational character of all stories about the past and promotes critical inquiry into issues of subjectivity and narrative. In the process, American Encounters strives to understand the context in which meanings related to nations, cultures, and political economy are continually produced, challenged, and reshaped.

KIRSTEN WELD

PAPER CADAVERS

THE ARCHIVES OF DICTATORSHIP

IN GUATEMALA

DUKE UNIVERSITY PRESS · DURHAM AND LONDON · 2014

Library of Congress Cataloging-in-Publication Data
Weld, Kirsten, 1982–
Paper cadavers : the archives of dictatorship in Guatemala / Kirsten Weld.
pages cm — (American encounters/global interactions)
Includes bibliographical references and index.
ISBN 978-0-8223-5597-7 (cloth : alk. paper)
ISBN 978-0-8223-5602-8 (pbk. : alk. paper)
1. Guatemala—Politics and government—1945–1985—Sources.
2. Guatemala. Policía Nacional. Archivo Histórico.
3. Guatemala—Relations—United States—Sources.
4. United States—Relations—Guatemala—Sources.
5. Archives—Political aspects.
I. Title. II. Series: American encounters/global interactions.
F1466.5.W45 2014
972.8105'2—dc23 2013026391

Photographs on cover and p. i by Daniel Hernández-Salazar
and used by permission of the photographer.

For the workers, past and present,
of the Proyecto para la Recuperación del
Archivo Histórico de la Policía Nacional

CONTENTS

LIST OF ABBREVIATIONS

AEU   Association of University Students, University of San Carlos (Asociación de Estudiantes Universitarios)

AFPC   Accord on the Strengthening of Civil Power and the Role of the Armed Forces in a Democratic Society (Acuerdo de Fortaleci-miento del Poder Civil y Función del Ejército en una Sociedad Democrática)

AGCA   General Archives of Central America (Archivo General de Centroamérica)

AGSAEMP   Archives and Support Services of the Presidential General Staff (Archivos Generales y Servicios Apoyados del Estado Mayor Presidencial)

AHPN   Historical Archives of the National Police (Archivo Histórico de la Policía Nacional)

AID   Agency for International Development

ARENA   Nationalist Republican Alliance, El Salvador (Alianza Republicana Nacionalista)

AVEMILGUA   Association of Military Veterans of Guatemala (Asociación de Veteranos Militares de Guatemala)

BIEN   Special Investigations and Narcotics Brigade (Brigada de Investiga-ciones Especiales y Narcóticos)

BROE   Special Operations Reaction Brigade (Brigada de Reacción de Operaciones Especiales)

CACIF   Coordinating Committee of Agricultural, Commercial, Industrial, and Financial Associations (Comité Coordinador de Asociaciones Agrícolas, Comerciales, Industriales, y Financieras)

CADEG   Anti-Communist Council of Guatemala (Consejo Anticomunista de Guatemala)

CCI   International Advisory Board, Project for the Recovery of the National Police Historical Archives (Consejo Consultivo Internacional)

CCN   National Advisory Board, Project for the Recovery of the National Police Historical Archives (Consejo Consultivo Nacional)

CEH	Commission for Historical Clarification (Comisión de Esclarecimiento Histórico)
CEM	Center for Military Studies (Centro de Estudios Militares)
CICIG	International Commission Against Impunity in Guatemala (Comisión Internacional Contra la Impunidad en Guatemala)
CNT	National Workers' Central (Central Nacional de Trabajadores)
CNUS	National Committee on Trade Union Unity (Comité Nacional de Unidad Sindical)
COCP	Joint Operations Center of the National Police (Centro de Operaciones Conjuntas)
COE	Special Operations Commando (Comando de Operaciones Especiales)
CRIO	Regional Telecommunications Center (Centro de Reunión de Información y Operaciones)
CUC	Campesino Unity Committee (Comité de Unidad Campesina)
DGPN	Director-General of the National Police
DIC	Department of Criminal Investigations
DINC	Criminal Investigations Division (División de Investigación Criminal)
DIT	Department of Technical Investigations
DNSA	Digital National Security Archive
EGP	Guerrilla Army of the Poor (Ejército Guerrillero de los Pobres)
EMDN	National Defense General Staff (Estado Mayor de la Defensa Nacional)
EMGE	Army General Staff (Estado Mayor General del Ejército)
EMP	Presidential Staff (Estado Mayor Presidencial)
ESA	Secret Anti-Communist Army (Ejército Secreto Anticomunista)
FAFG	Forensic Anthropology Foundation of Guatemala (Fundación de Antropología Forense de Guatemala)
FAMDEGUA	Association of the Families of the Detained and Disappeared in Guatemala (Asociación de Familiares de Detenidos-Desaparecidos de Guatemala)
FAR	Rebel Armed Forces (Fuerzas Armadas Rebeldes)
FERG	Robin García Student Front (Frente Estudiantil Robin García)
FRG	Guatemalan Republican Front (Frente Republicano Guatemalteco)
FUR	United Revolutionary Front (Frente Unido de la Revolución)
GAM	Mutual Support Group (Grupo de Apoyo Mutuo)
GOG	Government of Guatemala

HIJOS	Sons and Daughters for Identity and Justice and Against Forgetting and Silence (Hijos e Hijas por la Identidad y la Justicia y Contra el Olvido y el Silencio)
HRDAG	Human Rights Data Analysis Group
ICA	International Cooperation Administration
ICITAP	U.S. Criminal Investigations Training Assistance Program
IIAA	Institute of Inter-American Affairs
INTA	National Institute for Agrarian Transformation (Instituto Nacional de Transformación Agraria)
ISAAR	International Standard Archival Authority Record
ISAD(G)	International Standard for Archival Description (General)
JPT	Patriotic Workers' Youth (Juventud Patriótica de Trabajo)
MINUGUA	United Nations Verification Mission in Guatemala
MLN	Movement of National Liberation
MONAP	National Movement of Pobladores (Movimiento Nacional de Pobladores)
MP	Public Ministry
NOA	New Anti-Communist Organization (Nueva Organización Anticomunista)
ODHAG	Human Rights Office of the Archbishop of Guatemala (Oficina de Derechos Humanos del Arzobispado de Guatemala)
OPS	Office of Public Safety
ORPA	Revolutionary Organization of People in Arms
PAC	Civil Self-Defense Patrols (Patrullas de Autodefensa Civil)
PDH	Human Rights Ombudsman's Office (Procuraduría de los Derechos Humanos)
PGT	Guatemalan Workers' Party (Partido Guatemalteco de Trabajo)
PMA	Mobile Military Police (Policía Militar Ambulante)
PN	National Police
PNC	National Civil Police
PR	Revolutionary Party
PRAHPN	Project for the Recovery of the National Police Historical Archives (Proyecto para la Recuperación del Archivo Histórico de la Policía Nacional)
PSD	Social Democratic Party
PSP	Public Safety Program
REMHI	Interdiocesan Project for the Recuperation of Historical Memory (Proyecto Interdiocesano de Recuperación de la Memoria Histórica)

RMU	Master Location Registry (Registro Maestro de Ubicación)
SCUGA	Special Commando Unit (Unidad de Comando Especial del Ejército de Guatemala)
SEDEM	Security in Democracy
SEPAZ	Presidential Peace Secretariat (Secretaría de la Paz de la Presidencia de la República)
SIC	Criminal Investigations Section (Sección de Investigaciones Criminales)
SIPROCI	Civilian Protection System (Sistema de Protección Civil)
STUSC	University of San Carlos Employees' Union (Sindicato de Trabajadores de la Universidad de San Carlos)
UAE	Special Investigations Unit, Human Rights Ombudsman's Office (Unidad de Averiguaciones Especiales)
URNG	Guatemalan National Revolutionary Unity (Unidad Revolucionaria Nacional Guatemalteca)
USAC	University of San Carlos
USAID	United States Agency for International Development

| ACKNOWLEDGMENTS

I n *All the Names*, José Saramago conjures the labyrinthine archives of an un-
named city, its grim Central Registry of Births, Marriages, and Deaths. The
registry's musty depths are populated only by an archon—the all-powerful
Registrar—and the beleaguered clerks at his service. Such was the abiding
disorder and dereliction there that from time to time a bumbling researcher
would fall victim to the archives; one lost soul, a genealogist unable to find his
way back to the main desk, was only discovered, "almost miraculously, after
a week, starving, thirsty, exhausted, delirious, having survived thanks to the
desperate measure of ingesting enormous quantities of old documents." In
response, the Registrar, who had written the wayward genealogist off as dead,
did what bureaucrats do best: he issued an internal order. Thereafter, to avoid
other such unsavory incidents, it would be "obligatory, at the risk of incurring
a fine and a suspension of salary, for everyone going into the archive of the
dead to make use of Ariadne's thread."[1]

The notion of Ariadne's thread ties this work together in several ways. As
a methodology intended precisely for solving problems that suggest multiple
manners of proceeding, it pushed me to embrace inter- and multidisciplinary
approaches in tackling the National Police archives as a site of analysis. As a
metaphor, it could not be better suited to thinking about a sprawling warren
of records whose rescuers call its decaying storage facility *el laberinto* (while
the facility's former occupants, who used the space as a torture and detention
center, termed it *la isla*). Above all, though, the idea of Ariadne's thread serves
me best as a way of visualizing the lifeline—constituted by a dense network
of relationships, love, and solidarity—that has enabled me to navigate the archives of the dead.

First, I thank the archivists, who too often are left for last and upon whose
perspectives and labor this project relied. Chief among them were Thelma
Porres and her staff at the Centro de Investigaciones Regionales de Mesoamérica; Thelma Mayen de Pérez and her staff at the archives of the Tipografía
Nacional; Anna Carla Ericastilla, the director of the Archivo General de Centroamérica, a voice of reason and a friend; and, at the National Police archives,

Ingrid Molina and Lizbeth Barrientos. Anna Carla, Ingrid, and Lizbeth were themselves actors in the story I am about to tell, but their good sense and ideas also contributed to my approach in telling it. And Trudy Huskamp Peterson— tireless and engaged, the globetrotting gonzo archivist extraordinaire—enriched this study in more ways than I can name. I hope she will forgive the artistic license I have taken over the years in translating her discipline's foundational concepts both into Spanish and into this book.

In Guatemala, I was fortunate to draw upon the expertise of still more wise women: Tani Adams and Marcie Mersky, who gave me thoughtful advice at the early stages of this project, and Kate Doyle, a valued comrade and mentor without whom I would never have been granted anything approaching the access I enjoyed to the police archives. The fact that the Project's leaders accepted this stranger into their midst as warmly as they did, on Kate's voucher alone, is a testament to the invaluable work done by Kate and her colleagues at the National Security Archive. At the Project, many of those individuals whose commitment and friendship I most appreciate cannot be named here for confidentiality reasons. But some can: Gustavo Meoño and Carla Villagrán let me join their fledgling archival rescue initiative in early 2006, granting me nearly unfettered access to the internal workings of the Project along with their trust, which this work hopefully bears out. Alberto Fuentes urged me to focus on young workers' experiences of laboring in the archives. Enmy Morán provided an example of how academic historians' skills can be brought to bear upon contemporary political concerns, and I thank her for her friendship. Most of all, I thank the Project's rank-and-file workers for welcoming me as a *compañera*—especially the members of the 2006 historical investigations team and the 2007 Joint Operations Center table team, alongside whom I worked most closely. I am always moved by their tenacity and dedication to imagining a different future for their country. Other friends and colleagues outside the Project offered ideas, comfort, and camaraderie: Laura Arriaza, Míchel Andrade, Edeliberto Cifuentes, Iduvina Hernández, and Mario Castañeda. Thanks, too, to the talented photographer-activists whose images appear in this book: James Rodríguez, Jean-Marie Simon, and Daniel Hernández-Salazar, who work to make visible what Guatemala's powerful would prefer to obscure.

As I imagined and executed this project, Stuart Schwartz and Carlota McAllister offered constructive criticism, sound advice, and good cheer when it was most needed. Greg Grandin accompanied me on this venture from the moment of its inception, and along the way he taught me about power, about Guatemala, and about engaged scholarship. Michael Denning is a boundless reservoir of creative thinking and practical ideas, ever ready to turn a writing problem on its head in unexpected ways; I have benefited so much from his engagement with my work. And Gil Joseph is an incomparable mentor, fan, editor, friend, and sage. He was at my side at every step, and I am proud to be part of the generation of historians he has trained. More recently, Silvia Arrom, June Erlick, Joe Tulchin, Liz Oglesby, Jean-Marie Simon, Diane Nelson, and several anonymous peer reviewers read the manuscript and gave generous, indispensable feedback. Dagmar Hovestädt and Günter Bormann facilitated my enlightening visit to the Stasi archives in Berlin. My research and writing were supported by the Social Sciences and Humanities Research Council of Canada, the International Dissertation Research Fellowship program at the Social Science Research Council, Yale's Council on Latin American and Iberian Studies, Yale's MacMillan Center for International and Area Studies, the Andrew W. Mellon Foundation, and the Florence Levy Kay Fellowship in Latin American History at Brandeis University, where I was lucky enough to have Jane Kamensky and Silvia Arrom as mentors. The Harvard University History Department and the David Rockefeller Center for Latin American Studies have been most genial home bases from which to complete the process of crafting this book, a process expertly and empathically guided by the inimitable Valerie Millholland and Gisela Fosado at Duke University Press. Of course, as the refrain goes, any flaws in the final product are mine alone.

In New Haven, where this book was born, I shared dreams, frustrations, and bourbon with dear friends. My warmest thanks go to Caitlin Casey, Steve Prince, Julia Irwin, David Huyssen, Louise Walker, Jesse Franzblau, Alison Bruey, Lisa Pinley Covert, the 2005–2007 members of the Working Group on Globalization and Culture, Jack Hitt, Christopher York, Ezer Vierba, Jeffrey Boyd, the Connecticut Center for a New Economy, and the Graduate Employees and Students' Organization (GESO) at Yale, whose long and ongoing fight for recognition made my graduate school experience both possible and worthwhile. My New York Bureau—Patrick Guyer, Holly Beck, Seth Prins, and company— launched me on many overnight and early-morning flights to Central America. The world's best *suegros*, Susan and René Aramayo, helped me with footnotes (Susan) and cured the archivist's lung with which I would invariably return from Guatemala afflicted (René). Jesse, Louise, Susan, Lisa, and particularly David and Jeffrey read parts of this work in its earlier incarnations and offered a raft of suggestions for its improvement; David also provided critical last-minute help with editing and sources. As for my friends and family from back home in Canada, I thank Kate Lunau, Esmé Webb, Daniel Aldana Cohen, Jonah Gindin, Nick Hune-Brown, Krista Stout, Megan Dunkley, Wayne

Nadler, Lisa Nadler, David Wachsmuth, Sylvie Nicholson, Michael Wernikowski, Maxime Rousseaux, Sophie Rousseaux, Phoebe Rousseaux, and Judith Rae for their love, thoughts, and/or engagement with this project in various forms and at various times. It was Judith who, innocently, first brought me to Guatemala, not knowing at the time that she was setting me upon a much longer journey. And throughout, I have counted on the backing and hearty encouragement of my parents, Howard and Suzanne.

Finally, I thank Carlos Roy Aramayo, whose incomparable intellect, unerring revolutionary ethics, and irrepressible goofiness make every single one of my days better. Always with me as we navigate life, the universe, and everything, Carlos truly is my Ariadne's thread.

I n the dark of a restless night during the late 1970s, a young Guatemalan named Raúl Perera shot into wakefulness from a dream so unusual that he remembers it vividly thirty-five years later. He cannot quite recall the date. He knows that it was after he joined the Guatemalan Workers' Party (PGT), the outlawed communist party, and became a vocal leader of his Guatemala City trade union, but before the two attempts on his life that left a bullet scar along his forearm, a close friend dead, and no option for him but to begin a long exile in Mexico. Amid years of activism and war, that one night has haunted Raúl ever since because it brought him a vision so fantastical that it verged on the absurd. That night, his subconscious granted him entrance to a forbidden space: the archives kept by his country's feared National Police.[1]

Once inside, Raúl crept along the archives' labyrinthine corridors in the crepuscular light. He yanked open drawers and thumbed through file folders thick with surveillance photographs of loved ones and reports detailing informants' infiltration of leftist groups. He mined the files, learning how the police organized its death squads, what sorts of information they collected on citizens, and what could be gleaned about the fates of disappeared comrades. In Raúl's waking life—which he spent dodging, not courting, the attention of state security forces—such acts would have been inconceivable transgressions, sure to be met with lethal retribution. Generations of dictators and elites had long directed the National Police (PN) to suppress not only organized resistance but any and all forms of oppositional thinking, eventually using it to help execute the Cold War counterinsurgency campaign for which Guatemala will always be notorious. During that campaign, police administered spy networks; they crushed demonstrations; they did the dirty work of generals and political leaders; they followed, abducted, tortured, and killed. With a terrifying blend of clumsiness and zeal, they targeted schoolteachers, students, progressive priests, peasant farmers, social democratic politicians, street children, and Marxist revolutionaries alike. Raúl was hardly the only Guatemalan whose reveries the police tormented.

So it seemed unreal when, decades later, he found himself inside the police's archives once more. This time, however, it was no dream. "The very color of the pages, the fonts, and everything about the documents in my dream turned out to be exactly how they looked in real life," Raúl reflected incredulously after several years' work on a pathbreaking initiative to put the once-secret police records at the service of postwar justice.[2] In a serendipitous coup that none had ever imagined possible, a small contingent of human rights activists had gained access to the National Police's long-lost archives. Investigators from Guatemala's Human Rights Ombudsman's Office (PDH), while conducting an unrelated inspection on police property in July 2005, stumbled upon what seemed to be vast quantities of old papers. After surveying the sprawling warehouse—a former detention and torture center once known as *la isla* (the island), with spattered cinderblock walls and cell-like inner chambers—and navigating its maze of rooms piled high with bundles of moldy records dating back more than a century, the investigators realized that they had uncovered the largest collection of secret state documents in Latin American history.[3]

The news spread quickly in a country still deeply divided after nearly four decades of brutal counterinsurgent warfare, but the discovery raised more questions and controversies than it resolved. How would the find—an estimated eighty million decaying pages—be managed? Who would have control over this potentially explosive cache of records, believed to contain damning evidence of state abuses from an era of forced disappearances, political assassinations, and genocide? Could these archives offer a new chance at postwar reckoning, which remained stalled more than a decade after the end of a conflict that took the lives of as many as 200,000 citizens?[4]

Raúl was among the first members of a tiny team, soon to grow, that took stock of the find. Its members would take on the arduous task of sorting through the half-rotten, disordered heaps of paper, hoping to rescue a dark portion of their nation's past. Grasping for a manageable place to start, the earliest archival recovery volunteers began by rescuing a huge mound of personal identity cards that lay decomposing in a half-completed room at the building's rear. The majority of the 250,000 cards had survived, but only because sun and water exposure had transformed those at the top of the pile into a tough papier-mâché crust that protected the others beneath. As Raúl sifted through more and more records, on his hands and knees alongside fellow activists clad in face masks and rubber gloves, he routinely stumbled upon the names of friends and acquaintances now alive only in archives and memories. He did not know that a Central American archivist decades earlier had described such documents as "paper cadavers" in need of "resurrection," but he would have found the metaphor almost painfully apt; in some cases, the archives revealed companions' fates for the first time.[5] It was difficult labor, made no easier by the arson attempts and death threats that periodically reminded the volunteers of the real risks still faced in Guatemala by those seeking to unearth the war's history.

How had these mountains of paper, with all the power and social control they represented, never been destroyed? Why were they all but abandoned, yet still deemed threatening enough for the Guatemalan government to keep them secret from postwar truth commission investigators? Raúl's life story—his past and present encounters with the police and its archives in dreams and in life—encapsulated a tumultuous and unsettled half century of Guatemalan history. How had this political exile, after some thirty years of struggle and failed revolution, found himself in the company of others like him, using the files of their former victimizers as part of an unprecedented effort to rewrite history? And would their collective effort finally yield justice?

People study history in order to participate in contemporary politics; we recover the past in order to look to the future. As such, documents, archives, and historical knowledge are more than just the building blocks of politics—they are themselves sites of contemporary political struggle. We argue and disagree, ardently, about history. We interpret the same documents and events in myriad, divergent ways. We push for state records to be made public, decry their censorship, and support those whistle-blowers and document-leakers punished for violating the presumed sanctity of the state secret.[6] And while we can build consensus around the notion that we must learn from the past in order to avoid repeating our forebears' errors, we spar openly over that past and, especially, over who should bear the blame for those errors. The adjudication of history has serious consequences, including the payment of reparations, the offering of official apologies following atrocities, the settlement of land claims, and the integrity of national identities. This means that our engagement with history, whether or not in a professional capacity, is always suffused with our own ideological inclinations, personal interests, and present-day political ends.

This is all the more true for those communities in which matters of historical interpretation have immediate real-world stakes, such as the Guatemalan activists whose lives and labor form the subject of this book. As E. P. Thompson once wrote, "Experience walks in without knocking at the door, and announces deaths, crises of subsistence, trench warfare, unemployment, inflation, genocide. . . . In the face of such general experiences old conceptual systems may crumble and new problematics insist upon their presence."[7] In an unstable postwar Guatemala, the surprising appearance of the National Police archives presented all manner of new problematics, requiring new conceptual systems with which to confront them. Aging police and military officials implicated in war crimes walked free, enjoying impunity and ongoing political power, while the fates of thousands of citizens remained unknown. In such a context, the amateur historians exhuming this past had no choice but to get down to work, and the new conceptual system they developed for reckoning with the documents combined historical research, courtroom litigation, technical archival science, and impassioned advocacy. In the process, they set a model of political engagement with the past, one that channeled the spirit of an observation by anthropologist Michel-Rolph Trouillot: "No amount of historical research about the Holocaust and no amount of guilt about Germany's past can serve as a substitute for marching in the streets against German skinheads today."[8]

This book analyzes how the sudden reappearance of seventy-five million pages of once-secret police documents impacted the volatile Guatemalan political scene, bringing a historian's eye to bear upon how postwar activists use historical research and archives precisely as a way of marching in the streets today. During the peace process in the mid-1990s, then president Alvaro Arzú and his administration denied that any police archives existed. Arzú, defense minister Héctor Barrios Celada, and interior minister Rodolfo Mendoza stonewalled the United Nations–sponsored Historical Clarification Commission (CEH) charged with investigating the country's 1960–1996 civil war.[9] In theory, and according to the terms of the 1996 Peace Accords, the CEH had the right to access military and police records for its investigation. In practice, however, its petitions for access were summarily denied, and the CEH was forced to proceed without any documentation from the Guatemalan state.[10] The police archives, therefore, were a political bombshell, because while victims' families had long been armed with what Gloria Alberti terms "archives of pain"—the watchdog reports and testimonies of state violence amassed by human rights nongovernmental organizations and other nonstate actors—they had never before had large-scale access to "archives of terror," namely, the records used by state perpetrators.[11]

The archives' discovery renewed a national conversation about historical memory and transitional justice. It also provoked violent opposition from conservative sectors seeking to prevent the documents from coming to light.

Today, a foreign-funded activist initiative called the Project for the Recovery of the National Police Historical Archives (PRAHPN), hereafter "the Project," is rescuing the decaying records and analyzing their contents, with the aim of generating evidence to use in prosecuting war-era officials for crimes against humanity. Over time, the Project grew from its improvisational beginnings into a precedent-setting effort armed with hundreds of staff, state-of-the-art technology, and support from around the world.

It also operated from a position of political commitment; the Project's coordinator was a former guerrilla commander, and its work was animated by the goal of reframing the official narrative about the war—what Elizabeth Jelin has called the "master narrative of the nation"—that had been promoted for years by its victors.[12] This military-backed version of history held, not to put too fine a point on it, that state security forces heroically defended the fatherland from the evils of Soviet-sponsored communism. Lives lost along the way, the story went, were those of naive youngsters brainwashed by vulgar Marxism, who would have done better to stay at home (*se habían metido en algo*), or else of terrorists who deserved what they got and worse still. In this telling, if a high school student distributing leaflets for a leftist student group ended up as yet another defiled corpse with its tongue cut out and hands severed, dumped in a ravine or mass grave, the student had brought it upon herself. It tarred trade unionists, students, and peasant activists as traitors, deviants, and *vendepatrias* subservient to foreign ideologies.[13] But this interpretation could neither bury survivors' contradictory memories nor quell their expectations that a purportedly democratic state should offer at least an opportunity at justice. If the postwar project of building a democratic society where one had never existed was to succeed, this paean to the armed forces could no longer be its foundation myth.

In such a setting, the (re)writing of history *is* politics—politics with a definite sense of urgency, as statistical indicators unanimously warn that postwar Guatemala finds itself in an "emergency situation."[14] The country's major twenty-first-century preoccupations (inequality, violence, impunity, Maya disenfranchisement, out-migration) are driven by unresolved historical grievances: crimes not solved, socioeconomic disparities not redressed, power not redistributed, and perpetrators unprosecuted.[15] Only 2 or 3 percent of *all* crimes, political or common, are prosecuted at all.[16] And so history is lived as an open wound. Those who have plumbed its depths know all too well how *el delito de pensar* (the crime of thinking) invites punishment from those who would turn the page on the past and foreclose certain visions of the future.[17]

With the weak state scarcely able to protect its citizens' health and safety, entrenched affinity groups—oligarchs, business elites, foreign agro-export and mineral extraction interests, and the military—have made the resulting power vacuum their own jealously guarded domain. The question today for reformers, and regional systems like the Inter-American Court of Human Rights, is: How to dislodge them?[18] The Guatemalan military explicitly conceived the country's mid-1980s transition to procedural democracy as a counterinsurgency strategy; wartime power structures were never dismantled. Newer human rights organizations struggled to carve out spaces for debate in a crippled postwar society that was democratic in little more than name.[19] After the accords, these organizations focused on chipping away at a deeply corrupt political system, with results ranging from unforeseen successes—for example, the hard-won conviction of Bishop Juan Gerardi's murderers—to, more commonly, disheartening failures, particularly in security reform.[20] Framed against such a bleak landscape, a forgotten warehouse filled with rotting administrative documents seems an unlikely motor for substantive change.

But as with all tools, the archives' utility derives entirely from the manner of their application. This book seeks to make sense of the archives' importance in both the past and the present, investigating how these documents acquired their power and how they are being reimagined in a very delicate postwar setting. Though the documentary collection is composed of one physical set of papers, those papers have at different historical moments represented two distinct *archival logics*—two organizing principles, or two reasons for being. The first logic was one of surveillance, social control, and ideological management, a Cold War–inflected logic that used archives as a weapon against enemies of the state. The second logic, emerging from the records' rescue, is one of democratic opening, historical memory, and the pursuit of justice for war crimes—again using archives as a weapon, but to very different ends. I analyze how the varied uses to which Guatemalans have put these records over time—the evolution from the first archival logic to the second—offer a narrative arc that maps onto the country's broader transition from war to an unstable peace.[21] (In so doing, I suggest that we must expand the conventional chronology by which we define the Cold War, because in various parts of Latin America, such as Chile and Argentina, electoral politics and judicial cultures remain strongly colored by that period's legacies.)

Trouillot writes that the word "history" has two vernacular, mutually dependent meanings: the first refers to the materiality of the sociohistorical process ("that which happened," or what historians write *about*); the second refers to the past, present, and future narratives that are produced about it ("that which is said to have happened," or what historians *write*).[22] In this book, I explore these meanings and their interrelation. For example, did genocide happen in Guatemala—as the CEH and, in 2013, a Guatemalan court ruled—or is it only *said* to have happened? How would one go about proving it? Those accused of crimes against humanity have long argued that *no hubo genocidio*; as the website of Guatemala's Association of Military Veterans (AVEMILGUA) proclaims, "There are those who feel the need to manipulate history in order to justify their crimes and treasonously implicate those who prevented their terrorist plans from being realized. . . . They only disinform, and the truth will never change."[23] The police archives' reappearance, however, destabilized such confident claims. For the first time since formal peace was struck, human rights activists had access to abundant documentary evidence in the state's own hand, though they faced the risks of conflating "history" with a description of crimes and victims. In tracking how these activists made use of these documents—how they exhumed this mass grave filled with paper cadavers—this book not only details how the messy process of history-writing and rewriting functions but also makes an argument about why it matters.

THAT WHICH HAPPENED, OR, "*SÍ HUBO GENOCIDIO*"

Each year, the small town of Sumpango Sacatepéquez celebrates Day of the Dead with a festival of giant kites handmade from tissue paper and bamboo rods.[24] The round kites, the largest of which span an impressive six meters in diameter, are intricate works of art, labored over for months by all-male teams of community members late each night after their days in the field. From afar, the festival appears whimsical: the translucent kites' vivid colors shot through with sunlight, their tasseled edges ruffled by mountain breezes. Thousands of visitors crowd Sumpango's dusty soccer pitch, waiting for the climactic moment when all but the very grandest kites are taken down from their display mountings and flown. Each kite-building team sends its own opus aloft, with as many as five or six young men straining to control their creations with long ropes; the competition is fierce, but all in good fun. The beautiful kites are effectively destroyed in the process, half a year's work torn apart in a few delirious seconds. Once the prizes are handed out, the community celebrates with live music and cold Gallo beer.

The gaiety of the festival masks a dark obverse. Many of the kites appear brightly hued and merry at a distance, but upon closer inspection they depict detailed images of loss and suffering inspired by Mayan experiences of the war. "Guatemala weeps and struggles, searching for its peace," read one kite; it showed three generations of indigenous women standing in horror before three men's machete-slashed corpses whose raw tendons and bones lay exposed. Another's imagery stretched back to the Conquest. Beneath a tableau of Spanish conquistadors torturing captured Mayan warriors and burning pages of hieroglyphic script, it read: "They burned our codices and killed our people, but the flame of our culture was not extinguished; it continues burning." Yet another bore images of four weeping women, each captioned: "Pain, Sorrow, Loneliness" framed the topmost woman's weathered face, and below the profiles to the left and the right appeared "Poverty, Insult, Mistreatment" and "Violence, Insecurity, Crime." But it was the 2007 festival's most visually stunning kite, a many-pointed star adorned with swirling licks of color and patterns evocative of the *alfombra* carpets lain during Guatemala's Easter Week, which featured the most arresting message. "To be born in this immense world filled with evil is simply to begin to die," it proclaimed above dramatic, Dalí-inspired renderings of winged demons hovering, spectral humans locked in a desperate embrace, and a bleeding world cleaved in twain. "Guatemala," the kite affirmed, "lives under the shadows of death."[25] (See fig. Intro1.)

Death and violence in Guatemala are more than artistic metaphors; they are daily realities that hover uncomfortably close to life. Historically, the country's salient features have been a dramatically unequal distribution of wealth, a semifeudal labor system in which elites forcibly conscripted indigenous peasants into debt peonage on farms producing goods for export, a profound anti-Indian racism (though the census still classifies more than half the population as "indigenous"), and a long tradition of dictatorship.[26] Popular protest and a general strike deposed the tyrant Jorge Ubico and brought, in 1944, a decade of political opening, free elections, and economic redistribution referred to as the Revolutionary Spring.[27] It was short-lived. In 1954, the Central Intelligence Agency (CIA), fearing the spread of Soviet-sponsored communism and wanting to protect U.S. economic interests, worked with revanchist local elites to oust the progressive reformist president, Jacobo Arbenz.[28] A new military dictator, Carlos Castillo Armas, was flown into Guatemala on a U.S. embassy airplane to take Arbenz's place, ushering in decades of antidemocratic rule. As U.S. assistance flowed into military and police coffers, unrest over successive regimes' crusades against not just the tiny Marxist left but also unions, universities, churches, peasant cooperatives, and journalists exploded into rebellion during the 1960s and 1970s.[29] Four insurgent groups—the Rebel Armed Forces (FAR), the Guerrilla Army of the Poor (EGP), the Revolutionary Organization of People in Arms (ORPA), and the Guatemalan Workers' Party (PGT)—attempted to mobilize first urban and then mass rural support for revolution against an increasingly murderous state.[30] They united in 1982 under the banner of the Guatemalan National Revolutionary

FIG. INTRO1 Kite from the Sumpango Sacatepéquez Day of the Dead festival in 2007. It reads, "Guatemala lives under the shadows of death. To be born in this immense world filled with evil is simply to begin to die." Photograph by author.

Unity (URNG).[31] These groups, and anyone deemed to be their allies—trade unionists, students, Mayas—were defined as "internal enemies" and became the targets of a coordinated counterinsurgency effort on the part of the military, police, and paramilitary death squads, with the country's elites using Cold War rhetoric to justify a full-spectrum campaign against any form of democratic opening.[32] When all was said and done, the army and police, fortified with foreign guns, technical expertise, and political cover, crushed the weak insurgency and killed or disappeared tens of thousands of civilians.[33] The terms of the Peace Accords, only halfheartedly and partially implemented, were a better reflection of the insurgency's near-total destruction than of the victors' will to enact change.[34]

The bloodbath in the highlands provoked outrage among observers, many of whom sought to contribute by documenting the crimes to which they bore witness.[35] Rigoberta Menchú's testimonial memoir, as well as many hundreds of reports by human rights organizations both inside and outside of Guatemala, sought not only to publicize rural violence but to stop it from continuing. Mindful of ongoing repression within the country and the heat of Cold War anticommunism in the international sphere, these early reports necessarily minimized guerrilla and militant politics in order to make the more immediately pressing case about crimes against humanity; the narrative was simplified, stripped to the heart of the matter (army violence against unaffiliated Maya civilians), and framed to make the maximum possible impact upon the U.S. Congress, interested world citizens, and foreign governments. This version of the story, one so appalling that it stuck in the minds of people around the world, was an important political tool. Moreover, it was true, and it was substantiated over time by a wealth of forensic and testimonial evidence.[36]

It was not, however, the entire story. Not only did it tend to collapse the complexity of the war into a single type of victim (Maya), a single perpetrator (the military), and a single theater (the countryside), it stripped the dead of agency.[37] In the postwar period, it produced the ahistorical suggestion that, as Carlota McAllister writes, "to be counted as victims of the war, Maya had to be innocent not only of any crime but also of any political agenda."[38] Scholars and researchers both foreign and local have since amply deepened and expanded our understandings of this complex conflict, but the sound-bite version of the war tends, still, to reflect just a few takeaway points: genocidal military, apolitical Mayas, rural massacres.[39]

This study has a different focus. The institutional perpetrator explored here is the National Police—a wartime actor so understudied that mention of it barely even appears in most accounts—and the theater of conflict examined, both in wartime and in peacetime, is Guatemala City.[40] Founded in 1881 by liberal dictator Justo Rufino Barrios, the PN tied existing bands of urban gendarmes and rural night watchmen into a more cohesive corps that, alongside the military, defended the interests of private capital. Two of its early directors were U.S. citizens—José H. Pratt of the New York Police Department and Gustavo Joseph of the Washington, DC, Metropolitan Police Force—who, foreshadowing the 1950s, were brought in to help with professionalization and training. The historical record's silence on the PN can be partly explained by several factors: first, of course, that there were no police records available for would-be researchers to use until 2005; second, the common understanding that the counterinsurgency's primary architects and executors were the military, not the police. The first factor contributed directly to the perception of the second; while the military was indeed decisively in charge, the police were still involved in many of the conflict's defining crimes, which Guatemalans knew well at the time. Third, the emergence of the Maya movement over the course of the 1980s and 1990s stimulated interest in writing about the Maya experience of the war, and indeed, Mayas—including politically mobilized

Mayas, as Carlota McAllister, Betsy Konefal, and others have shown—made up a majority of the war's dead, raped, and displaced.[41] This led researchers to the rural areas where the military's massacres were concentrated, away from the urban centers that were the police's main theater of operations.

There is also a fourth factor, one that brings us back to the political nature of historical interpretation. The war in Guatemala City involved a different kind of violence—a surgical, targeted repression against specific sectors of civil society and popular movements—and often, consequently, a different kind of victim. Many of the forty-five thousand Guatemalans who disappeared during the war had lived and agitated in the capital city. They were trade unionists, schoolteachers, antipoverty campaigners, labor lawyers, radical students, Communist Party members, reformist politicians, liberation theology–influenced clergy, organizers and fund-raisers for the insurgency, and yes, in not a few cases, armed insurgents themselves.[42] The urban counterinsurgency, which featured heavy National Police participation, inflicted disproportionate repression upon thousands of city dwellers whose only crime was to be a student, a union member, or a victim's family member searching for her lost sister or son. It also, however, pursued sectors of society radicalized into fighting and fighting back, self-consciously and passionately, for revolution. Urban insurgents blew up police stations and supply convoys, assassinated police and military officials, and carried out high-profile kidnappings to draw attention to their cause and—they hoped—destabilize the state. Popular movement activists, organized in labor and student federations, decried the escalation of state repression and called openly for regime change. They died for it, and they should not have. They were well aware, however, that they might, and they knew that their police files would grow thicker with each passing day of their foreshortened lives. Around the University of San Carlos in the early 1980s, student leaders would half-jestingly ask each other, "¿A quién le toca mañana?" (Whose turn will it be [to die] tomorrow?). It was an admission that they knew what they were getting into, believed in what they stood for, and, for better or worse, were willing to become martyrs to their cause.[43]

The war's victims were not only, we now know, apolitical cannon fodder, nor was the U.S.-backed military the only agent of repression, nor did the entire conflict unfold in the *altiplano*. Yet these other components of the story have been comparatively little told in the war's aftermath, leaving us with a peculiar paradox: though the police's counterinsurgent role and the importance of the war's urban stages were well understood at the time—as documented in press and popular movement reports—both of these dynamics have largely disappeared from subsequent accounts. The discovery of the PN archives therefore promises a wealth of opportunities for new analyses and understandings—about the police's responsibility for war crimes, about urban social movements, about the geography of insurgency, about the institutional and social history of the police and its agents, about changing conceptions of crime and criminality over time, and more. Also, because of the toll taken by forced disappearance in Guatemala City, hopes run high, perhaps dangerously so, that the archives will help bereaved family members to learn what became of their loved ones, and to prosecute those responsible.

As the records are cleaned, reordered, and digitized—as of January 2013, some fifteen million pages of the total seventy-five million had been thus preserved—these and other stories will be written and rewritten. The Project's publication of a hard-hitting investigative report, *Del silencio a la memoria*, in 2011 represented an important first thrust. Other voices from the archives are emerging in various forms, including undergraduate theses written by young Guatemalans interested in excavating their country's past. By working toward the passage of a new national archives system law, building new diploma programs in archival science and human rights at the national university, sharing its technical means and expertise with other arms of government and NGOs seeking to preserve their own records, and collaborating on standing war crimes cases, the Project has argued for archives to occupy a new and different role in national culture—and, hence, for a different and slightly more equitable relationship between citizens and the state. By changing the way Guatemala archived, the Project sought to change the way Guatemalans lived.[44]

It is this trajectory of continuity and change that I have sought to document. Consequently, although this work treats the PN's structural history and the war in Guatemala City at significant length, it does not purport to be a complete social history of the police. Rather, I use the archives as a conceptual bridge with which to connect two very different periods of political ferment: the armed conflict, and the attempts to grapple with its legacies. As mentioned earlier, the PN archives have at different times represented two distinct archival logics, one of wartime social control and the other of postwar truth claims and democratic opening. The historical evolution of the first logic into the next parallels the transition from formal conflict to contractual peace (*paz pactada*). I therefore tell the history of the archives as a way of telling the history of the war, and I conduct an ethnography of the archives and the Project as a way of narrating the importance of this history in peacetime. In tracking how the very same raw documents, the police archives, engendered the production of very different historical narratives, I expose the interdependence of history's two meanings: *that which happened* and *that which is said to have hap-*

pened. In this case, what connects them is the archives. In every case, archives form stunning articulations of power and knowledge, which must be teased apart if we are to understand the stories we tell ourselves about the past.

ARCHIVAL THINKING

To put the archives at the center of my work and to consider them as a unit of analysis unto themselves rather than as a simple repository of historical source material, I had to learn how to think archivally. Archival thinking, as I define it, has a dual meaning: first, it is a method of historical analysis, and second, it is a frame for political analysis.[45] These correspond to the dual meanings of the word "archives" itself: the first denotes collections of objects, often but not exclusively documents, analyzed for their content; the second refers to the politicized and contingent state institutions that house said documents.

On the historical side, archival thinking requires us to look past the words on a document's page to examine the conditions of that document's production: how it came to exist, what it was used for, what its form reveals, and what sorts of state knowledge and action it both reflected and engendered. On the political side, archival thinking demands that we see archives not only as sources of data to be mined by researchers but also as more than the sum of their parts—as instruments of political action, implements of state formation ("technologies of rule"), institutions of liberal democratization, enablers of gaze and desire, and sites of social struggle.[46] Why a particular document was created *and* why it was grouped with other documents and kept in order to constitute an "archives" are mutually dependent questions. Any archive contains far less than it excludes, as archivists know, and every archive has its own history—one that conditions the ability to interact with it, write from it, and understand the larger systems of power, control, and legibility that record keeping necessarily enables.[47] The Enlightenment notions undergirding the concept of state archives, as both *a part of* and *apart from* modern societies, represent these institutions as neutral storehouses of foundational documents.[48] In practice, however, the politics of how archives are compiled, created, and opened are intimately tied to the politics and practices of governance, and are themselves historical in a way that transcends the content written on their documents' pages. This is especially so in settings where the "terror archives" of deposed regimes are reconceived as technologies of justice and/or components of state (re-)formation. In order to think archivally, then, we must place archives—with their histories, their contingencies, their silences and gaps, and their politics—at the heart of our research questions rather than simply relegating them to footnotes and parentheses.

This work does so by taking the PN archives as its central site of analysis, examining three different types of work done by the archives at the state, civil society, and individual levels. At the level of government, these records—like the military's records, a prize long fought for by activists—were tools of counterinsurgent state formation, rendering legible those sectors of society deemed to be enemies of the state in order to enable their elimination. Policing is, in its most basic sense, a process by which a state builds an archive of society. The work of policing—think, for example, of the criminal background check—would be impossible without the archival tools of fingerprint databases, arrest logs, and categories of circumscribed behavior. Hitched to Cold War objectives and local elites' efforts to shut down socioeconomic change, however, the oppressive power of police records assumed an intensified character. By producing a massive documentary record about Guatemala and Guatemalans, the National Police corps was transformed—with U.S. assistance in matters archival, technical, political, and material—into the shock troops of the hemisphere's most brutal counterinsurgency.

At the civil society level, the records' current incarnation as the objects of a revisionist recovery initiative makes them a space in which battered progressive sectors attempt both to reconstitute and construct themselves anew through archival practice. Increasingly, human rights activists have come to phrase their demands upon the state in archival terms: to obtain documentary access means to obtain truth, and to obtain truth means to obtain justice. Therefore, documentary access becomes equated with justice, even if the reality remains more complicated. There is no simple equation wherein more documents equals more truth, or more truth commissions mean more justice, and though these propositions ring true for a reason, critiques of audit culture suggest that the declassification of former repressive regimes' records serves ill as a mere barometer of state transparency or democratization.[49] I pursue a thornier question with this case study: What does the way a society grapples with an archive like this—the way it puts history to work—tell us about that society, its "peace process," the nature of its institutions, and the fabric of its relationships between citizens and state?

Finally, at the individual level, the police archives exert power over the subjectivities of all who come into contact with them. They offer up the ever-elusive promise of "revealing the truth" about the war's dynamics even as the archive's sheer dimension creates a totalizing illusion of counterinsurgent omnipotence, changing and reorganizing survivors' memories of their own political participation. As fetishes of the state, they generate desire for the forbidden state secret, whether a historian's craving for virgin documentation or a survivor's urgent need to learn how his sister died. But although we often assume a correlation between archived documents and historical facts, the police records, like those of any institution, are imperfect, incomplete, and riddled with misapprehensions and errors. They cannot align with survivors' memories of the war, owing to questions of perspective and the passage of time.

It is important to remember that at all three levels, the memory work represented by the police archives' rescue is more about knowledge *production* than it is about knowledge's recovery. At all three levels, the archives act—generating archival subjects, historical narratives, and state practices. I hope that this book's position in the interstitial space between history and anthropology, and its development of the concept of archival thinking, will encourage historians to think more ethnographically—and anthropologists to think more historically—about archives.

In the Guatemalan case, the conditions and contingencies of how these archives came to be *both* an implement of wartime social control *and* a site of postconflict empowerment tell us much not only about the country's history but more broadly about the conduct of the Cold War in Latin America. As the United States initiated police assistance programs in countries seen as potential "dominoes," its advisers in Guatemala focused specifically on security forces' need to improve their archival surveillance methods, enabling them to more effectively eradicate "subversion."[50] As Stoler reminds us, "Filing systems and disciplined writing produce assemblages of control and specific methods of domination."[51] And yet, the role of archival practice in the militarization of modern regimes is rarely considered by scholars, despite a raft of excellent studies on the uses of archives for social control in various colonial administrations.[52] This study argues for the integration of archives and archival surveillance into the pantheon of more obvious tools of international Cold War political influence. After all, the work of containment was not only carried out with guns, helicopters, and development programs: it was also carried out with three-by-five-inch index cards, filing cabinets, and training in records management. Archives, in Guatemala and elsewhere, were another front in the global Cold War.

This examination of archives' counterinsurgent uses also provides insight into postconflict transitions and societies' efforts to reckon with civil war's corrosive legacies. It demonstrates how a society's "archival culture"—the attitudes it fosters about archival access, and how citizens can conceive of putting information to use—is a revelatory indicator of the relationship between state and society, one that changes over time. Put simply, we can discern a lot about a society, particularly a postwar society, by looking at how that society treats its archives. As cultural theorist Jacques Derrida writes, "There is no political power without control of the archive, if not memory. Effective democratization can always be measured by this essential criterion: the participation in and access to the archive, its constitution, and its interpretation."[53] Accordingly, I use archival thinking to explore both the technologies of political repression and the practices of social reconstruction being deployed by survivors working to marshal the same body of records for different ends.

Guatemalans' practices of postwar social reconstruction have been multifarious; the rescue of the PN archives is simply a bright and recent star in a larger constellation of initiatives. As Mario Castañeda writes, "Memory is actualized in struggle, in rebellion, in the negation of our society's status quo," a notion that has produced enduring battles referred to by one activist group as a "memory offensive."[54] "Memory," here, is defined not as passive or recuperative but as active and engaged. The memory offensive has taken forms as diverse as *escrache*-style public denunciations of ex-generals; research projects on social movement history; efforts at criminal prosecution; raising public awareness through historical education; demonstrations and counterdemonstrations (for example, the annual protest march every 30 June, attempting to rebrand Army Day); exhumations of mass graves and inhumations of identified remains; the building of local museums and memorials; and ongoing work to combat corporate mineral extraction on Maya community land and oppose drug war–related rural remilitarization.[55] Within this array of practices, however, certain moments stand out as landmarks: the release of the Archbishop's Office on Human Rights report *Guatemala: Never Again!* in 1998; the publication of the CEH report in 1999; the leak of a high-impact army dossier dubbed the "Death-Squad Diary," or Diario Militar, in 1999; and, I submit here, the rescue of the National Police archives.[56] This book explores how the Project fit into this broader memoryscape, drew strength from previous initiatives, and laid the groundwork for subsequent advances.

This book is thus far the only one documenting the process by which terror archives are recovered, but this line of inquiry has regional and global resonance. As Louis Bickford wrote a decade ago, "An emphasis on archival preservation is often not explicitly highlighted as a key ingredient to deepening democracy and the long-term vibrancy of democratic practices in countries that have experienced traumatic pasts."[57] In recent years, however, an emphasis on preserving and declassifying archives documenting human rights abuses—and archives in general—has increasingly been folded into postauthoritarian strategies that previously focused more on lustration, the building of monuments, or securing apologies, though much distance remains to be covered. In virtually every country of Central and Eastern Europe, including the former East Germany, Serbia, Romania, and the former Czechoslovakia, political change impelled popular demands for access to secret police records, and Germany's decision to open the Ministry for State Security, or Stasi, archives after reunification was influential.[58] In 1997, the United Nations Commission on Human Rights adopted the Principles for the Protection and Promotion of Human Rights through Action to Combat Impunity. They included five principles on the "preservation of and access to archives bearing witness to violations," developed by jurists Louis Joinet and Diane Orentlicher, which established norms for victims', prosecutors', defendants', and researchers' access to archives containing information about human rights abuses.[59]

Latin American countries have now taken the Joinet-Orentlicher principles and run with them. In 1992, Paraguay's "Terror Archives"—the records of its secret police during the Stroessner dictatorship—were discovered, processed, and used in the country's truth commission.[60] (In 2009 they were integrated into the Memory of the World archival register of the United Nations Educational, Scientific and Cultural Organization [UNESCO], which as of that same year also included Cambodia's Khmer Rouge records, collected by the Documentation Center of Cambodia and made accessible to researchers at the Tuol Sleng genocide museum in Phnom Penh.)[61] In 2008 in Uruguay, President Tabaré Vázquez created the National Archives of Remembrance to make accessible records from more than a decade of military rule.[62] In Brazil in 2009, President Luiz Inácio Lula da Silva ordered the creation of the website "Memories Revealed," where his administration published declassified army records from the country's twenty-year dictatorship.[63] In January 2010, Argentina ordered the declassification of military records from its Dirty War and reversed its amnesty law for army officials.[64] Also in 2010, Chile's Michelle Bachelet inaugurated the Memory Museum; it features a large library documenting the years of the dictatorship, during which Bachelet herself was tortured.[65]

Beyond the Americas, Spanish president José Luis Rodríguez Zapatero passed a decree in 2008, part of his Historical Memory Laws, allowing Franco victims to retrieve documents about their families from the Spanish Civil War archives.[66] Farther east, the Iraq Memory Foundation today works to compile and preserve documentation from the long years of Ba'athist repression. (Its efforts are complicated by the fact that the U.S. military seized great quantities of Hussein-era intelligence files upon occupying Baghdad, and more were destroyed in the fighting.)[67] These many recent examples are interrelated, as nations at different stages of postconflict reckoning use each other's best and worst practices as models for their own approaches, with assistance from transnational networks of human rights NGOs.[68] In the wake of the Arab Spring, activists in Tunisia and Egypt, too, moved to secure the archives of fallen regimes with an eye toward their future use. One journalist reported from Tunis that an "unassuming whitewashed building . . . [is] crammed full of explosive material potentially more damaging, or vital, to Tunisia's democratic experiment than any incendiary device. The structure is not an armory packed with weapons. It houses the long-secret archives of the country's once-dreaded Interior Ministry."[69]

In the Guatemalan case, the National Police archives are a microcosm of the country's larger postwar dynamics: their existence denied, their rediscovery accidental, their future uncertain due to the threats faced by "human rights" initiatives in the country, their rescue initially completely ad hoc in the absence of government capacity or political will to exercise its constitutional responsibility over them, their processing funded entirely from abroad. The conditions of the police records in 2005 offered a sobering snapshot of the "peacetime" landscape; their recovery has provided another, capturing the incremental, hard-fought nature of political change on the ground. The archives' double nature thus reflects the tremendous tension of post–Peace Accords Guatemala. On the one hand, as Guatemalans know well, there has been so little substantive change; on the other hand, the very existence of the archival recovery initiative, however beset by challenges it has been, testifies to how much political opening *has* been achieved. As one activist commented to me, "Even ten years ago, they would have killed all the people working in a project like that."[70]

It is partly for this reason that archivist Eric Ketelaar likens archives to both temples and prisons. "In all totalitarian systems—public and private—records are used as instruments of power, of extreme surveillance, oppression, torture, murder," he writes. "The records themselves are dumb, but without them the oppressor is powerless." Following Foucault, he suggests that the panoptical archive of a terror state serves a carceral purpose, imprisoning society by making it known that the state is always watching and always filing; but, he notes, "paradoxically, the same records can also become instruments of empowerment and liberation, salvation and freedom"—they can serve as temples, as "safe havens," once the terror state falls.[71] This has certainly been the case in the post facto repurposing of the terror archives kept by, for example, the Nazis, the Stasi, the Khmer Rouge, or the KGB. However, close ethnographic attention to the process by which that repurposing takes place reveals the temples/

prisons dyad to be less black-and-white than we might wish. To be able to resurrect a paper cadaver in postwar Guatemala—to learn what became of a *desaparecido*, or identify a *desaparecido*'s remains, or write and reveal new histories—is a gift of inestimable value, a temple's treasure indeed. But for all that, what is rescued remains a paper cadaver, not a citizen: a testament to the repression suffered by that citizen, a thin and tragic representation of a once-full life, and a less-than-liberatory reminder that the military state succeeded in forcing social struggle off the shop floors and university campuses, down from the mountains, and into the filing cabinets. To walk the halls of a state's prison-turned-temple is a worthy goal for any citizenry; however, the salvation and freedom thus offered can necessarily only be partial, for the deeds chronicled in the archives have already taken place. The right to truth is critically important, but not more so than the violated right to life.

The National Police archives, we shall see, have many stories to tell, and most are not expressly written on its documents' pages. They are stories of politics, of collective action, of painful separations and reunions, of sacrifices made, of states and of people, of resistance and silencing and loss, of survival. Those engaged in trying to tell such stories carry out their historical work with the goal of a more democratic contemporary politics, and even the most impassioned advocates of a process referred to in Guatemala as "the recovery of historical memory" know that their efforts at rewriting history look more to the future than to the past. As Walter Benjamin has written, "To articulate what is past does not mean to recognize 'how it really was.' It means to take control of a memory, as it flashes in a moment of danger."[72] Historical memory cannot be "recovered" like data in a computer file; by its very nature, memory is a shape-shifter, morphing once an analytical gaze is brought to bear upon it.[73] Instead, memory's recovery is, fundamentally, about power. In this case, engaging the politics of memory is a way for a battered activist sector to articulate archival truth claims, seek reparations both material and symbolic, and reconstruct itself as the country's political conscience.[74] History and memory allow for the *reivindicación* (redemption) of the war's victims and the remaking of its survivors, both essential if Guatemala is to have any hope of building a more just society.

METHODOLOGY

In writing this book, my goals were twofold: first, to participate in the collaborative initiative of revealing new histories of repression and resistance, and second, to trace and analyze the process by which Guatemalans themselves made sense of the police records, their memories, their postconflict lives, and their visions for an uncertain future. When I began this work, it was not at all clear that I would emerge with anything. The first week I arrived to do preliminary research as a Project volunteer, in April 2006, unknown individuals threw a Molotov cocktail into the archives site under cover of darkness, making both front-page headlines and the point that the documents' survival was hardly guaranteed (see fig. Intro2). A few months later, a group of uniformed army generals marched into the PDH, demanding that the Project's director be fired and that they be given access to the Project's personnel information. These were the sorts of hazards one expected, and they underscored activists' fears that their archival rescue effort would be shut down for political reasons. But other threats to the archives' safety came as surprises. In February 2007, a hundred-foot-deep sinkhole, resembling the crater an asteroid might pound into the earth, tore open Guatemala City's Zone 6. The result of poor plumbing infrastructure, the yawning sinkhole just around the corner from the archives devoured an entire city block and several area residents overnight. It could easily have taken the precious police papers along with it. Despite the uncertain outcome, I soldiered on, as we all do when we believe in the importance of the task.

To reconstruct the U.S. role in producing a counterinsurgent National Police, with attention to the role of archival production, I used records from the State Department, the Department of Defense, the CIA, the National Security Agency, the National Security Council, and the U.S. Agency for International Development (USAID), particularly its Office of Public Safety. It bears highlighting that many of the records pertaining to this period and area of inquiry remain significantly redacted or classified altogether, underscoring the fact that state secrecy and hermetism where information is concerned are hardly the sole purview of the global South—as Chelsea Manning and the protagonists of Wikileaks, among others, might well attest if they were not in hiding or in prison. On the war more generally, I consulted long runs of Guatemalan newspapers; military and police publications; insurgents' communiqués and internal correspondence; student pamphlets and publications; guerrilla memoirs and testimonies; presidential speeches and radio addresses; Inter-American Court on Human Rights cases; reports from watchdog organizations like Human Rights Watch and Amnesty International; foreign police training manuals; and more. I complemented this documentary research with perspectives and memories shared by the older workers at the archival recovery project.

Much of my research was ethnographic as well, involving extended participant observation and interviews both formal and informal. I accompanied the Project as a volunteer worker, observer, translator, and colleague from

FIG. INTRO2 Early Molotov cocktail attacks at the police archives made front-page headlines. *La Hora*, 11 May 2006.

the spring of 2006 onward. Before doing my own formal research, I worked full-time for six months (May–July 2006 and June–August 2007) as a Project volunteer, the only foreigner to work as an everyday, rank-and-file member of the team. For the first stint, I worked on a historical analysis team generating preliminary reports on the PN's clandestine and semiclandestine units and death squads, including Commando Six (Comando Seis) and the Special Operations Reaction Brigade (BROE). For the second, I was a member of the team processing the records of the Joint Operations Center (Centro de Operaciones Conjuntas), the entity serving as the primary conduit for police-military communications. During these months on staff, I was able to experience for myself the range of emotions engendered by this painstaking work: the pride and excitement of finding a document of real importance, the anger and sadness provoked by nonstop reading about violence and vice, the boredom and frustration of long days spent sifting through bureaucratic minutiae. It was only after this initial phase, which also included a shorter visit in January 2007 and volunteer work on a compilation of declassified U.S. documents sent to the Project by the National Security Archive that same year, that I began conducting my own research, mostly during the 2007–2008 academic year when I lived in Guatemala City. I thus became, in a sense, a tiny part of the story. My early contributions to the historical analysis team were mixed into the basic building blocks of the Project's eventual, and much more substantial, public report on its findings. As a translator, I mediated a number of the interactions between international technical advisers and Project staff from 2006 to 2008. Most memorably, in one interview I conducted outside the Project I received an off-the-record tip about a warehouse full of forgotten police records in the town of Puerto Barrios. Passing the tip along led to the recovery and incorporation of thousands more documents into the archives (though not before a suspicious arson incident nearly derailed the process). Finally, of course, I am also part of the surge of international interest in the Project, placing me among a cohort whose commitment to assisting the Project carried its own imperial baggage and transnational power dynamics, key elements of the story too.

In addition to the archival research mentioned previously, I conducted dozens of interviews with the Project's workers and the figures involved in its orbit—in government, the diplomatic corps, and the human rights sector—and I took part in the Project's everyday life for a year and a half, watching it evolve and struggle and grow. This allowed me to observe the process of reconstituting the archives, work that expanded Project staffers' political consciousnesses and senses of themselves as political actors, contributors to a larger democratizing initiative, and opponents of an official history that had marginalized and criminalized popular agency. Many Project *compañeros* and *compañeras* had high hopes for the archives. They also struggled, however, with what Jelin calls "the labors of memory"—the active, demanding work of managing resurgent traumas, psychological burdens, and memories stirred by sorting through the archives, reading about violence for eight hours daily, and finding loved ones' names or photographs.[75] My interviews with Project workers took place all over the city, in bars and cafés and shopping malls and private homes, but I conducted the majority of them at the archives—a challenging environment for many reasons, not least of which being that it remains an active police base. The sounds of gunshots from the adjacent police firing range or barking dogs from the nearby canine unit are heard throughout my recordings, yet another testament to the tensions of the Project's workplace. There are pauses in the tapes, or moments of hushed whispering, when interviewees would see an officer walk by or thought one was within earshot. The interviews were thus conditioned by the same sense of unease and instability pervading both everyday life in Guatemala City and these amateur historians' particular line of work. As such, I have protected their identities; individuals are identified in the text by pseudonyms and in the notes by interview code number.

While I have had the privilege of reading, both as a volunteer and in subsequent visits, many thousands of documents from the PN archives, my work here does not involve engaging the archives as a historian customarily might. I wanted to document the *process*, not to process the *documents*. This was why the Project gave me such unparalleled access to its work and workers so early on, in the spring of 2006. I was allowed to join the team precisely—and only—because its leaders believed that it could help to have an on-site foreign observer present to document its efforts, and because I offered to work at the service of the Guatemalans' priorities before following my own. Had I asked for research access in 2006, or 2007, or 2008, I would have been denied (as others were), with good reason. Aside from the fact that the archives' state of disorder at that time made traditional historical research impossible, the Project was operating with a very low profile, hoping to avoid the release of any information that could provoke retaliatory attacks. At that point, even family members of the dead and disappeared were being refused access to the records; it was not a queue I was interested in jumping. As a result, all staffers, myself included, signed confidentiality agreements promising not to divulge anything about the documents' contents.[76] (Access has subsequently been opened to the approximately fifteen million documents that have been digitized; many historical studies will emerge from that body of documentation in the not-too-distant future.)

I constantly struggled with the challenge of making my research useful to the Guatemalans who had extended me such trust. "We need to have a high international profile, so that nobody can come and shut us down for knowing too much," one Project worker told me.[77] I hope I have repaid their faith in some small sense not only by honoring the confidentiality agreement I was asked to sign (which is to say, I have not quoted from documents I saw while the agreement was in effect, though I do use documents subsequently made public), but by writing a book that argues strenuously for both the historical and the contemporary relevance of their work. My central preoccupation was to make the case for this history's importance, and by extension for the importance of historical and archival knowledge to the conduct of contemporary politics. I wanted to trace the remaking of these archives from the ground up because I knew instinctively that once that process concluded, its messiness and complexity would forever be lost as the archives were transformed into an institution, a success story—considered a fait accompli, like so many of the other archives that historians visit. We would have a new historical narrative about the war—the one being generated by the archive's rescuers—but no account of the process by which that narrative was produced or of those actors' stake in it, and hence no sense of the powerful relationship between the two types of history.

STRUCTURE AND ORGANIZATION

In keeping with the dialectical structure outlined here, whereby I explore the tension between the two archival logics applied to the National Police documents over time, this study introduces the circumstances of the archives' discovery, closely examines both logics, and then turns to the synthesis produced over time by their opposition. The book is structured in four parts: "Explosions at the Archives" (chapters 1 through 3), "Archives and Counterinsurgency in Cold War Guatemala" (chapters 4 and 5), "Archives and Social Reconstruction in Postwar Guatemala" (chapters 6 and 7), and "Pasts Present and the Future Imperfect" (chapters 8 and 9).

Chapter 1 narrates the early days of the archives' reappearance, charting the beginnings of the rescue initiative and the Project's evolving ideas about how to build new knowledge about the armed conflict and the police's role in it. It shows how this process was microcosmic of larger questions about war and postwar political struggle. Chapter 2 demonstrates that rather than being a stroke of random luck, the discovery and marshaling of the PN archives were instead the culmination of decades of activism over access to state security records. These "archive wars," as I term them, established important precedents that informed how the PN archives would be put to use, and I outline the trajectory of the archive wars while also assessing the role of archival access in authoritarian societies. Chapter 3 returns to the Project, narrating its conversion from an ad hoc, scrappy effort into the professionalized and more stable initiative it would become. It attempts to answer the "million-dollar question" of why the archives were never destroyed by authorities while they had the chance.

Chapters 4 and 5 form a pair: by stepping back in time to analyze the role of the police and their archives in the conduct of the counterinsurgency, they show how the PN records acquired their power. (As the archivists at the Project quickly learned, one must understand the police's structural history in order to interpret the documents.) Chapter 4 reaches back to a decisive moment in the history of the PN: the 1954 overthrow of Arbenz and the subsequent initiation of a large-scale U.S. assistance program that converted the PN from a ramshackle assortment of thugs into a professionalized counterinsurgency apparatus. It examines the construction and use of the police archives historically, arguing that archival technologies were essential components of the state's campaign against civil unrest. Chapter 5 continues the story of the PN past the termination of direct U.S. police aid in 1974, arguing that the dramatic failure of security reform in the postwar era is a function of the PN's own institutional history. It traces the structural genealogy of the PN's militarized, semi-official wings, demonstrating how these structures were never dismantled and today continue to participate in extralegal activities like social cleansings and politically motivated executions. It introduces the term "post-peace" to describe Guatemala's unstable, violent postwar status quo.

Chapters 6 and 7 also form a pair, ethnographically following the experiences of the workers at the archival recovery project. Chapter 6, which focuses on the experiences of older-generation leftists working at the Project, argues that these veterans have played an instrumental role in the production of new narratives about the conflict's history. It also explores how working in the archives has impacted these survivors' subjectivities, generating new opportunities for social reconstruction and reckoning while reopening old wounds. Chapter 7 examines the experiences of the younger workers at the Project, a large group of under-thirty individuals who lived the war as children and who today bridge the conflict and postconflict eras. It shows how their time at the archives shaped their emerging senses of self, transforming some of them into lifelong activists. It argues that among the archives' greatest impacts on Guatemala may prove to be the *formación* of more than one hundred politically conscious youth leaders committed not only to postwar justice but also to privileging archival preservation and historical reconstruction in their visions for the future.

The final two chapters discuss other archival recovery initiatives, international collaborations, legal advances, and educational endeavors sparked by the Project. Chapter 8 looks at the ontological shift undergone by the police archives since 2005: from a ragtag project in the process of *becoming* a usable archive, through a dangerous historical moment in which the Project was nearly destroyed altogether, into the established Historical Archive for the National Police—an institutionalized state of *being*. It examines what that shift both promised and portended for national politics. Chapter 9 discusses the landmark legal advances from 2010 on to which the police archives contributed; exceptions that prove the rule, these successful few cases and the herculean efforts to secure them suggest that a fuller reckoning with Guatemala's history will be hard-won. The charged debates surrounding these legal cases speak to the connections between a society's archival culture, its engagement with historical knowledge, and its political conditions. They demonstrate both the possibilities and the limitations of archival thinking.

As one Project worker once told me, "Human beings need to write their own histories."[78] This book defends that proposition, while demonstrating that in delicate postconflict settings where the politics of history remain deadly serious, the act of doing so represents personal risk, collective courage, and, above all, a tremendous amount of labor. Project workers have worked, admirably and against the odds, to resurrect their country's paper cadavers in the hope of charting a new path forward. I wrote this book in the service of that larger aspiration: to resurrect lost archives, lost narratives, and, however abstractly, lost lives.

PART I │ **EXPLOSIONS AT THE ARCHIVES**

ONE | **EXCAVATING BABYLON**

While some of us debate what history is or was, others take
it in their own hands.
—Michel-Rolph Trouillot, *Silencing the Past*

Though today's National Police archives site gleams with fresh paint
and new flooring, hums with the noise of high-speed scanners, and
bustles with the energy of young workers and awed visitors, it was
not always so. When investigators from the Human Rights Ombudsman's Office (PDH) stumbled upon the archives in July 2005, what they found was,
according to one of the first to see it, "impossible to describe."[1] There was an
aura of decay about the massive unfinished structure, occupied only by small
armies of rats and bats and reeking of mold and mildew, where detainees had
once been regularly tortured to death. It lay in a scrubby field carpeted with
overgrown weeds and ringed by heaps of scrapped cars. The papers it housed
seemed endless, crude bundles by the millions spotted with vermin feces and
cockroach carcasses, their hand-scrawled labels barely visible beneath years of
dust, with puddles of cloudy water seeping up into the piles of paper and rotting them from within. The space summoned to mind images of entrapment:
a concrete labyrinth, a warren of windowless cells, a zone of haunting and
sepulchre. At the back of the edifice, humidity and neglect had conspired such
that verdant plant life coiled up the walls, sprouted from within the masses of
paper blanketing the earth, and hung down from the ceiling in long fronds.
This last, the Project's assistant director remembered, "was why we gave that
room the name 'Babylon.'"[2]

The metaphor was apt, for the archives—even in their putrefaction and incredible dimension, and perhaps all the more so for it—represented, to many
Guatemalans, their very own wonder of the world. The archives' existence had
been denied for years at the highest levels of government, and their reappearance, therefore, came as a shock.[3] They seemed at once to confirm long-held
suspicions and to challenge assumptions about the traces left behind by state

<figure>**FIG. 1.1** Photograph by James Rodríguez, mimundo.org. Used by permission of the photographer.</figure>

terror. Upon hearing of the find, people tended to have one of two reactions: to assume, based on the belief that such records had always existed and had been meticulously kept, that the archives would reveal great truths, or else to wonder why the records had never been destroyed and speculate that their neglect spoke to their lack of incriminating information. Would the archives open a new window into the past, or would they disappoint?

To find out, one thing was required: work. To make sense of what was estimated to be eighty million pages of records, all manner of work—in forms unforeseen by those who rolled up their sleeves in the earliest days—would need to be done. Grappling with the archives, a natural flash point for both interest and opposition, would ultimately require lobbying, funding, training, alliance-building, security, technology, staffing, supplies, perseverance, and hope. And though these varied types of work would eventually be performed by a team of more than two hundred Guatemalans, using state-of-the-art methods and aided by an enthusiastic network of international allies and donors, what became the Project for the Recovery of the National Police Historical Archives began as a tiny handful of volunteers with little more than shovels, an abiding faith, and a deep sense of their own histories.

Anthropologist Michel-Rolph Trouillot writes that conventional theories of history ignore how most history is produced outside of academia; "we are all," he reminds us, "amateur historians with various degrees of awareness about our production."[4] The staffers of the Project, over time, became not only amateur historians but also amateur archivists; these amateur historians and archivists sought, by rescuing the archives, to illuminate occluded stories from forty years' worth of civil strife. With backgrounds in activism, they knew the road ahead would not be easy. They were painfully aware of the conditions that had produced them as historians, witnesses, and human rights defenders; they were, likewise, painfully aware of the difficult conditions brought to bear upon their attempts to reclaim their histories. As Project workers—many of them veterans of the gutted Left, or else veterans' children—rebuilt the archives, they also built power; in learning to "think archivally," they came to claim physical and intellectual control over documents that had once been used to control them.[5]

But we have not yet arrived at that part of the story. To get there, we must follow the messy, uncertain path taken by our small group of volunteers at the outset, as they repeatedly confronted the same daunting questions: What, in a place like Guatemala, was to be done with an archive like this? What was possible, or thinkable, or even dreamable? Could the archives even be saved, much less put to use? What would it take, and what resources were available? Precisely because the Project stands, at the time of this writing, as an odds-defying success story, one might be forgiven for assuming that the road to such success, while perhaps long or slow, was mostly straight and linear, and that its travelers initially set out with a well-labeled map and the guiding compass of established precedent. Reality, of course, is rarely so simple—but, at the very least, it is usually far more interesting. With this in mind, part I of this book tells the story of the Project, first in its earliest days and then through its consolidation from an uncertain labor of love into a veritable institution with scientific bonafides, management hierarchies, an international reputation, and a critical role to play in a rapidly evolving national conversation about archives, human rights, and justice. The Project's journey out of Babylon, chronicled here, demonstrated the dizzying stakes of archives: not simply collections of dusty papers consulted by the odd professional historian but rather hotly contested shreds of information and evidence that could make or shatter families, legal processes, and national histories.[6] Along the way, we see how the erstwhile Cold War logic of these documents—their "prose of counterinsurgency"—was leveraged through blood, sweat, and tears into a different logic, one of agency and aperture.[7] The archives' rescue and institutionalization represent the fulfillment of its workers' and leaders' dreams that they could bequeath to future generations a set of tools that could never be broken and truths that could never be disappeared. But it is the preceding period, the interregnum between improvisation and institutionalization, that shows us the fundamentally processual character of historical production. The rebuilding of the PN archives by activists seeking to make truth-claims upon a contemporary state is nothing less than an object lesson in how, as Trouillot argues, "what history is matters less than how history works."[8]

NARRATIVES OF DISCOVERY, ENCOUNTER, AND CONQUEST

Amateur historians emerged as key actors later, but fate smiled upon the Guatemalan human rights community the day it sent a professional historian to investigate reports of improperly stored explosives on a police base. In June 2005, a series of massive explosions at Guatemala City's Mariscal Zavala military base lit up the night sky in Zones 5, 6, 17, and 18, filling the already pollution-thick air with toxic smoke. The weapons, more than a ton of projectiles left over from the war, had detonated at a rate of thirty per minute over four long hours, spurring mass evacuations from the surrounding neighborhoods.[9] When the dust had settled and the poisonous gas cleared, the PDH fielded a raft of complaints from local residents, who lived wedged between Mariscal Zavala and the National Civil Police's own arms storage facility, and into whose homes the blast's debris tumbled. Fearing a similar explosion at the PNC's munitions depot, the PDH immediately filed a request for the PNC to remove all explosive materials from its Zone 6 warehouse. Three weeks later, it sent investigators to the PNC installations to verify compliance and conduct a risk assessment of the surrounding area. It turned out that the explosives were still on-site, but they were not all that was to be found there.

The head of the PDH's investigations unit, Edeliberto Cifuentes, was the affable former head of the School of History at the University of San Carlos, a garrulous intellectual writing a biography of Guatemalan historian Severo Martínez Pelaez in his spare time. "Our standing orders at the Investigations Unit are to look at everything that can be seen, in order to find what can't be seen," Cifuentes related, sounding like a professor advising a young researcher on methods. After establishing the PNC's failure to remove the munitions, the PDH team set about examining the surroundings, looking for flammable materials that might increase the blast radius of an inadvertent detonation. They found heaps of junked cars, many with gasoline still in their tanks; they identified a school, a health center, and many private homes that would have been affected by a putative blast; and they saw papers, bundles upon bundles of papers piled up against the interior windows of the PNC office building. The thought that jumped first to their minds, which were focused on assessing risks, was that these papers represented a lot of flammable material. When Cifuentes asked the ranking PNC official there, Ana Corado, what sorts of papers these were and in what quantity they could be found, she replied, simply, "These are the archives of the National Police."

Corado made no attempt to hide the archives from the PDH; instead, she gave the investigators a full tour, one not unlike the tour today given to visiting donors and researchers, and explained where different bodies of documentation were stored—high-impact political cases here, administrative records there. When Corado led them to the warehouse's second floor, a vast chamber brimming with what Cifuentes described as "huge volcanoes of documents" spilling forth from rusty filing cabinets and buckled wooden shelves, the investigators realized what they had found. "It was very much an emotional reaction," Cifuentes recalled. "Because you can imagine, when one finds a document, a piece of information that is key in the construction of a case or a story or an investigation, that's one thing. But to find all of this documentation there—you say to yourself, this is a treasure that will help us to construct enormous histories. . . . My emotional reaction was that of a historian!"[10]

Cifuentes returned to the PDH and told his colleague Carla Villagrán of the news; she, the head of the PDH Analysis Unit, went upstairs and shared the news with Sergio Morales, the ombudsman. The ombudsman's office, an institution based around the figure of a congressionally appointed human rights defender, was created in 1985 as part of the "transition to democracy."[11] The ombudsman's mandate included securing evidence related to human rights abuses and conducting investigations accordingly; Morales understood the stakes of what his team had found and how his mandate permitted him to act.[12] The PDH could not customarily bring cases before the courts; that duty fell to the Public Ministry (MP), though the PDH could investigate cases and present its findings to the MP for its own use in prosecutions. There were, however, a handful of exceptions to this rule: *casos de averiguación especial*, special cases in which prosecutorial authority was ceded to the PDH's Special Cases Unit by the Supreme Court in the event of obvious state responsibility. One such case, the 1981 abduction of fourteen-year-old Marco Antonio Molina Thiessen, provided Morales with proximate cause to secure the archives in search of evidence.[13] The day after the PDH team's visit to the base, its (unarmed) members were sent back to guard the archives against any attempts to enter the site or remove documents until the PDH could take custody of them.

Morales's judgment call, for the PDH to assume responsibility for the archives, was bold. He believed that "if we hadn't taken control of them, the archives would have remained, discarded, on that site until the moment when a

FIG. 1.2 A National Civil Police agent toils among the documents. Photograph by Daniel Hernández-Salazar. Used by permission of the photographer.

bulldozer or tractor would have been sent to demolish the building and make way for something new. I think the archives would have been lost."[14] But his move raised serious questions. There was no precedent in Guatemala—or in Latin America—for finding such an immense cache of secret state documents. The PDH had neither funds to contribute nor any staff trained in archival methods; it was certainly not the proper institution to steward a mammoth documentary recovery project. However, Guatemala's national archives—the Archivo General de Centroamérica (AGCA), to which the task of rescuing the records constitutionally fell—was grievously underfunded and understaffed. The entire country was then home to fewer than ten certified archivists. It was difficult to know where to begin. Very little was known about the National Police—its structures, modes of operation, or forms of organization. And the pregnant sense of political threat, the risk that any attempt to delve into the police's past would invite retribution from the same entrenched powers who regularly attacked human rights defenders, only amplified the uncertainties.[15]

As a result, competing narratives about the archives' importance jostled for prominence from the beginning. State security forces and their representatives played down the discovery; interior minister Carlos Vielman scoffed, "Of course we have records. We are the police!"[16] Corado, the PNC official in charge of the archives, was also puzzled by the idea that the papers under her watch were a momentous "discovery," though for different reasons. Corado, soft-spoken and bespectacled, had been sent to join the team of mostly female agents toiling at the archives six months before the PDH arrived. This was no honor; being relegated to the archives, known within the PNC as *el basurero*, or "the dump," was considered a punishment. "I had a superior who didn't like me and he ordered that I be transferred somewhere where he'd never have to see me again," she recalled.[17] Just days before Cifuentes searched her workplace, Corado had been told by a superior to burn records that were no longer in use; the day the ombudsman took custody of the archives, the same superiors threatened her with termination if she gave any information to the PDH. To her credit, Corado disobeyed both directives.

Despite these efforts to silence both her own voice and that of the documents, however, she maintained that the archives were never "secret" in the way that activists claimed. "What happened is that since nobody knew that this archive existed, that's why lots of people said it was . . . closed. But this archive has never been closed, it's always been open," she said. She asserted that prior to the PDH's arrival, anyone could have solicited access to the records, though she conceded that the documents' disorganization rendered "access" a practical fiction. Nonetheless, the political decision taken by the Arzú government to refuse archival access to the UN truth commission diverged from the reality on the ground, in which the records rotted away in neglect. (The implications for citizens' access were the same.) Bereft of supplies or training, Corado and her team scavenged string and cardboard from their own homes to start bundling the papers, simply assuming that nobody was interested in the records beyond the group of women consigned to caring for them. "For me, this isn't garbage," Corado attested, "it's a treasure."[18] She thought she was alone in her opinion, though, because for her superiors the archives were a problem—not a political problem, but rather one of storage. Interest in freeing up the space occupied by the papers impelled Corado's predecessor to even phone the national archives (AGCA) and inquire about which papers could legally be destroyed. The AGCA team, led by its soon-to-be director Anna Carla Ericastilla, was *invited* to conduct a full assessment of the archives—welcomed and given unfettered access to the records—more than six months before the PDH's arrival on the scene. "So the word 'discovery' got my attention," Ericastilla remembered. "I think that the word 'discovery' should be used, in this case as in all others, with caution. Just because I don't know about something doesn't mean that nobody else does."[19] She pointed out, without minimizing the historical importance of the police archives, that abandoned bodies of decaying state records were nothing novel in Guatemala—they were the rule.

So was this an earth-shattering discovery of secret archives, or the routine appearance of yet another neglected set of administrative papers? It depended on who was being asked, and to whom it mattered. State security forces minimized the find, even as direct threats against the PDH and the archives' integrity in the days following the PDH's intervention suggested that powerful actors felt otherwise. To an archivist, the records were important, but their conditions were no different than the country's many other abandoned archives, and the word "forgotten" was a better characterization than "repressed" or "secret." To the police agents working away in *el basurero*, the records were a Sisyphean *cargo*, a punishment to be discharged in obscurity. But to human rights activists, July 2005 was a watershed. Decades of official denial had criminalized victimhood, obliterated hope that state documents would ever be released, and left thousands in limbo about the whereabouts of their disappeared loved ones. The Arzú government had refused to surrender records to the truth commission, and though few were fooled into thinking that archives therefore did not exist, neither could every abandoned building in the nation be searched to force the question.[20] The Mariscal Zavala explosions had been a cacophonous accident, fortuitously giving investigators a mandate to access a storage facility they would otherwise never have entered—one whose records would have been partially incinerated if not for the foresight of one rank-and-file agent. The appearance of the police archives was the product, like so many other linchpin moments in history, of a mix of felicitous political conditions, *longue durée* social struggle, and luck. For better or worse, the PDH began working first, and asking questions later.

EXCAVATING BABYLON

"In the beginning," assistant director Fuentes remembered, "we had all the enthusiasm and interest possible, but my impression was that this was a titanic task."[21] The period from July to December 2005 can be considered the first phase of the rescue initiative, in which the work was improvisational and its future profoundly unclear, but in which the stakeholders who would shape the future direction of the Project came together. To tackle the documents, the PDH loaned a few of the original seven or eight personnel from its existing units; the first archivist to work at the site, Ingrid Molina, had just begun working with Cifuentes's unit, and other early arrivals were transferred to archives detail by the PDH because they were considered people of *confianza*.[22] The remainder of the initial group was composed of volunteers from the tenacious human rights organizations Security in Democracy (SEDEM) and the Mutual Support Group (GAM), whose early contributions were crucial to the initiative's survival. These Project pioneers had no supplies, besides flimsy face masks and rubber gloves purchased at a local pharmacy, and they performed the earliest stage of their recovery work, the rescue of the *fichas* (file cards), crouched atop loose concrete blocks in a space choked with dust and vermin. SEDEM and GAM contributed chairs and tables, the first supplies, and the first computers; SEDEM then paid the salaries of more than thirty staffers once additional individuals were hired on.

These were major sacrifices for such underfunded organizations, but the justification was clear. SEDEM, GAM, and the PDH had previously collaborated on the partial rescue of the archives of the defunct Presidential Staff (EMP) in 2003 (see ch. 2); the police records, not as obviously "cleansed" of incriminating information as the EMP collection had been, promised more results.[23] As soon as the volunteers began to pull *fichas* out from beneath the crusted paper-pulp promontory protecting them, they saw notations of a political character, reading "Communist" or "subversive," scrawled on individual citizens' driver's license and *cedula* (personal identification card) forms dating back to the 1930s. "I was assigned to the crime *fichas*," remembered one worker, "and one of the things that impacted me the most was finding the *ficha* on Víctor Manuel Gutiérrez," an Arbencista and PGT leader murdered by the state in

FIG. 1.3 A Project worker pulls a Guatemalan's personal identification *ficha* (file) from a heap of decomposing records. Photograph by James Rodríguez, mimundo.org. Used by permission of the photographer.

1966. "His *ficha* said 'Communist #1' in red letters."[24] In an unsettling echo of the documents' original logic of surveillance, police agents shadowed this early archival work.

These volunteers' primary concern with justice rather than archival science, and the PDH's lack of technical archival expertise, led some to question whether it was appropriate for the PDH to shoulder the task. Constitutionally, custody of the records fell to the AGCA; Guatemalan law calls for all state records older than ten years to be incorporated into the national archives system. But the outdated law, Decree-Law 17-68, was never enforced, and the AGCA lacked the funding, personnel, or storage space to fulfill its own mandate. New documents had not been physically incorporated into the AGCA's holdings since the 1960s; Decree 17–68 lacked the strong foundations a national archives law needed, and the AGCA had no legal mechanism by which to compel the surrender of documents. In a country rife with corruption and impunity, state organs were in no rush to share their paper trails. Hence, the AGCA languished, victim to a studied societal indifference to the importance of archives.[25] It was in no position in 2005 to accommodate eighty million pages of uncataloged records.[26]

But this did not mean it was unwilling to try. A proposal supported by then vice president Eduardo Stein and the Presidential Human Rights Commission

(COPREDEH), argued that the state, namely, the AGCA, should take responsibility for the PN archives.[27] (Though the ombudsman post was a congressional appointment, it was meant to be semiautonomous from the sitting government.) The theory was that, thus handled, the archives "would not belong to one ombudsman or one government" but would instead be incorporated into the documentary patrimony of the state, while still guaranteeing access to the PDH for investigative purposes.[28] Physical and financial custody would be assumed by the Ministry of Culture, the AGCA's parent ministry, and the state would raise funds for the task; the technical work of organizing the records could be contracted out to a private outfit. The argument was that if the PDH were to simply take care of the problem using international monies, this would be an abdication of duty by the central government, an intervention that would let the state shirk its archival responsibilities. It would also politicize the archives. The COPREDEH proposal was intended to begin a new era of the AGCA, strengthening the institution and allowing it to eventually rescue archives from all state dependencies. But the proposal died in the Ministry of Culture, which was unwilling to commit to the risk such a project would entail. "It was a lost opportunity," reflected then COPREDEH head Frank La Rue. "It shows you the weakness of democracy in this country," he said, suggesting that cowardice and weak institutionality had blocked a timely chance at state-building.[29] Insiders at the PDH, though, saw the proposal as a tactic that would, advertently or otherwise, stall their investigation by consigning the archives to the care of an institution without the resources to guarantee access to them—or, worse, outsourcing the technical archival work to a third party, which would regulate access according to its own priorities.[30] A long-held mistrust of state institutions, exacerbated by the war, contributed too; as Ericastilla said, "Given the terrible things that public administration and the state have done to the Guatemalan people, I understand that confidence in State institutions is very limited."[31]

In the end, international donors' decision to fund a PDH human rights investigation in the archives settled the question, at least for the Project's first years. The PDH already had strong relationships with many foreign governments' development agencies, particularly European ones, most of which ran aid programs in postwar countries focusing on liberal mainstays: transitions to democracy, access to justice, and promoting human rights. When the PDH, far richer in political capital than the AGCA, convened a group of donors in the fall of 2005 to explore their willingness to support the Project, it found natural allies who were, because of their own priorities, very much inclined to assist.[32] The international cooperation programs of Switzerland and Sweden were the first to throw their hats in the ring, pledging several million dollars—a huge sum by local standards—and, more important, their political support. "Human rights have always been our main priority," said Åsa Wallton of Sweden's International Development Agency. "Of course when you discover an archive like that, nobody knows its potential but you have to give support."[33] As was customary with donor commitments to new projects, the decision by Sweden and by Switzerland's Program for the Promotion of Peace to participate created a domino effect, allowing other donors to justify their own contributions.[34] The German and Catalan development agencies followed suit, followed by Spain, Oxfam-UK, the Basque Country, and the Netherlands. Most donors channeled their funds through the United Nations Development Program (UNDP) to protect the Project from allegations of financial mismanagement.[35]

The donors did not, however, participate due to any particular interest in archival conservation; international aid agencies are not in the habit of paying for other countries to organize their old papers. "The interests of the donors are the same as those of the PDH: they didn't get involved because they were interested in archival science," said the UNDP's Christina Elich. "They all saw archival science as a necessary evil at the beginning."[36] The preservation of historical documents was considered only a means to an end, imagined to be useful only insofar as it would allow trial-minded investigators to marshal evidence. As one observer at Guatemala's branch of the UN High Commission for Human Rights told me, "The human rights angle, the investigation of past abuses, is a big hook for international interest in the project. I can imagine that that was the angle that was 'sold' in order to bring those donors to the table and [have them] sign over such huge amounts of money."[37] Donors' interest in the human rights aspect of the Project was as strong as their interest in its archival dimensions was weak, a function of the politics of international development aid. It highlighted what Louis Bickford identifies as a major lacuna in most transitional justice efforts: any emphasis on archives and archival access as critical functions of postwar transitions and truth-telling initiatives.[38] As Wallton bluntly said, "Funding depends on the sexiness of the project."[39] Archives, per se, were not seen as sexy; human rights discoveries were. And the PDH was not merely leveraging the overlap to attract donors; it, too, was initially uninterested in the work of archival description and preservation. In fact, these technical dimensions were seen by some as an *obstacle* to obtaining the desired information in a timely fashion; as one donor put it, "Lots of people wanted access, but nobody wanted to deal with the papers."[40]

This dynamic would soon change, and significant credit for that change lay with certain international actors, who echoed the concerns raised by domestic archivists but who had the clout to make their voices heard. The National Security Archive, a Washington, DC, research institute devoted to publishing declassified U.S. documents, had worked intensively in Guatemala for years; the thousands of U.S. government records its Guatemala Project, directed by Kate Doyle, obtained during the 1990s were a major contribution to the CEH report. Doyle visited the archives shortly after their discovery; realizing that the PDH's main deficiency was its lack of capacity for handling documentation in a legally and archivally sound manner, and that its failure to do so would fatally compromise its human rights investigation, she worked with the incipient rescue effort on analysis and strategy. She connected the PDH with several experts: the U.S.-based archivist Trudy Huskamp Peterson, a specialist in the preservation of truth commission records, and Ana Cacopardo and Ingrid Jaschek of the Memory Commission for the Province of Buenos Aires, an organization devoted to preserving the archives of the Argentine juntas' secret police forces.[41] Their input would confirm that archival science was not a time-consuming sideshow but, rather, lay at the heart of the proposed human rights initiative; it proved to be just the beginning of the assistance that the Project would receive from abroad. Soon, the PDH assembled an enviable constellation of international experts and attracted global media attention, notable when juxtaposed against the minimal play the archives' discovery received inside Guatemala. In part, this was by design—to conduct the work discreetly, to avoid reprisals or creating unrealistic expectations about what could be found in the archives. But the relative silence around the Project domestically, compared with the interest it sparked internationally, spoke to larger patterns of historical amnesia regarding the war.

The involvement of international specialists raised the question of precedents: What were other contexts in which similar "terror archives" discoveries had taken place, and what kinds of best practices might be imported into a Guatemalan setting?[42] A unified Germany had inherited the well-organized archives kept by East Germany's Ministry for State Security, or Stasi, a case often referenced by the Guatemalan activists with good-natured jealousy. (The Guatemalans, though, viewed the Stasi archives through rose-colored glasses; they were unaware that the Stasi had left behind more than fifteen thousand large sacks filled with shredded high-impact documents, and that teams of German workers would spend more than fifteen years reconstructing them by hand, a task still ongoing.)[43] Germany, eager to reckon with the atrocities of its past, created a federal authority in 1991 that would administer and guarantee public access to the records.[44] Timothy Garton Ash writes that it came to represent "a ministry of truth occupying the former ministry of fear," where citizens could consult the files kept about them, some numbering thousands of pages.[45] Greece, once its dictatorship fell, used the records produced by its repressive bodies to compensate victims and lustrate perpetrators. However, it then elected to destroy the documents, thus eliminating any possibility of their future use. Spain opted to transfer all political records left behind by the Franco regime to the National Historical Archives, thus preserving for private and academic use its files of repression.[46] In Paraguay, activists in the early 1990s discovered hundreds of thousands of records detailing the practices of dictator Alfredo Stroessner's secret police; the records were collected, organized, and made publicly accessible as a discrete terror archives in a room of Asunción's Palace of Justice.[47] Lithuania and the Ukraine both inherited KGB records, which they integrated into their National Archives. In Argentina, when the Intelligence Directorate of the Buenos Aires Police was disbanded in 1998, its records were closed for use in the country's ongoing judicial processes; they were then transferred to the Memory Commission, which opened them to the public several years later.

Comparative cases would prove useful in the longer run by providing examples of the sorts of special legislation other countries had drafted to protect their terror archives and institutional arrangements made for their custody, care, and access. Nonetheless, Guatemala's case was unique. Unlike in Germany, the Guatemalan government under President Oscar Berger was hardly eager to clarify past abuses, and the fact that Guatemala was still controlled by powerful military sectors ensured a chilly climate at the state level for such an archival recovery effort. Compared with Paraguay, where the accidental discovery of the records was an important parallel, the dimension of the find proved a critical difference; the Paraguayan documents, 600,000 pages' worth, could be accommodated in one room, but the Guatemalan records would require much more extensive capacity-building, labor, and fundraising.[48] Whereas in Argentina the state had mandated the use of surrendered records in judicial proceedings, such proceedings in Guatemala were blocked in 2005, with the government unwilling to step in. The PN records were simply too numerous, too decayed, and too much of a political powderkeg for any foreign model to be borrowed. Indeed, their peculiar conditions—their distinct politics and challenges—were functions of the history that activists were seeking, through the recovery effort, to clarify. Unlike the other countries, Guatemala had not completed anything like a "transition to democracy," at least insofar as questions of historical memory or justice were concerned.

This refusal to reckon with the recent past would reverberate at various levels of the effort to recover the PN archives.[49]

CONSOLIDATION, COMANDANTES, AND MOLOTOV COCKTAILS

Once donors had pledged sufficient funding to allow the PDH to envision a formal recovery project—for which no money came from the Guatemalan government—the PDH set about addressing staffing. The Project needed a director: someone with political savvy, the international connections necessary for fund-raising, leadership experience, and a personal commitment to the goals of historical clarification and justice. Gustavo Meoño was the ombudsman's pick; the two had met during their lobbying efforts for the UN body known as the International Commission against Impunity in Guatemala (CICIG).[50] Meoño, a strapping, avuncular man in his early sixties, was a well-known, polarizing figure with both loyal comrades and bitter enemies. As a teenager, he became involved with the Catholic student group Cráter, and his experiences in the countryside moved him to join the insurgency. Rising through the ranks of the Guerrilla Army of the Poor (EGP), Meoño served on the group's National Directorate, devoting his life, as he put it, "to fighting for respect for human rights, to the fight for democracy, to the fight for justice in this country, for the rule of law."[51] Meoño broke with the EGP shortly before the Peace Accords and then ran the Rigoberta Menchú Tum Foundation for a decade. He was, serendipitously, already leaving the foundation when the police archives appeared on the scene. "People with religious beliefs might say that this was a *providential* event," Meoño reflected, "something that arrived at the *exact* moment when I was looking for something"—not employment per se but a means of continuing what he saw as his life's work.[52] "Directing the archives project fits exactly with what I believe and think," he told me. "I don't pretend to promote impartiality or neutrality. Not at all."

Meoño's postwar objectives included the recovery of what he called "democratic memory"—a focus on the history of political struggle, rescuing and restoring the stories of those who had resisted dictatorship, even if their alternative visions had failed or been flawed in their execution. Without protecting this "democratic memory," Meoño believed, Guatemala would never construct a democratic national identity; instead, it would continue to criminalize those who fought for the right to think differently, discouraging future youth from politics and leadership. "The idea of the rights to memory, truth, and justice is not an issue of the left or of the right," he argued. "It's an issue of fundamental human rights, independent of ideology or political militancy."[53] Perhaps, but most of those working on questions of historical memory were clustered at one end of the political spectrum. Many who had been involved on the Left during the war found themselves reconstituted and represented as a peacetime "human rights sector," despite the many divides of ideology and praxis among them. (This essentializing of progressives was usually intended to discredit them; for example, conservative *Siglo Veintiuno* columnist Alfred Kaltschmitt slurred the employees of the government's National Reparations Program [PNR] as bitter ex-guerrillas who had failed to "install their Marxist-Leninist Shangri-La.")[54] As such, the PDH knew that "it could provoke some controversy" for Meoño to become the project's figurehead; "we did think about putting someone less political and less polemical in the job," Villagrán said.[55] In the end, Meoño's experience trumped his divisiveness, at least to the PDH.

With funds from the international community, the rescue could start to be conceived as a medium-term Project. The original volunteers and staffers borrowed from NGOs could be hired semipermanently, and could grow in number. Under Meoño, the Project began looking for appropriate individuals to work on this sensitive project: *gente de confianza*, trustworthy people who sympathized with its goals and understood the importance of discretion. As will be discussed in chapter 6, many of those hired under these guidelines were people already known to the PDH or Meoño, many of whom had strong personal links to the archives or had lost family members or friends during the conflict. By December 2005, they numbered more than fifty. They could be counted upon to honor the confidentiality agreement all Project staff had to sign, stating that they would not disclose any information contained in the documents.

But other sectors reacted less positively to Meoño's appointment and to the entire "human rights" cast of the initiative. In the first days after PDH investigators found the archives, a delegation from the PNC's Civil Investigations Section—its detective force, historically involved in investigations of a political character—arrived at the PDH's central office and shadowed its personnel, collecting their names and tracking their comings and goings. Days later, a drive-by shooting blew out the office's front windows; while the archives were the most controversial initiative then under way at the PDH, "neither did [the gunmen] leave a note saying, 'this is because of the archives.'"[56] As with many threats against human rights advocates in Guatemala, the messages communicated were ambiguous by design, making it difficult to clearly attribute responsibility or motive.[57]

Some attacks on the Project, though, were unequivocal. Generals from the Association of Military Veterans (AVEMILGUA) visited the ombudsman twice to pressure Morales in person, demanding Meoño's firing and information about the other people hired on at the Project.[58] (Morales refused both solicitations.) María Ester Roldán, the judge who granted the PDH access rights to the archives, was approached by a police lawyer and offered her price to reverse the decision. When she refused, she received death threats, her home was machine-gunned, and her office was ransacked.[59] The same week, someone threw a Molotov cocktail at the installation housing the archives, causing one of several suspicious fires on the site during the Project's first year.[60] Of course, the flip side of staffing the Project with rights activists and conflict survivors, as controversial as it was in certain sectors, was that these staffers had seen worse; their commitment to the initiative would not waver. "You hear about acts of violence all the time—deaths, murders, disappearances, kidnappings, even though we're no longer in this war, even though they've signed peace accords," said one worker. "But this work is part of the path we need to walk in order to build a different future for our children, for the next generations."[61] A few Molotov cocktails would hardly change their minds. Rather, most Project employees felt that the greatest danger they faced was simply "creating expectations that the archives can't fulfill"—erroneously giving the impression that every victim's case could be solved or every *desaparecido's* whereabouts determined.[62]

Threats to the young Project were not exclusively political. The physical conditions of the site posed health risks; respiratory problems due to the mold and dust plagued workers, who often showed up with hacking coughs or congestion caused by inflamed sinuses.[63] And in February 2007, area residents awoke in the middle of the night to a fearsome rumbling. Overnight, a city block–sized area just adjacent to the archives was swallowed by the earth, collapsing into a hundred-meter-deep sinkhole that consumed houses, businesses, and several local residents.[64] The disaster required the evacuation of nearly a thousand people; it also plunged the Project into chaos. "The uncertainty of the hole was terrible," said the Project's inventory specialist and guardian of its archival master location registry. "There were aftershocks, there was always a risk that it could get bigger. The ground felt like when you're going down on a Ferris wheel. Everyone was working, but with a terrible fear!"[65] Work teams were reorganized into an emergency boxing convoy, working extended hours to ensure that as many documents as possible were packed for potential evacuation. Ultimately the sinkhole stabilized, though the city did not repair the damage for years. But it did not escape Project workers' notice that on top of the political and environmental dangers they expected at the archives, Guatemala City always offered unforeseen hazards, now including the possibility that the ground might simply disappear beneath them. "Honestly, habit has made us get used to these sorts of things," said Rosario; as such, setbacks tended to strengthen workers' resolve, or at least to roll off their backs.[66] "In life, you always have to take the good with the bad," the inventory specialist reflected, "and look for the silver lining in any human situation. Because of the sinkhole, many of our documents got put into boxes for the first time!"[67]

The drama of the sinkhole was, in retrospect, a minor example of the physical challenges at play. Before any investigative work could begin, critical infrastructural modifications had to be made. From an archivist's perspective, the site was a nightmare. The warehouse, planned as a multistory edifice, was never completed. It was supposedly intended to be a police hospital, though the profusion of small, windowless rooms inside revealed that patient care was not its main purpose. Because construction had never progressed beyond the second floor, what served as the roof was insufficient for protection against inclement weather. The ceiling let water pour through like a sieve. Lacking windowpanes, the windows were simply open holes in the walls, through which rain, debris, and bats passed freely. Some window frames were stuffed with old, waterlogged eight-inch computer disks (ostensibly, if implausibly, to help keep the rain out); these warped, obsolete disks were revealed, much later and with a tremendous amount of effort, to contain valuable and salvageable data. The electrical wiring was shoddily strung, presenting yet another fire hazard. The bathroom facilities could only optimistically be described as rudimentary, and they were too few to accommodate the team. Several times, the women's bathroom flooded the building's rear, necessitating further emergency moving of documents and terse meetings among female workers about how to prevent future plumbing problems that might endanger the records. And as another rainy season approached in 2006, water continued to seep in and soak more documents.

Eager to begin case investigations but mindful of these logistical obstacles, the Project moved to exert physical control over the compound. Staffers exterminated rats and roaches; repaired and expanded the electrical system; did their best to improve the bathrooms, and later built a new bathroom structure adjacent to the main warehouse; painted, installed panes of glass to create windows, knocked down walls to allow air to circulate, and covered the dirt and concrete floors with vinyl; patched holes and replaced filthy, cracked skylights to let the sun stream through; cleared out huge quantities of trash; raised great mountains of documents onto wooden slats; gathered the outdated computer disks for later data retrieval; and installed fire extinguishers. Among the most pressing concerns were the junked automobiles piled up willy-nilly in the bald fields surrounding the site, in places stacked three or four high. The fields were the tow trucks' dumping grounds for all vehicles destroyed in the city's traffic accidents; stray dogs lived amid the twisted metal carcasses, which included decades-old cars and even the skeleton of a downed airplane. These wrecks, their tanks half full of gasoline, put the documents at grave danger of succumbing to fire—a risk made all the more evident after the Molotov cocktail attacks of May 2006—but the Project did not have the equipment, money, or legal authority to move them. Some of the site's problems were particularly vexing; two visiting Swiss conservation experts mused that while the persistent bat infestation endangered the documents by generating a profusion of acidic guano on the top sheets of record bundles, the bats also provided a worthy service by helping control the building's insect population. This led the experts to the (only half-jesting) conclusion that the ideal solution would be to outfit the winged pests with miniature diapers.[68]

Security, too, was a concern; how could the PDH guarantee the safety of both the documents and the workers? Unarmed guards had watched over the site since the PDH's arrival, but more substantial security infrastructure was needed. The Project installed gates both at the entrance to the archives area and at the entrance to the entire wing of the PNC base. The team of ten guards—still unarmed—now sat inside booths of glass and poured concrete, from which they monitored footage rolling in from the newly installed surveillance cameras around the site's periphery. Thick curls of razor wire now spiraled atop perimeter fences; inside the building, locking iron gates were fitted into the doorway of every workspace, ensuring that no police officials or other intruders could tamper with the Project's files and notes. These measures, though an improvement, were undercut by a simple fact: although the PDH had the right to consult the archives, as assured by the 2005 judicial order, the documents themselves still belonged to the PNC, and the police and the Interior Ministry could continue to use them as they saw fit.

This point was driven home during the summer of 2006, after Spanish jurists established a special ambulatory commission as part of their effort to prosecute eight Guatemalan generals and police chiefs for genocide in Spanish courts.[69] The event under investigation was the infamous 1980 Spanish embassy fire, a peaceful protest that ended in a raging inferno killing all but one of the protesters, who were barricaded inside the burning building by police. (The surviving protester was kidnapped from the hospital, his tortured corpse dumped the next day.)[70] The day after the Spanish judge arrived in Guatemala to hear witnesses, a group of police agents turned up at the archives and asked Project staff to show them any and all documents relating to the early 1980s police death squad Commando Six. (Commando Six was involved in the embassy fire, and its then chief, Pedro García Arredondo, was one of the eight individuals named in the case, along with then director-general of the PN, Germán Chupina.) This was an obvious attempt to bully the Project, but it also suggested that police and military interests understood the value of the documents and were looking to arm themselves against prosecution.[71]

Intimidation came in many forms at the Project, most tangibly in the daily surveillance of Project workers that PNC personnel carried out during the PDH's first months on the scene. The police carefully noted which documents Project staff consulted, what hours they kept, and what they discussed while they did it. While Meoño and his staff worked to maintain cordial relations with the police's own archival employees, tensions initially flared between the two groups, who hardly shared a history of collaboration. Again, Project staffers' activist backgrounds provided them with a key attribute—tenacity—that allowed them to put their heads down and ignore any interference. "When we started, the police were running around as though they were 'taking care' of the documents, but really they were making sure we weren't touching anything or looking at anything they didn't want us to see," said one worker. "But so we said fine, let's just work naturally, and talk to them normally."[72]

In the end, the task of remaking the archives—re-creating their system of organization and archival chain of custody while gaining intellectual command over their contents—would prove even more difficult than clearing the logistical and physical hurdles. Fixing up a building, cultivating international donors, and operating under the radar were things that the Project and its allies had done before in other contexts. But managing archives, turning a massive warehouse of decomposing documents into a usable resource, keeping track of the information being found, and decoding how the police had operated in order to decipher the records—these were new frontiers. Mastering this alien territory would force Project workers to expand their perspective on the archives, to gaze for the thousandth time at the papers and suddenly see something different: not just the potential for smoking-gun individual documents but, rather, the elaborate bureaucratic logic behind them. They needed to learn, in Ann Stoler's formulation, to see "archiving-as-process rather than archives-as-things."[73] Walking in the archival footsteps of their former enemies, these amateur historians needed to understand how the PN operated, to get inside the police's proverbial head and grasp how the institution *thought*, if they were to have any hope of reconstituting its archives. It would not prove easy, as we shall see in chapter 3.

Working in their favor, though, was the fact that winning the battle for the police records had been no accident of fortune. Instead, it was the product of more than two decades' worth of hard-fought political struggle over archives and access to information, which had imparted instructive lessons. Beginning in the mid-1980s, when family members of those disappeared and killed in Guatemala City began to organize around the collective demand for information about victims' fates, state transparency and archival access became important planks of their agenda.[74] The fact that activists had spent years attempting to gain access to state security records, with one important success in 2003, had laid the groundwork for grappling with the PN archives. The Project would build upon the folk knowledge accumulated over the course of those skirmishes, which I call the "archive wars," but it would also confront the same obstacles—state hermetism, military opposition, and a lack of citizen empowerment vis-à-vis state records that mirrored broader patterns of obscurantism and disenfranchisement. Before we can turn to the development of the Project, we must first look back upon how it became possible for activists to even dream of winning access to state security records. We must consider how—through the unlikely confluence of long political struggle, propitious historical circumstance, and good fortune (itself a rare commodity in postwar Guatemala)—the unthinkable could be made real.

| **ARCHIVAL CULTURE, STATE SECRETS,**

AND THE ARCHIVE WARS

I leave something written in order to attest to the fact that I did it—I write that we killed the following people because they were communists, and here's the proof. The necessity of leaving something written about one's activities is almost inherent in humanity. To link oneself with the past using proof. This causes archives to not be destroyed in their entirety, to at least be kept in part or brought together or even hidden—but not destroyed.

—Esteban, Project worker

At the corner of Guatemala City's central plaza sits the stolid edifice housing the national archives, the Archivo General de Centroamérica (AGCA). For years, the AGCA shared the corner with one of the rudimentary public urinals found throughout the city, whose metal door exhorted users to "¡Orine feliz, orine contento, pero por favor, orine adentro!"[1] The urinal's visitors did not always hold up their end of the bargain, however, and being forced to hop over streams of urine in order to enter the archives was not an uncommon experience for those who wished to look up a family tree or a property record. The situation worsened when the urinal was removed in 2007. The drain had vanished, but the cultural memory of the corner's principal use—the idea of the national archives as, above all, a place for excretion—endured. Such numbers of people started relieving themselves directly against the side of the building that knee-height stalagmites of dried uric acid soon ringed it. The AGCA was forced to ask its janitors to daily mop away the results, which obstructed access to the main doors. Windows had to be kept closed against the stench. One Project archivist was struck that of all the institutions bordering the plaza—the Metropolitan Cathedral, the National Palace, the army's pension authority—the archives bore this burden: "If they'd put the urinal in front of the cathedral, everyone would have been outraged—that it's a violation, it's indecent, it's disrespectful—so why is it acceptable to put it in front of the national archives?"[2] She read its placement as a sign that most Guatemalans did not appreciate the archives' importance. As the AGCA's director wearily remarked, "It's as though the people were pissing on their own history."[3]

This unfortunate tale speaks to larger truths about Guatemala's archival politics. We have seen how the National Police archives were, after the formal counterinsurgency concluded, left to neglect and disorder; agents assigned to the archives, consigned there as a punishment, called it *el basurero*.[4] But they were not an isolated case. Instead, documents in Guatemala were generally referred to as *basura*—trash to be eliminated, not resources to be protected.[5] The national archives were distressingly underfunded; from the 1960s on, state institutions ceased bothering to turn over their records to the AGCA, despite the constitution's stipulations. In fact, the dire conditions in which PDH investigators found the PN archives were, no doubt, replicated in the storage warehouses of every organ of government (hence why the archivists who first saw the PN records were comparatively nonplussed). The work of Ann Stoler and others has shown us that the *form* and manner in which archives are kept are as important as the *content* they reveal.[6] What did it mean that archives were considered garbage in Guatemala? What purpose did this attitude serve, and what does it reveal about the state's technologies of rule over time—or about everyday Guatemalans' efforts to change them? Scholars of archival and political science often link the accessibility of state archives to that state's levels of accountability; the more archival access, the more democracy. This observation has some truth to it, but it is not particularly interesting. Such a simple correlative elides the richness of information about a state's character—and the fabric of the relationships between state and citizenry—to be gleaned, historically and ethnographically, from the attitudes that state fosters about archives.[7]

"Castrated in history," argued one Guatemalan journalist, "we are a people without knowledge of ourselves." He distilled into a single scene what he saw as a disorder afflicting the body politic: "The image which best identifies us is that of a son, who arrives at the house after his parents die, looks at all the items his parents had kept, and says, 'Look at all this garbage they had.' Without sorting through their possessions, he throws them all in the trash, and cleans out the space with disinfectant."[8] The argument echoed the words of many workers at the Project, who knew that a long legacy of authoritarian rule had powerfully and purposefully disconnected society from its own history. Historical myopia served as a technique of governance and took many forms. "History," in school curricula and the Guatemalan academy, referred only to tales of great men—presidents, *ladinos*, independence heroes. Archives, which offered potential routes into what had long been silenced (while, as Trouillot points out, also creating new silences of their own), were devalued, dumped, or destroyed.[9] And postwar political opinion makers, some of whose hands were bloodied during the war, promoted two self-serving myths. One was that no archives existed to substantiate victims' claims; the other was that to advance as a nation, Guatemala needed to turn the page, leave the past behind, and not succumb to the "sickness" of memory.[10]

From the mid-1980s on, however, activists began confronting these myths as part of their efforts to demand justice for counterinsurgency victims. The issue of access to state documents was a charged battleground years before the appearance of the PN archives, and we must place the discovery of those records in that broader context. The main bone of contention was the concept of *secreto de estado* (state secrecy) enshrined in Article 30 of the Guatemalan constitution. The article stipulates that administrative information is public, save that pertaining to "military or diplomatic affairs of national security."[11] State authorities repeatedly refused petitioners' requests for archival access using Article 30 as justification; complainants challenged the legitimacy of such denials, often applied to requests having little to do with current national security.[12] In the process, the language of history, memory, and archival access became an idiom that war victims used to make claims on the state, particularly as popular movements were decimated by counterinsurgent terror. Conservative and counterrevolutionary forces in Guatemala had exploited the power of archives earlier than had the Left; however, progressives came to appreciate their use-value as well. This chapter traces the genealogy of their wars of position, in Gramscian terms, over archival access, which I refer to as the *archive wars*.[13] Archives in Guatemala, as elsewhere in the Americas, were not just technologies of rule; they were sites of battle between rulers and ruled.[14]

Tracing the evolution of Guatemalan archival culture provides a window into the shifting nature of postwar society. The language of archival access, and the actual manipulation and rescue of suppressed archives, came to represent and embody larger processes of contestation surrounding the country's postconflict trajectory, the relationship between state and citizen, and the role of history in contemporary politics. Archival culture is state politics; the keeping of records, granting of access to them, and denial of access to them lie at the heart of all systems of government, and examining these practices over the course of Guatemala's move out of armed warfare demonstrates the extent to which the Peace Accords did not much change the exclusionary, militarized nature of the state. The circumstances of the PN archives were, in many ways,

FIG. 2.1 Family members of the disappeared sought out state records in an attempt to answer their shared question: *¿Donde están?* (Where are they?). © Jean-Marie Simon/2012.

the exception proving the rule about the transition to electoral democracy; rescuing the PN records, and the challenges faced during the process, highlighted the poisoned nature of the country's archival politics. In working to valorize archives, the Project cast the stakes of fostering a national culture that defiled its own historical memory into stark relief.

GARBAGE AND NATIONAL PATRIMONY

In December 1992, a Central American woman walked into Manhattan's Swann Galleries—the best-known rare-document auction house in the United States—carrying ten documents in a portfolio case that she said had been passed down through her family. The records she offered for sale, worth tens of thousands of dollars, included a sixteenth-century coat of arms for the city of Santiago de Guatemala, a document bearing the signature of Spanish conquistador-chronicler Bernal Díaz del Castillo, and foreign treaties with Guatemala signed by the likes of Theodore Roosevelt, Woodrow Wilson, and Queen Victoria. The would-be archival entrepreneur, María Elisa Rohrmoser, successfully made the sale, though she was never able to collect her money; between signing the deal and picking up her check, Rohrmoser was arrested by customs agents, who had been tipped off that her supposed heirlooms were actually rare documents stolen from the Archivo General de Centroamérica.

And Rohrmoser was no garden-variety thief, but the spouse of Julio Roberto Gil Aguilar, then the director of the AGCA. It was an inside job.[15]

The AGCA's holdings, along with those of the Catholic Church and the municipality of Antigua, have historically been Guatemala's best preserved and institutionalized.[16] And the idea that a collection viewed by its own director as ripe for the plunder represents the best of Guatemalan archival practice is sobering indeed. On the bright side, the records purloined by Rohrmoser and Gil Aguilar had at least been sufficiently well kept as to remain saleworthy. In contrast, the Guatemalan Association of Archivists estimated in 2008 that some 90 percent of the country's archives were in a state of utter decay or abandon, and that statistic referred only to those archives still extant.[17] It was so common for outgoing government functionaries to destroy their records in order to conceal evidence of their own wrongdoing that another archivist supposed some 30 percent of all Guatemalan documentary patrimony had already been destroyed.[18] That by 2008 only ten archivists had ever graduated from Guatemala's only archival science training program was also revealing.

Indeed, in many respects, the AGCA was a banner achievement in a country inclined to let documents rot. Founded in 1846 as the Archivo General del Gobierno just after the consolidation of independence, the national archives became the premier document collection in Central America, specializing in colonial records from when Guatemala was an important administrative center for the Spanish crown.[19] In 1920, the Archivo General was placed under the jurisdiction of what became the Ministry of the Interior. What the institution lacked in funding and official support was compensated for by the dedication of its personnel. Beginning in 1935, longtime director José Joaquín Pardo, who administered the archives for three decades, personally cataloged— despite his lack of training or expertise—much of the holdings according to his own ad hoc organizational system, and the eclectic card catalog on the AGCA's second floor today remains the fruit of his labors. Prior to Pardo's efforts, the few researchers to brave the chaos of disordered documents worked, as one observer writes, "among mountains of old papers, in open warfare against rats, spiders, and other pests that infested the pages, prisoners of woodworms and abandonment. . . . Chance could reward the investigator with incredible surprises; or else, his time would be wasted uselessly in a tiring and fruitless search, *as though the task of researching our national history were nothing less than a punishment or a mythic act of supplication.*"[20]

In the 1930s, dictator Jorge Ubico—an early believer in policing a citizenry using records, and a master centralizer of power—ordered the transfer of state records held in Guatemala's departments back to the capital, to be housed in the national mint. The contemporary archives building was erected in 1956, and twenty-two linear kilometers of documents were moved there. In 1968, responsibility for the archives shifted to the Ministry of Education, and the national archives' function as the guardian of public administrative records was enshrined in Guatemala's first and only archives law to date, Decree-Law 17-68. In the same year, the institution was renamed the Archivo General de Centroamérica, the result of a meeting of the various directors of the Central American countries' national archives, who agreed that the Guatemalan archives, because its colonial holdings spanned other areas of Central America that had once fallen under the jurisdiction of the isthmian captaincy-general, deserved the status of being a *Central American* archives.[21] In 1985, the AGCA was administratively shuffled once more, incorporated into the Ministry of Culture and Sports, where it remains today.[22]

If 1968 was an important moment of growth for the AGCA as an institution, when it enjoyed at least lip-service support from President Julio César Méndez Montenegro, it was perhaps its last.[23] Though the new building erected in the 1950s provided space for the existing collection, its designers failed to anticipate the rapid escalation in the state's bureaucratic output due to technological advances like photocopiers and computers. It simply ran out of space to house new documents in the late 1960s, and this coincided with larger political trends. The 1966–1970 period saw a massive increase in the militarization of the state, the result of U.S.-funded fortifications of Guatemala's counterinsurgency apparatus. It was not a time of increased state transparency. Decree-Law 17-68, which regulated archival operating procedure for state dependencies, included no enforcement mechanism for its mandate that state organs turn over their records every decade, and since the AGCA building could not accommodate new records anyway, state dependencies simply left their files to rot in storage or destroyed those chronicling unsavory practices. "How does the state see archives? They see them as a site of potential accountability, where they'll be held responsible for their bad practices," said Project archivist Molina. "When you go to consult archives, they don't see you as a researcher; they see you as an auditor, looking for the abuses they're committing."[24] While security forces built painstaking surveillance archives of Guatemalans' political activities, "normal" state archives languished.

It was lazy practice with political consequences. "We archivists know that there are different factors that cause deterioration, in terms of documentary conservation, but the worst agents of deterioration are negligence, disinterest, and lack of knowledge about patrimony," said Molina. "For state institutions, all the issues of archival science are reduced to issues of space. An archive becomes a problem once the papers don't fit anymore. So they feel they have two choices: warehouse the documents or throw them out."[25] Both unsound storage and outright disposal imposed the same barrier to access. Were a citizen to visit, say, the Ministry of Agriculture and ask to see a particular set of records, an official might trumpet the ministry's transparency, directing the individual to a storage space heaped with millions of disorganized papers and wishing them good luck. It was archival access in name only. "I've come to believe that this is a deliberate strategy," said Project assistant director Fuentes—a cultivated attitude toward documentation that all too conveniently blocked citizens from exercising their rights. "How can we investigate if there are no documents? How can we know our history if there are no documents?" He ruefully recounted finding in the PN archives, along with directives ordering subordinates to burn certain quantities of records, a "rather grotesque" document prohibiting agents from using pages found in the archives as toilet paper, suggesting that the practice was sufficiently common to require a written proscription.[26]

The AGCA's holdings still largely stop in the late 1960s, though they remain a rich source for earlier periods. In the absence of a more robust archives law, the AGCA's twenty-strong staff relies upon a roving commission—a group of technicians who visit various state dependencies, remind them that the destruction of historical documents is illegal, and encourage them to maintain adequate and accessible archives within their own headquarters. Hanging on doggedly despite a decimated budget, so much so that their Internet access was cut off for several weeks in 2008 while bills went unpaid, the AGCA's staff gamely struggled to safeguard historical memory.[27] The roving commission, summoned regularly by state organs hoping for the go-ahead to burn old papers, conducted on-site assessments to help functionaries distinguish between "administrative" and "historical" records. Administrative records, archivally speaking, were those in ongoing use; historical records, commonly referred to as *dead archives*, were those whose administrative function had expired and whose primary value was as cultural-historical resources documenting institutional life.[28] In theory the AGCA would house and preserve these dead archives; in practice, it could simply encourage others not to destroy them. However, the nature of police archives makes it difficult to draw the distinction between "living" and "dead" records. Because so much of police work depends on access to individuals' criminal histories, documents that are forty or fifty years old retain administrative use, and cannot be considered "dead." Decree-Law 17-68's provision that all state records had to be sent to the AGCA every ten years, then, made no sense for police records; as Molina put it, "If a citizen, or a judge, asks for a background check on someone, what are the police going to do? Take a bus to the AGCA to look up their own records?"[29]

It was the AGCA's roving commission, brought in by the National Civil Police in January 2005 some six months before the serendipitous arrival of PDH investigators, that first laid eyes upon the National Police archives. That nothing came of this initial encounter with the records—that despite years of efforts by activists to secure state security archives, the archivists tasked with assessing the PN documents never thought to inform anyone of their existence—spoke to the depoliticized nature of "cultural patrimony" as an official concept of the state. The Law for the Protection of the Nation's Cultural Patrimony (1997) laid out the Ministry of Culture's standards for what qualified as the country's cultural heritage, noting that "it is necessary to legally promote the rescue, investigation, salvage, recuperation, conservation, and valuing of those goods which constitute Cultural Patrimony," whose destruction would be subject to punishment. Under the law, forms of patrimony both "tangible" and "intangible"—from Maya archaeological sites to musical instruments, local medicinal traditions to underwater paleontological remains, and including archives—were created equal and would theoretically be protected equally.[30]

In practice, however, the Ministry of Culture, like the AGCA beneath it, was afforded no meaningful enforcement mechanism with which to fulfill its responsibilities; it operated under extreme budgetary constraints while charged with too many tasks. This generated all manner of cruel bureaucratic farces. For example, just a year after the end of a war in which Maya culture and lifeways were systematically attacked by the state—with security forces using the destruction of indigenous graveyards, the rape of Maya women, and other forms of cultural violence to control or exterminate Indian identity—the cultural patrimony law stipulated that any act degrading Maya culture would be met with a fine of 5,000 quetzales, or about US$600.[31] As long as efforts to expand access to state archives were shunted into bureaucratic channels defining them as issues of "cultural patrimony," one could bet that they would be met with inaction. To this day, Guatemala has no national registry of its various archives; without knowledge of which documentary holdings even existed, how could the AGCA work to protect them?[32]

While the preservation of cultural patrimony was rendered toothless by the weakness of its guardian institutions, not all were blind to the value and potential of expanding public access to archives, especially those documenting the war. While the AGCA's struggle to save archives was a war of attrition, others engaged in direct battle over the issue. To the military, access to information had always been political. As Silvio René Gramajo Valdés indicates, hermetism and information security on the part of the army and the police were essential components of counterinsurgency strategy, particularly as the military engineered the for-show transition to democracy in the mid-1980s.[33] As successive civilian-led facade regimes performed the trappings of democratization, power brokers freed themselves from international opprobrium while tightening their grip on information—always using the *secreto de estado* provision as justification.[34]

This made access to archives a political minefield, generating a crisis of expectations that would prove difficult to contain. The contested process by which the state, the military, and civil society negotiated the liberalization of access to government information highlighted something archivists have long known, but scholars of transitional justice have, some argue, often ignored: the link between access to archives and authoritarianism.[35] Indeed, the debates over archival access were, ultimately, debates about the nature, and future, of the authoritarian and postauthoritarian state. And while NGOs and international donors had devoted considerable effort during the peace process to combating impunity in Guatemala, they almost never focused on archival access as one of the anti-impunity struggle's key battlegrounds—perhaps because *arcana imperii*, or state secrecy, is central not just to authoritarian rule but to democratic rule as well.[36] The military's use of Article 30, from 1996 on, to refuse solicitations for access to records provides a sense of how, as Bickford writes, "the vulnerability and lingering authoritarian characteristics of new democracies might be profoundly connected to authoritarian pasts."[37] In fighting to discover what had become of lost loved ones, activists combating dictatorship's legacies came, over time, to understand the role that archives could play in their struggle.

HABEAS DATA: A GENEALOGY OF THE ARCHIVE WARS

"We've always been interested in getting access to all state archives," Mutual Support Group (GAM) director Mario Polanco told me.[38] GAM formed in 1984, the result of encounters between family members searching for disappeared loved ones at the Guatemala City morgue, and it quickly became a leading advocate for victims.[39] Members of GAM were determined to discover what had happened to the country's *desaparecidos* and filed countless writs of habeas corpus (*recursos de exhibición personal*) with authorities to ascertain the whereabouts of those illegally detained, even as the answer was always the same: *sin efecto*, without result. The researcher today opening any bundle of PN records from these years finds it rife with these requests. In 1985 alone, GAM filed more than seven hundred such writs; it recognized that while the most disturbing acts committed by state security forces were unlikely to have

le los detectives

ronel de policía Pedro García Arredondo, destituido

PAGINA 8

pide proceso
funcionarios
PAGINA 6

icupan las
as del PR
PAGINA 10

reconoce a
de gobierno
PAGINA 11

cuatro cadáveres

as manos cercenadas

PAGINA 2

SINAS
CENTAVOS
LA CAPITAL
LOS
IENTOS

SECRETOS EN CASA DE DONALDO ALVAREZ. — Las autoridades descu-
brieron puertas y pasadizos secretos en la residencia del licenciado
Donaldo Alvarez Ruiz, ex ministro de Gobernación y líder del Partido
Institucional Democrático (PID). También hallaron listas con numero-

sos nombres de ciudadanos y centenares de fichas de personas con
sus fotografías y datos de identificación. En esta fotografía aparecen
25 de esas fichas, escogidas al azar por los periodistas. Información
en página 12. (Foto PRENSA LIBRE)

REVISTA
GUROS
Y TIRAS COMICAS
INCLUIDAS

"CONTE"

FUFAS
PROPANO   DESDE   CON 25

FIG. 2.2 Protesters discovered these files, of citizens under government surveillance, at the house of outgoing interior minister Donaldo Álvarez Ruiz. Guatemala's major dailies published photographs of the files in the days following the coup d'état that brought Efraín Ríos Montt to power. Photograph by *Prensa Libre*, 27 March 1982.

been documented on paper, police and army records could nonetheless provide important clues as to what had happened.

The point was brought home just after the military coup of 23 March 1982, when crowds of anguished protesters stormed the home of outgoing interior minister Donaldo Álvarez Ruiz and found stacks of files of individuals presumably targeted for elimination, which they displayed for publication in Guatemala's major dailies (see fig. 2.2). The discovery was a one-off window into the otherwise closed world of state archival surveillance; an easy way for military officials to discredit victims' claims was to note that they were "not sustained by documentary evidence."[40] In the late 1980s, GAM members filed a complaint with the Guatemalan Supreme Court denouncing the state's "kidnapping" of the archives of the police and the army, basing their demands on Articles 28 and 30 of the constitution. "They never even responded to us," Polanco recalled.[41] Only after the PN archives' reappearance thirty years later did GAM's surviving members learn that police officials had, as of 1980, instructed agents never to share police detention logs with judges, thereby guaranteeing that no habeas corpus request would ever yield results.[42]

Because of public officials' intransigence, activists put aside the issue of archival access for a number of years. But in 1993, tensions over documents twice flared anew. First, in March, personnel from the National Police's Identification Bureau (Gabinete de Identificación) anonymously denounced the plans of PN authorities to destroy the archives of the Department of Technical Investigations (DIT). The DIT, in existence from 1982 to 1986, was that period's incarnation of the police's elite detective squad, charged with executing politically motivated operations. Though the DIT was abolished by Vinicio Cerezo in 1986, renamed, and its personnel supposedly *reciclado*, or purged, its successor institutions maintained the squad's long-standing notoriety for carrying out forced disappearances and social cleansings. The DIT's archives would have offered considerable insight into some of the cases that most concerned the leaders of GAM, including those of GAM founder María del Rosario Godoy de Cuevas and her husband, Carlos Cuevas Molina; GAM founder Nineth Montenegro's husband, Edgar Fernando García; and GAM leader Héctor Gómez Calito, all of whose deaths or disappearances in 1984 and 1985 were subsequently linked to the DIT. Therefore, when the Identification Bureau chief, Luz Hernández Nova, informed her staff of her intention to destroy the DIT's criminal files, one agent sent a whistle-blower's letter to the press.[43] It expressed concern, and not necessarily a left-wing concern, that the archives "contain reports on individuals who under previous governments committed crimes," and if they were destroyed the criminals "would remain in impunity"; it indicated that "the information in the archives could serve in the investigation of acts committed during the tragic years of violence" and urged that authorities not be permitted to "make the documents disappear."[44] When word of the plan leaked, PN director-general Leopoldo Guerra insisted that it was "all a rumor." In response, GAM called on the PN to turn the archives over to either GAM or the PDH, "so that we can review them and be able to investigate for ourselves whether or not these archives contain any information about our loved ones."[45] Months later, when the furor had died down, PN officials shut down the DIT archives; another anonymous complaint to the press from within PN ranks blamed subdirector-general Fernando Ligorría for the move, calling it a "virtual amnesty" for the thousands of criminals whose acts were chronicled in the files.[46]

Also in 1993, after former human rights ombudsman Ramiro de León Carpio assumed the presidency, word traveled to human rights groups that the military had decided to destroy a large number of documents. In response, GAM worked with Nobel Peace Prize laureate Adolfo Pérez Esquivel, an Argentine activist, to bring a new kind of legal appeal to Guatemala: the writ of habeas data.[47] Habeas data holds that an individual has the right to access any information about herself or her family that is held by her government. It grants the individual access to, say, military files about the army's killing of her brother, just as a writ of habeas corpus would give that same individual the right to ascertain if her brother was being held in army facilities.[48] The concept's genesis is Latin American, first implemented by Brazil, then by Colombia, Paraguay, Peru, Argentina, and Ecuador, all countries that experienced internal conflict—and, importantly, forced disappearances—during the Cold War. (In 2007, the writ of habeas data was exported beyond Latin America to the Philippines, written into the constitution to address the high numbers of Filipinos killed and disappeared during years of internal separatist battle.) In affirming the right to habeas data, the Argentine Supreme Court argued that the right to information touched upon "the rights to identity and to reconstruct one's own history, which are closely aligned with human dignity."[49]

Taking a page from this initiative, GAM decided to import habeas data, if unofficially, to Guatemala. Seeking to prevent the destruction of the military records, GAM presented its own writ of habeas data to the Supreme Court and the Constitutional Court "for symbolic value." Polanco noted that it was "more of a moral appeal than a legal appeal," and the military eliminated the files anyway.[50] But the idea of archival access as a central aspect of postconflict justice would endure; the Commission for Historical Clarification (CEH) included in its final report a formal recommendation that the Guatemalan state pass legislation enshrining the right to habeas data and penalizing "the gathering, storage, or concealment of information about individuals, their religious or political affiliation, their trade union or social activism and any other data relating to their private lives."[51] (To date, no such legislation has been adopted.)

The peace process generated another space for contestation regarding archives. As mentioned earlier in this work, the CEH found its theoretical access to military and police records stymied. The commission, established in the 1994 Oslo Accord between the Guatemalan government and the URNG, was tasked with "the historical clarification of the human rights violations and acts of violence that have caused suffering to the Guatemalan population."[52] In order to carry out this mandate, the commissioners needed to examine security forces' files, and the Oslo Accord placed no restriction on the CEH's right to solicit information from government and military archives. However, it did not grant the CEH subpoena power, leaving the commission powerless to enforce compliance. As an initial salvo in what became a prolonged affair, head commissioner Christian Tomuschat filed a written request to defense minister Héctor Mario Barrios Celada and President Alvaro Arzú on September 9, 1997, for information on five well-known "paradigmatic cases": the case of "Los 28," the mass disappearance of some thirty PGT leaders in 1966; the mass disappearance of six PGT leaders in 1972; the mass disappearance of twenty-seven National Workers' Central (CNT) union members in 1980; the mass disappearance of seventeen more union leaders later that same year; and the 1989 disappearances of ten University of San Carlos student activists, members of the Association of University Students (AEU), five of whose corpses later appeared bearing signs of torture.[53] (Incidentally, the National Police was directly involved in all five cases.)

What ensued was an increasingly hostile war of letters between Tomuschat and various Ministry of Defense officials, in which army authorities responded to the CEH's requests by buck-passing, obfuscation, denying the records' existence, claiming that such access would violate Article 30's *secreto de estado* provision, and squabbling that the CEH, in investigating the military and police, was violating the "universal juridical principle" of presumed innocence and had therefore compromised its objectivity.[54] The National Police offered nothing in response to CEH solicitations, its collaboration "insufficient" and "superficial."[55] (Later, as Project workers labored in the PN records after their rediscovery, they found documents with "do not send to the CEH" scrawled at their top margins.)[56]

Ultimately, Tomuschat concluded that the commission's efforts to obtain archival evidence from the state were "conspicuously unfruitful." "On the whole," he wrote, "one may characterize the contribution made by the Government of Guatemala to the process of clarification as next to nothing. In particular the armed forces pursued a deliberate strategy of obstruction without admitting this." After first asserting that the CEH had no right to consult military archives, the army then contended that "the archives consisted of a black hole for the period under investigation by the CEH." Tomuschat concluded that the state's position "can only be explained by the fact that, during the long years of democratically elected presidents from 1986 onwards, the Armed Forces and the Secret Services, which had lost any sense of justice and equity, were largely able to maintain their roles as major power centers of the country," again revealing the connection between archival politics and the character of the state. The government's conduct toward the CEH, he argued, was a "black stain" upon the Arzú presidency.[57]

It also boded ill for the implementation of the Peace Accords, as the 1996 Accord on the Strengthening of Civil Power and the Role of the Armed Forces in a Democratic Society (AFPC), which abolished the PN and restructured the army, also called on the government to pass a law "regulating access to information regarding military or diplomatic matters of national security . . . with an eye toward avoiding any abuse of power and to guarantee respect for citizens' rights and liberties."[58] (Ironically, the CEH itself produced voluminous archives, but the UN deemed it too dangerous for those records to remain in Guatemala, and therefore ordered them sealed in a warehouse in New York for fifty years. They can only be opened with the written permission of the UN secretary-general in response to a petition from the Guatemalan state, and thus far, for reasons that should by now be obvious, no petition has been made. Archivists are not even allowed in to maintain the records' condition, such that by the time they are opened in the late 2040s, the 1990s-era computer disks and databases may well be obsolete and unusable.)[59]

The CEH commissioners' skepticism about the state's stewardship of its archives was borne out in 1999, shortly after the release of the commission's report. In a news item that dominated headlines for weeks, a fifty-four-page file chronicling nearly two hundred forced disappearances and political killings orchestrated between 1983 and 1985 by the Presidential Staff's intelligence unit—auspiciously known as "El Archivo"—was smuggled out of the army's archives and given to human rights activists in the United States, who published it.[60] The victims' entries featured their photograph, name and pseudonyms, information on their political activities, whether or not they had informed on their comrades during detention, and the dates of their capture and execution (or, occasionally, release), using the code "300" to indicate death. It was a gruesome document, in some cases revealing victims' fates for the first time. Its impact was explosive. Defense minister Marco Tulio Espinoza denied that the "Diario Militar," as it came to be called, belonged to the armed forces, while pressure from victims' advocates, who demanded access to the rest of the military archives along with army personnel registries from the 1983–1985 period, mounted.[61] Curiously, Espinoza fell back upon archival science in an effort to absolve the army of blame, claiming that attributing the Diario Militar to the army was a misidentification of provenance. He argued that all military documents were printed on letterhead, sported an identification number, and bore an official seal. Since the Diario had none of these features, Espinoza asserted, it could not be an authentic file.[62]

But the defense minister was forced to abandon his claim that the file was inauthentic, as the former leaders of the PGT, FAR, ORPA, and EGP came forward to confirm that the individuals in the Diario indeed had been militants in their organizations. Instead, the army took a new tack: stating that "we neither accept nor reject" the Diario as its own, it then alleged that all army documents

FIG. 2.3 By Fo, originally published May 1999. Used by permission of Fo/*Prensa Libre*.

from the war had already been destroyed, making this one a fake.[63] Ex-dictator Oscar Humberto Mejía Víctores, in power from 1983 until 1985, emerged from retirement to proclaim his innocence, insisting, "I never ordered that anyone be killed" and suggesting that the media firestorm was "like an Alka-Seltzer: it bubbles up for a little bit and then everything calms down again, because they have no proof, these are false testimonies."[64] Army officials scrambled to contain the public-relations disaster; after the National Security Archive's Kate Doyle accused Espinoza of destroying records regarding disappeared ORPA commander Efraín Bámaca Velásquez, a spokesman backtracked to announce that, in fact, the military had never destroyed *any* documentation from the armed conflict and had instead dutifully turned it all over to the CEH.[65] Defense minister Héctor Barrios Celada, who preceded Espinoza, was "evasive and nervous" at a press conference when attempting to walk the rhetorical line of neither accepting nor rejecting the file's veracity.[66] Others were less circumspect: the director of military intelligence, Colonel Mario Mérida, accused victims' groups of having fabricated the Diario themselves, and right-wing presidential candidate Luis Ernesto Sosa Ávila claimed that those named in the Diario had indeed been murdered, but by guerrilla leaders, not the army.[67]

Despite the army's vigorous disavowals—or, perhaps, because of them—the Diario Militar represented the human rights community's first real victory in the "archive wars" of the 1990s. In the wake of the Diario's release, family members of the 183 individuals named in the document called upon President Arzú in his role as commander in chief of the army to release more files from the military archives.[68] The human rights ombudsman, Julio Arango, convened the Multi-Institutional Authority for Peace and Understanding (Instancia Multi-Institucional para la Paz y la Concordia), a group uniting some sixty-five human rights organizations with the objective of, among other things, fighting for archival access as it pertained to justice.[69] The Diario galvanized activists and bolstered the claims they had been making for years. But its greatest impact was, of course, on the family members and friends of the 183 men and women who stared out from the file. "I remember it very well, because when this document appeared, I was about sixteen or seventeen, and it caused a major crisis in my house," remembered Camilo, a young worker at the Project whose parents had both been Communist Party militants. "My mother was extremely upset—because you could just download the Diario from the Internet, and in it appeared all her friends from the PGT," lost comrades by the dozens, their destinies finally uncovered.[70] The dossier both wounded and soothed. It was traumatic to learn that a fallen compatriot had, under torture, turned in two *compañeros*, who were subsequently hunted down and killed. But finding out that a disappeared brother had, in fact, died offered new, if bittersweet, possibilities for closure for families forever left in a state of limbo. The nonagenarian mother of the disappeared trade unionist Rubén Amílcar Farfán, for example, had left her home's garage light on for the thirty years following his 1984 disappearance, so that if her son ever returned he would find the doorway illuminated and welcoming.[71] And the abundance of evidence contained in the Diario offered promising material for courtroom justice. In 2007, the Myrna Mack Foundation (FMM) and the Berkeley Human Rights Law Clinic filed a case before the Inter-American Commission on Human Rights on behalf of a group of family members of thirty Diario victims. (As of this writing, the case was still pending.) In October 2008, the commission held a hearing specifically regarding the right of victims' families to access state documents about their lost loved ones; more than five hundred documents from the police archives containing information about those named in the Diario were submitted as evidence.

Much as the national conversation about the Diario owed its intensity to the struggles over access preceding it, so too did it influence the next major archival flash point: 2003, when the long-overdue, Peace Accords–mandated dissolution of the Presidential Staff (EMP) presented the question of how to deal with the organization's records.[72] In fine Guatemalan security-reform tradition, the EMP had its name changed to the Presidential Intelligence Secretariat in 1993 to deflect criticism, but the intelligence service never changed its shady modes of operation. The CEH and REMHI reports fingered the EMP, and particularly its "El Archivo" intelligence unit, as having directed political terror in Guatemala City; it was responsible for some of the highest-profile crimes of the war and postwar periods, including the murders of anthropologist Myrna Mack and Bishop Juan Gerardi.[73] When then president Alfonso Portillo announced that he would finally disband the EMP and replace it with a civilian intelligence service, the news was warmly received. However, it came accompanied by whisperings that the EMP's archives would be destroyed in the process. In response, GAM and the Human Rights Office of the Archbishop of Guatemala (ODHAG) jointly petitioned to have the EMP's archives saved, turned over to the PDH, and opened for consultation and analysis. And in 2003, something unprecedented happened, as Portillo was leaving office: the petition was granted. Investigators overseen by the PDH would be permitted to enter the Zone 10 military base where the records were kept, under the custody of the Army General Staff, to photograph the EMP papers. It was a stunning coup for human rights organizations, in a country more familiar with coups of another sort entirely.

Members of GAM, Security in Democracy (SEDEM), ODHAG, the Center for Human Rights Legal Action (CALDH), and Sons and Daughters for Identity and Justice and Against Forgetting and Silence (HIJOS), sporting PDH jackets, arrived at the military base in February 2004 to begin work. Out of fear that the army would change its mind—team members witnessed, while at the base, the destruction of other groups of documents they were not allowed to consult—they opted to digitize as many pages as possible, as quickly as possible. After many discussions of how best to proceed, the activists opted to take pictures first and analyze the documents later.[74] Armed with digital cameras, several dozen workers—extremely nervous about working on an active base, where "they took your name and your time of entry, you knew they knew your license plates, where you were coming from, everything about you"—set themselves to photographing the documents.[75] They spent nearly two years, at varying levels of intensity, taking photos of more than a million pages of records that were stuffed in grain sacks and heaped willy-nilly in a leaky chamber.[76] "It was very . . . *artisanal*," explained one team member.[77] Although the EMP archival recovery initiative had indirect support from the international community—in the form of advising from the National Security Archive and the fact the NGOs that stayed until the end, SEDEM and GAM, were largely funded from abroad—it never elicited the kind of applied technical assistance, money, or attention that the Project would two years later. In retrospect, it was a trial run for the PN archives' recovery.

Instructive errors were made in the handling of the EMP archives. Because archivists were not included in the process, the EMP documents were photographed without maintaining the original order, ascertaining the provenance, or preserving the chain of custody of the records. Therefore, in a court of law it would have been too easy to dismiss the images as fabrications.[78] At the end of the initiative, the PDH and the NGOs were left with more than seven hundred compact disks of images, without any sense of the documents' order or the spatial relationships between different records, both important tools for their interpretation.[79] Divorced from their original contexts, the documents would be much harder to analyze after the fact.[80] Additionally, when the PDH was asked by human rights groups to take physical custody of the records—to which the National Defense General Staff (EMDN) actually consented—the PDH refused, citing financial constraints and a lack of space, leaving itself with only the disks of disordered images.[81] GAM and SEDEM were unable to fund an analysis of the images; the PDH kept the master disks because it had the original legal authority to digitize the records, but it never made a serious attempt to put them to investigative purposes or open them to researchers from other organizations.[82] In fact, the possibility of granting access to the images down the line was never even considered, which also affected how they were gathered. As Project archivist Lizbeth Barrientos attested, "Scanning for scanning's sake represents a double risk."[83]

These pitfalls—the uninformed archival practice, the PDH's ambivalence, the improvised nature of the initiative—meant that the opportunity of the EMP records was never fully capitalized upon. Warts and all, though, the experience with the EMP archives laid groundwork for the police archives project that would follow it. It conferred upon the PDH, GAM, and SEDEM a "certain level of moral authority regarding these types of archives," in the words of SEDEM's Iduvina Hernández, establishing these human rights organizations as "natural" stewards of documents pertaining to the war, even though the constitution (and professional archival prerogative) assigned that role to the AGCA.[84]

When the PN archives were discovered in 2005, the PDH convened the Human Rights Convergence, an umbrella group uniting many of Guatemala City's major human rights NGOs, to devise a strategy for grappling with the find. And when the PDH asked Convergence members to lend their organizations' employees to be volunteers in the nascent police archival rescue, groups like GAM and SEDEM had natural candidates to offer: those who had worked on the EMP initiative. Over the course of the Project's existence, easily a dozen veterans of the EMP archives ended up working on the police records, building upon past experience to help develop better practices for the future. Additionally, the army's decision to allow a group of activists onto an active base to sift through its documentary dirty laundry—an unprecedented move, though probably indicative of how thoroughly the records had been "cleansed"—rendered thinkable the idea of launching a project to rescue the police archives. It created political, intellectual, psychological, and juridical possibilities. "There was a lot of fear about doing this kind of work," said one GAM staffer who participated in both the EMP and PN initiatives. "Before Portillo, we never thought we could pull this kind of thing off."[85]

The Project, therefore, owed the dedication of its workers and leaders, as well as the support of domestic and international allies, to twenty years' worth of struggle over access to archives. It was, ultimately, a contest about citizenship, competing conceptions of justice, and the nature of the transitional state. This war of position over documents and history—an attempt not to overthrow the system but to wrest information from it—came into being just as Guatemala's war of maneuver, the armed struggle, ended. (In the mid-1980s, when GAM was founded, the URNG had already been effectively defeated on the battlefield.). And while the lessons learned over the two decades preceding the appearance of the National Police archives had been valuable ones, the Project would, in the following years, confront far thornier challenges for which no precedents existed. As we have seen, activists jumped at the opportunity to make use of the police archives, even as their efforts were bedeviled by the perversities of Guatemala's archival culture and politics. But to make headway in the service of a new objective—to actually *change* Guatemala's constricted archival culture by bringing the documents meaningfully to bear upon postwar society—would take new levels of creativity, grit, and hard work. It would require archival thinking.

| **HOW THE *GUERRILLERO*
BECAME AN ARCHIVIST**

We move around the archives like rats; I move like a rat,
looking for information, looking, looking.
—José Antonio, Project worker

B y mid-2006, as the first anniversary of the archives' discovery approached, the Project's staff began thinking not only of short-term emergency preservation but also of longer-term planning. The work had begun in a comparatively simple, targeted manner with the rescue of the mammoth pile of encrusted personal identity *fichas*. It had depended upon the folk knowledge that activists had accumulated over the course of the archive wars. Once significant headway had been made with the *fichas*, however, the work became more complicated. The Project would need a staged work plan, a systematic approach to archival organization, a speedier way of getting the work done, and a leadership structure to accommodate a staff that was, thanks to the sponsorship of countries like Sweden, Switzerland, and Spain, quickly expanding. At least for the moment, and in defiance of its protagonists' fears, the Project was free to grow. But how should it grow?

To begin addressing these questions in a more centralized manner, Gustavo Meoño, the former EGP commander in charge of the Project, asked a group of trusted workers to form a *coordinación*, or leadership team, which would make the major decisions concerning day-to-day operations by consensus. The exact composition of the *coordinación* varied over time, but it consistently included Meoño himself; the jovial, cherub-faced assistant director, Alberto Fuentes; the soft-spoken archivist, Ingrid Molina; the Project's historian; and four or five others. In conjunction with the PDH, whose influence lay more in overall strategy than in the nuts and bolts of project management, the *coordinación* established the priorities for the months to come. The Project would orient its work toward three fundamental and familiar goals: clarifying the history of the war, rescuing historical memory, and promoting justice. The investigation would focus on the period from 1975 through 1985, on the well-founded hypothesis that it would yield the bulk of the evidence on human rights abuses; a later statistical sampling of the documents would bear out this decision.[1] Because the ombudsman was up for reelection in mid-2007, the Project had to assume that its access to the records would last only through his tenure.

As such, the coordinators prioritized the human rights investigation, aiming to work as quickly as possible. But with the exception of Molina, few of them had experience in working with office documents, much less familiarity with the precepts of archival science. These were, for the most part, not individuals who had ever held office jobs, and decoding the bureaucratic logic of the police's documentary flow seemed like a distraction from the human rights investigation. Molina, and the AGCA's Ericastilla when she was invited to give archival training seminars to Project staff in 2005 and early 2006, had gamely attempted to impart the principles of archival organization to their unorthodox group of pupils, who for the most part failed to see their relevance. Because the police had been a large, sprawling bureaucracy comprising many substructures, Molina and Ericastilla emphasized that would-be amateur archivists had to pay close attention to archival science's two core concepts: original order and provenance.

Provenance, the basic principle of any archives, refers to how "records of one organization that created and maintained records in the conduct of business *must not be mingled* with the records of any other organization that separately created and maintained its records."[2] The files of any individual record-creating entity within a larger bureaucracy would become, in an organized archive adhering to international standards and using official archival terminology, a "fond"; its substructures' records would be organized as different "subfonds" within it. For the PN, this meant that documents kept by the Detective Corps, for instance, had to remain separate from documents kept by the Radio Patrol, or the subdirector-general, or Procurement Services, or the Fourth Corps, all mini-bureaucracies with their own leadership structures and records, though part of the larger police hierarchy. The postwar archives needed to be organized exactly as they had been during the war, such that a hypothetical former police chief, back from the grave, could walk into the PDH's reorganized archives and know precisely where to find everything. But provenance could be difficult to establish. To which fond did a record belong if it bore no evidence of receipt, or if it was one of six copies sent out by the director-general to various subdependencies, or if the sender had not included its information at the top corner of the first page? Establishing provenance meant learning how to mimetically grasp and reproduce the police's logic, to read between the lines.

The second principle, original order, requires respecting the original arrangement given to a body of records by the office that maintained them. If the First Corps kept its files on sex worker arrests arranged by internal filing number rather than chronologically, and indexed them accordingly, then respecting the original order would mean *not* rearranging the files chronologically. This would permit the police's own index to remain useful in locating files and would provide clues to how the PN organized its information, what the relationships between different records were, and how the PN made use of the voluminous data it kept. It would reveal how the organization thought.[3] Preserving the documents' original order also required an additional metastep: tracking any and all changes made to the physical placement of the records as staffers moved bundles of papers from unlit back corners to their worktables. Maintaining a chain of custody within the Project as the investigators conducted their work, moved boxes, or changed the storage layout after making infrastructural improvements would ensure that all PDH interventions into the documents would be accounted for, critical for assuring the documents' admissibility in legal proceedings. Any movement of a document from one room to another had to be recorded and witnessed, its archival path itself archived.

But archival principles do not exist in a vacuum. Instead, they are profoundly and inherently relational. To understand and deploy the concepts of original order and provenance, any archivist—amateur or professional— needed to understand how the PN itself had functioned. The documentary flow within any bureaucracy reflects that bureaucracy's structures, relationships between substructures, and internal hierarchies. A faithful archival restoration— "respecting records' creators as the authoritative voice in terms of record organization," as an early bible of archival science put it—demanded an understanding of how the institution and its agents behaved.[4] But because the PN had always worked in relative secrecy, an arm of a national security state with certain subsquads' operations unknown even to other members of the force, outsiders had never known much about how it operated. What was, for example, the relationship between a corps and the director-general's office? How many corps existed at different moments, and why? What was the role of the subdirector general? Was Commando Six, an infamous death squad, part of the Second Corps or a stand-alone entity? During which years was it active? What did the number "32," which appeared handwritten on certain documents and not others, mean? How did the PN interact with the military and with presidential intelligence structures? Who sent copies of their documents to whom? These questions had to be answered not only to re-create the organization of the documents but to grasp the secrets the archives had to tell.

As Lizbeth Barrientos, hired as the Project's second staff archivist in 2008, observed, "An archivist can't work alone. An archivist needs to work with a historian."[5] And in the fall of 2005, two specialists (the staff historian and an external expert in security issues) compiled an internal report based on their initial findings at the archives, a review of the PN's general orders, and the near-nonexistent secondary materials.[6] They struggled to piece together more than a hundred years of police history, with the archives still a disaster zone. At the outset, the Project's historian keenly felt the weight of her responsibility, exacerbated by the team's limited time frame; in the early months of the work, she had nightmares about the road ahead. "One dream I will always remember," she recalled, "was one in which I was surrounded by huge piles and piles of white dinner plates, which I had to clean in a certain amount of time. And of course what I was really thinking of was the piles and piles of documents that I was working on every day."[7]

Based on their preliminary report, which pointedly noted that "it will not be possible to conduct a more detailed investigation regarding the police's structure if the scope of the investigation is not reduced," a small historical investigations team was assembled in early 2006, and for more than a year it worked to clarify the PN's shifting structural history.[8] I worked on this team during my first months at the archives, and I quickly came to recognize the looping scrawl of PN ex-director Germán Chupina, who ran death squads from PN headquarters during the late 1970s and early 1980s. Our team's work was challenging because the structures we were most interested in investigating—death squads, rapid reaction forces, and riot police—were mobile and unofficial entities, quickly put together and taken apart, and so they generated little in the way of a paper trail.[9] The riot squad that had opened fire on a particular group of striking workers in 1981 would have been assembled quickly with officers culled from elsewhere in the police who then returned to their regular posts, thus not producing or receiving correspondence as a standard body would. Nonetheless, the historians advanced in their task over time. As the police's structure came into focus over the months, one work team used the wall of its work space to build an elaborate construction-paper tree, with the different branches and leaves representing different PN structures and substructures—a graphic organigram for workers to consult. New leaves were added and old ones taken away whenever new relationships between squads and sectors were revealed, thus charting the Project's evolving knowledge.

FIG. 3.1 Project workers improvised, and constantly amended, their own organigrams as they sought to understand the administrative structures and bureaucratic functioning of the National Police. Photograph by author.

When the tree eventually became too obsolete in its central assumptions—its main branches—to be amended, it was taken down, not without some wistfulness on the part of the team whose cinderblock walls it had brightened.[10]

While the historians worked to decipher PN structures, the activists, who had not yet come around to seeing the use-value of seemingly abstract archival principles, set about cleaning documents and organizing them the way that seemed most natural to them: chronologically. New *costales*, or grain sacks, of papers were opened and divided up by year, not by police subunit. Workers were divided into teams—one per year from 1979 through 1985, one working on the PN's ledger books, one each for the Second and Fourth Corps, one continuing with the *fichas* from the Identification Bureau, one with the documents from the Quetzaltenango departmental headquarters, and another working on the PN's daily reports.[11] The table teams regularly found pages or files that were badly degraded by mold, water, or time, and they improvised methods of archival preservation that, they thought, would help preserve documents for posterity. In this, the staff archivist served as an archival policewoman. When she informed workers that adhesive tape could not be used to bind torn pages because the glue would attract insects, they used staples. When they learned that stainless steel staples were not available in Guatemala, and that the staples they were using would further corrode the pages, they began replacing rusted old staples by literally sewing pages together with needle and thread. "Bueno, the men didn't know how to sew!" one worker remembered. "And so that was another thing, and we had to teach them how to sew! And they would say, 'Oh my God, I can't, I can't do it!' And we would say, 'Well, you have to learn, because you need to work!' And now they know how to sew."[12] (Once stainless steel staples were imported from abroad, the sewing was abandoned.)

Before description and filing systems were put in place to record the locations of important documents, workers would make their own notes on scrap paper, recording the salient facts of the record and where it could be found anew. When workers had difficulty recalling which PN code words referred to which positions (in the coded documents, mainly telegrams and radiograms, terms like "Kidar," "Kobof," or "Vupom" referred to "chief," "subchief," or "judge"), they made poster-style memory aids.[13] Workers' methods were artisanal and collaborative, relying on collective knowledge within teams to conduct the detective work of interpreting whatever happened to issue forth from the next flea-ridden sack of papers. It was a deeply human response to facing the inner workings of terror's bureaucratic machinery.

Each day at the archives presented new challenges for which workers lacked precedents. "If a document is getting wet because there's water on the floor, what do I do?" asked one. "I can't just move the paper because of the chain of custody. But the document is just getting wetter and wetter. What are you going to do?"[14] When a worker opened one of the large ledger books in which the PN tracked incoming and outgoing correspondence, and found live worms contentedly burrowing through the paper, what was the procedure to be? When one *ficha* was pulled from the stack bearing, instead of fingerprints, actual shriveled pieces of dessicated flesh sliced from the fingertips of one unlucky citizen and stapled directly to the file card, how was that *ficha* to be preserved?[15]

In most cases, questions of archival practice and documentary interpretation were resolved by collective reasoning, either in meetings or within teams. One worker, an elderly former EGP organizer, reminisced about stumbling across a file on one of Che Guevara's lovers alongside several younger employees, two women in their early twenties, and watching as the younger workers realized what they had found. "Let me tell you how beautiful it is when someone finds a document about a particular event, and they ask the group, 'How should I interpret this?' You get to see how young people from today try to interpret the events of the past," he remembered fondly.[16] These quotidian exchanges did more than provide clues about PN operations. They also impacted the subjectivities of Project workers, who found themselves retrieving their own dusty memories as they labored over equally dusty papers. "In the moment when a document appears with X information," said one, "it gets shared among the work group, and that generates learning—I can say, 'Look, I lived that, I went to that demonstration, and in that photo of the demonstration, I was marching behind that group you see there.' That is formative education. And when you tell them about who marched ahead, who marched behind, who was there, what was happening—that is political education. Hearing how this demonstration was conducted, that teaches them something."[17]

The communal spirit of the early days was not limited to the exchange of political and historical understandings, though many older workers remembered these interchanges with deep satisfaction. Staffers also collaborated on brightening their grim work space and managing the labor's emotional toll. When a stray dog, living amid the junked cars surrounding the compound, began hanging around at lunchtime, workers named her (La Lechu) and looked out for her by gathering leftover food from the modest *comedor* where most staffers ate lunch. The dog, scrappy and good-hearted, became a mascot. When La Lechu became pregnant, the 1979 table started a collection fund, raising money to build a little doghouse for her and her puppies as the rainy season approached. Soccer was another welcome diversion; to release stress during breaks, workers played pickup games on the pitted concrete joining the site's two warehouses. And to improve the physical work space, which still resembled a dank jail, many pitched in to bring leafy plants, political posters, colorful textiles, and photographs to spruce up the long gray halls. The archivist banned the plants—they generated humidity and attracted insects. But later, when the Project converted a parking lot outside the building into a garden, each worker was encouraged to contribute a plant to it. Soon, tall, symbolism-rich corn stalks and vibrant roses greeted visitors. New bulletin boards featured photocopies of articles showcasing the Project's work, and activist posters bore slogans like "Where There Is Little Justice, It Is Dangerous to Be Right . . . But When One Is Right, Justice Is Possible." Individual teams' work areas came to feature hand-drawn announcements of members' birthdays and soccer season calendars; older workers brought in art made by their children. Before long the musty building was, if not exactly a pleasant space, certainly a friendlier one whose appearance reflected the staff's personalities and interests.

These holistic aspects of the first year at the archives were highly valued, both psychologically and politically, by those who were doing the work. It was difficult, traumatizing labor, and the early solidarity of a few dozen workers served as critical social glue, sustaining them as they faced an uncertain future.[18] But the Project could not function this way in the long term; the posters and friendships would remain, but the artisanal methods became obsolete. Increased funding in 2006 allowed the Project to expand and systematize its work along three interconnected axes: the archival, involving the description and organization of the records; the quantitative, a sampling project under the supervision of the U.S. statistical analysis outfit Benetech; and the investigative, namely, the research into human rights abuses.[19] A year into its existence, with the foundations for these lines of work established and basic infrastructural problems solved, the Project would blossom in earnest—though not without suffering growing pains.

PROFESSIONALIZATION

"It's easy to imagine that when the Project publishes its first report, someone could try to discredit it by saying, 'It's just a bunch of Commies working there,'" said Jorge Villagrán, the Project's technology coordinator. "But the most beautiful part about the scientific rigor, about the quantitative elements of the investigation, is that that risk doesn't exist."[20] Indeed, the Project—always trying to anticipate where attacks would originate—embraced scientific methods as a means of shoring up its credibility. Early allies were members of the Human Rights Data Analysis Group (HRDAG), then a part of Benetech, a California organization placing technology and statistical analysis at the service of human rights initiatives around the world.[21] Their work with the Guatemalan truth commission, as well as in the historical accounting of human rights violations in Colombia, East Timor, Yugoslavia, Burma, Sierra Leone, and Peru, made HRDAG a natural partner of the Project, and an early visit by director Patrick Ball set in motion a long relationship.[22] Ball conducted an assessment of the archives, developing plans for a multistage random sampling of the documents and for the safe storage of the sample data at remote foreign sites.[23] A quantitative analysis of the PN's documentary output would eventually yield statistically sound results.

The random sampling, based on a three-dimensional topographical map of the archives site, was taken from computer-generated location points, to which trained staff would navigate and extract a preset number of document units. To generate those points, the computers relied upon an archivist's tool called the Master Location Registry (RMU), a global and ever-shifting three-dimensional map of the entire site that accounted for every bundle stuffed in every cranny. The RMU team preserved the documentary chain of custody, tracking every time a bundle or sack of records was moved from one room to the next for processing. Randomly extracted documents in hand, a team of codifiers would capture all the data from those documents: sender; receiver; any names mentioned (prisoners, criminals, officers); any actions (captures, releases, deaths) referred to; and all other details. The results were strictly calibrated using a series of exercises to ensure that codifiers captured the same pieces of information in the same way, eliminating bias. Villagrán explained why achieving precision in the quantitative sampling required such extensive training and standardization:

> We're just taking down the facts from the document; we're not interested in doing any interpretation. So if a document mentions that a decapitated body was found, how do we interpret that? Maybe in the qualitative analysis, one could conclude that this was torture, that this was extrajudicial execution, or something else. But in the quantitative analysis, the first fact is that this is a dead body. And then you have issues of consistency even with that objective fact: maybe to you that's a death, maybe to me it's a cadaver. That means we have zero consistency, that we don't understand the fact in the same way. When you have a group of fifteen people, it gets even more complicated.[24]

The captured data, once analyzed, would support any number of conclusions: for example, what percentage of the documents contained evidence of human rights abuses or had passed through the director-general's office? Such data could allow the Project to prove that the high command of the police was kept informed about all police actions, thus assigning them responsibility for abuses committed under their watch and kneecapping common protestations that any violations were simply the isolated result of a few bad eggs. The former director-general Chupina, pursued for genocide by Spanish courts until his 2008 death, repeatedly claimed that if the police had ever committed abuses, he was unaware of them; after Chupina died, his son told reporters that his father "told us he felt responsible for what the police did, but the way a father feels responsible for the actions of his children—not directly for what happened."[25] The statistics would allow—and did allow, upon their publication in 2011—the Project to debunk such claims by pointing to the archival chain of command. They would also protect the Project from accusations of bias. "If someone arrives and says 'Oh, this codifier slanted the results, so they're not legitimate,' I can point them to the standardization exercises," said Villagrán. "Or they can try it for themselves." This was crucial, politically, as it rendered the data, and qualitative deductions drawn from them, far harder to discount. "Of course," Villagrán continued, "the science just provides the math, the statistics, the method. But the end result is that you have a scientific process used to draw a political conclusion."[26]

Scientific and technical approaches would impact the Project in other ways, too. With Morales up for reelection in 2007, and hence the Project's long-term viability in doubt, everyone's top priority was the digitizing of the records. Digitized, the documents' contents would forever be available, even if access to the physical records fell victim to politics. "That's the only aspect of this that is irreversible," Meoño said, "the aspect where no matter what happens, those documents will never be lost."[27] The first computers were delivered in mid-2006, and scanners followed soon behind. (Staffers hotly anticipated the arrival of the first scanner, but when the delivery men showed up with the unwieldy box, they dropped and shattered it, delaying the scanning process by another precious month.) Setting up a complex server and scanner network in Guatemala, however, was tricky. Given the maintenance that scanners in constant use would require, they needed to be sourced locally and covered by local warranties; the same was true of the software for organizing the digital documents, significantly reducing the range of available options. Villagrán and his team, looking for machines that would fulfill their very specific needs, surveyed local scanner users to find the appropriate equipment. It was in the office of a credit card company where they found the only locally available brand of large planetarium scanners, needed to scan the giant PN ledger books. The smaller scanners also required careful consideration: most makes used a paper feed that pulled pages from above through small wheels and flipped them out the other side. Such a mechanism would destroy the archives' wispy, ultradelicate carbon papers. In the end, the Project opted for a fleet of small Kodak scanners (without the offending feed mechanism) for use on letter-sized documents, developing a work rotation of two shifts—one from seven in the morning until two in the afternoon, and the other working well into the evening—of workers feeding papers into ten scanners. The task was repetitive and boring; workers reassigned to scanning were often disgruntled at being displaced from analytical, interpretive work to the rote task of feeding pages into a machine, far too quickly to read any of their tantalizing content.[28]

The more high-tech aspects of the rescue work, which most directly confronted the constraints of local conditions, were finessed with significant assistance from the international community. A Swiss expert in digital records preservation helped set up the scanning system and image databases; HRDAG specialists trained the staffers engaged in the random sampling; U.S. statisticians helped design the statistical analysis. International contributions were not only technical; the foreign experts who made up the Project's International Advisory Board, assembled in March 2007, advised the Project on comparative archives laws, strategic planning, political concerns, and more.[29] But the technical assistance proved especially crucial. For example, the eight-inch floppy disks that had been stuffed into open windows to keep out the rain dated to the late 1960s; they could no longer be read, certainly not by any computer manufactured in the last twenty years. But a U.S. programmer and forensic data analyst, Hugh Daniel, cobbled together a complex disk-reading system and then shipped it, and himself, to Guatemala. The disks were so old that they predated the ASCII text encoding system, requiring Daniel to build computer connectors that would "translate" the disks from VISIDIC coding into ASCII before they could be read using a custom-made hardware setup composed of scavenged parts from various obsolete, painstakingly sourced vintage machines. After several weeks of trial runs, hardware adaptations, juryrigging, and sheer sweat, Daniel and the *compañeros* assisting him were able to render legible copious amounts of data from more than a thousand disks.[30]

Introducing archival science and international archival standards into the work rhythm proved more vexing, however, because it could not be managed by a few specially trained workers as were the random sampling project and the digitization initiative. Instead, every single worker needed to assimilate the concepts of original order and provenance, observe the documentary chain of custody, and master the norms of archival description as outlined in the International Standard for Archival Description (General), or ISAD(G).[31] They would have to learn, in the words of staff archivist Barrientos, to "think archivally," or *pensar archivísticamente*—a new mode of analysis that would forever change the way they looked at documents.[32] Rather than first reading what the document actually *said*, archivally thinking workers' eyes would immediately scan for clues to its provenance and original order—its sender, any seals or stamps indicating receipt, how many copies were sent and to whom, any filing numbers in the upper corners, the document type, notations in the margins. Additionally, Project coordinators needed to assign archival fonds and subfonds status to the different record groups, after decoding enough about the PN's structure and operations to determine which subentities maintained their own filing systems.

The Guatemalan archivists had emphasized these goals since the Project's inception. But because the PDH's *gente de confianza* did not yet understand the importance of archival methods to accomplishing their research objectives, the local archivists' counsel, coming from relatively young Guatemalan women, fell on deaf ears.[33] One young worker particularly impacted by the war—his father murdered by state forces, his mother detained by the army while pregnant with him—referred to himself only somewhat jokingly as a member of "the radical anti-archivists," an imagined affinity group of those who saw the archivists' cajoling and the internal seminars on archival methods as a waste of time.[34] The initial priority for many was to extract damning information and digitize the documents as quickly as possible, without tarrying over the details of organizing it all. "It was kind of de-motivating, because nobody listened to Guatemalan archivists," said Barrientos. "The people who were super gung-ho to scan everything disregarded the technical advice because they didn't want to hear it," because it was perceived as slowing down their high-pressure race for information about human rights violations.[35] "The first staff members were angry when I arrived and told them what to do!" remembered Molina. "There was tension, there was resistance to the archival science; people basically treated me like an irrelevant voice who periodically said things about archives and then they just went on doing things the same old way."[36]

It seemed easier to organize all the documents together chronologically, minimizing the time spent on understanding arcane new concepts. The problem, of course, was that such an approach would destroy the documents' original order, muddle their provenance, and thus damage their validity as evidence in court—with courtroom use of the documents being the entire point of the Project. The documents' archival bonds would be shattered. When Ericastilla, the AGCA archivist, was brought in for a few training sessions, she noted "the grave issue of how people weren't understanding archival science as a critical tool without which their investigation would be impossible. There was a strong resistance, that people didn't want to do archival work, they wanted to do their human rights work. They didn't understand that you couldn't do one without the other."[37]

Here, another foreign specialist—the U.S.-based archivist Trudy Huskamp Peterson, whose work with police and truth commission archives had taken her around the world many times over—played a decisive role in changing the Project's course. Peterson, a no-nonsense midwesterner with a cheery, matter-of-fact manner, wrote a preliminary assessment of the archives in 2005. But in May 2006 the Swiss government began funding monthly visits by Peterson, allowing her to provide consistent, hands-on training in the application of archival principles to the human rights investigation. And where the exhortations of local archivists were ignored, Peterson's prestige and voice were better heeded, resulting in major modifications to the Project's archival praxis. Referred to as "La Doctora" and marveled at for her comparatively towering height, Peterson, with the aid of a translator, issued directives, explained concepts, provided examples, and brooked little resistance.[38] It was a slow and strained process, and to some it was an unwelcome shifting of gears just when rank-and-file staffers had grown accustomed to their ad hoc methods of archival organization. Though Peterson had more extensive experience than her Guatemalan counterparts, Ericastilla also chalked the discrepancy in influence up to "a lack of national self-esteem, a national insecurity complex" in which Guatemalans were inclined to revere international experts while paying less mind to their own.[39] "I didn't have enough experience to force people to listen to me," Molina reflected. "Everyone just said 'yes, yes, Ingrid.' But with Trudy they couldn't do that!"[40] Molina and Peterson began working together, joining forces to overhaul workers' archival practices.

By November 2006, after nearly six months of intensive training, the Project was able to shift into a new phase of archival organization.[41] The three hundred boxes' worth of documents that had been organized chronologically would be, for the time being, set aside, an albatross of compromised provenance known as the *depósito documental*.[42] Henceforth, all the labor, from scanning and cleaning all the way up to case investigation, would be reorganized along archival principles, as opposed to simply using techniques of archival preservation. The table teams organized by year were now a thing of the past. Working with the archivists and historian, Project leaders assigned archival fonds and subfonds status to what they now knew were the major internal structures of the PN: its director-general's and subdirector-general's offices, the General Inspector's office, the Identification Bureau, the Department of Criminal Investigations (including the records of its institutional predecessors: the Judicial Police, Detective Corps, and Department of Technical Investigations), the Joint Operations Center, First through Sixth Corps, all the departmental offices, and the remaining substructures. Teams were reorganized to reflect the priority fonds, where they focused on those fonds' 1975–1985 documents. Each team used common reference materials to help interpret the records distributed to them by the document-cleaning teams: the historians' reports, secondary sources like the CEH report, an ISAD(G) manual, and a procedures manual that laid out guidelines for determining document type, original order, and provenance. The teams identified documents according to these criteria and then generated technically adequate descriptions of document series within their assigned fonds and subfonds, using ISAD(G) guidelines to structure their descriptions. They began to impose a standard order upon the records.

"After La Doctora Peterson came," remembered one older worker, "we had to do our work in a different way. It was difficult to understand."[43] Some complained, arguing that original order and provenance were perhaps important in well-organized First World archives, but did not apply to the Guatemalan records. "Now it makes me laugh, but at the time it made me want to shoot someone—today they tell you that we're going to organize the documents in a certain way, and then four days later they tell you we have to do it another way," remembered another.[44] In general, younger workers grasped the new concepts more easily; they were generally more educated and more conversant with modern organizational methods. This created strains during the transition away from improvisational work practices. As one worker and ex-guerrilla in his midsixties said of the youngsters quickest to master the new approach, "They thought that because they were political science students, they had the right answers all the time."[45] Older veterans brought in for the infraknowledge accumulated through long trajectories of political involvement struggled to apply their life experiences under a new division of labor, one that made most employees' daily work into a quota of minute tasks rather than a broad collective project. Workers in their early twenties were fast-tracked into leadership positions; the march of archival professionalization felt to some like a devaluation of their political acumen and experience.[46]

Nonetheless, archival thinking took hold in unexpected ways. Once it became clear that archival organization and description practices could improve workers' ability to locate and analyze the documents—that archival practice would expedite the human rights investigation—staffers came to embrace the logic of thinking archivally. A few of the original doubters even signed up for university courses in archival science, taught by Molina and Ericastilla, which they attended evenings and weekends on top of their full workdays. After the archival fonds were standardized, some workers even found themselves slipping when wanting to reference an arm of the PN—say, the Joint Operations Center—and referring to it as a *fondo*, or fond, rather than as a police entity. (As one told me, "Some *fondos* of the police were really just used to repress.")[47] *La archivística* was, as the most die-hard activists came to believe, the only way investigative work could successfully be done. "When the archives first appeared, we said, 'Okay, there's the archives, let's go do our investigation,'" remembered Fuentes, himself a late convert to archival methods. "The first lesson we learned was that it was *impossible* to do any kind of research given the condition the archives were in."[48]

Archival categories came to be important lenses through which Project workers interpreted the police's structural history. But they also affected the way that workers understood themselves, the history of the war, and their relationships with one another. Archival thinking was a tool, but it was not without its own powerful effects—it mediated identity as well, hailing workers as archival subjects in a new and different way from that intended by the police in the first place. One embassy staffer from a Project donor country remarked of Meoño that the former EGP leader, after enough exposure to finding aids and archival descriptions, began to manifest symptoms of "Stockholm syndrome, like someone who was so close to his kidnappers that he came to understand their reality. Now he knows so much about archival science. Trudy [Peterson] infected everyone!"[49] Peterson identified the end of the Project's first phase as the moment when, in early 2008, she "heard Gustavo Meoño give a tour of the archives and explain the concepts of 'chain of custody' and 'provenance' and 'original order' absolutely perfectly. I would guess that three years ago Gustavo had never heard of those concepts, and today they are a fundamental part of the vocabulary of everyone at the Project."[50] The *guerrillero*, while in search of paper cadavers, had become an archivist.

Interestingly, integrating archival practices into the Project was no one-sided compromise. The idiosyncracies of the archives demanded flexibility and adaptation from not only the activists but also the archivists. "A group of archivists," said Barrientos, "would have identified the fonds first, classified the papers, organized the papers, described the papers, placed the papers in their storage locale, and only *then* scanned them."[51] In such a scenario, needless to say, analysis of the documents would come even later, once all the other steps had been achieved. The question facing the Project was, as the PDH's Carla Villagrán put it, "how to introduce the idea of human rights investigations into a technical-professional tradition that's so rigid in this sense."[52] The specificities of the PN archives—which compared to, say, the Stasi archives, had been encountered in a frightful state—required Project archivists to accept a new and unprecedented order of operations. Waiting to clean, organize, and describe the entire archival holdings *before* commencing scanning or analysis would have involved a wait of something like twenty years, and would probably never have happened at all, since foreign governments interested in transitional justice would never have funded an archives project lacking an immediate human rights component.[53] The Project's funding, dependent on the whims of the international community, was then guaranteed only through the fall of 2007; on top of that, if Morales lost his bid for reappointment, the PDH would only have two years' worth of access to the documents. Because the Project existed in a permanent "emergency situation," in Walter Benjamin's words, it required a more contingent and specific modus operandi, drawing from both archival and investigative toolkits.

As such, it was necessary to "create a concept, and an innovative methodology, in order to develop both the *archivística* and the investigation in a simultaneous and complementary manner."[54] Workers in charge of archival description were trained to identify documents of interest to investigators, passing photographs of them along to the investigative team and ensuring, by accurately identifying the document's provenance, original order, and RMU location, that they would be correctly interpreted and located in the future. Training was constant and ongoing. Meanwhile, the archivists had to adjust their technical priorities. "It's not the same to tell a researcher to wait a couple of months for a document as it is to tell a citizen to wait, someone who has already waited ten, fifteen, or twenty years to find out what happened to their loved one," said Molina. "I think this is very important, and in the field of archival science this element has really been left to one side." Although archivists were trained to see all users of archives—and all documents—as equal, in a country like Guatemala this was not always so.[55] For the purposes of the PDH's investigation, records from 1975 to 1985 were simply more valuable than the rest; an archivally sound methodology had to be developed to prioritize their treatment.

Finally, foreign archival consultants adapted to the political and technical limitations of local circumstances. "La Doctora comes from a very modern country with lots of resources and lots of awareness about archives' importance and value," Molina explained. "We wanted the same things here, but you come up against the reality that, say, there is no acid-free cardboard in Guatemala for archival boxes, and we can't afford to bring it in from the outside."[56] Politics intervened into ideal visions of archival practice as well: while Peterson had initially recommended making copies of mold-infected records and then destroying the originals to avoid contaminating other documents, the PDH did not own the records, and so lacked the authority to destroy even a single page.[57] The investigators came to accept archival science as a friendly intervention; the archivists came to understand the concerns of those focused on the human rights investigation and the constraints of the PDH's time frame and resources. As Meoño put it, "The documents aren't an end in themselves—they're things that need to be put at the service of people, so that those people can exercise their rights."[58]

THE "MILLION-DOLLAR QUESTION"

The tools of archival science—conservation practices, modes of document organization and analysis, finding aids, and instruments of description—allowed the Project, in rebuilding the archives, to build power.[59] As Peterson writes, "The purpose of describing archives is to gain intellectual control over the records"—a control that, by describing records' contents, creators, and locations, would permit researchers to find the answers to their questions, or defendants to find evidence.[60] By restoring the site's physical infrastructure, deciphering the PN's institutional history, and organizing and describing the documents, Project investigators literally took control of the archives, reclaiming them from abandonment and putting them at the service of a new mission. This archival power would allow Guatemala's beleaguered human rights sector to envision unprecedented advances in war crimes prosecutions and historical reckoning, as discussed in chapters 8 and 9. As one staffer reflected, "All this work we've done on the archives has given us a new vision of the world. It's given us many tools—now we can see who had the power. You just have to sit down and read the documents."[61] The archival and technical professionalization the Project underwent during its first year and a half represented, on the one hand, incredible progress—indeed, a new vision of the world, opened up by the possibilities of archival thinking. "When I arrived," recalled one worker, "we were surrounded by garbage; today, that's been converted into a garden."[62]

On the other hand, however, the journey from garbage to garden, or from decrepit Babylonian garden to one filled with roses and cornstalks, was littered with stumbling blocks. While it was a victory in a certain sense—the *guerrillero* had become an archivist—it was one born of a constricted set of political possibilities and the crushing of efforts to win broader socioeconomic change. Was it, in fact, a good thing that the *guerrillero* had become an archivist? Did this new identity empower, or enclose? As for the notion that we may assess a society's level of democratization by analyzing the conditions of its archives, the circumstances of the PN archives suggested a mixed "democratization" indeed. The archives were stumbled upon accidentally, the result of an investigation into mishandled explosives that typified the sorts of infrastructural dangers daily threatening lives across the global South. Different wings of government were indifferent to the records, which were technically their responsibility, or else wanted to help but lacked the resources and political will. An outfit with only the barest experience dealing with archives, the PDH, took on the task of restoring the records—funded entirely, like so many initiatives related to truth and justice, by the international community and staffed by private NGOs. Dangers both political and structural threatened the Project; sticky politics, powerful personal interests, and the odd Molotov cocktail put its survival in jeopardy. More than simply a barometer of the sitting government's commitment to transparency, the PN archives' context was a sobering reflection of Guatemala's postconflict social and political fabric.[63] The rescue of the archives was a tremendous step forward in Guatemala's benighted postwar landscape. But it was not the sort of change that had, just a few decades earlier, animated hundreds of thousands of citizens.

Throughout the rescue of the archives, one stubborn question remained in the minds of most everyone who visited them: Why did the police, or the military, not destroy the files while they had the chance? At the Project, nearly all the amateur historians and archivists had an educated guess. Many chalked the archives' survival up to a pervasive culture of impunity; as one worker commented, "Political power in this country can be a little blind, no? And sometimes when people believe they have power in a given moment, they assume they'll retain it for their whole lives."[64] One analyst ascribed the phenomenon to military shortsightedness: "I think nobody ever thought of it, not the heads of the military—their vision never went further than their own personal benefits or their particular job description, and they never thought that someone, someday, in Guatemala, would break through into their very own buildings and go through their records. It just never occurred to those little minds."[65] By this logic, then, military and police officials would have assumed that nobody would ever intervene to seek out the records, and would have known that whether or not they did was irrelevant. Because security forces effectively enjoyed immunity from prosecution, it would not matter whether the documents came to light. They would never suffer any consequences.[66] (In contrast, Stasi officials spent the two months leading up to the Berlin Wall's fall feverishly destroying their high-impact files—first using industrial shredders and then, when the shredders gave out, tearing apart the records by hand, aware that the arc of history was bending toward a new era.)

Others, more historically inclined, attributed the archives' survival to a fundamental human need to keep records, to leave traces. "The necessity of leaving something written about one's activities is almost inherent in humanity," one Project worker said. "To link oneself with the past using proof."[67] And to the most archivally thinking individuals on the scene—including not only the archivists themselves but also some members of the Project's leadership and international advisory board—the answer lay in the essence of bureaucracy itself. "We've got to remember," Meoño said, "that no matter how atrocious the acts were, they were administrative measures. And administrative actions have to be documented. The only way a state functionary can prove that they've done their job is to compile a written record and file it away. . . . What are for us shameful crimes against humanity, for the perpetrator it's simply a matter of complying with patriotic duty."[68] International adviser Hassan Mneimneh, of the Iraq Memory Foundation, put the matter most crisply: "Ultimately these files are the institutional memory of the bureaucracy. To expect a bureaucracy to destroy its files is to expect it to commit suicide."[69]

But the best way to answer what Project insiders called the "million-dollar question" of the archives' survival is to page backward in the history book. Documents both *represent* power and *are* power—not in some deracinated, postmodern sense but all too concretely in their creation, keeping, and use by political actors.[70] As such, they are customarily not destroyed unless they represent a proximate risk or inconvenience to those who control or produce them. Police records in particular serve their function of social control long after the infractions they record have passed; a police background check, for example, relies upon a large corpus of antecedent documents to generate an individual's criminal history. Even though the National Police was disbanded in 1996, the new National Civil Police needed the former agency's archives in order to perform its basic duties. Most acts of policing rely directly, and inseparably, upon acts of archiving.

And the National Police archives were rich with information on supposed "enemies of the state." Especially since the days of Jorge Ubico's dictatorship, police records were used as tools of political control, tracking "subversives" and "Communists" with a militarized logic of surveillance and ideological management. In 1954, when the United States backed Castillo Armas's coup d'état against Arbenz, CIA operatives raided Arbenz's files, compiled a blacklist archive of more than seventy thousand suspected Communists, and turned it over to Castillo Armas's secret police in order that these enemies of the new state could be exiled, jailed, or killed. Subsequent generations of PN officers, under the watchful eye of military intelligence, relied on this blacklist as late as the 1980s to pick off exiled Arbenz loyalists as they trickled back into Guatemala. As the next chapter shows, the PN received additional special training in records management (again courtesy of the United States), ensuring that its leadership was well aware of the critical role archives could play in what soon became the most brutal counterinsurgency in the hemisphere. Crudely put, in order to kill university students or community organizers, one had to keep track of who they were, who their friends and relatives were, and what daily routes they traveled. The history of the armed conflict and of the PN's participation in it demonstrates the importance of the police records, which compiled these very types of intelligence information, to the "successful" execution of the counterinsurgency.

Because the Guatemalan peace process represented such an utter defeat for the URNG—as one Project worker put it, "you entered the guerrilla with fifty cents and you left with nothing"—the counterinsurgent mentality among oligarchs and generals and businessmen never came to an end.[71] The heavy weight of history maintained its dominance over peacetime politics; state terror had been a tool of state formation, producing a postwar social and political world in whose creation oppositional voices had not been permitted to participate. Well after the Peace Accords, progressives of every stripe continued to face persecution. The military remained an influential source of political and financial clout, and a reconstituted police force only exacerbated its predecessors' reputation for viciousness and corruption.[72] Impunity reigned; everyday violence, sometimes perpetrated by state security forces, terrorized and distracted the population. Ergo, why bother destroying the archives, such a useful fount of information about those who sought—and continued seeking—to articulate political alternatives?[73] Ignored, and culturally understood as garbage, no old papers could possibly threaten the status quo where forty years' worth of hard-fought political militancy had failed.

Or could they?

PART II | **ARCHIVES AND COUNTERINSURGENCY IN COLD WAR GUATEMALA**

FOUR

BUILDING COUNTERINSURGENCY ARCHIVES

We have, of course, no desire to interfere in the internal affairs
of Guatemala.
—U.S. secretary of state William Pierce Rogers, 1971

Soon after Colonel Carlos Castillo Armas flew into Guatemala City on
a U.S. embassy plane to oust President Jacobo Arbenz Guzmán, the
strongman sought technical support from his American friends in
intelligence-gathering and countersubversion tactics.[1] Since the 1954 coup,
Castillo Armas had busied himself by cutting a deep swath through Guatemala's democratic Left using a ramshackle assortment of rival security services,
and he was keen to rationalize his crusade. In response, the International Cooperation Administration (ICA), USAID's predecessor, sent a consultant, Fred
G. Fimbres, to assess the capacities and deficiencies of the National Police
with an eye toward designing a U.S. assistance program. Fimbres's report
noted his counterparts' "almost neurotic hypersensitiveness to communist
activity and threatened attack," chronicling the areas in which local law enforcement did not pass muster: vehicle maintenance, radio communications,
interagency coordination, disaster readiness—any and all routine functions
not immediately related to the apprehension of suspected communists.[2] This
subordination of civilian policing to partisan political terror did not, in and of
itself, trouble Fimbres; the very purpose of his visit was to evaluate how the
United States could assist in controlling "subversion" in the post-coup period.
Fimbres's concern, rather, was that the PN's sagging infrastructure, organizational inefficiencies, and budgetary constraints might limit U.S. allies' ability
to clean house in Arbenz's wake.

In his report, Fimbres made special mention of the sorry state of the PN's
general filing and records system.[3] At PN stations, he observed "piles of documents, files, etc. dumped on the floor"; others were heaped in crude bundles
or "arranged somewhat" on the floor, amounting to a central records unit he

deemed "hopelessly inadequate," falling "far short of its most treasured and prized objective—that of [being] an aid to the law enforcement function and investigative process."[4] Fimbres's gut assessment of the importance of record keeping was dead-on. He criticized the archival practices of the amateurish PN general staff, but when evaluating the Section for Defense against Communism, an elite intelligence unit that "secure[d] evidence in subversive matters," Fimbres noted that its archives and record control were "most excellent," the result of a provision in Castillo Armas's Preventive Penal Law against Communism (1954) that required the section to keep files on individuals linked to "communist" groups or activities.[5] Fimbres's observation implied a connection between effective record keeping and effective social control, a connection lost neither on his successors at the U.S. Agency for International Development (USAID) nor on their Guatemalan pupils. Record keeping, and the surveillance of "enemies of the state" that good archival practice permitted, would prove indispensable.

In his recommendations, Fimbres advised that U.S. assistance focus specifically on records management, both by providing training—he suggested offering courses in "Police Records," "Police Property Records and Control," and "Police Records and Report Writing"—and by supplying raw materials like filing cabinets and file cards.[6] To build a modern, effective police force, the Guatemalans would need to learn how to build modern, effective archives. As U.S. support for the police and military expanded over the course of the Cold War, the question of record keeping remained in play, with the Americans ever mindful of how Guatemalan security forces "could improve their operation through the use of records."[7] Once Fimbres submitted his report, U.S. technicians began conducting daily classes in records management for PN agents, installed cabinets for safe document storage, and implemented a property registry so that the PN could keep track of weapons and matériel—the stockpiles of which ballooned as AID shipments began rolling in.[8] In 1959, U.S. advisers boasted that the "new [police] records bureau" set up by ICA's Public Safety Division was "probably the greatest and most productive improvement made by the National Police since the inception of the Public Safety Program."[9] The archives later fell into neglect, accounting for their calamitous condition in 2005. But, ironically enough, U.S. intervention deserves some credit for there being police records left for postwar investigators to find at all.

Lest something so seemingly banal as records management assistance be dismissed as a neutral component of interstate collaboration, a 1957 letter from the State Department's R. Richard Rubottom to a colleague at the ICA spoke to the intentions of U.S. police aid in all its forms. "We do not undertake programs to improve the efficiency of Latin American police forces per se," Rubottom emphasized. "Where we do render them technical and material assistance, it is for the stated objective of increasing their capability to combat communist subversion."[10] U.S. intervention in Guatemala is better known for bloodier feats: deposing a democratically elected president; arming "neurotic" anticommunists to the teeth; offering political cover for state-sponsored terror; and providing technical assistance to security forces while knowing, at every step of the way, that those forces were using U.S. aid and political capital to commit crimes against their own citizens. But record keeping, too, belongs on that list. U.S. aid impacted both the *form* of the police (and military) archives—their comprehensiveness, storage and organizational methods, and materials used—and their *content*, the history of repression revealed by the documents today. The United States led the restructuring of the PN from 1954 until the shutdown of its global police aid programs in 1974, a period that saw the force transformed into the shock troops of a newly mechanized urban counterinsurgency. U.S. assistance in matters archival cannot be separated from U.S. assistance in matters more broadly counterinsurgent, which is why both subjects are treated together in this chapter.

U.S. support for Guatemala's twentieth-century dictatorships, particularly its military aid, would surely have had even more disastrous ramifications absent the extensive reporting carried out by a generation of activists, journalists, and academics. Meanwhile, though, aid to the National Police has gone understudied and underpublicized.[11] Army generals were the main architects of the counterinsurgency, including its genocidal period, 1981–1983, after urban counterterror forced the insurgency into the countryside.[12] But the PN were direct protagonists in many of the state's most brazen acts of political violence: the March 1966 mass disappearance of "Los 28," the Spanish embassy fire, the murders of Manuel Colom Argueta and Alberto Fuentes Mohr, the suppression of the Coca-Cola bottling plant strikes, the 1980 mass abduction and disappearance of National Workers' Confederation trade unionists, the Mutual Support Group disappearances of 1984 and 1985, and more. To ignore the PN's role, particularly in the methodical destruction of the urban labor and student movements, elides the complexity of Guatemala's armed conflict. The police, alas, were no mere sideshow.

This chapter tells the story of how U.S. advisers took a "trigger-happy" force with a habit of shooting submachine guns "indiscriminately" into crowds of peaceful demonstrators, spent nearly twenty years in close collaboration with them, and exited the scene under congressional fire in the mid-1970s.[13] They left behind a National Police with the barest of increased competence in civilian law enforcement, but which had been significantly restructured in the service of counterinsurgency priorities. U.S. advisers consistently recommended and enacted the rationalizing of those operating procedures most central to U.S. Cold War objectives: assembling a surveillance archive, streamlining political investigations, encouraging tactical collaboration and intelligence-sharing between the PN and the military, and constructing a regional telecommunications network that would link the highest echelons of the hemisphere's fiercest counterinsurgency apparatus.[14] The transformation of the PN during the war's first phase began with the transformation of its archives.

POLICING THE AMERICAS

The notion that the United States should advance its geopolitical interests by training and funding foreign police forces originally drew inspiration from European colonial practices. The theory became reality during the U.S. occupations of the Philippines, Nicaragua, Haiti, and the Dominican Republic during the early twentieth century.[15] The long-term institutional character of U.S. international police aid, however, was forged slightly later, under Franklin D. Roosevelt. Roosevelt created the Institute of Inter-American Affairs (IIAA) in 1942 as part of the Office of the Coordinator of Inter-American Affairs (OCIA). Both outfits were designed as wartime vehicles for promoting economic development and improvements in hemispheric public health, with no prima facie involvement in questions of security. Their creation was part of the Good Neighbor Policy and indicative of a U.S. shift, if largely rhetorical, away from gunboat diplomacy.

The twin menaces of Bolshevism and fascism, though, made maintaining hemispheric "stability" a high priority, not only for ensuring economic dominance and improving health indicators but also for anticommunist political retrenchment. In the early 1940s, the FBI began establishing a presence in Latin America, on the assumption "that surreptitious police contacts could be used as intelligence sources for keeping track of Nazi activities inside Latin America"—contacts that could be kept and used to advantage after the end of the Second World War.[16] Both the FBI and the CIA pursued covert relations with Latin American police forces, and although the IIAA was ostensibly geared toward economic development, it would not avoid the polarization of the Cold War. The IIAA became the International Cooperation Administration, the State Department's economic development agency, in 1955; it also, somewhat counterintuitively for an economic aid outfit, coordinated foreign police assistance programs. Six years later, the ICA became USAID, and the Kennedy administration's 1962 move to create the Office of Public Safety (OPS), consolidating diverse police programs into one administrative unit housed within USAID, was unpopular among officials who had joined the organization to build wells, not distribute guns. But despite USAID director Hamilton Fowler's position that "a police program had no place in an organization whose mission was to provide economic and technical assistance in such areas as agriculture, public health, and education," and his colleagues' discomfort with working alongside "redneck cops and spooks," the USAID officials were overruled.[17]

In 1957, when Inter-American Affairs approved the expansion of the ICA's existing "Guatemalan project," it did so only provided that a set of conditions be met. These included the following:

1. That it be made clear that the ultimate objective of this program is "to strengthen the capability of internal security forces . . . with the purpose of enabling them more effectively to counter (communist) subversion". . . .
2. That the technicians to be sent to Guatemala be briefed to this effect prior to their departure.
3. That the highly political nature of their work be made clear to the technicians assigned to Guatemala.
4. That an instruction be sent to Guatemala . . . directing that a special relationship be established between the police mission and the Embassy in view of the political nature of its work.[18]

These directives set the tone for what became a long and dynamic relationship between the United States and Guatemala's police. U.S. advisers' work with the PN involved some initiatives that, divorced from their broader context, seemed perfectly benign—providing extra uniforms, so that working-class agents who previously slept in their only uniforms could rotate outfits; training in vehicle maintenance for safer patrolling; implementing tour-of-duty schedule changes, so agents could spend more time with their families.[19] However, these were incidental details within the larger paradigm of a global strategic program to internationalize police assistance, whose goal was to construct a "combined U.S.-indigenous defense system" that would deeply involve Third World police in the effort to contain communism.[20] As Martha Huggins notes, it was no coincidence that the National Security Council's 1290D police assistance expansion, which foreshadowed the Office of Public Safety, was proposed in the very year of the Viet Minh victory at Dien Bien Phu and as the CIA was completing its plans to overthrow Arbenz.[21] The escalation of U.S. international security aid was designed to prevent further such "losses"—and to facilitate its own intelligence gathering, the fruits of which today lie in the U.S. National Archives. The list of receiver countries for police aid programs reads like a marquee of potential dominoes: South Vietnam, Brazil, Uruguay, Colombia, Greece, South Korea. In Guatemala's case, U.S. objectives mapped all too well onto local elites' desire to crush any move that stunk, to them, of the "exotic horrors" of the Revolutionary Spring.[22]

In 1955, when Castillo Armas first solicited technical assistance with intelligence-gathering from the United States, the ICA identified no fewer than ten different formal "countersubversion" bodies: the Civil Police, the Secret Police, the Treasury Police, the Government Investigative Police, the Investigative Squad of the Civil Police, the Presidential Police, a unit called "Coronado Lima's Investigative Group," the Immigration Investigative Service, the Army G-2, and the National Committee for Defense against Communism.[23] These groups carried out the post-Arbenz purges, in which some nine thousand people were detained and ten thousand forced into exile.[24] Some of these rival groups were already well known to the Americans, because CIA agents had collaborated with the National Committee for Defense against Communism in compiling the blacklist, mentioned in the previous chapter, of Arbenz loyalists, PGT members, and other perceived enemies.[25] Here, archival surveillance was consciously being used, and taught, as a technology of social control years before the war began. When Major Enrique Trinidad Oliva, Castillo Armas's coordinator of technical cooperation with the ICA and the "number 2 man in government," complained to the ICA about the absence of a central police records system, embassy officials pointed out that although they had already established a file system on subversives—the CIA blacklist—"doubtless the Embassy's revelation that there were a number of persons with communist records among a group of exiles cleared recently by the Government for re-entry into Guatemala highlighted this problem for Major Oliva." In other words, the embassy not only built a hit list for the regime but pointed out when the Guatemalans had missed one. But this was apparently not good enough; Oliva's central records bureau would materialize too, in short order.

Along with the organized intelligence structures, ICA observers noted, most government ministers and the heads of the aforementioned groups employed their own confidential agents, many of whom spent "a certain amount of time spying on each other." From an efficiency standpoint, this was a mess; embassy second secretary William B. Connett Jr. characterized the intelligence services as "dispersed, pragmatic, uncoordinated, built to a large degree around personalities, untrained in investigative techniques, hampered by political intrigue and, in general, relatively ineffectual."[26] Security forces were brutal but inefficient; zealously anticommunist but poorly trained and equipped; willing to act but territorial and mistrustful of rivals. The proffered remedy was, in a word, *professionalization*, as it would remain for generations of police reform through century's end and beyond.

With so many areas in need of "professionalization," one might imagine that the incoming U.S. team would hardly know where to begin. But while the initial phase of U.S. assistance was more limited than at later points, its priorities were clear: special investigations, information management, and the centralization and streamlining of political policing. These were also Castillo Armas's objectives. In 1956, he created the General Directorate for National Security (DGSN), a secret service that would coordinate and consolidate state efforts to repress what it considered to be communist subversion. It inherited the blacklist archive generated by the CIA and the National Committee for Defense against Communism.[27] (The DGSN also worked to assemble new lists of its own, requiring, for example, the proprietors of hotels and inns to nightly submit their guest lists, to facilitate the tracking of foreigners from "suspicious" countries and individuals on the run for political reasons.)[28]

Also in 1956, Fimbres recommended that the United States immediately send a specialist to provide training in physical and technical surveillance (including records management), interrogation techniques, and the use of scientific methods in special investigations.[29] However, the specialists first sent, David Laughlin and John Popa, soon realized that they would need to spend the Public Safety Program's initial phase undertaking far more basic forms of professionalization—improving working conditions and trimming patrol rosters—to strengthen the PN's "very low morale and lack of esprit du corps" and boost retention in order to make the training worthwhile.[30] The aforementioned early development of the PN's record keeping was one of the principal gains from this first stage of assistance, and the Guatemalans were quick studies, keeping suspect individuals' files at the ready if the time to act arose. The first entry in the police file on social democratic politician Manuel Colom Argueta, for example, was made in 1957, and twenty-two years' worth of archival surveillance later, Colom was assassinated at police hands.[31] By the late 1950s, the training had made significant inroads in rationalizing police operations; it was clear who had come to run the show at PN headquarters, and quickly at that. In 1958, when Major Piloña left his post as the police's director-general, he issued a press release touting seven major areas of advancement under his tenure. Laughlin noted, in a memo back to Washington, that six of the seven accomplishments Piloña cited were, in fact, "the direct result of programs initiated and carried out by the Public Safety Division of ICA."[32]

Though the initial phase of Public Safety Program (PSP) assistance was originally slated for phaseout in 1961, the U.S. Operations Mission decided in 1959 to "wait and see" before shutting down the program, owing to concern at the triumph of the Cuban Revolution.[33] For domestic elites, it was a felicitous move, as internal unrest swelled with President Ydígoras Fuentes's decision to allow the United States to train the Bay of Pigs invasion force in Guatemalan territory. Ydígoras was widely viewed as a corrupt, weak leader, and his Bay of Pigs move smacked of opportunism and pro-U.S. servility. In August 1960—just three months before the 13 November revolt by army dissidents that sparked the war—Ydígoras Fuentes went to the United States for assistance in responding to the "recent disturbances, the probable source of the agitation, and the threat it poses for the stability of constitutional government."[34] By suggesting that Soviet-backed communists were nipping at Guatemala's heels, Ydígoras marshaled U.S. support for the repression of legitimate social and economic grievances. The ensuing recommendations, made by PSP adviser Rex D. Morris, provided the template for continued U.S. security assistance; the double threat of Cuba and a homegrown insurgency was seen to justify extreme measures.[35] Morris's recommendations, which were endorsed and eventually implemented in various forms, became the foundation of security forces' urban counterinsurgency strategy for decades to come.

COMMON THUGS AND ASSASSINS

Morris's 1960 counterinsurgency blueprint called for U.S. advisers to create within the PN a Special Investigations Bureau and a Central Records Bureau. The Special Investigations Bureau, to be staffed by specifically trained personnel, would be constituted by presidential decree and granted authority to apprehend anyone suspected of "crimes threatening constitutional Government." Its responsibilities would be as follows: "To investigate and be informed concerning A) political interests of social, business, and labor organizations as these effect [sic] the government, B) political activities of foreign nationals (e.g. communists and other agents with interests adverse to the State's, C) Guatemalan citizens with outside political interests and/or allegiances, and D) Guatemala [sic] citizens who otherwise have political interests contrary to the interests of the country."[36] An "Intelligence Coordinator," reporting directly to the president, would manage the bureau's activities.

Along with the Special Investigations Bureau, Morris proposed a Central Records Bureau "for the purpose of collecting, filing, and evaluating all records pertaining to persons involved in any form of criminal activity, such as fingerprints, arrest records, photographs, personal descriptions, alias files, and the like."[37] It would allow the PN to build detailed criminal histories of particular individuals, track their activities over time, and make full use of a standard law enforcement tool: the background check. However, what sounded like routine policing—keeping track of lawbreakers—took on a sinister cast when designed primarily to apply to those with "political interests contrary to the interests of the country." The Central Records Bureau, or central archives of the National Police, was consolidated in 1967, organizing data to be searchable both by surname and by crime type.[38] For example, in addition to maintaining files on individuals of interest, the police's Master File Registry indexed agents' and informants' reports by category of interest; these indices included "Communist Agitators," "Subversives," "University Campus," "Demonstrations," and "Cadavers."[39]

The final recommendation pertained to a favorite cause of U.S. advisers, though one that would not be implemented until the late 1960s: the integration of the feared Judicial Police into the organizational structure of the PN. The National Police was founded in 1881, but the Judicial Police's particular brand of social control was a more recent development; the "Secret Police," its institutional ancestor, first appeared in 1900.[40] Dictator Jorge Ubico famously relied upon this "auxiliary army," almost always run by military personnel, which cultivated its reputation for savage efficiency in the dispatch of enemies. (For this it was disbanded after the 1944 revolution and reinstated after 1954.)[41] Variously incarnated over time as the Judicial Police, the Judicial Guard, or the Judicial Department, to ordinary Guatemalans its goons, who were organizationally separate from the PN, were collectively dreaded and derided as *La Judy*.[42] Its leaders were notorious: one Judicial Police head under Ydígoras Fuentes, Jorge Córdova Molina, was also a ringleader of Mano Blanca, perhaps the most infamous of Guatemala's 1960s death squads.[43] Córdova Molina, described in U.S. documents as a "common thug and assassin," and other Judicial Police officers had close ties to the far-right Movement of National Liberation (MLN), itself responsible for numerous extrajudicial executions of labor, student, and popular movement leaders throughout the armed conflict.[44] When the Judiciales were disbanded (on paper, but not in deed) in 1966, papers reported on their newly revealed torture chambers at Zone 1's La Tigrera compound, from whence screams had regularly echoed along the thoroughfares outside its gates. Reporters noted that the exiting *jefes* had taken their hoods, tins of insecticide (*gamexán*), garroting cords, and other torture implements with them upon vacating their positions.[45]

As the theory went, integrating the Judiciales into the National Police would eliminate redundancy vis-à-vis the "overlapping intelligence and 'po-

FIG. 4.1 A plain-clothes *judicial* (special agent) of the Judicial Police. © Jean-Marie Simon/2012.

litical' functions" they shared. It would centralize political policing and, allegedly, separate countersubversive activities from civilian policing.[46] It also provided an opportunity, as recommended by the Americans thereafter, to create a separate intelligence unit fulfilling Judicial Police functions that would report directly to the president: "La Regional," the U.S.-established communications network allowing security forces to share intelligence and collaborate on special ops. Here, however, theory and praxis diverged: the separate intelligence unit was indeed created, and the Judicial Police were indeed fused into the PN structure. But the old Judiciales never changed their ways; rather, they continued to collaborate with military structures in extralegal operations.[47] The implications of melding the Judiciales and the National Police were clear for the future of civilian policing. Weaving an autonomous political force into the PN without bringing it under control would have disastrous results. From 1966 on, the Judiciales—"the principal agent of political repression," in one newspaper's words—would operate in close coordination with a newly resurgent army, from within the heart of the civilian police.[48] The moniker of "Judiciales" would be shed, but its modus operandi would not.

The USAID advisers were well aware of the Judiciales' abuses. In a 1962 memo, public safety chief Herbert O. Hardin noted that "it was not uncommon for the police to open fire on the participants in disturbances on the slightest provocation, and the results were usually tragic." Demonstrating the confused logic of U.S. police aid, Hardin then discussed how "in order to discourage the use of such weapons and tactics, 700 revolvers were furnished to the National Police in Guatemala in 1957."[49] He went on to describe how the Judicial Police were sent in ahead of the PN to control the peaceful anti-corruption protests known as "Las Jornadas de Marzo y Abril de 1962," or the Days of March and April 1962. In these demonstrations, thousands of workers, politicians, and students poured into the streets to denounce the Ydígoras regime in the largest street protests since Ubico's 1944 overthrow.[50] In one such demonstration, he wrote, Judicial Police chief Jorge Córdova Molina "engaged in indiscriminate behavior, firing his submachine gun into the mob. This had a chain reaction on the rest of the Judicial Police who also began firing indiscriminately at the rioters." Once the Judicial Police began firing, the PN rear guard began spraying their own, USAID-supplied bullets into the crowd—"directly contrary to the advice and teaching which the police had received through the US Public Safety Program," Hardin huffed. Never one to miss the silver lining on a dark cloud, Hardin believed "that the actions of the USAID Public Safety Advisor in prevailing upon the National Police to cease using rifled firearms and rely on depressed fire from riot guns resulted in the saving of numerous lives and probably lowered the number of casualties considerably." U.S. assistance bore no responsibility for the casualties, Hardin implied, because the PSP had not worked with this particular Judicial Police chief. He neglected to mention that the PSP had developed an "interesting exchange of relations" with the Judiciales two years earlier, providing scholarships for its agents to receive special training in Puerto Rico and having an ICA adviser teach a class at its training academy in the very handling and use of firearms.[51]

USAID worked with the Judicial Police and other repressive police sub-entities again and again. A constant problem, in fact, was that the Guatemalan state was consistently less interested in funding the police than the United States was. Over the course of the PSP, U.S. documents repeatedly lament the

Guatemalans' "inertia" when it came to supporting the police, mainly because the military was loath to fortify its perceived rival, particularly after General Enrique Peralta Azurdia assumed military rule in 1963. (This, too, occurred at the behest of the United States, which pre-cleared Peralta's seizure of power to dodge a democratic election that progressive ex-president Juan José Arevalo stood good odds of winning.)[52] At times, impatient Public Safety officials simply could not wait for the Guatemalans to get their act together, ultimately opting not to require the official disbanding of the Judicial Police before pushing to create the centralized intelligence apparatus designed to supplant it. The Guatemalan state was dragging its heels because, "despite recommendations for abolition of the Judicial Police, each regime has found it expedient to retain it as an organization to carry out questionable and distasteful tasks."[53] And so, rather than replacing the Judiciales, the new intelligence organization simply ended up incorporating them into its strategy. As early as 1963, "very encouraging progress" had been made in establishing a "centralized intelligence organization along [the] lines [of the] FBI [with] some features [of the] CIA." U.S. advisers ensured that any chief named by the government to head this unit would be "acceptable to us."[54]

In the meantime, popular discontent led to the formation of the Rebel Armed Forces (FAR) in 1962. As insurgency filtered into Guatemala City, U.S. advisers, domestic business elites, and the military finally agreed that it was indeed worth beefing up the PN's specialized forces. Serendipitously, John F. Kennedy had backed a substantial expansion of the Public Safety Program in 1962, in the form of USAID's Office of Public Safety, granting it powers greater than those of any other division of USAID. The president and Robert F. Kennedy also backed the creation of the Inter-American Police Academy in the Panama Canal Zone, later moved to Washington and renamed the International Police Academy. In Guatemala, therefore, on-the-ground political escalation dovetailed with an expansion of U.S. police aid worldwide. The Guatemalan police program would become among the largest and highest-profile OPS initiatives in the hemisphere.

A 1964 document drafted by the OPS's director spoke to rising concern over guerrilla incursions into the city, noting that while the preceding two administrations had "done little" to improve the PN, the Guatemalan government "now indicates its desire, with Public Safety assistance, to reorganize and improve the police."[55] Some of the sense of escalation was manufactured: USAID adviser D. L. Crisostomo noted in a report that various of the supposed "terrorist bombings" in the city were actually the handiwork of state forces, blamed on FAR guerrillas "in order to preserve a certain climate of tension" that would justify state terror. Some of the violence was certainly authentic, but the Guatemalan state used the crimes of a small cluster of insurgents, who in the Americans' estimation were nowhere near strong enough to threaten the existing regime, to justify a broader campaign against urban civil society.[56] The government studiously ignored the mounting activity of death squads like Mano Blanca, fronts for coordinated action between security forces and the MLN against not only suspected communists but also mainstream political parties like the Revolutionary Party (PR), the MLN's main rival.[57] As discussed previously, Mano Blanca's commander was a Judicial Police chief, but this was not the only level of interconnection between the extreme Right, death squads, the state, and U.S. assistance. As Greg Grandin writes, though the United States tried to distance itself from growing death squad violence, "the wrath of these private avengers was just as fundamental to U.S. goals as were the zeal and enthusiasm of PGT activists to the democratic achievements of the [1944] October Revolution."[58]

This new consensus, based on the police-military cooperation prioritized by U.S. advisers since the outset, required the technical means for interagency coordination. In 1964, PSP aide Alfred Naurocki led the creation of a Guatemala City–based telecommunications network connected to a Central America–wide system, linking various state security forces with U.S. counterpart facilities in the Canal Zone; Michael McClintock writes that the development of communications networks within Guatemala's security forces was the most significant assistance ever provided by PSP personnel.[59] Soon after Naurocki's arrival in May, Peralta created a "Presidential Intelligence Agency" housed in his official residence. By October, the agency was fully in operation, culling intelligence and sharing it with other Central American security forces. It sent the Judiciales to approach government agencies with requests for information on long lists of citizens supposedly belonging to "leftist factions," seeking to determine and monitor their whereabouts.[60] By the spring of 1966, the Regional Telecommunications Center, its staff later known as "La Regional" and eventually as "El Archivo," connected on a private frequency the leadership of the National Police, Treasury Police, Judicial Police, Interior Ministry, the presidential residence, and the military communications center. It was moved next door to the Casa Presidencial and placed at the disposal of the defense minister and the Army General Staff, becoming the nerve center of state terrorism. It represented the very streamlining sought by U.S. advisers and provided a newly empowered military the tools to assume direction of the war and make use of a restructured National Police.[61]

As the urban firefight escalated, USAID pulled a crack counterterrorism adviser, John P. Longan, out of Venezuela to lend a hand. Longan arrived in November 1965 with the aim of establishing a PN rapid-response unit that could quickly and flexibly handle disturbance control and special operations. He developed a new raid tactic called the Frozen Area Plan, designed to "force some of the wanted communists out of hiding and into police hands," and trained trusted agents in its implementation. Longan's oeuvre would come to be known as Operación Limpieza, a set of March 1966 raids in which security forces kidnapped and tortured more than thirty labor and peasant activists before dumping their bodies into the sea.[62] Operación Limpieza bestowed upon the Guatemalan state the dishonor of having invented the forced disappearance, a tactic soon to spread among Latin American dictatorships as anticommunist terror became both industrialized and exportable. The "Communist big-leaguers," in one U.S. advisor's words, who were murdered in the 1966 raids, including PGT leaders Víctor Manuel Gutiérrez and Leonardo Castillo Flores, had been identified more than a decade earlier by CIA operatives and included on the Castillo Armas regime's blacklist.[63]

This mass disappearance was a watershed. From 1966 on, state violence became mechanized, incautious, and seemingly unstoppable—not that U.S. advisers ever tried to halt it. After the 1966 disappearances, the embassy ran political cover for the Guatemalan state, denying having information on the crimes despite having been kept apprised at every step; in fact, in 1965 Longan had emphasized that it was "a must" to maintain the ability of U.S. personnel to "influence police operations," in order to maintain the ability to defend U.S. interests at a moment's notice.[64] U.S. advisers built the unit responsible for Operación Limpieza from the ground up; they established and maintained the telecommunications network allowing the military, the police, and the OPS to share intelligence leading directly to the captures. They kept in close contact with the Judicial Police, even though (or, perhaps, because) it was Judicial Police agents who, in coordination with military high command, raided the Zone 12 house in which Víctor Manuel Gutiérrez—archived as the country's "#1 Communist"—was hiding, abducted him, tied a hood over his head, and ran electric currents through his slim body until his heart stopped.[65] Though the government kept quiet about the killings, the Left knew who bore the blame: a month after the March 1966 disappearances, the head of the Judicial Police, Alberto Barrios, was forced into exile by attempts on his life. According to U.S. ambassador John Gordon Mein, the March abductions were "a considerable success"; the murders, and the embassy's blithe attitude toward them, were avenged with the death of Mein himself at the hands of the FAR two years later.[66] Mein's assassination spurred increased U.S. engagement. Following the Mein killing, the number of Public Safety in-country personnel jumped to seven from its previous average of three.

"TRANQUILITY AND PEACE"

The 1966–1970 period saw a tremendous escalation in the counterinsurgency and the military's consolidation of power, with Colonel Carlos Arana Osorio, the "Jackal of Zacapa," bringing scorched-earth tactics to the countryside for the first time.[67] But March 1966 also ushered in a significant expansion of police assistance and police-military activity in the capital, as Operación Limpieza had demonstrated what real collaboration between the military, the police, and U.S. advisers could achieve. Perhaps no act of stagecraft better represented the new counterinsurgency consensus than a blessing performed in front of the Metropolitan Cathedral on 13 March 1967. Under a high, late-summer sun, Guatemala's conservative archbishop, Monseñor Mario Casariego, sprinkled holy water onto fifty-four new Ford Broncos and Falcons acquired from the United States for the PN's radio patrol corps.[68] As the strains of the national anthem bled out into the plaza, the archbishop blessed each vehicle individually, expressing his pleasure at a purchase that would, he opined, bring "tranquility and peace" to *capitalinos*. After receiving the church's blessing, the patrol vehicles paraded around the park, across to Sexta Avenida, and south to the Plaza Italia. In attendance were the vice-minister of defense, Colonel Manuel Francisco Sosa Ávila; the entire PN leadership, including director-general Colonel Víctor Manuel Gamboa and third director Colonel Hernán Ponce Nitsch (later the PN director-general under Ríos Montt, a close friend); and Peter Costello, chief public safety officer for USAID in Guatemala.[69] (The year before, the PN had given Costello a special award recognizing the "useful services" he had provided to the organization.)[70]

Colonel Sosa, the vice-minister of defense presiding over the ceremony, was a major player in the U.S.-led streamlining of the counterinsurgency. Embassy documents identify Sosa as the Guatemalan "counterinsurgency coordinator," charged with administering the joint military-police operations that had made the late 1960s so productive in the detentions and executions of supposed communists.[71] Sosa, a friend of Méndez Montenegro's dating back to their military training in Chile, was an elusive character, deeply enmeshed in extralegal activities but with a low public profile. He never attained the notoriety of his contemporaries, though he deserved to. It was a measure of the PN's counterinsurgent importance—or, at least, of the importance of certain PN subsquads—that a figure like Sosa was named director-general of the National Police (DGPN) in March 1967. The USAID team was encouraged by

Sosa's appointment; over lunch that July, OPS chief Byron Engle assured the colonel that he would be pleased to assist him in arranging "the most expeditious method" of procuring equipment in the United States.[72] The CIA's Special Operations secret intelligence handbook from 1967 also mentioned the colonel. It noted approvingly that since Sosa's appointment as DGPN, the police had "been filling its responsibilities more effectively, particularly its counterinsurgency role. The police are more active than previously and are cooperating with the army in forming special counterterrorist squads which operate clandestinely against leftist insurgents."[73]

Translated, this genteel language of productivity meant that Sosa was using the PN as a base from which to run death squads, and not only involving the Judicial Police. Within the PN's corps (*cuerpo*) structure, four major corps were responsible for much of the city's policing.[74] Sosa selected the Fourth Corps (Cuarto Cuerpo) as the institutional home for "a special police unit that operated largely without reference to legal procedure," selecting loyalists to fill its ranks.[75] The unit was fully operational just a few months after Sosa began as DGPN, working with the army's Special Commando Unit (SCUGA); led by Colonel Máximo Zepeda, SCUGA, established in January 1967, was a key player in the military's urban apparatus.[76] One of the Fourth Corps' most significant hits, besides its takedown of Mano Blanca leader Jorge Córdova Molina in an act of interagency rivalry, was the abduction, torture, and murder of PGT leaders Rafael Tischler Guzmán, Cayetano Barreno Juárez, Julio César Armas González, and Enrique de la Torre Morel.[77] By October 1967, the Fourth Corps was "widely regarded by Guatemalans as the headquarters of the government's hush, hush anti-insurgent squads."[78]

Sosa's effectiveness would have been no surprise to the Americans, given their knowledge of how in 1966, as vice-minister of defense, Sosa was responsible for setting up joint army-police operations in city and countryside. On top of that, Sosa created the first death squad "phantom groups"—organizations like the New Anti-Communist Organization (NOA) and the Anti-Communist Council of Guatemala (CADEG), propaganda fronts behind which ad hoc coalitions of retired and active-duty army and police officers conducted extrajudicial executions. These squads also disseminated literature designed to terrorize. As one CADEG pamphlet read, "[We] must search until we find the castro-communist traitors who must pay with their lives for the crimes against their country that they have committed by returning [from Cuba], and without any piety they must die like rabid dogs, and their filthy corpses should not be given shelter by the blessed earth of Guatemala, but instead they must serve to stuff vultures' bellies."[79] That the CIA's special operations manual of 1967 indicated how "President Méndez is aware of the activities of these squads and is willing to gamble that they will not get out of hand" suggests that the embassy, too, was aware of the activities of these squads and gambled that they would not get out of hand.[80] As on other occasions, it was an unwise, self-serving bet.[81]

In the late 1960s, as at various moments throughout the armed conflict, U.S. advisers tolerated lapses in the legality of *covert* counterinsurgency operations, and at times registered their disapproval of same, even as they provided enthusiastic assistance for the police's *overt* counterinsurgency operations. Though no OPS official would ever have claimed to support the seamier side of antiguerrilla activity, their ongoing cooperation in "legit" operations—at times barely distinguishable from the extralegal—provided ample cover for dirty deeds. One instance of OPS participation in what Longan referred to as "overt" counterinsurgency measures was the office's close collaboration with Sosa in the development of a 1967 "pilot plan" for implementation in Guatemala City's Zone 5, a working-class barrio and PGT stronghold.[82] In the pilot plan, more than two hundred foot-patrol agents and dozens on bicycles and motorcycles—with "all the equipment to be provided by the Public Security Division of [US]AID"—would establish "an absolute control over the zone."[83] When Sosa announced the Zone 5 pilot plan in a press conference, he stressed his desire "that the National Police be a respectable and respected institution, that the institution provide a full guarantee of citizen safety, and that our citizens feel closer and closer to the police, without any sort of fear." (Citizens should well have felt closer to the police, as PN agents were now tracking all manner of public activities, including local fairs, concerts, lucha libre matches, church sermons, and community meetings, in order to learn the contours of daily life in different neighborhoods.)[84] In his description of the plan, Sosa dropped USAID's name several times.[85] When the specially trained pilot plan agents were honored with USAID diplomas, the U.S. national anthem was even played at the award ceremony.[86] The Zone 5 raids were overt, but what happened to those detained—not to mention the subsequent uses of the guns, vehicles, and ammunition provided for the operation—was never made public.

The contortions in logic caused by this apparent disjuncture—and the confusion of the military and police when embassy officials publicly reprimanded them for "excesses" OPS advisers had privately tolerated—were microcosmic of the larger schizophrenia of U.S. development policy. Stephen Streeter writes that the entire Alliance for Progress initiative in Guatemala was characterized by an internal contradiction between its "soft" democratization efforts, theoretically aimed at developing democratic liberalism, and its massive military buildup, devoted to liberalism's bloody repression.[87] A similar tension existed between U.S. efforts to generally professionalize the PN—by providing filing cabinets, records training, vehicles, and the like—and U.S. efforts to deploy the PN as the frontline executors of a war against the segments of civil society it saw as politically suspect. Ultimately, the former aid not only legitimized the latter; it was adapted to its purposes. But while there may have been tension between soft and hard approaches for those on the "soft" side who thought of themselves as democratizers, in fact, rather than representing an "internal contradiction," the two approaches were mutually dependent.

Sosa himself served as DGPN for only a year, until his prestige fell victim to public outrage over the kidnapping of Archbishop Casariego in March 1968. Initially decried by the military as an act of the FAR, the kidnapping was revealed to be a faux *secuestro* designed to discredit the Left; rumors flew about the army's responsibility. Though the archbishop eventually went home unscathed, two civilians involved in the imbroglio were taken away in a police car; in transit the car stopped and the police agents exited, spraying the car with more than fifty bullets and killing the handcuffed prisoners. The crime shocked the country, and the resulting scandal spurred even Méndez Montenegro, a weak leader who ruled subject to a pact giving the military full discretion over the counterinsurgency, to action. Because the army's role in the plot became impossible to deny, the president opted for a symbolic gesture that suggested a reining-in of extralegal tactics. The state's "three top counterinsurgents"—Sosa, defense minister Arriaga Bosque, and Zacapa commander Colonel Carlos Arana Osorio—were all packed off to low-profile diplomatic positions.[88] Sosa was shipped to Madrid as Guatemala's military attaché to Spain, supposedly punished for having employed unacceptable tactics.

For a year, that is: in June 1969, Sosa returned to Guatemala, lured back by Méndez Montenegro and appointed interior minister—head of the ministry overseeing his former charge, the PN. His return sparked protests from the University of San Carlos (USAC) Association of University Students (AEU), which issued a statement in *El Imparcial* condemning how Sosa's appointment "condones . . . the bloody acts that have brought mourning to thousands of Guatemalan homes."[89] The embassy speculated that Sosa was reinstalled to mollify the MLN hard-liners accusing Méndez Montenegro of being a soft-on-crime leftist sympathizer.[90] But MLNistas were not the only ones pleased by Sosa's return. Ambassador Davis, who was aware of Sosa's "illegal operations" involving the Fourth Corps, NOA, and CADEG death squads, wrote that "Col. Sosa is undoubtedly a stronger figure than his predecessor . . . and may inject needed vigor into police operations in a time of prospective troubles."[91]

The dissolution of the Judicial Police, the OPS objective nearly a decade in the making, would prove the first major case of institutional recycling within the National Police. Méndez Montenegro officially disbanded the Judicial Police, with great fanfare, in August 1966. Officials promised an end to the methods of the past: the reviled Judiciales would be replaced by the Detective Corps (Cuerpo de Detectives), a new squad to be characterized by technical professionalism, not political revanchism. Yet the Judiciales did not cease operations until 1970, and when the Detective Corps was finally constituted in its place, it was evident that the new structure differed from the old in name only. Army colonel José Vicente Morales, the head of the Judicial Police until the day of its actual demise in November 1970, continued on as the inaugural chief of the Detective Corps.[92] A number of the former heads of the Judiciales—themselves living archives of political knowledge, and hence powerful—were murdered in the years immediately following the switch, suggesting internal power plays and the continued use of "old" tactics with which to dispatch not only "subversives" but also rivals.[93] The Detective Corps would achieve its own notoriety in the coming years until 1982, when it was disbanded, or rather renamed, anew.

The year 1970 was also when Arana Osorio, another of the late-1960s counterinsurgency directors briefly rotated out of Guatemala by Méndez Montenegro, was elected president on the MLN ticket. U.S. advisers saw Arana as a tough, nationalist caudillo with little political acumen and "a reputation for relentless anti-Communism [and] political naïveté, a simplistic point of view, and a willingness to adopt extremist solutions when he feels they are necessary."[94] If forced disappearances and bustling death squad activity had come to Guatemala under a civilian regime, they would remain under a military one: the colonel brought his Zacapa allies, the "civilian extremists" who collaborated in the rural antiguerrilla campaign of 1967–1968, to serve as his personal security force. Their "history of violent, irrational activity," combined with the MLN's tight control over Congress and the military's support for Arana's law-and-order modus operandi, meant that the terror state would take no quarter in crushing dissent.[95]

Arana declared a state of siege in November, suspending the few remaining civil liberties and imposing a curfew "as complete as ever has been witnessed in Guatemala." In the first week of the siege, security forces picked up miniskirted girls and long-haired young men off downtown streets, yanking down the skirt hems of the former and shaving the heads of the latter. Ponytailed men, stereotyped as rebels, were a favorite target of Arana: "Is it too much to ask that people make the temporary sacrifice of going to the barbershop and cutting their hair?" the president wondered in a late 1970 speech, entreating honest Guatemalans to help security forces separate citizen and criminal by trimming their locks.[96] Arana's army also violated USAC autonomy by raiding university buildings later that month. Arana was particularly loathed on the USAC campus, known to radicals around the university as "El Araña," or "the Spider."[97] The USAC rector, Rafael Cuevas del Cid, outraged at the invasion, told his colleagues: "Autonomy does not reside in the university buildings, but rather resides in human dignity. Dignity that they can piss on. Dignity that they can massacre. But dignity that will not be destroyed. Intelligence, my friends, does not die, with buildings or without them."[98] The general, however, begged to differ. "Some of you already know by now," Arana intoned in his 1970 Christmas radio address, "that we are disposed to pacify Guatemala now and not later; that our present actions are like an unstoppable machine, which is to say, that we must pursue the goal until we achieve it."[99]

The U.S. Agency for International Development opted to join the fight. In 1970, the OPS approved significant allocations to the National Police— $410,000 for the construction of a training academy and $378,000 in "contingency funds" for a Rapid Police Development Project—despite nagging concerns about the new government's propensity for the extralegal.[100] After Arana's ascent to the presidency, and the accompanying spike in extrajudicial executions of students, journalists, and labor leaders, it became clear to some USAID and embassy apparatchiks that the United States could not avoid blame, or at least bad press, for its association with Guatemalan security forces.[101] Two years earlier, the outgoing embassy chief of mission, Viron P. Vaky, had lamented the U.S. decision to condone "indiscriminate" and "brutal" tactics, arguing that this had irreparably damaged the U.S. image and wondering, "Is it conceivable that we are so obsessed with insurgency that we are prepared to rationalize murder as an acceptable counterinsurgency weapon?"[102]

In March 1970, FAR operatives abducted Sean Holly, the embassy's second secretary. Speculating as to his captors' motives after his safe release, Holly reported that they were "particularly unhappy [with], as a matter of fact they hate, the Military Group and our assistance to the police. They hold us responsible for the repression by the military and the repression, murder and torture of their people by the police. They went on to talk about why we were giving cars, the radio room [Regional Telecommunications Center], and all this to the Guatemalans when they knew that we knew this was being used for repression." Over several hours of free-ranging debate on the topic between Holly and the young guerrillas guarding him, the American came to face his nation's culpability for how Guatemalan officers had been using their guns and training. "I think that what we have got to look at here," Holly testified subsequently, "is the whole view of theirs that we are responsible for police repression, and police ill-treatment of prisoners and for military repression. It does, at least in my mind, raise the question of our moral responsibility for this."[103]

In May 1970, after reading an embassy report on the Ojo por Ojo death squad's murders of several leftists—in which it was noted that Ojo por Ojo was made up primarily of members of SCUGA, which had worked closely with the PN under Sosa—one U.S. official scrawled in the margins of the report, "This is what we were afraid of with increased Public Safety support."[104] These voices of doubt within the U.S. advisory corps were important for two reasons: first, because they showed that there were indeed dissenters within the diplomatic community, and second, because they demonstrated that OPS officials cannot claim to have been oblivious to their efforts' bloody consequences. It was now obvious to all that the greatest danger to "peace and tranquility" came not from the Left but from the extreme Right, and USAID was helping to foot the bill.

ENDGAME

USAID allocated nearly a million dollars in police aid that year, to say nothing of the larger amounts being funneled into the military by other agencies. The agency committed itself to funding a new police training academy and also continued with its regular invitation of selected officials to the International Police Academy in Washington, DC, for instruction in operations planning, investigation, public relations, control of civic disturbances, marksmanship, transit control, and narcotics investigation.[105] The idea, charitably interpreted, was that by funding the academy and training the officers who would become its teachers, the OPS would be encouraging the development of civilian policing, inculcating in a generation of PN agents a well-rounded, ethical conception of a police officer's duties.

But, as usual, police and military leadership took the funds and training and adapted them to their own priorities. At the local police academy in 1970, only 100 officers were trained in "Basic Policing" and 196 in "Driving," while 393 were trained in "Riot Control and Use of Chemical Agents," 797 in "Target Shooting with the .38 Crossman and .38 Special Revolvers," and 1,200 in "Military Corps and Section Instruction."[106] Some products of U.S. assistance would indeed have improved civil investigations—particularly the establishment of a fingerprinting bureau, which was upgraded under U.S. supervision to the modern "Henry" system of fingerprint recording and analysis from the

Vucetich system previously in use—had civil investigations been the Guatemalan state's main priority.[107] (Others were harder to explain, such as the PN's 1971 decision, pushed by AID's Arlen W. Gee, to require all Guatemalans applying for their required *cedula* identification cards to have their fingerprints taken and entered into the force's databases, thus growing the archive of individuals' files enormously.)[108] And neither, frankly, was civil investigation the Americans' priority. Contemporaneously, a U.S. consultant advised hiring a full-time weapons technician to advise the PN in firearm use and help the Guatemalans increase their "hit capabilities."[109]

The OPS and USAID continued funding the PN despite its violations of its civilian mandate because, at the end of the day, the Arana regime was accomplishing U.S. goals, if with unsavory methods. And not every U.S. official had come around, like Vaky or Holly, to adjusting his cost-benefit analysis when it came to collateral damage. In July 1970, USAID director Robert Cuthbertson claimed that the Guatemalan Left was composed of "hard-core communist terrorists who are criminally oriented and love guns, love to kill." When questioned by fellow staffers about whether the United States should associate with a regime that so privileged security buildup over socioeconomic development, Cuthbertson offered a strident defense of Arana's development plans, presaging Ronald Reagan's famous "bum rap" comment about Ríos Montt fifteen years later.[110] Most advisers simply accepted the assertion that violence was being generated in equal measure by the extreme Left and the extreme Right.[111]

In the meantime, however, evidence abounded that U.S. allies were using U.S. taxpayer dollars to attack unarmed progressive sectors. In October 1971, the Ojo por Ojo death squad threatened the life of university rector Rafael Cuevas del Cid; U.S. officials knew that the government itself was behind the threats.[112] (Cuevas del Cid would later lose his son and daughter-in-law to state violence.) On 26 September 1972, Arana's security forces, in this case mostly PN agents, captured half of the PGT's Central Committee, making martyrs of Bernardo Alvarado Monzón, Hugo Barrios Klee, Mario Silva Jonama, and five others. The leaders were captured during a meeting in a private home and taken to the headquarters of the Detective Corps; they were never seen again. Shortly after the incident, the FAR kidnapped PN detective Abel Juárez Villatoro and forced him to sign a statement revealing the details of the operation. The eight prisoners had been captured by the clandestine operations team of Detective Corps subchief Arnolfo Argueta and turned over to the Fourth Corps' infamous chief, Juan Antonio "El Chino" Lima López, to be tortured and killed. As embassy documents indicate, "Police sources privately confirmed to us that the statement was essentially true."[113] And in late 1972, a new death squad appeared: Buitre Justiciero (Avenging Vulture), a front for the police elimination of common criminals.[114] In response to an internal report in October 1972 suggesting that a "Special Action Unit" had been formed within the National Police "to assume death squad functions," USAID director Byron Engle noted, without any apparent irony, that the news was "disturbing," and that "the time for stopping something like this from developing is before it gets started."[115]

Yet OPS advisers were not blind to the problem of state terror. A 1972 memo notes that the PSP's "major issue #1" moving forward was, "How can the [U.S. government] best assist the [government of Guatemala] to keep insurgency in check, while at the same time encouraging it to minimize use of illegal methods and use of repression against non-insurgents?"[116] But the National Security Council's Country Analysis Strategy Paper (CASP) for Guatemala in the 1973–1974 fiscal year clearly stated U.S. priorities. Security aid was designed "to assist the armed force and police to develop as rapidly as possible internal security capabilities sufficient to deal with the threat posed by violent opposition from the left," and "to enable the United States to maintain influence in the [Guatemalan] military establishment." (The next paragraph clarified some of the reasons for the U.S. investment in Guatemalan pacification, relating to the purchase of Guatemala's electrical company and to disputed trade and resource extraction deals involving the nickel-mining outfit EXMIBAL, the United Fruit Company, PanAm, and International Railways of Central America.)[117] The CASP suggested that the United States "discreetly use its influence" to discourage the Guatemalan state from committing extrajudicial executions but provided no clarity on how to obtain results, given that elsewhere it acknowledged that the United States' ability "to influence the political behavior of key power groups" was "marginal." The CASP provided only slight evidence, a trend projection measured according to "the Embassy's admittedly far from perfect index," for a claim that would release the United States from moral compromise: "We believe the GOG involvement in extralegal activity will decline."[118]

If U.S. officials were not acting, beyond privately suggesting to the Guatemalans that they be mindful of their growing image problem, international organizations began to take notice. In February 1971, Amnesty International first raised the "disappearances and murders of the opposition" of the Arana government with the Inter-American Commission on Human Rights, submitting documentation on hundreds of cases of "extralegal detention and disappearance." In December of the same year, the Latin American Studies Association passed a resolution condemning U.S. support for "semi-official and official rightist terror in Guatemala," singling out police and military aid programs as signifying U.S. complicity in repression.[119] Also in 1971, the U.S. House of Representatives made early forays into what soon became a larger conversation. A staff report on Guatemala and the Dominican Republic, evaluating the effectiveness of U.S. security assistance, noted that this aid's real impact was to legitimize state terror. "The argument in favor of the public safety program in Guatemala," the report noted, "is that if we don't teach the cops to be good, who will? The argument against it is that after 14 years, on all evidence, the teaching hasn't been absorbed. Furthermore, the U.S. is politically identified with police terrorism."[120]

By the early 1970s, the relationship of U.S. aid to police terrorism was being debated in a global context.[121] In 1969, the International Commission of Jurists charged that up to twelve thousand people were being held as political prisoners in the makeshift jails of Brazil's da Costa e Silva dictatorship, and in 1970 the *Washington Post* editorialized that there were "too many reports by too many reliable witnesses . . . about the torturing of 'subversives' for anyone to doubt that it goes on" in Brazil.[122] Senator Frank Church opened a Senate Committee on Foreign Relations investigation into U.S. police aid to Brazil in 1970; journalists Jack Anderson and Joseph Spear ran an investigative series disclosing CIA ties to the OPS, denouncing violence committed by OPS-backed foreign security forces, and calling for the program's abolition.[123] South Vietnam was another flash point, as regular reports of torture and murder committed by U.S.-supervised South Vietnamese police sparked further outrage.[124] By the time Greek director Costa-Gavras's film *State of Siege* (1973), which depicted the Tupamaros' kidnapping and murder of USAID counterinsurgency trainer Dan Mitrione, was nominated for a Golden Globe, Congress was ready to act. *State of Siege* ignited a firestorm among lawmakers, dramatizing U.S. involvement with Uruguay's police torturers and offering a strong denunciation of the International Police Academy, the OPS, and the entire principle of U.S. collaboration with dictatorships abroad. By 1973, the evidence and bad publicity could not be ignored. Senator James Abourezk (D-ND) met with political prisoners and conducted investigations that revealed, among other pieces of information, that the OPS had funded South Vietnam's infamous "tiger cage" cells, in which prisoners were hung from their arms in body-sized underground cages.[125]

Abourezk led the charge on two amendments to the Foreign Assistance Act of 1961, prohibiting foreign police assistance (1973) and banning any U.S. training of foreign intelligence services (1974). The Office of Public Safety, which had "trained" more than one million police officers worldwide, was dismantled in 1974.[126] In his presentation to the Senate Foreign Relations Committee, Abourezk decried how "this country is involved in an activity which is totally divorced from the scope and intention of U.S. foreign aid. The Office of Public Safety and the International Police Academy mocks the purpose of other USAID programs and has inflicted an indelible blemish" on U.S. credibility worldwide.[127] An era had ended, though not soon enough. In many cases, however, the taboo police assistance was merely rebranded as counternarcotics assistance, which, as historian Jeremy Kuzmarov writes, employed many former OPS personnel. (One Special Forces officer, dispatched to Colombia with a counternarcotics training team during the 1980s, reported: "The training that I conducted was anything but counter-narcotics. It was updated Vietnam-style counter-insurgency, but we were told to refer to it as counter-narcotics should anyone ask.")[128] This dynamic would evolve into the hemispheric "War on Drugs," but before that, its effects would continue to be felt in Guatemala.

THE WAGES OF COUNTERINSURGENCY

In 1974, after Congress settled the question, the OPS conducted a phaseout study assessing the Public Safety Program's impact on Guatemalan policing over the course of its nearly twenty years. It noted the following achievements: streamlining the PN from sixty-six operational units down to thirty-four, establishing La Regional, standardizing vehicles and armaments, institutionalizing riot control techniques, improving the archiving of personal identification files on more than one million citizens in a country of about eight million, building a new training academy, and convincing the Guatemalans to properly maintain their new vehicles. Over the course of the program, USAID directly invested $4.5 million in training, commodities, and advising for the PN, making Guatemala's police assistance program among its largest—to say nothing of indirect investments in, for example, the training of the army generals who would run the PN throughout the war.[129] In addition, USAID trained more than four hundred Guatemalan police at the International Police Academy and more than three thousand more in-country.[130] Indeed, technical improvements were made in the PN's civil policing capacities. But AID's primary impact on the PN was not the result of weapons shipments, uniforms, or traffic management instruction. What McClintock notes about U.S. aid's principal effect on the military also holds true for the police: "The U.S. security assistance program's introduction of sophisticated wherewithal for sowing the 'counter-terror,' such as computers, submachine guns, or helicopters was, in its influence on events, secondary to the Guatemalan military's whole-hearted adoption of the U.S. doctrine that it is correct and necessary for governments to resort to terrorism in the pursuit of certain ends."[131]

This would prove to be the only message that stuck. When U.S. advisers first arrived, they noted that the PN's operational capacities were woefully deficient. Indeed, as Fimbres's initial report indicated, the National Police was "acutely geared to security against subversive activity and communist attack, with the primary police function taking a secondary role." The following major problem areas identified by Fimbres in 1956 were:

> A lack of professional training, unwieldy spans of control, absence of good executive management, poor budgeting practices, poor personnel administration coupled with lack of concept of human relations in management, very low morale and esprit de corps, improper deployment of line personnel, lack of adequate and centralized police records, inadequate office and housing facilities, and lack of preventive maintenance and care of motorized equipment.[132]

Assistance from USAID did achieve modest improvements in some of these fields. But in their more honest moments, PSP personnel conceded that the training in civil policing was not taking hold. Instead, what USAID intervention accomplished was to make the Guatemalans see how its long-neglected "primary police functions"—better archives, modern equipment, vehicle maintenance, professional training, and improved personnel administration—were, in fact, *not separate* from the struggle against subversion. Rather, as OPS advisers instructed their counterparts, the struggle against subversion could be best carried out *only once* these primary functions, seen by the Armas-era leadership as low-priority pencil-pushing, were optimized.

Likewise, when the ICA first began to assess the PN, it took note of the mistrust and lack of collaboration between different security forces and intelligence groups. With U.S. assistance, particularly in constructing the technical means enabling interagency coordination, antisubversive operations were consolidated under military control, with specialized PN cadres integrated into a new executive hierarchy of terror. Staffers from OPS, who manned desks in PN headquarters, instructed police and military officers in the benefits of collaboration, systematizing intelligence, and maintaining the tools necessary (vehicles, files, guns) to get the job done. U.S. advisers rarely attempted to "curb the excesses" they observed in the process—and in which they at times participated directly—at any point during the Public Safety Program's twenty years, even as they were uncomfortable with the extrajudicial uses of what

Thomas Lobe calls U.S. "social control aid."[133] As embassy chief of mission Vaky wrote after leaving his post in 1968, "We have not been honest with ourselves. We *have* condoned counter-terror; we may even in effect have encouraged or blessed it. We have been so obsessed with the fear of insurgency that we have rationalized away our qualms and uneasiness. This is not only because we have concluded we cannot do anything about it, for we never really tried."[134]

The United States did not invent political polarization, class struggle, or police brutality in Guatemala. However, in their quest to maintain U.S. influence, protect U.S. business interests, and contain global "communism," Public Safety Program advisers abetted and encouraged domestic elites' efforts to obliterate any voices calling for change in society. As Stephen Streeter writes, for the highest echelons of Guatemala's power structure, "the communist threat was in fact a rationalization for bolstering the armed forces against a popular revolution against the oligarchy."[135] Even John Longan agreed. "It seems evident," he wrote, that the Guatemalan security forces "will continue to be used, as in the past, not so much as the protectors of the nation against communist enslavement, but as the oligarchy's oppressors of legitimate social change."[136]

As we shall see in the next chapter, the habits established during the Public Safety years died hard. Specialized PN units, under the direction of a U.S.-fortified military intelligence, continued their frontline involvement not only against the insurgency but also in the suppression of a broader social world based primarily in Guatemala City: trade unionists, students, professors, the urban intelligentsia, the press, and a growing chorus of human rights activists pushed to risky speech by the tortured bodies turning up in the city's gutters and ravines. Thousands of these people never reappeared, damning their loved ones to indefinitely suspend the grieving process while hoping against hope—and against the odds—that their family members would one day return. One of the best known of these *desaparecidos* was Víctor Manuel Gutiérrez, the PGT Central Committee secretary-general kidnapped during the March 1966 raids and then tortured to death.[137] The Project for the Recovery of the National Police Historical Archives cautiously began to reveal some early discoveries to the media in 2006 and 2007; one of the first documents it shared with the public was Gutiérrez's personal file, which was annotated to read, "#1 Communist of Guatemala."[138]

Gutiérrez's file spoke eloquently to the importance of archives in the counterinsurgency campaign. Though the PN had long maintained surveillance records, the filing system it used in the lead-up to the March 1966 disappearances was the result of records management training initiated in 1957 and 1958, wherein U.S. advisers set up a "Records Room," filled it with filing cabinets and supplies purchased by the Public Safety Program, and conducted daily training sessions in record keeping for their Guatemalan students. U.S. influence over the PN's archival practice extended to the very size of Gutiérrez's file card and the categories of information it collected about him—his physical characteristics, address, family members, movements inside and outside the country.[139] Moreover, Gutiérrez had been one of the Arbenz-era Communist Party members included in the first blacklist assembled by CIA operatives and handed over to Castillo Armas in the aftermath of Arbenz's ouster. As such, Gutiérrez's personal file, the first of many thousands to eventually be revealed by the Project, stands as a documentary artifact not only of political repression but also of the profoundly important and often neglected role of archives in processes of social control—the relationship of knowledge to power. The National Police archives, which reveal the dark nature of the PN's institutional history beyond a shadow of a doubt, have this and many other stories to tell.

FIVE

RECYCLING THE NATIONAL POLICE IN WAR, PEACE, AND POST-PEACE

The head of the National Police was named Chupina. One joke going around was, Did you hear Chupina had a twin brother in the womb?—Yes, stillborn, showing signs of torture and a *tiro de gracia*, a coup de grâce, in the head.

And in another Chupina and General Lucas are fishing, and Lucas catches a tiny fish and he's about to toss it back but Chupina says, Wait, give it to me, and he takes the fish in one hand and starts pummeling its head with the other, saying, OK, talk, where are the big ones?

—Francisco Goldman, *The Long Night of White Chickens*

n February 2007, Guatemalans were scandalized by a series of killings so unusual that they stood out among the capital's daily grind of homicides. The Central American Parliament, or Parlacen, was holding its annual meeting in Guatemala City; on 19 February, three Parlacen deputies, all Salvadoran representatives of their country's right-wing ARENA party, were found murdered in their car thirty kilometers outside the city. Forensic analysis revealed that before the car's torching, which burned the bodies so thoroughly that dental records had to be flown in from El Salvador to identify them, two of the deputies had been executed by *tiro de gracia*—a single bullet in the back of the head. In a coincidence too poignant to ignore, one of the slain deputies was the son of Roberto d'Aubuisson, ARENA's founder and wartime death squad leader best known for having ordered the 1980 assassination of Archbishop Oscar Romero.[1] Salvadoran president Tony Saca's reaction was historically resonant: he claimed that the killings had been "premeditated and planned by people who don't want freedom. We are not going to allow irresponsible people, communists, to achieve power." He went on to thunder, "On the list of heroes of ARENA"—a pantheon of martyrs now presumably including the murdered deputies—"there are many, many who gave their lives and blood to move this country away from communism."[2]

Despite Saca's eager leap back to Cold War rhetoric, the culprits fingered in the killings were no leftists. Instead, authorities arrested four Guatemalan National Civil Police (PNC) officers, members of the elite Criminal Investigations Division (DINC) squad, whose patrol car's GPS system had tracked their trip to the remote murder site. The four agents, one the head of the DINC's organized-crime investigations unit, were apprehended and incarcerated at El Boquerón prison on 22 February. That night, despite the maximum-security conditions and before they were able to testify about the murders, all four suspects were shot to death. A group of prison gangsters stepped forward to claim responsibility for the hit, but other inmates testified that a commando group of masked, armed men had entered El Boquerón and breezed through seven layers of security to dispatch the policemen. "We *mareros* [gang members] don't get ourselves involved in politics," one such whistle-blower told the press.[3] The plot thickened as more players in the case were suspiciously slain. The Parlacen killings, credited with overcoming domestic opposition to the creation of the UN's International Commission against Impunity in Guatemala (CICIG), inspired one journalist to argue, rightly or wrongly, that Guatemala was "the Somalia of Latin America, or, more precisely, the Haiti of Iberoamerica"—a failed state. Guatemala's representative from the UN High Commission for Human Rights agreed.[4]

The DINC was the PNC's special investigative unit—a semiautonomous wing staffed by detectives. When the Parlacen scandal ended the careers of interior minister Carlos Vielman and PNC director-general Erwin Sperisen, it also impelled calls to disband the DINC, which the PDH referred to as "a parallel body within the PNC . . . dedicated to executing individuals with total impunity."[5] The DINC weathered the storm, but some 60 percent of its agents were fired.[6] This narrative will, by now, sound familiar: an elite investigations arm of the Guatemalan police, composed of detectives and deeply involved in extralegal activities involving national politics and organized crime, is retooled in response to public outcry. The force is, supposedly, purged of criminals; the offending agents are recycled into other divisions; and the tainted unit is allowed to continue as before once the bad press subsides. One police chief likened attempting to reform the National Police to being a member of "the salmon club"—since the salmon, he explained, "is the only animal that swims upstream."[7]

Tracing the DINC back through its various cycles of *depuración* and *reciclaje*, or purging and recycling, offers historians clues as to why the DINC was involved in this complex crime at all. Before being repackaged as the DINC during the Berger administration, the PN's detectives unit was known as the Criminal Investigations Section (SIC), until Berger was forced to dissolve it due to persistent rumors about its use of torture.[8] The SIC was created in 1997 as part of the Peace Accords–mandated transformation of the PN into the PNC, succeeding the Department of Criminal Investigations (DIC), which had a similar reputation. The DIC had been in operation since 1986 and was itself designed to supersede the notorious Department of Technical Investigations (DIT), which then president Vinicio Cerezo had shuttered and whose officers he had mass-arrested in a dramatic raid designed to bolster his reformer's image, even as most of the ex-DIT agents were recycled back into the new DIC.[9] The DIT, in existence from 1982 through 1986, had in turn been conceived to replace the deeply corrupt Detective Corps, which itself had supplanted the Judicial Police, as discussed in chapter 4. In short, from an institutional standpoint, the DINC was the perfect unit to be tasked, on orders from higher up, with carrying out the Parlacen murders. The police's detectives unit, under this cumbersome array of monikers, had been executing similar crimes since the 1930s.

The story of how the Detective Corps became the DINC is not simply an acronym soup or a genealogy detailing the evolution of police structures over time. Rather, it is the social and political history of how a militarized, semi-independent force operated within the regular police, and it sheds light on the development and conclusion of Guatemala's armed conflict, the perils of police aid, the hypocrisies of the country's democratic transition, and the importance of recovering the PN's archives today. National Police agents were not the counterinsurgency's architects; neither, however, were they merely its handmaidens. The period from 1975, when direct U.S. police assistance was temporarily terminated, through the war's end saw the police participate wholeheartedly in the army's crusade. (The Project's decision to privilege the processing of the police records dating from 1975 to 1985 reflects how urban violence, and the police's role in it, accelerated during these years.) As one former G-2 military intelligence officer told the UN truth commission, "What the G-2 says is what the National Police does, they carry out military orders, only they do it in a more dirty way."[10]

The thorny case of the Parlacen murders demonstrates continuity rather than change, illuminating how and why the very security forces responsible for human rights violations during the war's earliest days still perpetrate similar atrocities. This chapter explores how the PN evolved from a wartime counterinsurgent force into a purportedly civilian National Civil Police, arguing that the failures of this evolution are emblematic of greater postconflict failures to build representative institutions, demilitarize, and redistribute power.

The army's decision to use "democratization"—relinquishing formal military rule and establishing the bare bones of a polyarchic electoral system—as a counterinsurgency strategy in the mid-1980s had devastating implications for the nature of the society Guatemalans would inherit.[11] Examining this trajectory not only writes the National Police back into recent Guatemalan history but also destabilizes triumphal narratives of postconflict transition. It is not the case that "'democracy' is only a mask for [a] military rule" unchanging across space and time; indeed, the very existence of the Project speaks to how dramatically the country's political landscape has changed.[12] However, the mechanisms used to repress Guatemalans' attempts to force open democratic spaces are remembered institutionally within the National Police.

The title of this chapter alludes to a third phase of transition: post-peace. Charles Call and William Stanley remind us that it is common, indeed normal, for violent crime to increase in the *immediate* aftermath of a peace process, as in El Salvador and South Africa.[13] However, they warn that if meaningful security reforms are not undertaken in the years following an armed conflict, longer-term prospects for peace and stability will be seriously undermined. Indeed, nearly two decades after the Peace Accords and following a brief early dip in violence, Guatemala today finds itself in a state of purgatory: neither in open conflict, nor truly at peace. As of this writing, the country's homicide rate stands at 48 per 100,000 nationally and more than 100 per 100,000 in the capital, exceeding the violent death rates of the war years; only between 2 and 5 percent of crimes result in prosecution; so-called parallel powers permeate state institutions; and Guatemalan psychologists declare that the constant barrage of shootings and murders has driven *capitalinos* to a state of "collective neurosis."[14] Morales Ramírez, a rank-and-file PNC agent exhausted after a twelve-hour shift, told a reporter in 2009 that when faced with such dramatic civilian insecurity and state impotence, "the only thing left is to entrust one's life to God."[15] The discovery of the PN archives, occurring alongside an ongoing debate about security reform, offers a critical opportunity not only to excavate the lost stories of victims but also to provide historical explanations for why the National Civil Police, despite millions of dollars in postwar international aid, remains mired in a paradigm so dark it impels its own agents to derive their hope from the heavens.

THE POPULAR MOVEMENT RESURGENT

In 1974, USAID closed down its Public Safety Program in Guatemala; no more official assistance would be given to the PN for the time being, though the CIA remained covertly involved in local affairs. But the United States' exporting of policing expertise was not forgotten. A year later, at the inauguration of the police training academy built with AID funds, defense minister Leonel Vassaux Martínez praised the U.S. contribution to "a renewed stage of *tecnicismo*" and professionalization within the PN. "Fifty years ago," he lectured, "the city was a tranquil place of moderate and sober customs, whose inhabitants—peaceful by nature—were scandalized by any act of delinquency." No longer, he told his listeners; by 1975, "delinquency [had] assumed alarming proportions," and demographic growth had brought "undesirable elements into society."[16] The National Police, Vassaux emphasized, was prepared for this shift. Some twenty years of U.S. assistance had produced counterinsurgency-geared innovations that had streamlined police operations, particularly the Regional Telecommunications Center. The PN also created the Joint Operations Center (COCP) in 1972 as a communications conduit with the National Defense General Staff (EMDN), permitting extensive collaboration in the dwindling days of Arana's state of siege.

But regime change, and the crushing of the FAR's first incarnation, brought a modicum of moderation. General Kjell Laugerud García, a graduate of U.S. training programs at Fort Benning and Fort Leavenworth, defeated Efraín Ríos Montt in a 1974 presidential election widely decried as fraudulent. Laugerud was a "close friend and confidant" of the outgoing Arana, with whom he cut his teeth in the Zacapa antiguerrilla campaigns of 1968.[17] His vice president was Mario Sandoval Alarcón, patriarch of the Movement of National Liberation (the self-proclaimed "party of organized violence") and a Franco-admiring hard-liner who backed death squads during the 1960s. Yet despite the conservatism of the new government and the chaos of the electoral campaign, official anticommunism and antisyndicalism ebbed under the new regime, at least initially. In early 1974, Laugerud, normally an enthusiastic red-baiter, pledged to improve his administration's relationship with organized labor, stating that he would "respect trade union freedoms and the organization of labor guilds."[18]

Laugerud was forced into this conciliatory position by organized labor's resurgence toward the end of the Arana regime. The mid-1970s saw significant growth in popular organizing, union-based and otherwise, as Arana's defeat of the rural insurgency gave him the confidence to cede a slight political opening in his administration's waning days; this coincided with a surge of popular mobilization around OPEC-related cost-of-living increases.[19] As the prices of basic goods spiked, urban government workers, beginning with primary school teachers, began agitating for wage increases. Their three-month strike won a salary hike; more important, it stimulated a wave of new organizing and the building of a broader labor movement, the National Committee on

Trade Union Unity (CNUS), in 1976.[20] In the first two years of Laugerud's rule, many small unions achieved legal recognition, and some strikes were allowed to occur, a palpable change of atmosphere. And it was not only unions that blossomed in the mid-1970s; the National Movement of Pobladores (MONAP), which worked with shantytown dwellers in the capital, and other popular organizations, often with a Catholic orientation, took hold. As Deborah Levenson-Estrada writes, "What distinguished the Laugerud years was not that the state guaranteed rights, but that compared to the extraordinary levels of violence of the 1966–73 period, death squad, army, and police actions killed fewer people. This definition of a 'political opening' may have been peculiar to Guatemala," but those progressives who had survived the Arana years were determined to take advantage of it.[21] It was under Laugerud that the "waves" of terror experienced under Méndez Montenegro and Arana Osorio became a "system" of terror characterized by selective assassinations—enabled by the intelligence-gathering, archiving, and communication capabilities recently acquired by security forces.[22]

The lively popular organizing of the early Laugerud years took an unexpected turn on 4 February 1976, when a powerful earthquake tore through central Guatemala. Some thirty thousand died, and hundreds of thousands more were left homeless. The *damnificados* of the quake, predominantly the poor and working classes, took matters into their own hands. Primary and secondary school students mobilized to rebuild their schools; university students self-deployed into marginal areas to dig latrines, provide medical care, distribute water, run pirated electricity lines, and generally do the recovery work.[23] As with natural disasters in other contexts, notably Mexico in 1985, the earthquake galvanized society's popular sectors, building consciousness and fomenting solidarity among newly mobilized citizens.[24] And the timing of the earthquake was provocative: not only did it expose the very inequalities to which the recent spate of organizing had been responding, but it occurred less than a year after the Guerrilla Army of the Poor (EGP) had formally announced its presence on the national scene by executing landowner Luis Arena, the "Tiger of the Ixcán," in El Quiché.[25] The EGP used the quake's aftermath for a call to mass action, interpreting the disaster as just "a tremor for the rich, [but] an earthquake for the poor." As one of its pamphlets argued, "The quake of February 4 dealt its blow to the Guatemalan population disproportionately, at the same level of magnitude with which control over the means of production and wealth among the distinct social classes are distributed. The working people suffer all the impact." The article concluded that popular warfare was the people's only alternative.[26]

It was not only the insurgency that built power during this tumultuous time. The CNUS formed just weeks after the earthquake, hoping to unite unions and union federations "into a broad coalition that could confront the state."[27] The next year saw more strikes than ever before, culminating with the massive Ixtahuacán miners' strike and march from Huehuetenango to the capital.[28] University of San Carlos law faculty advised new and expanding unions, while USAC students worked on popular organizing projects with the city's women, *pobladores*, and high school students. The Association of University Students (AEU) developed the capacity to mobilize mass numbers of students, growing its organizational abilities with help from the clandestine armed Left. In the countryside, organizing among indigenous campesinos flowered in the early 1970s as well, the result of rapid rural modernization in the 1960s and the efforts of Catholic Action and other catechist groups.[29] Political polarization and popular mobilization were rising to proportions not even seen in the street protests of 1962. A broad consensus of citizens rejected military rule, explored myriad means of expressing discontent, and, in their best moments, articulated alternatives. As at other junctures, however, the state and its allies, sensing danger and fortified with foreign firepower, pushed back against the winds of change.

THE CITY AS WAR ZONE IN THE AGE OF MARTYRS, 1977–1982

The year 1977 saw tremendous consolidation on the Left. It also saw a marked escalation in state-sponsored assassinations, both inside and outside the city, of those individuals at the forefront of efforts to crack open democratic political spaces; the Laugerud regime decided that such bold dissent would no longer be tolerated.[30] The growing list of the dead included prominent labor lawyer Mario López Larrave and student leaders Robin Mayro García Dávila and Aníbal Leonel Caballeros Ramírez, all assassinated by security forces in 1977. López Larrave was gunned down in his car by a group of armed men in a red Datsun. Caballeros's beaten body appeared two days after his abduction, and even his death did not bring a close to his police file: the PN spied on his funeral and on those who attended a memorial marking the anniversary of his murder.[31] The nineteen-year-old García was kidnapped too, his mutilated corpse dumped on a highway outside the city. Social democratic sectors, still vibrant during the late 1970s, were able to mobilize massive protests in response and, in García's case, a fifty-thousand-strong funeral march in which protesters shouted the slogan "Queremos a Robin vivo" that would later morph into the demand of *desaparecidos'* families, "Porque vivos se los llevaron, ¡vivos los queremos!" (Because they were taken away alive, we want

FIG. 5.1 National Police agents confront a demonstration. © Jean-Marie Simon/2012.

them back alive!)[32] A primary target for popular anger was Laugerud's reviled interior minister Donaldo Álvarez Ruiz, the titular head of the National Police, which had maintained López Larrave under close surveillance.[33] Banners at the demonstrations read, "Señor Álvarez Ruiz, you are the one responsible for the death of Leonel Caballeros," "Donaldo Álvarez Ruiz, assassin," and "The AEU holds the government responsible for all this violence."[34] Battle lines were drawn between the police and the people.

In response, the PN, like other militarized state institutions, deployed what Stanley Cohen terms "double discourse." Official state speech not only denied actions in which the government was clearly involved but also manipulated language to construct "a social reality that distort[ed] facts and events," combining literal denial with ideological justification to "re-arrange truth."[35] In his essay "The Police Institution Faced by Defamers," PN death squad commander Juan Francisco Cifuentes Cano sought to explain why radical youth were attacking his "glorious Institution," providing a window into a nationalist state-security ideology that saw its own agents as saviors and its opposition as threats to family, country, and God.[36] Cifuentes Cano divided his analysis into sections, including "Who Attacks Us," "Why They Attack Us," and "How They Attack Us." He posited that those protesting the PN were "not the best citizens nor the faithful compliers with the law," but rather "the enemies of peace, order, and progress in the country, those painted in various doctrinaire colors who eternally march in search of a universal dictatorship." He outlined a typology of those who considered themselves opponents of the PN, deriding them as "ambitious people who struggle only for their own economic gain," "the same opportunists as always, who lack moral values," "the bitter ones who, when political situations come to rise, lose their faculties," "errant romantic idealists who see defense institutions as those opposed to the establishment of the paradise promised by the fathers of socialism," and "youth in whom vibrates the desire for adventure and who, when they find it, dye themselves the color of the moment and call themselves 'real men.'" Cifuentes Cano dismissed the idea that the popular movements he caricatured posed any significant risk to the state or its armed institutions; instead, he wrote, "At the present hour, together with the NATIONAL ARMY, we form a wall in opposition to the uncontrolled currents of a world in convulsion."[37]

In reality, however, the insurgency's escalation and the increasing radicalization of the middle to late 1970s seriously undermined the state's ability to maintain order in the capital. Mario Payeras, founder of the EGP, may have been waxing poetic when he described the early days of the EGP's urban assault as "a ray of lightning which struck where it was least expected," but he was right to assert that the armed Left posed a real threat to the Laugerud regime, and later the Lucas regime, in the city.[38] The Otto René Castillo Front, the EGP's urban wing, carried out its first execution in December 1975 and began "armed propaganda" missions as early as May of that year, distributing printed materials in workplaces, educational institutions, and working-class neighborhoods. On 12 November, the EGP bombed the central offices of the National Institute for Agrarian Transformation (INTA). In April 1976, a raid on the El Bizonte arms warehouse netted the EGP not only a substantial cache of weapons and ammunition but also press attention, made all the more effective by the fact that defense minister Vassaux Martínez had indignantly denied the EGP's existence to the media just a day earlier. Two weeks later, the group executed Elías Ramírez, a former police chief it deemed "directly responsible for the kidnapping and assassination of hundreds of revolutionaries."[39] As the urban insurgency grew, PN agents, officers, and installations were frequent targets of efforts to destabilize the military state.

But 1978 was a definitive moment of rupture, as the military's massacre of unarmed Q'eqchi peasants at Panzós on 29 May shifted the conflict into a new register.[40] General Romeo Lucas García assumed power on 1 July, reappointing the much-loathed Álvarez Ruíz as interior minister and selecting School of the Americas graduate Germán Chupina to take over as PN director-general. The changes in PN functioning as a result of the 1978 leadership rotation closely mirrored the military's decided turn toward mass violence under

Lucas. While at other moments the PN played more of an adjunct role in the counterinsurgency, the Chupina period (1978–1982) was distinguished by the extraordinary autonomy and direct authorship over urban violence exercised by PN authorities, all military men. Even the influential General Héctor Gramajo, Guatemala's defense minister from 1987 through 1990, conceded that during these years, "there was [great] fear of Donaldo Álvarez Ruíz and Colonel Germán Chupina Barahona, who together had control over all the army and police forces."[41]

When the austere Chupina took command of the PN, he informed his officers that he would tolerate "neither sloppy ones nor lazy ones" among them, and announced that he would supplement the strength of those in uniform by creating a "civilian corps of police collaborators" composed of "honorable people in the different zones of the capital city" who would "inform the police institution of everything that takes place in their respective zones or *barrios*."[42] The use of *orejas* (spies) was, from this moment on, a matter of official PN policy. Civilian collaborators carried identification carnets, branding them as "Special Agents," issued by the Detective Corps, the handlers of government spies since the Ubico/Judicial Police days.[43] One example of a typical Chupina-era *oreja* report reads as follows:

> There is knowledge that the well-known subversive delinquent PATRO-CINIO POCON, originally from Huehuetenango, is currently living in the house of his sister MAURA POCON DE MINERA, wife of the doctor VICTOR MINERA, located at the address 45 Calle 12-22 Zona 12, Colonia Villa Sol, and in an apartment that this sister owns at the address 15 Calle Final Zona 21, Colonia Justo Rufino Barrios. Mrs. POCON DE MINERA works in the Municipal Training School "ECAM," located in Zone 8.[44]

Such a report would be routed, at the orders of the director-general and by way of the COCP, to the PN subbranch that was to be tasked with investigating the tip (in this case, the Detective Corps). Often, the Presidential Staff (EMP) would be copied on the communication. The PN received informants' reports directly or from above, handed down by the military to the police for execution; Chupina himself would write instructions in the margins, indicating whether a particular lead was to be pursued by the detectives or another squad. Another representative *oreja* report contained more details as to the nature of the accusation:

> There is knowledge that the individual known by the name of ELMER TOLEDO PINEDA, originally from the town of San Mororo in the jurisdic-

tion of San José Pinula, Department of Guatemala, disappeared from the area approximately one year ago. It is certain that he was the one who planned and directed the acts committed at the Chevron gasoline station in the town of Don Justo, and that he had planned other acts on the same occasion. As such, he is a dangerous SUBVERSIVE ELEMENT, [and] it is known that he works at the INCESA ESTANDAR factory located in Villa Nueva, on the highway to San Miguel Petapa.[45]

The year 1978 was also when Commando Six, a special operations unit appended to the PN's Second Corps, began operations, quickly becoming known as a leading executor of political crimes. (Commando Six would, during its four years in existence, be controlled by some of the PN's most infamous figures, including Pedro García Arredondo and Juan Antonio Lima López.) The COCP, in operation since 1972, was strengthened and more closely incorporated into the network of intelligence agencies at both the PN and military levels by Chupina, who dictated a new set of COCP governing regulations formalizing both its everyday functions and its close coordination with the Army General Staff (EMGE), the defense minister, and the EMP.[46] As well, Chupina promised a thorough *depuración*, or purge, of the PN and of its Detective Corps in particular, so that it would be staffed exclusively with "honorable persons."[47] Chupina only permitted individuals who had performed military service to be hired as PN officers.[48]

Chupina's vision of police rationalization produced an increase in both common and political violence. The second half of 1978 saw Guatemala City's streets and outgoing highways littered with corpses, their faces smashed in, hands amputated, backs pierced by bullets.[49] Popular movements took increasingly hostile antigovernment positions, inspired both by concrete acts of repression (for example, the extrajudicial execution of labor activist Mario Rolando Mujía Córdova that July) and by a broader economic context that saw urban bus drivers strike for higher wages using the USAC campus as their base. Demonstrations, tolerated during the early Laugerud years, were now being shut down by the PN's elite riot-control squads, who were fond of firing directly into crowds of striking workers. In October 1978, the PN's Model Platoon (Pelotón Modelo) antiriot squad broke up a demonstration of IGSS strikers by shooting into the crowd, wounding fifteen, and kidnapping the strike's organizers, including Emergency Committee of State Workers (CETE) leader Marco Antonio Figueroa. A day later, the police attacked a meeting of municipal water authority (EMPAGUA) workers debating whether or not to continue their strike, opening fire on them and wounding ten.[50]

All this served to radicalize unarmed popular sectors, their ire exploding when the city council approved a hike in bus fares in September. Residents of working-class neighborhoods erected street blockades, the CNUS declared a general strike, and protesters engaged with riot police in an increasingly confrontational manner, throwing Molotov cocktails and setting cars on fire. As Paul Kobrak writes, "The importance of the 1978 mobilizations had gone beyond the issue of bus prices. In its slogans and graffiti, protesters advocated revolutionary change, inspired by a sense of popular power achieved during the protests."[51] They won the battle—the original bus prices were restored—but they would soon lose the war. The Lucas government was in crisis; the specter of a Sandinista victory was on the minds of revanchists and revolutionaries alike, and the looming threat that the urban mass movement would unite with the rural strength of the EGP and the resurgent FAR inspired a redoubled reliance upon death squads by the state.

The Secret Anti-Communist Army (ESA), one such squad allegedly run out of Chupina's office, debuted in the second half of 1978, publishing hit lists of prominent left-wing and social democratic figures similar to the lists circulated by the MLN-backed squads of the 1960s.[52] In press releases, the ESA vowed, "For every anti-communist who falls in a cowardly attack, we will dispense justice to twenty [communists]." In August 1978, the Christian Democrats denounced the existence of a "Batalion of Death," which, it charged, was carrying out political assassinations with the government's approval.[53] In early 1979, another clandestine squad, Organization Zero, began claiming credit for executions using the slogan "Killing for Justice."[54] The PN reported that six hundred Guatemalans were murdered in February 1979 alone, most of them executed by yet another squad, the redundantly named "Escuadrón de la Muerte" (Death Squad), another secret outfit devoted to eliminating "known criminals."[55] By March 1979, extrajudicial murder was so public and frequent that it spawned its own neologism: those slain by clandestine armed groups were now referred to in press accounts as *escuadronados*—literally, "squadded."[56]

Among the death squads' victims in these years stand some of the Left's most beloved figures. They included AEU president Oliverio Castañeda de León, who was gunned down at the anniversary march commemorating Guatemala's October Revolution while PN agents, allegedly including Chupina himself, stood by and watched.[57] The archival record demonstrates that the police tracked Castañeda's activism closely before his murder; his name appeared on hit lists kept both by the police and by the Secret Anti-Communist Army. The PN's file on him tracked his presence at demonstrations and included several informants' reports on his activities. (Informants regularly reported on protests, noting carefully which organizations had turned out the greatest numbers of participants.) Posters and pamphlets from slain activist Mario Rolando Mujía Córdova's funeral, for example, were kept in Castañeda's file along with an informant's transcriptions of the slogans on demonstrators' banners and eleven photographs of the participants. A month before the twenty-three-year-old's assassination, labor and popular groups had converged on the Plaza Italia to express solidarity with Nicaragua; the police archived another informant's report on the event along with flyers distributed there by student groups and by the Central American Glass Industry union (CAVISA), soon to be decimated by extrajudicial executions. In addition to the *oreja's* observations, the report included thirteen photographs of the protesters. One such photo was enlarged and reprinted to reveal a more detailed image of Castañeda; on the reprint, a cross was scratched onto Castañeda's leg, presumably to identify him among the crowd.[58] Little imagination is required to connect this archival record to its subject's death.

Next, social democratic politician and United Revolutionary Front (FUR) leader Manuel Colom Argueta—whose police file dated back to 1957 and whose siblings, family, and friends were also under PN observation—was shot to death in Zone 9 by the occupants of a car whose license plates would turn up in the National Police archives thirty years later.[59] Progressive economist and Social Democratic Party (PSD) leader Alberto Fuentes Mohr met a similar fate, mowed down in front of the old Politécnica on Avenida de la Reforma; his murder and Colom Argueta's were attributed by CIA observers to the PN's Commando Six.[60] Student leaders Ricardo Martínez Solórzano, Manuel Lisandro Andrade Roca, Julio César Cabrera y Cabrera, Antonio Ciani, Alejandro Cotí, Ivan Alfonso Bravo Soto, and hundreds more were killed or disappeared; new information has emerged from the PN archives on some of their cases.[61] And so many members of the FUR and PSD parties, the remaining legal opposition to the Lucas regime, were assassinated that the parties ceased to exist.[62] The United States kept close track of the Guatemalan state's involvement in this explosion of death squad activity; each of these murders, local though they may have been, was very much "part of the Cold War," as Carlota McAllister writes.[63] As if to bring the point home, in the days after Colom Argueta's murder, unknown individuals decapitated the bust of Colonel Castillo Armas in the Guatemala City cemetery, smashing its stone head to pieces on the asphalt.[64]

The city had become a war zone, with confrontations between urban guerrillas and the PN, Mobile Military Police (PMA), or army nightly shattering an otherwise cowed silence. But death squad crimes—forced disappearances, selective executions—were committed quietly, leaving behind little evidence and few witnesses, hardly marking the cityscape until the moment a corpse was dumped. Carlos Figueroa Ibarra points out that within the country's "geography of forced disappearance," Guatemala City was a central theater, particularly during the late 1970s and early 1980s as the mass popular movements of students and workers were systematically annihilated.[65] For forensic historians, though, forced disappearances are difficult cases in which to assign individual responsibility, as their perpetrators were nearly always dressed in civilian clothing and therefore less readily identifiable by witnesses. (By contrast, army massacres in rural areas were carried out openly by uniformed troops, facilitating eyewitness identification by survivors.) In Figueroa Ibarra's study of more than six thousand forced disappearances, he notes that in some 60 percent of the cases, "unknown men" were reported to have been the victimizers, a phenomenon he terms "clandestine terror."[66] It is not difficult to imagine who, broadly speaking, committed these crimes; what remains unclear is whether a particular disappearance might have been carried out by Commando Six, the Detective Corps, another police unit, or directly by G-2 military intelligence, with individual responsibility even harder to pinpoint. That the PN's special squads conducted much of their business in plainclothes is thus one factor contributing to the minimizing, in many accounts of the war, of the police's role.

But police involvement in certain other acts of violence was more clear-cut. In 1980, the CIA reported that the "highest levels of the Guatemalan government through the National Police hierarchy" were "fully aware" of a clandestine burial ground, outside Comalapa in the department of Chimaltenango, used by the Detective Corps to dump bodies. The CIA cable, evincing the logical contortions of official denial, contradicted itself: it stated that the dozens of corpses found at the site were of "common criminals" only, yet elsewhere it noted that the Detective Corps disposed of bodies there "after interrogation."[67] (Of course, common criminals were unlikely to merit extended interrogation.) The dumping ground, U.S. observers reported, belonged to the detectives alone, and it spoke volumes about the Corps' modus operandi. In 2011, a series of human remains were exhumed from the Comalapa mass graves and their DNA analyzed. As of this writing, five victims have been successfully identified; they were all abducted in 1984 and were all among the detainees archived in the Diario Militar—the army document chronicling extrajudicial executions that was leaked in 1999—offering further evidence of close police-military collaboration.[68]

The year 1980 saw several urban mass murders bearing the PN's imprimatur, the Spanish embassy fire in January, and the abduction of twenty-seven workers from the National Workers' Central (CNT) in June, the anniversary of which is now Guatemala's annual Day against Forced Disappearances. In the case of the CNT unionists, a joint military-police action squad used a "Frozen Area Plan"—the method taught to Judicial Police detectives by USAID adviser John Longan in the 1960s—to cordon off the area around CNT headquarters and ensnare the union leaders in what survivors described as a "lightning strike" (*operación relámpago*).[69] The PN had been threatening the CNT for months, and in February 1980 had arrested seven of its leaders. They followed the June disappearances with another mass disappearance, under the direction of the Detective Corps' second-in-command: this time, police detained seventeen members of the USAC's Labor Orientation School, which Mario López Larrave had led before his assassination.[70] The CEH report describes how those taken were tortured in PN installations just adjacent to the present-day site of the police archives. As one U.S. embassy report stated, "It is believed that Government of Guatemala security forces killed all of them."[71]

The PN were just as involved in the Spanish embassy massacre. The incident began when a coalition of EGP-allied USAC students (from the Robin Garcia Student Front, named for the murdered student leader) and Campesino Unity Committee (CUC) activists occupied Spain's embassy, demanding an end to state terror in El Quiché. Rather than negotiating with the occupiers, security forces stormed the building, provoking a massive blaze that took the lives of all but one of the demonstrators. (The lone survivor, Gregorio Yujá Xoná, was abducted from his hospital bed that night and executed, his body dumped on the USAC campus.) The facts of precisely what occurred within the embassy—how the fire started, whose fault it was—have been hotly disputed, though the consensus opinion holds that police agents instigated the fire by launching gas canisters into the building.[72] What is not disputed, however, is that it was the PN's inspector-general who received the order from Lucas to break down the doors and remove the protesters by force, that PN agents prevented firefighters from entering the building, and that dozens of them stood by and watched as the thirty-seven peasants and students within were burned alive. The Spanish ambassador, who was inside during the incident but survived, later testified that "the police impeded the departure of all or some of those who found themselves trapped."[73] The incident resulted in Chupina's and Commando Six chief Pedro García Arredondo's inclusion in an international court case brought by Spain thirty years later against eight military and police officials for genocide and crimes against humanity.

The National Police's participation in these acts did not go unnoticed by the popular Left; shortly after the embassy fire, the USAC's governing body wrote an open letter to President Lucas demanding the firings of Chupina, Álvarez, and Detective Corps chief Jesús Manuel Valiente Téllez.[74] Neither, however, did the PN's role escape the attention of the armed Left. While the prevailing postwar narrative about culpability has focused almost exclusively on the army, the PN's responsibility was well understood during the conflict itself. Police substations were routinely targeted by insurgents in incidents that almost daily resulted in the deaths of the rank-and-file agents on night duty.[75] And the armed Left set its sights higher than killing night guards; guerrillas executed the second-in-command of Commando Six, the notorious torturer José Antonio "El Chino" Lima López, in January 1980.[76] (On the day of his death, Lima López sported a U.S. Army signet ring.)[77] In early February, just after the Spanish embassy fire, one police guard was killed in an unsuccessful EGP attempt to kill the PN's subdirector-general at his home.[78] In July, EGP cadres from the Otto René Castillo Front assassinated Miguel Angel Natareno Salazar, the head of the Fourth Corps, along with three other PN agents.[79] But the insurgents never won their greatest prizes, though not for lack of trying. In February, the EGP attempted the assassinations of Donaldo Álvarez (by car bomb) and Germán Chupina, while in July the FAR announced its own plans to kill both Chupina and Valiente Téllez in retaliation for the CNT abductions.[80] "These two assassins are profoundly despised by all the workers of this country, for many reasons," read the EGP's report on its attempt. "We regret having failed, and we know that the great popular masses regret it too."[81]

Interestingly, urban guerrillas were not the only ones targeting police officers, and PN extralegal activity did not eliminate only leftists. U.S. documents note that in 1980, "internecine rivalry claimed almost as many policemen as terrorist actions did," due both to internal power struggles and to agents' involvement in the illicit economy.[82] One of the most storied feuds in Guatemalan political history, between Detective Corps chief Jesús Manuel Valiente Téllez and Commando Six chief Pedro García Arredondo, claimed more than thirty lives, spelling the beginning of the end for the Detective Corps—in name, at least. Valiente was well known for both nepotism and butchery; on the side, he ran a private security firm, Los Vigilantes, staffed by dozens of members of his own family, which enjoyed near-total impunity in its settling of scores.[83] García Arredondo, after several years of bad blood between Commando Six and the Detective Corps in which the two frequently tripped over one another in the course of their clandestine work, decided to launch a hostile takeover of Valiente's turf. In 1980, numerous members of Los Vigilantes were murdered and several attempts were made on Valiente's life, with García Arredondo narrowly escaping similar aggressions.[84] On 22 August 1980, Valiente resigned under pressure, returning to the full-time administration of Los Vigilantes; however, the violence continued after his resignation, as fired Valiente loyalists were executed one by one.[85] In November, Valiente's home was attacked by armed gunmen; in July 1981, his brother was killed while waiting in a lunch line; and at the brother's funeral, PN detectives attacked mourners, gunning down eight members of Los Vigilantes. In early December 1981, Valiente was wounded in a sniper attack; in late December, a sustained grenade and machine-gun siege on his home killed his wife and daughter and left Valiente with only one eye and partially paralyzed.[86] Valiente fled to Miami, where he denounced García Arredondo's methods and confirmed that many of the recent murders attributed to death squads were, in fact, carried out by regular security forces, some under his own direction.[87]

García Arredondo's bloody takeover provoked a structural change within the PN. Previously Chupina, nominally subordinate to interior minister Donaldo Álvarez, had reported directly to the president while Valiente, nominally subordinate to Chupina, had reported directly to the interior minister. Hereafter, the two separate chains of command would be united into one, and for a brief period, the Detective Corps would be renamed the "New Detective Corps."[88] "It is called the New Detective Corps," police public relations officials indicated, "by virtue of its having been completely *depurado* [purged], with a total reorganization of personnel, and the new elements who have been admitted were selected because they are honorable people with a strong desire to work on behalf of the citizenry, in this way providing a new image to the Corps."[89] The *depuración* and *reciclaje* pattern appeared here in spades, a function of internal rivalry, not reform. Those familiar with García Arredondo's crimes were unimpressed by the change. As one U.S. embassy report indicated, "If the good news is the removal of a notorious human rights violator, the bad news is that his replacement, while possibly less venal, is every bit as ruthless."[90]

EVERY BIT AS RUTHLESS:
THE PN UNDER RÍOS MONTT AND MEJÍA VICTORES

Pedro García Arredondo would head the "New" Detective Corps for a year and a half, presiding over the July 1981 final offensive against the urban insurgency that all but obliterated the capital city's guerrilla presence.[91] By March 1982, when the coup d'état took place that saw Efraín Ríos Montt emerge as junta leader, the state had driven most insurgents out into the *campo* for a battle that would, Ríos Montt threatened, see not "scorched earth" but rather "scorched Communists."[92] The police dismantled guerrilla safe houses, or *reductos*, throughout the capital, and each fallen safe house was trumpeted by the regime as a further shift in the war's balance of power.[93]

Upon assuming power, Ríos Montt, an evangelical Protestant, set about conducting his own *depuración* of Lucas-era moral failings.[94] "There will be no more assassinations, and no more corruption," he proclaimed with millenarian conviction.[95] Many Guatemalans, even progressives, had been so horrified by the Lucas regime that they were relieved, at least initially, to see Ríos Montt take over.[96] The junta deposed and arrested twenty government officials, aiming to curb the police's death squad activity. Donaldo Álvarez Ruíz, after fleeing the country, had his home sacked by Ríos Montt's troops, revealing an arsenal of weapons and files; Pedro García Arredondo was removed as head of the Detective Corps and replaced by International Police Academy graduate Oswaldo Xolón Yat; and the indomitable Germán Chupina was rotated out as PN director-general and replaced by Hernán Ponce Nitsch, a "close friend" of Ríos Montt and former School of the Americas instructor.[97] The Detective Corps was disbanded, replaced by the Department of Technical Investigations in March 1982.[98] The Detective Corps, the new authorities decided, had been employing "inadequate empirical procedures" and stood accused of "anomalies in service, poor precedents, and having committed crimes." Its *depuración* involved the firing of some 150 detectives, many of whom reappeared on DIT personnel rosters soon thereafter.[99] La Regional, the intelligence-coordination service, was renamed the Archives and Support Services of the Presidential General Staff (AGSAEMP), or "El Archivo" for short. The nickname was appropriate, since within El Archivo, "archive and computer files would continue to be kept on students, political activists and leaders, human rights activists, journalists, [and] trade unionists, among others."[100] Ríos Montt seemed determined to rein in, or at least establish his own control over, violence in the capital, seeking to bring order to a chaotic city. Indeed, an incredulous *El Imparcial* ran an unusual headline a few days after the coup, spotlighting a piece of news so rare that it merited front-page placement: "No Gun-Related Deaths Today."[101]

The DIT under Ponce Nitsch, however, would not stray far from the coop. Ríos Montt's professed commitment to reducing death squad murders would last only a few months, while state-sponsored killing in the countryside escalated massively. (One editorial cartoon in the USAC's satirical *No Nos Tientes* student publication pictured the 1982 coup as a relay race, in which Lucas passed forward a baton to Ríos Montt.)[102] Ríos Montt's concern was not, ulti-

FIG. 5.2 Ríos Montt takes power. © Jean-Marie Simon/2012.

mately, that political homicides decrease; as he warned in July 1982, "Whoever is against the instituted government, whoever doesn't surrender, I'm going to shoot. It is preferable that it be known that 20 people were shot, and not just that 20 bodies have appeared beside the road." Rather, he desired that it take place according to his own guidelines and priorities.[103] Ríos Montt's innovation in criminal prosecution was to establish the Tribunales de Fuero Especial—special closed, Star Chamber–style military courts, to try accused subversives. But in practice, the process simply provided a thin procedural veneer for the same arbitrary executions conducted under Lucas. Ríos Montt instructed his elite operatives from El Archivo to "apprehend, hold, interrogate, and dispose of suspected guerrillas as they saw fit."[104] Toward that end, the dictator decreed that the responsibility for administering the PN be transferred, in early 1983, from the Interior Ministry to the Ministry of Defense, to render the police's militarization formal.[105] Administration of the "often unruly" DIT was taken over by the Army General Staff; instituting military discipline was seen as a way for the new regime to distinguish itself "from the corrupt Lucas García-Álvarez-Chupina model."[106]

But the lived relationship between the PN and society changed little. In March 1983, Ponce Nitsch announced that any journalists who wrote news items "confusing the population" risked indefinite imprisonment.[107] Police and military operations on university territory, whether under the pretext of combating narcotrafficking or with no pretext at all, continued under Ríos Montt even as the urban insurgency had already been all but defeated. Between July and October 1982, for example, more than twenty USAC students and professors were disappeared.[108] To say the urban insurgency had been all but defeated did not mean that occasional attacks on police substations, bombings of state installations, or guerrilla interceptions of FM radio stations did not continue. Nevertheless, the organizational network of safe houses that had sustained the insurgency through July 1981 had been broken by security forces, which continued to use the quest against subversion to justify ongoing residential raids and vehicle checkpoints.[109] As for internal PN matters, the DIT endured another round of *depuración* in April 1983, which saw some twenty officers arrested on corruption charges.[110] The phrase used by the U.S. embassy to compare Pedro García Arredondo to his predecessor—"possibly less venal, [but] every bit as ruthless"—could also have been used to describe the conduct of the police under Ríos Montt.

Patience for Ríos Montt's diversions from the military's pacification plan—and for his increasingly fervid religious pronouncements—waned quickly, however, and generals deposed him by coup in August 1983.[111] The new head of state, General Oscar Humberto Mejía Víctores, was a military strongman cut from Lucas García's cloth, with one difference: his desire for the reinstatement of U.S. aid, which led him to conduct a public relations campaign to rehabilitate Guatemala's reputation abroad. (Under Mejía, the state challenged Amnesty International, accusing the authors of its reports of having "an interest in distorting the reality of our country.")[112] This meant backing off from the "official" killings of Ríos Montt; instead, Mejía Víctores disbanded his predecessor's special military tribunals and returned to the practice of clandestine murder and forced disappearance.[113] But Mejía's PR push was half-hearted at best. When the United Nations passed a resolution condemning Guatemala for human rights violations, the government laughed it off. "We aren't taking the resolution that seriously," spokesman Fernando Andrade Díaz-Duran shrugged.[114]

General Héctor Rafael Bol de la Cruz was selected to replace Ponce Nitsch as director-general of the PN, and Bol de la Cruz's PN would be deeply involved in state efforts to crush a new wave of urban organizing that began in late 1983. That November, USAC rector Eduardo Meyer denounced the disappearances of more than fifty members of the university community in the preceding weeks.[115] As Paul Kobrak writes, "More than at any other time during the armed conflict, under Mejía Víctores the cruel practice of forced disappearance became the State's preferred method of combating the opposition."[116] Security forces met the resurgence of PGT-linked labor and student activism with harsh measures.[117] In May 1984, for example, seven members of the AEU's Executive Committee were disappeared in quick succession; earlier that year, several kidnappings took place in which the circumstances "clearly suggest[ed] they were perpetrated by government security forces."[118] As one U.S. document indicated, the National Police, particularly the DIT, "have traditionally considered labor activists to be communists," and acted accordingly.[119]

The grieving family members of these student and labor organizers, who met in the course of their anguished visits to the morgue looking for the bodies of their loved ones, came together to pressure the state for their *desaparecidos'* safe return by forming the Mutual Support Group (GAM) in June 1984.[120] The group's demonstrations, meetings with officials, and tireless advocacy pressured the Mejía Víctores government to make at least symbolic gestures toward investigating forced disappearances. However, rhetorical attacks on GAM began almost immediately, with Mejía Víctores tarring the organization as "subversive" and suggesting that many of the disappeared were "perhaps in some Communist country with some scholarship or in Havana, Cuba."[121] Soon, GAM became the target of violence, with the DIT being central in efforts to crush the organization. Héctor Gómez Calito, who joined GAM after his brother's 1982 disappearance, was kidnapped in broad daylight in March 1985. His tortured, burned body appeared soon after, hands tied and tongue cut out, and it became known that DIT agents had been inquiring after Gómez in his hometown of Amatitlán shortly before the murder. As U.S. accounts indicated, the body of Gómez—"an extremely non-violent person"—had been disfigured to an even greater extent than was customary in state-sponsored executions, "to make a point to the GAM group."[122] Rosario Godoy de Cuevas, another GAM member whose husband, Carlos Cuevas Molina, was abducted in 1984 by armed men who self-identified as DIT agents, spoke at Gómez's funeral.[123] Her eulogy, part of which was broadcast on television, decried his murder and blamed the state for perpetrating it. Days later, Godoy de Cuevas herself went missing; DIT agents telephoned her parents to inform them that the bodies of Godoy de Cuevas, her brother, and her two-year-old son were at the morgue. Although the police report claimed the three perished in a "traffic accident," autopsies showed that the young mother had been beaten and raped; her infant's fingernails had been pulled out.[124]

The "Holy Week murders," as they came to be known, of these GAM activists shared a modus operandi with hundreds of other killings under the Mejía

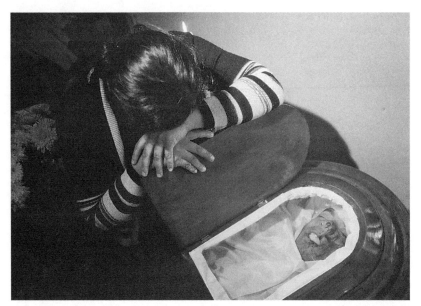

FIG. 5.3 At the funeral of Héctor Gómez Calito. © Jean-Marie Simon/2012.

FIG. 5.4 Rosario Godoy de Cuevas denounces state-sponsored executions before her own state-sponsored torture and assassination. © Jean-Marie Simon/2012.

FIG. 5.5 The Grupo de Apoyo Mutuo protests the murders and disappearances of its members in the wake of the murder of Rosario Godoy de Cuevas. © Jean-Marie Simon/2012.

Víctores regime. They were ordered and designed by military intelligence, but often carried out by specialized police units like the DIT.[125] Triangulating data from the Diario Militar and the National Police archives has since demonstrated this pattern. Under Ríos Montt and Mejía Víctores, the police structures relied upon for the execution of such "dirty work"—the DIT, the Fourth Corps, BROE/Fifth Corps, and Second Corps, to name the most prominent among them—did not change significantly from earlier periods. The DIT, despite its *depuración* and the new name it was given in 1982, continued the work of its predecessors, the Detective Corps and the Judicial Police. For its role in political killings between 1982 and 1986, the DIT would in turn meet its end, with newly installed civilian president Vinicio Cerezo attempting to score a public relations coup by disbanding the tainted entity. But the DIT's institutional successors would not break with its history.

DEMOCRATIZATION AS COUNTERINSURGENCY: FROM CEREZO TO THE PEACE ACCORDS

As Ronald Reagan suggested to the outgoing Mejía Víctores in a personal letter written in 1985, "successful elections and continued further improvement in respect for human rights in Guatemala are essential to securing from the Congress the economic and military assistance needed by your country."[126]

The letter sent a clear message: the Reagan administration was sympathetic to the objective of crushing communism, but congressional concern over human rights abuses tied the hands of U.S. hawks who wanted to reinstate military aid. If the Guatemalans could restore some semblance of democratic rule, thus solving the country's image problem, Congress could authorize increased assistance to its "friend and ally." "We would like to do more. Unfortunately, at this moment, the amount of help we can provide is limited," Reagan wrote. "I can assure you, however, that we are sensitive to your needs."[127]

Within Guatemala, the private sector and reformist currents within the military had already found that after years of bloody rule by coup, international isolation, and mismanagement of the national economy, it also served their interests to promote a return to constitutional government. As Rachel McCleary writes, while Arana had maintained good working relations with the private sector by actively promoting interregional trade through the Central American Common Market, Laugerud García and Lucas García had antagonized the private sector by clinging to import-substituting trade strategies that transformed the economy into a centralizing patronage system marked by clientelism, inefficiency, and corruption.[128] These regimes ran the economy into the ground, in the eyes of the power brokers composing the Coordinating Committee of Agricultural, Commercial, Industrial, and Financial Associations (CACIF). U.S. assessments put the mid-1980s economy at its weakest point in fifty years, and Guatemala's oligarchs and *terratenientes* were none too pleased with the situation, withdrawing their uncompromised support for military rule.[129]

On the military side, a group of forward-thinking officers based at the Center for Military Studies (CEM) had concluded in 1982 that they lacked a military solution to an insurgency that both internal and external analysts estimated as having between 350,000 and 500,000 rural sympathizers. Therefore, beginning with the social development–oriented regime of Ríos Montt, they set about incorporating democratizing elements into their long-term plans to defeat the armed Left.[130] Additionally, the CEM strategists saw establishing a democratic cover as necessary to the military's very survival. While the army could keep the insurgency contained, it could not muster the strength to truly defeat it without a significant increase in U.S. military aid, for which it would need to win over the U.S. House of Representatives.[131] The Guatemalan military was, as one CIA report indicated, "stretched to the limits of their resources."[132] As McCleary notes, therefore, "this return to procedural democracy did not occur because the military suddenly developed democratic values."[133] Mejía Víctores, no great proponent of democratic values when it came to policing the streets of Guatemala City, was reluctantly persuaded to tolerate the November 1985 presidential elections. He made sure, however, to pass a general amnesty for military officers in his final days in office, in case the *apertura* got out of hand.

The transition to civilian rule, then, was not won by the popular sector. Instead, "democratization" was a central plank of the army's counterinsurgency plan. As Schirmer puts it, the army "learned to play its electoral-constitutional cards internationally while continuing to practice its sui generis counterinsurgency campaign domestically."[134] This did not escape the Left: in its *Verdad* newsletter, the PGT pointed out in 1984:

> The counterinsurgent project implanted by the imperialists and the army continues on the march: on the one hand, we have repression and terror, and on the other hand, the National Constituent Assembly presents its show of "opening" with the desperate goals of giving a democratic appearance to the regime's reactionary, fascist, and pro-imperialist politics; legitimizing the counterinsurgency strategy designed by the United States; re-establishing U.S. military and economic assistance to Guatemala; neutralizing popular discontent; and stopping the advance of the Popular Revolutionary War headed by the URNG.[135]

The piece ran accompanied by a crude editorial cartoon, in which a leering general stands beside a ragged-looking detainee, who hangs suspended by his feet. The dangling prisoner yells out denunciations of the military's abuses; the smug general retorts, "Lies! I'm even putting something about human rights in the Constitution!"

Such a scheme required a figurehead. Vinicio Cerezo, the first civilian president in decades, was elected to accolades in 1985's presidential race.[136] Cerezo declared himself to be a "fanatic of democracy," and by October 1986, his devotion had netted the desired results: more than $400 million in aid commitments in the 1986 fiscal year alone, including more than $100 million from the United States.[137] Cerezo went to great lengths to demonstrate his efforts to gain control over the hard-liners responsible for extralegal acts in previous administrations. One of his first decisions as president, in February 1986, was to disband the DIT. By presidential order, agents from the PN's Special Operations Reaction Brigade (BROE)—no saints themselves—were sent to raid DIT headquarters, arresting more than six hundred agents and officers.[138] "We had heard rumors about kidnappings, automobile thefts, and other crimes being committed by members of the DIT," Cerezo diplomatically declared to the press in justification.[139] (A year later, PN spokesman Carlos

Rafael Soto admitted that the DIT had indeed led death squad activities and had "even carried out torture in National Palace headquarters.")[140] By governmental accord 88-86, the DIT met its end, replaced by the Department of Criminal Investigations.

But Cerezo's power was severely constrained, as reflected in his efforts at police reform. Of the 600 ex-DIT agents detained, 115 were fired from the PN for "flaws in service," and some 20 more quit. However, the overwhelming majority of them, 470 agents, were sent back to the PN's training school for reinsertion. Most of the former DIT agents were recycled directly into the new DIC, rendering Cerezo's initiative more show than substance.[141] The DIT's three chiefs were escorted back to their homes, thanked for their service, and assured that they would not be prosecuted.[142] Higher up, Cerezo briefly attempted to appoint as PN director-general a retired general without active military ties. But defense minister Héctor Gramajo pushed through his top choice, the controversial general Julio Enrique Caballeros Seigné—a career intelligence officer, former head of El Archivo, and close Gramajo associate. (Caballeros Seigné was described by one newspaper columnist as "a strange mix of Batman, Ubico, and Ríos Montt.")[143] Military dominance over civilian policing, then, was not about to change; military intelligence structures like the G-2 and El Archivo were left intact, free to continue their muzzling of politically sensitive investigations and control of counterinsurgency policy. As one PN detective told Jennifer Schirmer, "Publicly, the spokesperson says we are not related to the army and that we are in charge of criminal investigations in Guatemala. But there are always two investigations going on simultaneously: that of the police and that of the G-2 watching the police."[144] As Cerezo told the foreign press shortly after his inauguration, if he were to attempt too much change too quickly, "you'll be interviewing me in Miami."[145]

Certain Cerezo-era innovations in policing had slightly more staying power because they better served military interests. Over the course of the 1980s, the U.S. government had become interested in furnishing aid to help fight narcotrafficking, an easier sell to Congress, and one early focus of restored U.S. aid to the National Police through the U.S. Criminal Investigations Training Assistance Program (ICITAP) was the creation of an elite PN antinarcotics squad. The Special Investigations and Narcotics Brigade (BIEN) was established under U.S. guidance in 1986, and some of its officers were trained in the United States.[146] Guatemala's enthusiastic participation in the United States' hemispheric antinarcotics crusade, which in practice rather resembled the United States' hemispheric anticommunist crusade, won it points with the U.S. military. Indeed, the narcotrafficking angle allowed the Reagan administration to continue funneling funds to the Guatemalan police, circumventing congressional restrictions. "In response to your government's interest in anti-narcotics assistance," wrote assistant secretary for inter-American affairs Elliott Abrams to interior minister Rodil in July 1986, "we have approved a pilot anti-narcotics training program for Guatemala. This program will provide funds for vehicles and mobile radios *to improve the logistical capabilities of your specialized police.*"[147] Abrams, a staunch anticommunist, made clear his chagrin at the limitations imposed by Congress, writing, "I regret that existing U.S. legislation severely restricts our ability to provide most forms of police equipment and basic training."[148]

When urban violence, after a brief dip following Cerezo's inauguration, began to rise dramatically, the administration implemented another change that sought to bestow a democratic patina upon ongoing military control. The Civilian Protection System (SIPROCI) placed police and other civilian security forces under the direct coordination of the minister of defense and, above him, the president. This protection system integrated twenty-six thousand agents from military intelligence, Civil Self-Defense Patrols (PACs), the National Police, the Treasury Guard, the Mobile Military Police, and the Presidential Guard into joint army-police patrols, and though it was in theory controlled by Cerezo, it operated out of the offices of El Archivo and functionally subordinated all internal security matters to the authority of military intelligence.[149] SIPROCI was the result of an ongoing power struggle between the military and the police. When foreign aid for police reform started to pour in at the outset of Cerezo's term, it raised concerns that the government aimed to strengthen the police at the expense of continued army dominance. Disgruntled officers made this point clearly when, in a 1989 coup attempt, they occupied PN headquarters; Cerezo survived the coup by acceding to a variety of its demands, including the tightening of military control over the PN.[150] Two months later, SIPROCI was inaugurated, and the narrative that the military needed to participate in civilian security due to PN incompetence prevailed from that point onward. Later, under president Jorge Serrano, the joint military-police patrol system would be renamed the Hunapú Task Force—in the tradition of security forces giving Mayan names to their operations—and would integrate thousands of ex-soldiers as "police officers."[151] The joint patrols were most regularly deployed in "cleansings" of street youth and attacks on student and labor demonstrations, for which the patrols would become a major target of reformers through the 1990s.[152] Though SIPROCI was packaged as Cerezo exerting control over internal security, SIPROCI's structure was conceived by the army as a means of leaving Cerezo holding the bag in case any abuses made it into the public eye. As defense minister Gramajo laughed years later, "Within this scheme of ours [SIPROCI], the President is responsible for everything. I informed Cerezo of all the activities of Intelligence . . . so that he would take the blame, not me!"[153]

As these changes were made, designed more to serve the army's interests than to improve civilian security, public safety worsened. The "White Van" (Panel Blanca) murders of the late 1980s, in which Treasury Police officers were revealed to be abducting and killing USAC students, were only the most blatant example of the state's ongoing death squad activity, and of the PN's inability (or unwillingness) to control common crime.[154] Indeed, it suited the military well to maintain the general forces of the PN in a state of purposeful neglect, even as it made use of certain PN subgroups as skilled hit squads. When one U.S. diplomatic attaché visited PN headquarters in 1987, he reported that it "was like travelling back in time about a century. Adjectives that jumped to mind were old, primitive, inefficient, unresponsive, disorganized, and hopeless. This organization is at square one and it is now understandable why the crime wave rages on."[155] Director-general Caballeros Seigné of the PN blithely blamed the escalating violence on "alcoholism and transit accidents" and the vice-minister of the interior attributed it to "the passions of Guatemalans."[156] But CIA observers knew that the spike in homicides was the handiwork of police and military death squads ambiguously linked to front groups like "Avenging Jaguar" (Jaguar Justiciero).[157] One CIA report expressly linked the practice of police personnel recycling with the existence of social cleansing squads within the PN, echoing the military's practice of using *rebajados* (ex-officers) to conduct especially unsavory work.[158] "Former PN officers who had left the PN for a variety of reasons were rehired into the Department of Criminal Investigations (DIC) of the PN for the specific purpose of capturing and killing individuals with long criminal records," the cable reported. "These groups are responsible for the rash of murders recently publicized in local newspapers."[159] Rather than preventing urban crime, the police were a root cause of urban crime, and the phenomenon was systemic. As the cable continued, presaging the DINC's involvement in the Parlacen case, "given PN proclivities, it is unlikely that these PN officers are acting on their own. They must be acting on the orders of the PN chief or possibly a higher authority."[160]

The situation threatened to derail the preliminary peace talks between the Guatemalan government and the URNG. The international community viewed as critically important the twin aims of reducing violence and strengthening civil policing in order to weaken the army's chokehold on society. As a result, the decade between Cerezo's inauguration and the Peace Accords saw foreign

countries eager to contribute funds, matériel, and training toward profession-
alizing the National Police. The United States reinitiated police aid through
ICITAP; Chile, Germany, Belgium, and Spain also participated, as did the UN
through its MINUGUA mission. Much of this police training included a focus on sensitivity to human rights concerns.[161] But as Marie-Louise Glebbeek
writes, "Extensive international support . . . did not lead to significant progress in real reform," with the police remaining involved in human rights violations, much of the donated funds being diverted or inappropriately used, and
foreign-trained agents ultimately deciding to leave the police altogether.[162]
This new wave of police assistance, much like the United States' first major
police aid initiative during the 1950s and 1960s, was a failure, at least with
reference to its *stated* goals. "The general feeling within the U.S. government,"
ambassador Thomas Stroock told Caballeros Seigné, "is that much of our effort has been wasted."[163] Stroock admired Caballeros and expressed hope "that
he succeeds in turning the police force into something more than a uniformed
gang" but noted that, "unless he gets strong political support from the [gov-
ernment of Guatemala], we have real doubts."[164] The military continued to
maintain "spies" within the PN in order to retain control over police operations, and the institutional traditions of illegal activity, profiteering, high turn-
over, staff recycling, and the absence of political support for reform plagued
successive efforts to *depurar* and demilitarize the PN.[165] As peace negotiations
evolved, consensus emerged that the National Police was so far beyond repair
that it needed to be scrapped.

THE END(S) OF THE NATIONAL POLICE

The Peace Accords, signed on 29 December 1996 after years of negotiations,
established a broad framework for postconflict transition. Drafted in the context of the URNG's defeat, terms of the accords reflected that power imbal-
ance. Nonetheless, the signing of the accords was a moment of hope for many
Guatemalans. Luisa, a worker at the police archives project who fought in the
EGP for fifteen years, remembered that the accords "created a space in which
citizens can speak, can say what we want, can protest—we can have the October 20 protest again, the May Day march. . . . I can tell you that yes, after the
signing of the accords in 1996, yes, there was peace. I can swear to you that
there was peace just a year later—peace, tranquility, a different life."[166]

Luisa went on, however, to say that the tranquility did not last. "Another
year later, the collapse began again," she observed. "Now we're even worse
off than [during the conflict], with the violence and all that. Today, we're
screwed."[167] Indeed, one of the most maligned aspects of Guatemala's transi-

tion has been security reform, the failure of which has led to the "post-peace" environment of insecurity and impunity described at the outset of this chapter.[168] On paper, things seemed promising: the National Police was disbanded and supplanted by the National Civil Police, whose operational framework was outlined in the Accord on the Strengthening of Civil Power and the Role of the Armed Forces in a Democratic Society (AFPC). "Peace rests," the document's opening lines read, "upon democratization and the creation of structures and practices that, in the future, avoid political exclusion, ideological intolerance, and the polarization of Guatemalan society."[169] The AFPC specified the civilian character of policing, protected human rights in the exercise of internal security, required that the new PNC reflect Guatemala's multiethnic and pluricultural nature, and barred the military from participating in internal security. Plans were made to establish new police facilities, a new training academy, and a close collaboration between international donors and MINUGUA to oversee significant increases in PNC agent salaries.

So what went wrong? Three key factors contributed to the police reform's lack of effectiveness, all of which were deeply embedded in the PN's institutional history. First, as Susanne Jonas writes, many aspects of police reform were predicated upon constitutional reforms affecting the military and the justice system, which themselves were delayed or blocked in their implementation due to infiltration, corruption, or a lack of political will. Second, the PNC remained subordinated to the army during the transitional period, with former soldiers reappearing within PNC ranks and as part of ongoing joint military-police patrols. Third, and most important, the *depuración/ reciclaje* dynamic that had characterized a half century of police reform was not shed with the signing of the accords. Up to 90 percent of the former PN agents—whose incompetence and criminality were decried during the peace process by everyone from the URNG to the military—were recycled back into the PNC. Originally, the Arzú government planned to retrain these agents in a six-month program, but when security demand exceeded the supply of trained officers, the curriculum was slashed to three months. Over MINUGUA's protests, more than two hundred former army and Mobile Military Police officers were also integrated into the PNC, including a sizable contingent of ex-Archivo intelligence specialists.[170]

The Department of Criminal Investigations also died with the Peace Accords. The AFPC stipulated that the PNC's criminal investigations capabilities be strengthened and regulated by a civilian authority; as a result, the besmirched DIC was replaced by the Criminal Investigations Section in 1997, which received extensive ICITAP training.[171] But according to a MINUGUA assessment several years later, the SIC was overworked, undersupplied, ill-trained, and implicated in political crimes. In short, the SIC strongly resembled the old DIC—and the DIT, Detective Corps, and Judicial Police before it.[172] By 2000, the SIC was being critiqued for its infiltration by "parallel powers" and its use of torture and extrajudicial execution, along with more quotidian crimes like running car theft rings; in 2006, it was abolished in response to public outcry.[173] It was replaced by the Criminal Investigations Division, which underwent one last *depuración* of 60 percent of its members—but not until after four of its antinarcotics and criminal investigation specialists died mysteriously in El Boquerón prison after the 2008 Parlacen murders.[174] The journey from the Judicial Police, to the Detective Corps, and eventually to the DINC thus brings us full circle: from Jorge Ubico's dictatorship, to Castillo Armas's soliciting of U.S. police assistance, through the long decades of the war, and into nearly two decades of its bittersweet peace. As of this writing, the future of a new police reform initiative, headed for a time by human rights activist Helen Mack, was uncertain, with president Otto Pérez Molina promising that his *mano dura* approach to public safety would prominently involve a reinvigorated military.

This genealogy of the National Police, and particularly of the stubborn institutional persistence of its fiercest special squads, reveals much about the country's political pitches and rolls over the past half century. David Bayley's insight that "the police are to the government as the edge is to the knife" suggests that larger truths about the relationships between state and society can be gleaned from examinations of what Egon Bittner calls the "low" and "tainted occupation" of policing.[175] In Guatemala's case, the survival of the Judicial Police in its various forms speaks to the unwillingness of military regimes and, later, of civilian governments, to relinquish their ability to kill arbitrarily. This expedience—the casual ease of murder, the lazy scorn for opponents, the vacuum created by impunity, and the seductive sense of power conjured by terror—proved difficult to surrender. It is what renders deeply problematic the fact that procedural democracy was instituted in Guatemala as a counterinsurgency strategy; the persistence of a counterinsurgent mentality is a defining characteristic of the post-peace era. Confronting it is among the goals of the Project, which has sought not only to rescue the PN's archival paper trail but also to deploy the archives in efforts to eradicate impunity. To accomplish both tasks, the Project has had to exhume the forgotten history of the PN's role during the war, the outlines of which I have sketched here and which other historians will fill in over time.

The National Police did not run the counterinsurgency; it did not, for the

FIG. 5.6 A makeshift memorial to the disappeared in Guatemala City. Photograph by James Rodríguez, mimundo.org. Used by permission of the photographer.

most part, decide which political opponents would die and which would live. But it formed an integral element of a state terror apparatus that left the country's social fabric in tatters. The PN's low-level agents were overwhelmingly poor and working-class, uneducated, poorly paid, and regularly sent into situations they were not adequately trained to handle. Their histories remain to be written, and they will emerge from careful study of the eighty million documents in the police archives. What we know now, however, is that the PN's agents, under orders from the generals and colonels who commanded them, tortured political prisoners; they rounded up street children, addicts, and other undesirables in social cleansing sweeps; they dumped bodies like refuse in clandestine mass graves, in the city's ravines, or at the entrance to the University of San Carlos; they were ambushed, blown up, shot, and hunted by urban insurgents; and they abducted young idealists from grocery stores, hospital beds, public buses, and high schools. They were, too often, the plainclothes *hombres desconocidos* who, with a few moments' scuffle and a plateless Ford Bronco, set parents, lovers, siblings, and children on long and desperate searches for, to borrow Carlos Figueroa Ibarra's phrase, "los que siempre estarán en ninguna parte" (those who will always be nowhere). For this, the National Police must be remembered and its records painstakingly combed, for what remains to be learned page by disintegrating page, by the hopeful.

PART III | **ARCHIVES AND SOCIAL RECONSTRUCTION IN POSTWAR GUATEMALA**

I want to tell you that when I arrived at the archives, it had a strong psychological effect on me. I began to remember many things, things that had happened during the time of the repression, the time of my participation in the movement. Many, many things began to bubble up, things I thought I had truly forgotten. And so I started to see the archives as a possibility, as a way to tell future generations that this happened—and not just because some person here or there said so, but because there is now documentary proof of how it took place.

—Gregorio, Project worker

In the Project's early days, conditions at the archives were precarious at best. Lacking chairs, workers sat hunched over for eight hours daily on concrete blocks; they inhaled clouds of dust and assorted molds, which lay heavy and bright across the rotting pages like strokes of paint; and they were exposed to the waste of rats, bats, and other vermin. Riskiest of all, in light of the retribution faced by other activists who sought to plumb the depths of the state's wartime abuses, they affiliated themselves with a potentially dangerous initiative whose future was uncertain.[1] One might wonder why anyone would endure such circumstances, or what might qualify one to do this sort of work. In a country with fewer than ten trained archivists, previous archival experience was impossible to demand; no available training, whether in criminology or history or forensic science, would have been adequate preparation for the unprecedented task of rescuing eighty million documents under such dramatic constraints. Instead, the original volunteers and workers were evaluated by one measure: *confianza*. In this setting, *confianza's* literal translation as "trust" was a thin description; its deeper connotation was a certain level of dedication to human rights work and memory politics. *Confianza*, explained the Project's assistant director, was not easily quantified, but it essentially meant "that the people are referred to us by people or organizations we trust; that we know their trajectory, their level of commitment; that they've been linked to the causes that are worth fighting for in this country."[2]

As such, the initial volunteers and workers at the archives—later to become a minority as the team grew—were no average citizens plucked off the streets. Some had been combatants or clandestine actors in the organizations composing the URNG; others had been active in the student movement, or trade unionists, or community organizers. Some were born into families with histories of activism stretching back to the Revolutionary Spring; others had their political consciousnesses forged in the mass strikes of the 1970s, the 1976 earthquake, or simply by growing up as *campesinos*.[3] (As one worker told me, "We didn't fight because it was in style. I fought because I was poor and had no chance to go to school, and that either kills you from hunger or kills you from ignorance.")[4] They had lost family and friends; they had moved in and out of exile and clandestinity. The experience of working to rescue the archives was thus distinct for them, and the reconstitution of the archives was conditioned by their living knowledge. As Raúl, a Project case investigator, put it, "What affects me most is that the area of the archives in which I work, and the years which I work on, are years in which I wasn't just a witness—I was an actor, a victim, a part of all of it. And the victims who you find in the archives were your friends, your *compañeros*, your neighbors."[5] Rosa, a longtime EGP combatant who joined the insurgency as a teenager, attested that "those of us who were *metidos* in the conflict, *metidos* in it full-time, we have a different vision of the archive."[6] These workers' life histories were inextricable from their labor at the Project, an essential dimension of the archival rescue process.

This chapter explores how these individuals, ranging in age from their early forties to their early seventies, underwent and understood the work of producing and reproducing the PN archives. My discussion suppresses and alters details about informants' identities for their protection, but it does not omit information about the nature of their past political participation, experiences they universally remember with pride.[7] They worked as amateur historians, archivists, conservationists, and detectives. However, they did so informed by powerful personal histories of loss and militancy, which made being in the archives a complex experience indeed. The work challenged established knowledges and memories at the individual level for those workers who daily read records written, in part, about themselves. As María Elena, an ex-guerrilla, recalled:

> It's impossible to describe how I felt when I first saw the archives. . . . It offered the possibility that, for the first time, we could come to see ourselves

from a distant point of view, from the perspective of the Other—to learn what the Other thought. . . . How was it that we young people, whose only desire was social justice, came to be considered a problem of the State, a problem of state security? It's impossible to see yourself, from your own perspective, as a delinquent or as a terrorist, if everything you did was in the hopes of creating a better country, a more harmonious and equal society.[8]

Many reported that working in the archives had provoked the resurgence of long-repressed memories and the recurrence of dreams or nightmares. Gregorio, the odd-job man around the Project, said that his "contact with this history, manipulating these documents," acted as a finger in the wound, compounding pains still acutely felt: "There were times I didn't want to show up at work, times when I cried there. It makes you re-live many things."[9] But while the labor made workers vulnerable, it also engendered processes of social reckoning and reconstruction. Workers found themselves learning about facets of the war never before understood, and they grew accustomed to sharing stories, debating the unfolding of the war, and working side by side with once-reviled police officers. These survivors' embodied encounters with state documents occasioned new and sometimes frustrating forms of engagement with their pasts. Not only did they reread their own histories from the "Other's" perspective; they worked to write new chapters with an eye toward justice, finally confirming with documentation experiences long denied by the state's "double discourse."[10]

It was not a linear process. Sociologist Stanley Cohen notes that "memory is less a filing cabinet that we open to examine a pre-selected file (*my childhood, the war*) than a book we are writing and editing."[11] This was especially true in a setting where survivors' memories did not necessarily square with the omissions, silences, and bureaucratic language of the documents. The rescue of the archives thus offers several levels at which to consider these dynamics of memory making and history writing—all of them profoundly contingent, messy, and incomplete, as history and memory necessarily are. After reading the surveillance file kept on him by the Stasi, Timothy Garton Ash wrote of "how a file opens the door to a vast sunken labyrinth of the forgotten past, but how, too, the very act of opening the door itself changes the buried artifacts, like an archaeologist letting in fresh air to a sealed Egyptian tomb."[12] This chapter explores how the act of opening that door not only changed these workers' buried artifacts but also marshaled them for renewed use in the present.

Guatemala's tendency toward silence regarding the war and present-day climate of violence deterred many citizens from engaging with history. But a small number of people refused to succumb to this oblivion, even as it required them to spend their days on a filthy police base, echoing with the martial soundscape of gunshots and barking dogs, sifting through the dusty remembrances of atrocities past.[13] Given their backgrounds, these older Guatemalans' interest in the archives was hardly surprising. "The archive really got my attention," Luisa told me in a near whisper, afraid that the PNC agent nearby might hear. "I was interested in working here, because we have family members, friends, acquaintances—many people who were disappeared, who were captured, and we never knew what happened to them. With that, I don't want to say that I had the idea that I could 'do something' about that, but at least, within that history, I wanted to learn what happened, how they died, who took them."[14] Luisa had spent much of her adult life as a combatant in the EGP, which she called her "first school." She fought, married, bore children, and learned to read during her time spent serving in two of the guerrilla group's rural fronts. She was not alone in hoping to learn what had happened to lost loved ones there; while this was rarely workers' sole motivation, it was never far from their minds. Dolores, an ex-EGP case researcher who grew up steeped in the Rebel Armed Forces (FAR) militancy of her stepfather and uncle, reported that "even people who are new at work, they come with photos of their husbands, the same way I have a photo of my brother, and they tell me, 'I want to find out what happened to my husband.'"[15]

Others were drawn to the archives by a more general commitment to historical clarification and justice; they remained pessimistic about the possibility of solving specific cases. "I think that the things that happened here in the war years can't be found in those archives," Rosario said. She had been a trade unionist in the capital during the 1970s and early 1980s and was driven into a decade-long exile for it. Though she was normally reserved, volunteering few details about her experiences, discussing the archives made her voice swell with emotion. She marveled about how, back in *la época*, "we never would have thought that one day we'd have access to these papers. This is back when it was terrifying to even speak of the police. And to think that we'd be working there on a police base, with those papers in our hands." She was amazed at the luck of the archives' survival but knew that the answers the documents offered would be only partial.[16] Jacinto, a younger veteran of what remained of the urban student movement of the 1980s, shared Rosa-

FIG. 6.1 A Project worker sifts through the files. The labor was both physically and emotionally taxing. Photograph by James Rodríguez, mimundo.org. Used by permission of the photographer.

rio's doubts about solving specific cases—including the case of his own dis-appeared brother—and tempered his expectations accordingly. "I've never looked to find documents about my brother," he said. "I arrived hoping to find documents that could serve society."[17]

Humberto, a case investigator, envisioned his participation as part of a broader *compromiso*—a fundamental moral position, a political consciousness linked directly to his decades of involvement in the FAR and the EGP: "It was purely a question of *conciencia*," he said. His militant past meant that he "already had the *conciencia* to do this kind of work, I already sympathized with these types of projects."[18] *Conciencia* was what all the initial Project staffers had in common—a sense of moral engagement forged during the war that sustained them through months of volunteer labor before the international money began to flow. *Conciencia* was the electric connection between past struggles and the present day.[19] Rosa, who fought in the EGP until demobili-zation in 1996, felt she could not refuse the opportunity to volunteer in the archives, even in tough economic times: "I decided that it was fine . . . be-cause I felt something there, like a hope, that this could contribute to Guate-mala. I feel like I am working toward the same goals, but now with different conditions."[20]

It was common for these older staffers to speak of the recovery work as *un regalo de vida* (the gift of a lifetime).[21] They used words like "precious," "beautiful," and "marvelous" to describe a daily labor that involved thumbing through grisly photos of decaying cadavers, scanning seemingly endless lists of police duty rotations, and other tasks both morbid and mundane that few outside the Project might ever imagine as marvels. However, the opportunity to act in the service of one's conscience after the revolution's defeat seemed, indeed, a great gift. Esteban, a former student activist and PGT militant, made the link expressly:

> It's very gratifying [to work at the Project], because in these difficult con-
> ditions, we continue doing the same work, but in a different form. That's
> how some of us consider it. This work is a continuation of what we did
> before. We're subverting orders, no? And we continue. Maybe not with
> the explosive, incendiary effect of the past. But at that time, we were the
> youth; now, we're not so young anymore. And yes, it's been very rewarding
> to see it that way. Those of us who are still around are here. We've always
> been very few. If there had been more of us in this country, our conditions
> would be very different. They never let us be many, but those of us who are
> still here continue on the same path—if not here in the archives, then we
> do it in an NGO, or a committee, or by being teachers or clandestine actors
> in our communities. *Ahí está la gente, siempre.*[22]

Working at the Project offered those who defined themselves as bearers of *conciencia* an opportunity at political participation independent from post-war party politics, viewed widely as craven and corrupt. The *regalo de vida* concept highlighted what for progressives was a bitter postwar truth: aside from the problem of high unemployment across the board, ex-militants in particular had a difficult time finding paying work that conformed to their ethics and engaged their histories. Demobilization was a shock for some who were not yet prepared to lay down arms; even more difficult, particularly for those who had joined the insurgency at a young age and had no conventional job experience, was reintegrating into normal life and finding safe spaces in which to express their convictions.[23] Edeliberto Cifuentes, the historian and PDH investigator who stumbled across the police archives in 2005, told me, "There are a lot of people who are unemployed in Guatemala because they aren't willing or able to work in anything except human rights. I include myself in that group. I can't find anywhere to work besides the academy or human rights—I can't work in just any part of the government. And I think that happens to a lot of us."[24] The difficulties of the reinsertion process belied the idea that a "postwar transition" could occur neatly, the fruit of top-down decisions that instantly erased wartime divisions. Instead, dissidents' histories, and their own condition as living archives of an armed conflict, continued to contour their anything-but-"normal" lives. "The private sector would never have me!" exclaimed one worker and ex-PGT militant. "I'm in a bunch of photos from the '80s, lighting buses on fire with Molotov cocktails. And in the private sector, they have connections and they can easily find out who you are. You think [Project director] Gustavo Meoño could get a job in the private sector? What a joke!"[25] Ex-militants were naturally drawn to the Project, but they were also pushed into it by the dearth of compelling alternatives.

DEATH, ARCHIVES, AND MEMORY WORK

History, *conciencia*, and necessity brought these workers to the archives; once there, however, many found that their experiences challenged their expectations, and that the archive's necessary relationship to death and history haunted them in ways that were difficult to bear.[26] Achille Mbembe writes of the archival/historical reconstruction process that "following tracks, putting back together scraps and debris, and reassembling remains, is to be implicated in a ritual which results in the resuscitation of life, in bringing the dead back to life by reintegrating them in the cycle of time."[27] But resuscitating the dead—a process operating concretely here at levels beyond those considered by Mbembe, Derrida, or other theorists of archives—is dangerous business, and it puts a tremendous burden on human rights workers who are, by virtue of their own sacrifices, victims too. If traditional manipulations of archives bring the dead back to life, then for former militants, working at the Project brings *their* dead back to life.

An example: Esperanza, as a lower-middle-class young woman in the early 1970s, began her political life as an organizer in Guatemala City's secondary school system. She was radicalized in the aftermath of the 1976 earthquake, which laid bare the deep poverty and exploitation lived in marginal sectors of the capital. From that point on, she incorporated herself into the PGT, putting up a "communication barrier" between herself and her family and devoting herself to organizing students in night classes "to achieve change in our country, to build a society with different values, different principles."[28] She worked as a PGT organizer for nearly a decade, interrupted by a brief period of exile provoked by a botched attempt to kidnap her from the school where she was based. Esperanza was no stranger to exile, having spent the first ten years of her life there as a result of her father and uncles' opposition to the Armas regime. To exile she returned in the mid-1980s; during this final exile, her father and uncles were murdered. When she returned for good after the signing of the Peace Accords, she and her husband sought to avoid politics, opening a small restaurant. But they found themselves unsatisfied by apolitical life, closing the restaurant and reengaging with their histories. When Esperanza arrived at the police archives in 2005, she found the work of constantly reading about violence to be an immense strain; for her, it was easier to "see the pages as nothing more than just papers that I was cleaning, cleaning, cleaning," shutting herself off emotionally from what she was reading. But after some time spent working in this manner, Esperanza decided one day that she would begin to *read* again, actively attempting to prevent herself from becoming desensitized by the sacks and sacks of files about death. "So all of a sudden, I decide to return to the reading," she said, "and I open a new bundle of papers, and it turns out that the very first sheet I find is the report from when the bodies of my uncles were found." Her two uncles, beloved elders in her family, were together when they were shot. Though the report Esperanza had uncovered contained no new information on the case, simply stating that her uncles had been killed by *desconocidos*, the shock of finding their names archived stirred her anger and sorrow anew. "That day, for me, was a horrible day."[29]

Esperanza was not alone in finding information about a murdered family member during a regular workday; others also found references to dead or disappeared parents or siblings.[30] Most commonly, ex-militants would stumble across the name of a former *compañero* in a writ of habeas corpus (*recurso de exhibición personal*), filed by family at the time of a disappearance. In the majority of cases, mentions of loved ones did not bring new information but simply offered an "official" version of what had transpired—that an individual was killed by "unknown individuals," or else nothing more than a brief mention of the name. "I have found documents about my closest loved ones dead, their photos, very painful things," María Elena told me, trailing off in tears as gunshots from the police firing range pounded in the background. "But without necessarily finding any truths; sometimes you find nothing more than the stamp of repression upon their bodies."[31] New truths or not, no snippet of information was without value, even if it offered no new leads. As Raúl attested, "Many of the things the documents say weren't secrets to us. We knew them. What we didn't know was the details of exactly what had happened. . . . Now we have all the details, and better, we have confirmation. If I go and claim that the police kidnapped X person, nobody will listen to me; but if one day, all of this is documented, people won't want to believe it, but they will have to. That's the difference."[32]

While Raúl was clear about the potential gains of working at the archives, the work still took its toll on him, as it did for the others. He spoke of how the stress generated by the work had physiological effects ("your spine hurts, and it means that your whole system is altered. . . . It sends off physical alarm bells") and emotional consequences ("it affects you; at times, it alters your character. Involuntarily you get irritable sometimes, you get angry. It's a permanent struggle not to let yourself get carried away by these feelings").[33] Another worker described how she had been trying to "put everything that had happened behind me," but when she began at the Project, the memories "hit me like a giant headache. . . . I felt that it was very hard, psychologically, for a human being to do this work."[34] Jacinto, the younger PGT activist, became enraged after finding a document mentioning an erstwhile neighbor, a fellow student activist assassinated during the 1980s: "It makes me so angry to see the documents attesting to how they followed X or Y person. You say to yourself, look at this whole structure, all lined up against one person. It makes you angry, because it wasn't fair, it wasn't one-on-one—it was a structure. Hundreds of people against one. It's frustrating and it makes me so angry."[35]

Workers struggled not only with the content of the documents but also with the physical space in which the documents were housed: *la isla*, as it was called in the 1980s when the police used it to detain and torture dissidents. One area of the site in particular, the prison-like *laberinto* (labyrinth) mentioned in chapter 1, was especially difficult to handle with its windowless, dirt-floored rooms, suspicious small holes blasted in the walls, and sections fitted with what appeared to be brackets for manacles or other bindings. "Entering that space gives you a sensation like...a life experience," Gregorio recalled. "Like one of your friends had been there, that this was where they had been tortured, that maybe there were bodies buried there. . . . There were subjective elements in that space that could lead someone to say, 'Here is where my friends were tortured,' and that affected us very much."[36] When Leonora, a case investigator, was summoned to the cramped space on her first day, she found herself with "the urge to get up and run right out of there."[37] Evincing the undercurrents of guilt and disempowerment infrequently discussed openly by former militants, Gregorio spoke of how "the fact of entering this place made me remember, it makes you remember and it makes you think that your friends were once there, and you couldn't help them, you couldn't do absolutely anything for them."[38]

To a certain extent, the emotional strain was inherent to the work. Spending eight hours daily reading not only about political repression but also about sexual assaults, armed robberies, accidental deaths, and other "archival sliv-

FIG. 6.2 A warren of windowless, cell-like rooms at the warehouse's rear spoke to the site's former use as a detention and torture center. Photograph by author.

ers" of violence would tax the coping skills of even a disinterested reader.[39] As José Antonio, the Project's inventory specialist, told me, "When you read something, you visualize it, you visualize the suffering of this person in your head, you see in your head where they fell. You see the suffering of the widow, the children." He spoke of recurring dreams he began having after he started working at the Project, in which identical scenarios to those in the documents would replay in his mind with his own children as the subjects.[40]

In the case of these war survivors, however, this strain was compounded many times over by the fact that the names appearing in the documents were *theirs*, belonging to *their* friends, *their* acquaintances, *their* schoolmates, *their* loved ones. Guatemala is a small country, and even a well-informed foreigner does not have to spend much time skimming through the records before recognizing a name. Humberto, in stumbling across a reference to a fallen *compañero* from the EGP, found that "it brings sadness to remember a friend, even though you already knew what had happened to him. . . . And when you find the name there, you react; you read the report where it says that he was shot repeatedly, but it's reported as an act of common delinquency, you don't know why. You find it there like whatever murder."[41] And some workers learned from the documents, for the first time, how a close relative was killed. "In there, I found out how my brother had died," Dolores told me. "I had never known. And still today in my house, my mother, my siblings and I, we can't talk about our brother. We've been living with this for twenty years, and we still need to learn how to talk about him as he was. . . . I was one of the lucky ones, to have been able to learn this."[42] Reencountering the war through the Other's eyes blurred comfortable distinctions between present and past, memory and history. In Esperanza's words, the archives were "a space where we all return to the past, and we all come to relive the pain or to awaken what's asleep inside each and every one of us, and to face the reality of what we lived."[43]

Wartime activists who in peacetime labored for justice bore a double burden. Not only were these individuals themselves victims, having lost family or friends to state repression and revolutionary campaigns, but they continually relived past experiences while performing contemporary memory labor. They simultaneously wrestled with and reified their losses, all while seeking to marshal them for the purposes of effecting change in the present. This dynamic was by no means unique to the Project; the Guatemalans who worked on the CEH and REMHI projects, for example, were deeply impacted by the pressures of taking victims' testimonies, as many had themselves suffered gravely.[44] Fredy Peccerelli, director of the Forensic Anthropology Foundation of Guatemala (FAFG) and a member of the Project's advisory board, pointed out that survivors often actively sought out such work as a dynamic way to grapple with their wartime experiences. "You don't do this sort of work for professional advancement," he noted.[45] Neither, though, did they do it out of a desire for vengeance. As one Project staffer put it, "I am interested in bringing [perpetrators] to justice, but not in treating them the same way they treated us, because that would be sinking to their level, becoming their equal, and I never want to be equal to them."[46]

A similar dynamic pervaded the Project, where workers often sublimated their emotional reactions in order to get the job done. Luisa, cited earlier as saying that resurgent memories hit her "like a giant headache" upon starting

FIG. 6.3 Work at the Project involved frequent contact with grisly images of decomposing cadavers, many exhibiting signs of violence or torture. Photograph by James Rodríguez, mimundo.org. Used by permission of the photographer.

to work at the Project, remembered: "My head hurt so much. But I told myself that we had to work as hard as we could, because this work needs to get done. If I want to learn the history, I need to do this work; I just need to throw my-self into it, and once I do, I'll get accustomed to it. And so it was."[47] Survivors, drawn to memory work because of past experiences, found themselves both aided and constrained by those same experiences; this double-edged sword took its toll. And because these individuals were employees, instead of pri-vate citizens visiting a public archive to seek specific information, they had to daily press ahead with cleaning and ordering the documents, despite whatever pain the papers brought—eight hours a day, five days a week. As Esperanza observed, "It's not as though I can leave my baggage at the door, like they tell you in some jobs, 'You came here to work, so leave your problems at home and concentrate on what you have to do.' That's not possible anywhere—much less in this kind of job."[48]

Project workers deployed a variety of strategies to manage the strain. The simplest, of course, was talking: talking at the worktables, sharing experiences with coworkers, venting frustrations over a cigarette or a cup of instant coffee at *la refa*, the midmorning break. But talking was never enough, and some did not feel sufficiently comfortable with their colleagues to do so. After a year and a half of operation, when the collective strain became palpable, the Project instituted group discussion–based, mandatory, monthly mental health workshops. In terms of group approaches, however, the Project's most effective means of managing the burdens of the work was soccer. At every *refa* and lunch hour, boisterous workers—male and female, young and old—would take over the pitted concrete mall between the two archives buildings and play hard-fought games of pickup *fút*, which everyone else watched and cheered. "Because of the way the games are played," commented one member of the scanning team, "you know that people are there for catharsis. Many of the people yell, they fight, they kick, they laugh, precisely because it's a way to escape from the tensions provoked by this routine, which is a routine of violence."[49] The Project's coordinators encouraged the informal games and the more competitive rotating tournaments they led to, well aware of their workers' need for release.[50] Others, less athletically inclined, found relief by focusing on the end goals of the Project: Luisa, who was older and suffered from chronic health problems, told me that what had helped her "get through" was imagining how, someday, there would exist an archive where Guatemalans would be given the opportunity to search for their family members. "It's something beautiful, like a daydream," she said. "It lifts your self-esteem, it lifts your energy, it lifts your desire to do your work and accomplish all the things we're accomplishing today. That's how we talk about it among ourselves—that one day there will be a real archive here. That is our collective thought process, and it helps us keep ourselves working as we should."[51]

Some were more inclined than others to embrace the darker thoughts occasioned by the "routine of violence." Rosa, whose immediate family suffered no fewer than five disappearances, conceded that it made her heartsick to find lists of detainees, or to read about locations where a safe house had fallen or a botched propaganda-distribution activity had led to a capture. "But still, I say: what a good thing that some information remains about these people, and that someday we'll be able to clear up what happened to them," she enthused. "What a good thing that we have the chance to do this work, because we knew these people. If someone just reads a name and doesn't recognize it, they keep reading and everything remains the same. For me, it's different. So that makes me think that the small contribution I can make in the archives, even if it's really very small, has a huge value."[52] Similarly, when I asked Esteban if it was difficult for him to read so much evidence of violence, he replied:

No, it's fascinating! I've taken advantage of that opportunity; for those of us who continue to live the past, reading these papers allows our latent traumas to flower, allows us to remember that one of these cadavers we see in the photos could have been a *compañero* who had been at one's side. Because all of the cadavers that turn up as xx or unidentified, all of those cadavers had names. And they were killed, and things were done to them, and that was because they had names. It wasn't because they were nameless. To see that, it causes old traumas to surface anew. . . . But that's a very good thing, because it doesn't permit them to accumulate, it doesn't permit them to bottle up and create strong pressure; rather, it means you can release some of the pressure from time to time.[53]

In Esteban's interpretation, the reencounter with the companion via the document could provide both relief and vindication: relief in the sense of offering a release valve, and vindication (*reivindicación*) in the sense of reassigning agency, subjectivity, and identity to the dead.[54] The police archives brought these workers' dead back to life; once revived, how might they be put to rest?

TRUTH-VALUE AND TRUTH'S VALUE

The *reivindicación*, or restoring of honor and agency to the dead, was a major motivating force for nearly all the ex-militants with whom I spoke. Even in the face of the testimonial and forensic evidence compiled in the CEH and REMHI reports, the Guatemalan air still hung thick with a homegrown holocaust denial: the charge that the genocide of the 1980s and the urban counterinsurgency were the invention of "subversives" seeking to discredit Guatemala on the international stage. Efforts by the state, business elites, and some journalists to discredit and attack war victims had always drawn their strength from the idea that nobody could "prove" the truth-value of the events in question, and therefore the victims were making it all up. Victims and testimony givers were accused of lacking patriotism—of being "traitors to the homeland"—or being too stupid to realize that their "disappeared" husbands had probably just taken up with other women outside the country.[55] In 1986, after the Mutual Support Group (GAM) had spent several years advocating for the live return of their disappeared loved ones, the military released a statement calling GAM's accusations slander precisely because—importantly, in light of the PN archives—they were "not substantiated by documentary proof."[56] Ex-president Alvaro Arzú, once a member of the ultra-right-wing Movement of National Liberation, rejected the hardest-hitting conclusions of the CEH's final report; at the report's presentation ceremony, the generals in attendance turned their backs to head commissioner Tomuschat as he announced the findings.

The state's constant expressions of contempt for the Left (armed or otherwise), for socialism, for intellectualism, and for the families of the disappeared were part of its counterinsurgency strategy, and these tactics affected popular movements from without and within. In peacetime, similar language was used to discredit those who continued seeking justice, often based on the charge that victims had no "proof" of what they claimed. Esperanza emphasized the extent to which militants internalized the state's disdain for their ideals: "We played the game too, feeling that what we were doing was subversion, it was clandestine, it was something not accepted by society, and so we've been carrying this around like a burden of guilt ever since. I would even say it's a shame that we carry, a shame that we've built up over time."[57] A daily reading of the terror archives, however, renewed ex-militants' resistance to such tropes by providing new evidence of the state's disproportionate responses to their activism—in the state's own hand. As Raúl said, "We shouldn't have to feel shame for what we did. We got involved because we saw injustice, and the injustice was so great that it could not be tolerated. The very word 'subversive,' which was seen as an insult, as a serious charge, really isn't such a bad thing. Because if the system doesn't work, you have to change it, you have to subvert it."[58] Workers who participated on the Left were generally clear, proud, and defiant about their reasons for having taken part in efforts to resist military rule. "I didn't join the EGP to screw around," Victoriano said. "The dignifying of the *guerrillero*, not of the assassin—that is where the archive will contribute."[59] Raúl explained how this idea motivated him:

> I hope we can at least reveal that the person who was accused of being a criminal, a delinquent, felt obligated to do what they did, and that any other person would have done the same if they'd been there in that moment, faced with all the shame and dishonor that we've now documented. It will be impossible to say that we were lying, because we have the proof in the documents. It will restore the histories and memories of so many people who were dismissed as being *metido en tonteras*, people who were written off by others who said, "If they'd just stayed at home, nothing would have happened to them." People need to know that these people who were called dangerous delinquents were very noble, people who did a duty knowing that their commitment would cost them their lives. They had no egoism. . . . The papers don't say it, but I lived and worked with some of the people in these documents, and they were people who would give up their own food so that others could eat. Their commitment was real.[60]

The abiding need to restore honor to the armed conflict's victims—and, by extension, to themselves—inspired Project workers' daily labor of sifting through gruesome photos and endless pages of bureaucratic minutiae in search of nuggets of evidence. Rosa, who happened to stumble across several documents about a particular *desaparecido*, was assigned the task of continuing to look for information on this person, whom she had never known personally but whose case was high-profile. She found searching for records about this specific person to be a "beautiful" experience, because "you say to yourself, this is a person who was fighting because they wanted to change this country. It's a person who has the same ideas and the same beliefs as you about living in this country, wanting it to develop, wanting it to be different." (Her comment was a post facto gloss over the very real factional divisions that characterized the wartime Left.) "And so when you become aware of these elements linking you to another person, it gives you a very strange feeling, but at the same time it makes you very interested in continuing to search for information," she said.[61] Rosa's interaction with these documents was inseparable from her own history—in fact, it made her feel more connected to her history—but not strictly in the sense of "learning about the past."

Particular documents and cases aside, the simple fact of the archives' existence, and the assumption that it "proved" a set of truths known to the Left all along, was seen to finally deny nonbelievers the ability to write off justice seekers' truth claims. "In this sense," a PDH analyst told me, "there is a profound satisfaction in being able to say, 'I did not invent this. This is how it happened. And I can prove it with documents that the state itself generated. . . . You told me all this was a lie but no, it was true.'"[62] The potential for corroborating what was already known about the war, to say nothing of revealing new information, offered the powerful hope of vindicating testimonies long discredited. It could not right the errors of the armed Left, nor could it restore the lives of those who fell in the service of a more utopian Guatemala. But resurrecting paper cadavers—demonstrating with the state's own records the extent of its repressive security structures—brought comfort to those who had upended their lives for political change. "It gives value to people's struggle. We weren't wrong," said Jacinto, defending his movement's goals even as he regretted aspects of their execution and felt *engañado*, or cheated, by its leadership.[63] "We were deceived, maybe, but we weren't wrong."[64]

The notion of proof value, however, was more complex than it seemed. Even a supposedly "normal" archive's ontology is complicated by the fact that "what is recorded is never simply 'what happened,'" and that what one finds there is necessarily incomplete, unreliable, and/or indefinite.[65] At the PN archives, relatively few "smoking gun" documents were ever unearthed. Rather, most case investigation rested upon complex processes of triangulation among multiple sources. This challenge was exacerbated by the fact that researchers regularly encountered amateurish and occasionally indecipherable records scribbled by semiliterate police agents and informers on unsigned scraps of paper, not to mention the pages obscured by mold and rot. As discussed earlier in this book, these records' legal proof value depended on how effectively the Project workers "constructed an archives," and maintained the documents' archival bonds, in the midst of the chaos of their discovery site. But even at the level of the individual document, researchers were thwarted in their efforts to "prove" what they "know" happened—to square their memories and histories with a police force's institutional memory and its ill-kept, partial (as both *self-interested* and *incomplete*) history.

A particular aggravation for workers was reconciling their memories of the conflict with the lacunae, silences, and bureaucratic euphemisms of the documents. The very life experiences that workers cited as a motivating force dogged the task of soberly interpreting each document according to the Project's abstracted methodology. "I might know something, but if the document doesn't actually say it outright, then I can't speculate," complained Jacinto, who worked as a document codifier. "I struggle with that, I struggle with it very much. Because sometimes, even if a document doesn't explicitly say something, it's still obvious!"[66] An example was the scores of documents that referred to mass detentions of individuals for public drunkenness. During the early 1980s, PN squads regularly reported entering particular zones of the city—often those known, like Zone 5, for being hotbeds of guerrilla activity—and emerging a short time later with hundreds of people in custody, all supposedly for being drunk.[67] "Bueno," Jacinto exclaimed, "el chapín es bolo, pero siempre la suspicás!" Guatemalans might indeed like to drink, he joked, but such mass arrests were highly suspect.

The codification methodology in particular, quantitative in nature, was designed to literally transform each document into a set of data points. It allowed workers only to record what the document *actually said*, not what they thought the document implied or euphemistically suggested. It could not capture a former militant's infraknowledge, revealing the tension between the quantitative and qualitative aspects of the investigation—between the observations of a professional researcher and the convictions of an aggrieved victim. One worker spoke of how he had come to see the documents as "hypocritical," after reading multiple reports on well-known assassinations stating that the individuals in question had been shot to death by *gente desconocida*, "even though everyone knew that the police were the killers."[68] "You don't know, in the long term, whether or not the methodology will end up revealing what you know, with the experience that you have," Jacinto concluded.

More commonly, though, the disjuncture between scientific methodology and lived experience simply translated into frustration at the worktable: for example, the shock of reading that Oliverio Castañeda de León had been executed by *desconocidos*, even though multiple witnesses attested otherwise. Such official turns of phrase served the same function as what Hannah Arendt has called the "language rules" of Nazi Germany, wherein the bureaucratic terminology of extermination ("deportations," "special actions," "cleansing") was both brutally clear and purposely euphemistic, intended to sow feelings of doubt and disempowerment.[69] That survivors still struggled with these linguistic strictures decades later spoke to the enduring strength of terror's double discourse. Stanley Cohen, following Michael Taussig and Marguerite Feitlowitz, outlines terror states' strategy of simultaneously denying responsibility for atrocities, denying that atrocities are occurring at all, and maintaining "the hermetic mythology about the dangers posed by 'subversives,'" thus ensuring that even external criticisms serve only to "make the denials stronger and the ideology more sacrosanct."[70] In this sense as in others, being a former militant at the Project was a double-edged sword—it implied a privileged knowledge, but not always one that found a technical use, as researchers were forced to depend upon and, ultimately, to reproduce the chilling linguistic traps used by the National Police.

THE LABORS OF MEMORY

Elizabeth Jelin writes eloquently about the labors of memory, which she defines as the active psychological efforts made by survivors of violence in order to, in a Freudian sense, "work through" their past traumas.[71] At the Project, such labors were inseparable from the larger enterprise, as discussed earlier. However, the Project was more than a space for individuals to work through their memories. It took the notion of "labors of memory" to a whole new level because it was also a workplace with salaried employees, management hierarchies, productivity targets, and divisions of labor—which often conflicted with the private, personal emotional work Jelin describes.

The secrecy of the coordinators regarding the investigation, arguably a judicious discretion with information given Guatemala's ongoing political instability, proved challenging for some older workers, who had waited decades for the truth to be made known. José Antonio, who administered the archives' Master Location Registry and therefore had some of the most universal access to documents of anyone at the Project, felt his patience tested upon finding "good documents" and then being told to keep quiet until the time was right to reveal them, rather than trumpeting the discovery to the nation as his heart might wish. "I move around the archives like a rat," he told me, "looking for information, looking, looking, looking." Once, when he found a document of high investigative importance, he was instructed to simply note its location and put it back without telling anyone else about it. At the time, the Project had been trying to avoid giving "them"—right-wingers, the Partido Patriota, the Otto Pérez Molina campaign—any ammunition during the run-up to the 2007 presidential elections. The rationale was that if information leaked to the public about any particularly revelatory documents it could provoke retaliation against the Project. Fair as the reasoning may have been, it was still difficult for workers to tolerate, forcing them to juggle both strategic interests and personal desires. "I felt deceived, disappointed," José Antonio said. "I wanted to go public, but it wasn't possible. . . . It's hard to wait. Sometimes it makes me want to leave this job, because I'm so curious and I get lost in the documents and it's so hard to be patient. I know that as a professional I have to wait."[72]

Others, relegated to what they saw as the baser tasks of the archives—scanning, or codification—resented that these positions did not allow them to apply their life experience to the job. As the Project professionalized, its division of labor became much starker, and those at the bottom of the hierarchy were resentful. They almost universally spoke of the case investigators and researchers, who got to work analytically with the documents, with jealousy. And the verticality of the Project's organizing structure, particularly its case investigations, meant that the workers not integrated into the investigative structure felt shut out—as though the very infraknowledge for which they had been hired was being wasted. Gregorio, once the head of an important worktable but later transferred to building maintenance, insisted that he would serve in whatever capacity he was needed. He admitted, however, that he "would have preferred to continue working in contact with the documents."[73] Those with backgrounds in militancy were drawn to the PN archives, but they wanted those backgrounds to factor into their daily labor. They wanted their opinions to be heard, they wanted to be kept abreast of where the case investigations were headed, and they wanted access to what José Antonio called "the most precious things"—incriminating documents. They were not always satisfied with their positions as the Project expanded; operating the photocopier for eight hours daily, or feeding sheet after sheet of fragile carbon paper into a scanner so quickly that there was no time to read them, wore upon those eager to bring their analytical skills and mental databases to bear upon their work.

The division of labor affected the morale of older workers in other ways.

While in its earlier days the Project's operating structure had been collaborative and horizontal, the Project became increasingly streamlined and hierarchical by early 2007. Initially, everyone in the relatively small group of workers had thought of themselves as peers and had participated more or less equally in the daunting task of designing a way forward. But the rapid move toward the compartmentalization of tasks divided types of work and grades of pay. Here, the tensions between the Project-as-human-rights-initiative and the Project-as-place-of-employment ran deep for those who had signed on out of a sense of moral commitment and who resented being excluded from the decision-making process. Some attributed the increasing verticality to the Project's leadership, partly composed of ex-insurgents, reverting to military forms of organization. As Victoriano put it, "Information had become so centralized in the *coordinación*, that those of us who were doing the work and knew more about it were kept out. Everything had become so secretive, and my personal opinion was that these were the operating methods of the guerrilla, this compartmentalization!"[74] Because the Project was a human rights project, workers expected it to be democratic; because it was a workplace operating under conditions of duress, the coordinators leaned on older organizational models as a way of keeping incendiary information closely guarded. The conflict between the two models was never fully resolved, and in difficult moments, it soured some *compañeros* on the whole initiative. "The archives have come to be seen as a business," complained Jacinto, "and the people who work there are seen as the workers in a business, workers for an employer who requires a product. . . . But I am a thinking person, and I fought for my ideas, and I keep fighting for my ideas, and I would like for that to be respected."[75]

There were also uncomfortable realities to be gleaned from the documents themselves. The sheer volume of information about state social control— about informants, surveillance, unmarked cars, plainclothes officers, urban raids and sweeps, international advisers, shipments of weapons and communications technology, trips made by PN agents to U.S. training centers, and the like—brought home yet again bitter memories of a divided insurgency, militarily outmatched, unprepared for the wholesale slaughter the state was willing to unleash upon the civilian population.[76] This is not to say that the organized Left, armed and otherwise, did not have its areas and moments of strength during the war—quite the opposite—and the immense scale of the archives risked overdetermining both the PN's historical power and the "doomed" nature of the revolutionary movements. Nonetheless, when I interviewed Victoriano with his wife, Dolores, they spoke movingly of how dispiriting it was to understand, only now, what exactly they had been up against:

VICTORIANO: I am from the EGP, I was basically born with it, I gave my whole life to it, and when I discover in the archives information about the spying they did on the revolutionary organizations, I realize—

DOLORES:—That we were only in diapers!

VICTORIANO: And so that's how I came to truly understand the dimensions of the war, the repressive character, the information they had, the training they received from the Israelis and all this. And at the time we thought, look at these police, they're so stupid, we shouldn't be afraid of them, we're *más chingón* than they are.[77]

Despite these and other challenges, however, the archives remained one of just a few spaces where ex-militants felt they could keep advancing what they saw as lifelong goals, such that, despite the labor tensions and psychological stresses and bitter realizations, they would persevere. "This belongs to us and we bear responsibility to make sure that this work is brought to fruition," reflected Rosa, sounding world-weary at the thought of the task ahead, and at the thought of the task left behind. "Look, if you give up in the face of something difficult, you have lost. So we have to keep fighting. That's how it is."[78]

UNEXPECTED DIALOGUES

These workers may have entered the Project with their *conciencias* fully formed, but this did not mean that their contact with the documents was a static experience. Rather, their reencounters with the past—whether traumatic, vindicatory, or both—had unexpected results.

We have seen how memory workers' labor at the archives brought new information about their histories, galvanized those who sought ways to enact their hopes for Guatemala in the context of a neoliberal peace, and opened possibilities for justice. It also, importantly, occasioned interpersonal reconciliation between ex-militants and agents of the National Civil Police (PNC)—a productive collaboration that would have been unimaginable before the archives. The PNC maintained a team of more than ten police agents at the archives full-time, and they shared close quarters with the Project team. Working with the police was not an easy transition for many Project staffers. When I asked María Elena what kinds of contact she had had with the police before the archives, she laughed heartily. "Ha! Running away! Escaping! Being in protests where they were shooting at us!"[79] Raúl, leaving the USAC campus with fellow union leaders late one 1983 night after a long meeting, was ambushed by PN agents who opened fire when they reached the university gates, killing Raúl's companion and wounding Raúl in the arm. Many

FIG. 6.4 A National Civil Police agent scrutinizes a public display of the war's dead and disappeared. Photograph by James Rodríguez, mimundo.org. Used by permission of the photographer.

former militants had little love for the police, and the prospect of working on a PNC base alongside PNC agents tested the limits of their tolerance. There was institutional tension as well, between the Interior Ministry, the PNC, and the human rights ombudsman's office. As Fuentes put it, "There's a historical reality there—the PDH and the police haven't exactly walked hand in hand through this country's history!"[80]

Having PDH employees occupying a police base and examining documents that, despite the judicial order granting them user privileges, remained PNC property was naturally a strained process. Police agents assigned to the archives shadowed Project workers closely in the early days. Ana Corado, the officer in charge of the archives, said that this was "to help them out, to tell them what needed to be done with the documents," but workers saw it otherwise.[81] One staffer with an especially sensitive role reported being followed home by plainclothes officers on multiple occasions; when he complained, the incidents ceased.[82] Most PNC surveillance took place at the worktable level under the guise of "protecting" the records. "When I started," Dolores recalled, "we were put in a room with a police officer who would keep watch over us. They would note down every time we went to the bathroom, they would note down everything we did, what we talked about. I saw the notebook once, and it had notations on all of these things."[83] "When we started," said Rosa, "the police were running around as though they were 'taking care' of the documents, but really they were making sure we weren't touching anything, looking at anything they didn't want us to see."[84] Being *vigilado* (surveilled)—all over again—led workers to modify their behaviors and guard their words. "There were often police agents with us, spying to see what we were up to, seeing what papers we were looking at," Jacinto remembered. "When they weren't there, we would talk, we would chat about politics or whatever, and as soon as they came back in, boom! The doors closed and we would only speak of trivial things."[85]

But the PNC agents were nobody's fools, and they responded poorly when treated with suspicion by people whom they, in turn, mistrusted as interlopers. Ana Corado and her agents had invested considerable effort in managing the heaps of abandoned records before the PDH had arrived, in defiance of their superiors' orders, attempting to bring some modicum of order and organization to the dumped papers. As a result, Corado was protective of the documents under her charge and was unconvinced that the PDH's intervention in the archives was to the benefit of the records. Because any request to see a new group of records had to be cleared with Corado, bad relations quickly translated into bad access. Inquiries about sensitive bodies of records—those of the Second Corps, the Joint Operations Center, or the Department of Technical Investigations—regularly put the two sides at loggerheads.

Project staffers soon realized that to get their work done, they needed to cultivate better relations with their counterparts, despite their negative past experiences. In the process, they became more sensitive to how "these papers, these archives, belong to the police, and we were working in a space that also belonged to them," as Rosario put it.[86] An atmosphere of tentative mutual respect slowly began to emerge, based on a shared valuing of the archives and fostered by the Project's directors in order to speed the pace of progress. Change came in the small details: before the Project had funds to install water cisterns or a microwave on-site, PNC agents shared theirs with Project staffers. In turn, it pleased and impressed the archives agents that the PDH was willing to provide supplies, introduce computers, and generally improve the archives' conditions, even if the two sides had different goals in mind.

It was the slow accretion of small gestures like this, in response to the difficult working conditions all the parties shared, that led to an unprecedented relationship being built between a hodgepodge group of leftist activists and state security agents. The necessity of forced coexistence, in police space, provoked two new forms of understanding among Project staff: as one worker put it, "First, you start to understand the logic of it all; second, you start to put yourself in their shoes, to see them as human beings."[87] When Project workers learned that it was due to Corado's efforts, not in spite of them, that the archives existed at all, the animosity dissipated further still. Workers found something in common with the agents: they all believed that the archives were, in Corado's words, "a treasure."[88] "We respect them for precisely this reason: because they really wanted to preserve these documents," said Gregorio.[89] It stunned many at the Project to learn that the plastic cord binding document bundles together had been purchased by the PNC agents at their own expense, and that the scissors and staplers in daily use had been brought from the agents' own homes.

Walking in police agents' shoes and spaces, and coming to appreciate their dedication to the archives, pushed many who began as ideologically opposed to the PNC toward an amplified understanding of their counterparts' lives. As Victoriano recalled of an early workshop held with Project workers and PNC archives staff:

> That was when I came to understand for the first time that the police were also victims of the system. With the solidarity that the police provided— Doña Ana [Corado] and the rest of them—we came to see their commitment to their institution from a more human perspective, seeing their children, hearing about their lives in very working-class barrios, knowing that their children can't tell anyone that their mothers are police officers because of the gangs, knowing about their loans. . . . They would give us water, which was scarce, and we would share space with them, and that was how things started to change for the first time, how the relationship advanced. And that's how you open up ideologically.[90]

Nearly everyone I spoke with stressed the idea that the police were also victims of the war, and if this did not mitigate the PN's abuses, it partly served to explain them. (All were careful to specify that this applied only to regular agents, and not to the death squads or the generals who actually controlled the police.) "Knowing the conditions in which the agents had to live, you can see that the police themselves had to be dehumanized in order that they could perform certain objectives or act in certain manners against victims," reflected Raúl.[91] Project workers saw firsthand that PNC barracks, some of which abutted the archives, were "in the most unbelievable state of filth and abandonment"—filled with rats, cockroaches, broken sanitary facilities, and "intolerable odors," amounting to "miserable, subhuman conditions."[92] Mattresses were filthy and filled with fleas or else nonexistent; agents often worked twenty-four-hour or forty-eight-hour shifts only to be forced to wait in line for a bed on which to rest. Most low-level agents came from the interior, shipped to the capital to work and send money home to their families; they were, in Christopher Browning's words, "ordinary men."[93] Their pitiful salaries did not cover rent, so they slept and lived at work. "In these conditions, people are not formed; they are dehumanized," Raúl said. "A dehumanized person is much more likely to commit crimes or other violations."[94] It was a difficult mental and emotional leap to make, but ex-militants came to see the police as human. María Elena found herself starting to think about the individuals who had, in the past, made up the police's rank and file, realizing that they had joined the police out of economic necessity, much as contemporary entry-level PNC agents—including those consigned to the *basurero*—were forced to do as well. "This was one of the hardest parts for me, coexisting with them, thinking that one of them could have been a torturer, one of them could have killed a *compañero*, and then to start discovering and building in these daily interactions a respectful human relationship. . . . It makes you see yourself differently, and see the relationships differently, and see that we were all victims here."[95] She was not alone in asserting that her vision of the police "from before" had changed.[96] Victoriano put it curtly: "I no longer think that we should line them all up against the wall and shoot them."[97]

That progressives and ex-revolutionaries could work alongside a group of police officers in the pursuit of a common goal—in this case, the preservation of archives—was almost stranger than fiction. It bespoke the extent to which social reconstruction, rather than being generated by governmental accords or reparations programs or the building of monuments, is necessarily a slow, patient, on-the-ground process requiring at least a partial sharing of goals and some degree of mutual compromise and trust. The reckoning achieved on one police base in Zone 6 of Guatemala City, wherein two formerly opposed groups met in the middle to construct a new kind of collaboration around the National Police archives, demonstrated the critical difference between social "reconciliation" and social *reconstruction*. Reconstruction represented the building of something new and distinct, of a "transformational element," rather than a return to a poisoned status quo after some official ritual of forgiveness and contrition.[98]

The fact that these former militants could make their fragile peace with a group of rank-and-file police officers did not mean that the age-old hostilities dividing the country had melted away. Not all state security forces were created equal; not all hands were equally bloodied. When I asked workers if they could imagine a similar rapprochement with army soldiers who had served during the war, some laughed and others frowned while giving the same response—no, of course not, absolutely not, never. But it bears pointing out that ten years earlier, they likely would have said the same of the police.

HUMAN NETWORKS AND THE NEXT GENERATION

The social and spatial world created on the police base derived its richness and energy from the dynamic, shifting relationships between past and present that the work engendered at every turn. The historical animosity between the human rights sector and the police was, in this space, redefined; for Project workers, their own psychological barriers between past and present were challenged by their immersion in the records of their former lives. It was the human resonance of these archives, the unfinished lives they depicted and the restoration of subjectivity and agency they were seen to promise, that gave the archives such texture and depth. The records are invaluable resources for scholarly analysis on a range of themes, to be sure. But to understand the *process* by which they were given new life, we must recognize that it was the people revolving around them—the militants turned memory workers, the police agents, and the thousands of dead who spoke through the yellowed photographs and crumbling pages—who represented the archives' heart. Their relationships both stretched forward and reached back in time, defining the archival work being done even as they reconstituted bonds of solidarity and visions for the future.

Many of the workers who speak in this chapter already knew each other before starting at the Project. Some were spouses, some had been *compañeros* in the EGP or FAR or PGT, some were old university friends, and others were simply acquaintances "from before" who reconnected upon arriving. Establishing these bonds anew represented, for some, a reinscription of past identities, a reconnection with their former lives. Alberto lost his brother, a revolutionary combatant, during the 1980s; in chatting with a coworker who had fought alongside his brother, they were able to connect based on their memories of their shared companion. "For some of the people who have rescued relationships of solidarity, of much caring, it has meant that we reidentify ourselves," Alberto said. "For example, I was talking with a *compañero* from the Project; it turned out that he had known my brother, they worked together, and we've proceeded to build a very beautiful friendship, based in this past detail. 'Oh, your brother was so-and-so, I worked with him, I remember him very well, he taught me a lot, et cetera.' Now we're friends, real friends."[99]

These types of experiences highlighted how the processes of social reconstruction at the archives were collaborative and quotidian, based in reading documents but also in sharing and interpreting those readings. "Reliving some of the things I lived and then chatting about it with a *compañero* is a pretty beautiful experience," Esteban told me. "To remember precisely these moments is part of the reconstruction of memory, and even better if you're able to do it with people who also lived it with you, or when you remember it with someone who lived it too, but who you didn't know at the time. There's a whole mountain of experiences there to talk about, to share, to chat about—and it becomes part of your daily life."[100] Interpreting the dates and names in the documents required sharing knowledge within work teams, whereby workers jogged each other's memories, older workers told war stories to younger ones, and questions were both asked and answered. "People come," Jacinto said, "they hear you talking about something, and they ask, 'hey, did you know so-and-so?' And you say yes, and they say, 'well, he was with me in this demonstration,' and it gives us a little bit of an opportunity to de-compartmentalize ourselves and to say *bueno*, you were there too, that's great, we're *compañeros*."[101]

Personal ties between workers extended not just horizontally among older ex-militants but also vertically between generations, again for reasons linked to the history of the Left. During the late 1970s and early 1980s, when state repression made political life in Guatemala City nearly impossible, many activists went into exile in Mexico City, where the insurgent leaderships were partly based—so many that a significant exile community developed there.[102] Exiles set up mutual assistance groups, communal houses, day cares, and job-seeking networks in their new city, aiming to ease the transition for political refugees not only from Guatemala but also from the other Central American nations riven by Cold War conflict.[103] Others spent their exile years in Nicaragua and Cuba, where they established similar networks. Both María Elena and Esperanza, during their time in Mexico in the 1980s, worked in these communal day cares caring for the children of *compañeros*. It was a delight for both women to find, upon beginning at the archives, that some of the babies whose diapers they had changed in exile were now grown up and working by their side among the Project's flood of young hires. Of the roughly forty children for whom María Elena cared in one Mexico City safe house, no fewer than three ended up at the archives. "In one way or another, seeing them working here makes you feel like you left interesting seeds, seeds which grew into a sense of social commitment," she said. "Even though [exile] was such a hard experience and there were so many negative aspects which could have scarred them, I think that it also provoked for them some overarching questions, which brought them here."[104]

In some cases, the intergenerational ties ran even deeper. Rosa, whose revolutionary commitments forced her to send her children outside the country for the duration of the war, found that having her two sons work with her at the Project helped them to finally understand why they had grown up abroad without the regular presence of their mother. It allowed them to move past feeling resentful and abandoned, wondering if Rosa had left them because she truly was just a "bad mother," as family members on their father's side would tell them. "Now that they have read the documents," she told me, "now that they know how the war played out, they say to me, 'Mamá, how terrible. How did this happen? How did you endure all this? And how did we survive?' Only now are they really starting to absorb this knowledge, but only because they're in this reality of the archives—if they weren't there, they would have continued thinking as they did before." Rosa's sons' ability to hold, in their own hands, evidence of the state's ferocity allowed them to reconstruct a relationship with a mother they had scarcely known as children. "I cried so much at not being able to be there all the time with my sons. I didn't want to be apart from them; it was a decision. But this seed that I planted, one way or another, has grown," she said, echoing the language of germination often used to describe the younger workers. "And now they are also adding their own contribution."[105]

The optimism these women felt about the promise of new generations was not theirs alone; many of the ex-militants with whom I spoke expressed great hope for Guatemala's youth, cheered by the experience of working alongside nearly a hundred young students who were committed to the Project and its goals. The violence of la época meant that many of those who were politically active on the Left had been forced to suspend their studies; in today's generation, they saw youth with better training and knowledge than they had been able to obtain for themselves. "Some of these young people are more academically qualified than compañeros who have entire lifetimes of experience in the struggle," said María Elena, suggesting that collaborations between better-educated youth and older veterans yielded a hybrid skill set that itself was an interesting result of the recovery process.[106] Others feared that the next generation had lost sight of progressive values, though they believed that the youth exposed to the archives were likely to become "stronger" in their ideals, to "act more intelligently," and to emerge with a heightened social consciousness. "I often chat with them about what we did, and the possibility that they, too, can find ways to express themselves and what they live," said Esteban. "We have the responsibility to tell them what we did, but also to tell them what we really think about it, in order to sustain it."[107] Sharing knowledge was, in this interpretation, another way older activists could reivindicar their struggle—by passing it on to others who might take up its mantle.

Hope for the next generation masked a darker truth for some older workers: a belief in their own obsolescence and contamination by war, trauma, and infighting over ideological differences. "I think that the generation of older folks [*viejitos*] just needs to die off," said Jacinto. "We need to die, and we need a new generation of young people who fight for different ideas. Because the older ones of us, we're not going to save the Left. Our own resentments limit us."[108] "Today there are different actors," Raúl explained, "the youth, those who need to learn—perhaps very painfully—the same things that we learned, and who need to avoid committing the same errors that we committed."[109] Young people, Esteban suggested, were not as "poisoned" as their forebears: "We older people already have a set of elements that have determined our actions—because we came from this organization or that organization, that's how we think. And we don't change, because often we don't want to change."[110] The pride many felt in having joined the organized Left existed alongside a tremendous sadness and bitterness at the sacrifices those decisions had demanded. "We're resentful, yes," said one member of the Project's advisory board, a well-known activist. "I carry around a lot of resentment. I lost a lot. I lost part of my own life, the part of my life shared with my friends, my *compañeros*, with my own husband, who was assassinated. So yes, I am resentful. But resentment is not a crime. Genocide is."[111]

Continuing to labor for justice, by working at the archives and sharing their experiences, was how many of these veterans tried to exorcise, or at least wrestle with, the demons of the war. As Jacinto told me about the murder of his brother, a PGT activist, during the 1980s, he broke down in tears, and we stopped our conversation while he recovered his composure. When he did, he said:

> That's what motivates you, it motivates you to keep fighting—not for myself alone, but for many people. We hope that what we're doing serves a purpose for many people, so that this can continue to be clarified, even if the perpetrators are dead or no longer here. Many are already dead, but others continue to live. Maybe the perpetrators in my [brother's] case are no longer living, but there are others who are, and we work for the opportunity for them to face punishment. It isn't vengeance, it isn't vengeance at all—it's justice, and it's so that the state can offer reparations to the families of the victims. If they don't, then it's as though the human life has no value. And the life of a human being who fights for their ideas is invaluable.[112]

In the run-up to the 2007 presidential elections, when it seemed possible that General Otto Pérez Molina could win the presidency, whispers circulated that if he triumphed, it would put the archives project in grave danger. (Pérez Molina did not win the presidency until 2011, and the Project has, at the time of this writing, survived his administration.) But the idea that an army general—one trained at the School of the Americas, who had commanded troops in the blood-soaked Ixil Triangle under Ríos Montt, had headed the secret intelligence service of the elite Presidential Staff, and was implicated in the intellectual authorship of Bishop Gerardi's murder—could take away yet another *regalo de vida* from these survivors was unconscionable. This new chance at postwar justice, at proof and vindication, would not be surrendered easily, not after so many other defeats. "If they want to close down the archives, then they'll have to drag us out of there themselves," Rosa vowed, smiling. "And they will have to drag us out of there dead."[113]

| **ARCHIVES AND THE NEXT GENERATION(S)**

I am an optimist, and so I believe in the young people. We lived it, but they can interpret it in new ways.
—Victoriano, Project worker

L atin American writers share a long tradition of addressing the hemisphere's youth, affectionately passing along the sage advice or bitter truths of generations gone by. Otto René Castillo, Guatemala's best-loved revolutionary poet, was no exception. Castillo, a PGT activist forced into exile by the coup against Arbenz, returned in 1966 and joined the FAR. Apprehended by the military during combat, he was tortured for four days and burned alive during the late-1960s Zacapa counterinsurgency campaign.[1] Ever since, the martyr's poems have resonated with progressives, with none striking a deeper chord than "Vámonos patria a caminar," the work that presages Castillo's own death. Addressed to his *patria*, it invokes Castillo's aspirations for the generations that would succeed his own. *I will remain blind so that you may see*, he wrote; *I will remain voiceless so that you may sing. I have to die so that you may live, so your flaming face appears in every flower born of my bones. Ay, homeland, the colonels who piss on your walls, we must pull them up by the roots, hang them from the tree of bitter dew, violent with the anger of our people.*[2] Castillo, still young himself, hoped his death would not be in vain. His poem hailed the youths who would follow in his footsteps, calling on them to walk with workers and campesinos to fight tyranny in the land of eternal spring. He would, he assured them, be at their side in spirit.

One of the most distinctive aspects of the Project was that the majority of its workers were under the age of thirty. By August 2007, the team had grown to more than 200 strong, though it would later settle at a stable size of about 150; with equal representation from men and women, some 65 percent of its members were youths.[3] These were individuals who came of age in the context of the war but never participated in it as insurgents, trade unionists, community organizers, or student activists as had many of their older counter-parts.[4] Many had only spotty recollections of the war. But studies of political violence's long-term effects indicate that those who grow up in a wartime milieu are nevertheless affected by it in myriad ways, carrying the war with them both consciously and unconsciously.[5] In general, Guatemalans between the ages of twenty and thirty have found themselves a generation in transition: not quite one of the long conflict's several cohorts, yet neither entirely part of a postwar one, and hence lacking an obvious way to define themselves. Many of them, encouraged by the discourse of page-turning reconciliation and abetted by a deficient educational system, not to mention distracted by the necessities of economic survival, rejected engagement with the past. As one Project worker in his midtwenties put it, "Most young people today are in their houses watching television, eating McDonald's."[6] Given the perception of widespread apathy regarding the war and its legacies, then, it is remarkable that such a sizable group of youths would endure the conditions at the Proj-ect to toil reading dusty documents, under the twin psychological burdens of mass death and a binding confidentiality agreement. What impelled the Proj-ect's next generation to connect with this history? Was this its way of heeding Castillo's call to pull up the colonels by their roots?

This chapter explores how youth experiences factored into the rescue of the archives. As this work argues more broadly, the conditions of a country's archives suggest greater truths about its history, social fabric, and politics. The nature of youth participation in the Project, with the Project itself micro-cosmic of a larger conversation about the war's legacies, reveals much about how coming generations will interpret, internalize, debate, embrace, and reject varied aspects of their country's twentieth-century history. Holocaust scholar Eva Hoffman posits that the recent "phase of fascination with collec-tive or group memory" regarding traumatic historical events in both academic and popular spheres emerged from what she calls the "'post' generation" or "the generation 'after'"—a group in which she includes herself, for whom the Second World War and the Holocaust were crucially formative events, but events which its members did not themselves experience.[7] The extent to which the Holocaust, academic literature's touchstone for analyses of the relationship between memory and history, may fruitfully be compared to the Guatemalan context is limited.[8] But Hoffman's point that defining the roles of memory and history in contemporary politics will necessarily fall to this "post" generation—in Guatemala's case, to several "post" generations—rings true. She cautions against the reification of "memory itself as something of value . . . a kind of late post-modern moral good," but stresses the importance of the "post" generation's engagement with "terrible histories which are close to us, but are not ours."[9]

Young workers at the Project came from diverse backgrounds in terms of their experiences of the war. Many had no direct, immediate-family connection—no *desaparecidos* in the family, no parents who participated on either side. Others did; they grew up partially in exile, were raised in communal safe houses while their parents fought, or lost close relatives to political repression, and they identified strongly with those connections. In terms of the general panorama of Guatemalans, however, the under-thirty workers were hardly diverse; nearly all were part of the urban middle class. Most had a university education, usually from the USAC, the national public university long associated with leftist politics, and proudly defined themselves as *sancarlistas*.[10] Many intended to continue in human rights, expansively defined, for the rest of their lives. They would be the progressive lawyers, journalists, and academics of their country's not-too-distant future—the opinion makers, the intellectuals, the definers of an evolving conversation about rights, social justice, and memory. They were the very people who would have been targeted for assassination had they been alive thirty years earlier.

Work at the archives, whether an initiation into such themes or the continuation of a path already trodden, provided a space for these children of the conflict to negotiate their complex subjectivities as part of a minority interested in historical memory, to understand the workings of their society, and to build, based on firsthand contact with state security documents, visions for change. Their experiences at the Project matter; they also, in important ways, surprise. This chapter presents the stories and dreams of a group of young amateur historians and archivists; it discusses the relationships and tensions between different generations of activists, comparing their conceptions of memory, history, and justice; it analyzes labor relations at the archives as a means of exploring these young workers' struggles for self-definition and respect; and it considers their debates over progressive or activist politics in terms of the larger challenges of reconstituting a functional Left in the post-peace era. Francis Blouin and William Rosenberg write that "what goes on in an archive reflects what individuals, institutions, states, and societies imagine themselves to have been, as well as what they imagine themeselves becoming."[11] If Otto René Castillo had to remain blind in order that his *patria* might have eyes, what might it mean that these young Guatemalans chose to put those eyes to work reading documents?

Like the older workers in the Project's early days, selected because they were considered politically trustworthy, many of the small number of under-thirty workers at the Project's inception joined the effort as no strangers to the human rights sector. A few had worked in other divisions of the PDH, several in its Unified Register of Forced Disappearances, the attempt to build a master registry of the disappeared.[12] A few others, through NGOs like the Mutual Support Group (GAM) or Security in Democracy (SEDEM), had even worked on the 2003 effort to digitize the archives of the defunct Presidential Staff (EMP), discussed in chapter 2.[13] Others, however, had no experience at all with memory work. They simply had the connections affording them access to a coveted commodity: a well-paying job. Each young worker's experiences were distinct; each revealed a different facet of a generation in transition, one deeply touched by a war it never had the choice to embrace or reject.

Héctor, a round-faced and cheerful Project worker in his midtwenties, was born in Nicaragua to EGP cadres; his mother's first partner, the father of Héctor's brother, had disappeared in combat some years before. Héctor's first eleven years were spent in exile, oscillating between Nicaragua and Cuba, during which he changed homes dozens of times. He spent some of this time in *colmenas*, communal houses for Guatemalan exiles in Nicaragua where groups of revolutionaries' children were cared for together, though his memories of this were hazy.[14] Educated by his parents about why their lives had taken such twists and turns, Héctor never resented them for the instability of his childhood; "Our parents never left us behind, no matter what they were doing for the Organization," he said, "and I value that a lot." But his return to Guatemala proved difficult. In Cuba, he remembered, "We lacked for nothing— we could play, we had food, we had education, we had health care, we could go outside whenever we wanted, with our friends, and not be afraid!" Integrating into a volatile pre–Peace Accords Guatemala was hard for Héctor and his siblings. They longed to return to Cuba and quickly had to modify their Cuban-inflected Spanish to fit in at school (and avoid suspicious looks from other parents). Moreover, when he and his parents returned, they were met with criticism and rejection from their extended family—cousins, grandparents, aunts, and uncles—who disapproved of his parents' insurgent participation, a common source of family fragmentation during the war and after. Yet despite the dislocations of his childhood, Héctor felt that the economic and racial injustice in his country was intolerable, and believed that it justified the sacrifices made in his name. "I think that if I'd been alive during the armed conflict, I would have incorporated myself [into the insurgency] too," he said. "Working at the Project is like following in my parents' footsteps."[15]

Camilo, a USAC sociology student of the same age as Héctor, had a similar childhood. His parents, student activists and PGT members, lived clandestinely for nearly twenty years, constantly moving and switching false identities, before leaving for a six-year exile in the early 1980s. Because the war remained ongoing when the family returned, they maintained strict security conditions; outside the house, they trained themselves not to be noticed. But, Camilo said, "inside the house, there was a lot of trust, and my parents would tell us stories—my mother would often tell us stories about university, about people who had disappeared, about victories they had won, happy stories and sad stories." His mother, especially, took care to explain everything—why she saw the struggle as necessary, why they had to live abroad, and why they decided to return from Mexico, where Camilo was cared for in an exile-run day care by a group of women, including several who would later work with him at the Project. Camilo was an activist in what he called the contemporary youth movement, a tight-knit group advocating not only for postwar justice but also against a neoliberal economic orthodoxy that saw Guatemala signing on to free-trade agreements and ceding indigenous land to foreign resource extraction interests. He defined this movement as a collective project of "all these young people who had returned from exile and were searching for an identity," youths who sought to make sense of their childhoods by engaging with social justice. His mother, Camilo said, was proud of his activism: "My political involvement is a function of hers; it's like a continuation of what my parents started. We're a family that has a certain path, and I am following the path of my family."[16]

For Rafael, the family connection was most explicit of all. He was born in Nicaragua to parents who were relatively high up in the EGP; like Héctor, his childhood had unfolded in Nicaragua and Cuba, and the move away from those idealized revolutionary lands in 1995 was tough on him too. "I didn't want to leave Cuba," he said. "Everyone looks out for their own interests here in Guatemala. The wealthy in Guatemala have never cared about the rest. Cuba's not like that. We had education, health care, a house—we didn't have luxuries, but we had everything we needed, which is the most important thing, right?" He was beaten by the teacher in his first Guatemalan school for doubting the existence of God, and he struggled to fit in. His parents were absent for much of his childhood, and he resented them—particularly his mother—for years.[17] But when Rafael and his mother, Rosa, found themselves in 2006 working side by side at the Project, he came to see for himself, in the documents, why she had left him behind to fight. A later convert to memory work, Rafael chose not to wear the political T-shirts, long ponytails, or goatees of many other young male activists, avoiding their revolutionary machismo, and he found his lifelong imbrication in a small community of leftists stifling at times. "At a certain point, I really wanted to separate myself from this group," he commented. "Because it was always the same thing—the people from work were the same people at the bar, the same people from childhood." After some time at the Project, however, he came to appreciate his networks, which provided him "comfort, and a sense of security." Rafael felt he could let his guard down among youths who had similar experiences, and he rebuilt his relationship with his mother. Over the course of the work at the Project, he made peace with the instability of his upbringing; he came to see, in the documents as much as in his daily life, why his early years had been spent the way they had. "If someone came to me tomorrow and said 'look, we're starting an armed group to fight against the government,' I would join up," he said. "I wouldn't think twice. . . . I think that even though many errors were committed, I fully defend the actions of my parents. I would participate in a similar struggle at any moment."[18]

Young workers from militant families, then, saw the Project as a way of continuing the struggle—much as the older veterans of popular movements saw it as a way to continue their previous political engagement and engage their *conciencia*. Youths like Héctor, Camilo, and Rafael were raised with the revolution and schooled in its essential principles; some, while in exile, even underwent structured programs of *formación política* (political training), particularly those who had lived in Cuba.[19] Rafael described his Cuban *formación* as follows:

> We had spaces specifically set apart in which we could talk about politics, depending on our age. They kept us informed, they told us what our parents were fighting for. They would take us to the house where all of the Organización's bulletins were mimeographed, so we could see what they said. They explained to us the situation of our country, and they explained to us that we might not win this struggle. They also trained us in security conditions, what we should and should not talk about. . . . But I understood the reasons for the struggle. I knew that my parents were fighting in a revolution, and I likened that to the revolution in Cuba—fighting against the United States, even though technically that wasn't how our revolution worked. I knew it was a struggle for the masses. I knew that they were fighting for the common interests of society—the only thing was that I had never seen the society![20]

Young adults with these sorts of pasts joined the Project with their political identities well established; they were, in North American parlance, red-diaper babies, positioning themselves as inheritors of their parents' revolution even though conditions had changed.

Other young people were drawn to the Project not by family continuity but by family loss. Davíd, a law student in his late twenties, could only speculate about his father's involvement in the war. He knew his uncle had been a member of an insurgent faction, though he did not know which one, and surmised that because his uncle and father had lived together at the end of their lives, perhaps his father had joined too. What he did know was that his father had been extrajudicially executed, his body found tortured with teeth missing, hands and feet tied, and a *tiro de gracia* in the back of the head. His uncle disappeared around the same time, when Davíd was just six months old. "All of this fills me with a strong need to know the truth, to find out what happened," Davíd told me. "And any one of those files at the archives might be the file of a disappeared person. Any one of those files could be the file of my father." Each file, he said, "is the story of a life, maybe of a truncated life, one which remains forgotten in the past," and he hoped to resurrect their stories. He even believed that the Project should have exclusively hired individuals with a disappeared or murdered family member, because he thought direct victims would toil much harder than nonvictims to mine the archives for details of state violence. He likened this to training police dogs, like those that Project workers saw daily as they passed the PNC's canine division to enter the archives warehouse: if the dogs were familiar with the smell of grenades, then they would learn to search buildings for grenades. "If you don't have a need to look for something, then you aren't going to look for it; you're just going to spend your days here flipping through the papers," Davíd said. "But if you really feel that need to look for someone—for your father—then it's going to run through your mind whenever you read the documents, 'I need to find my father, I'm going to find him, I'm going to find him.'" (When Davíd broached this staffing idea with the Project's coordinators, they disagreed, telling him that such an approach would turn the workplace into a "funeral.")[21]

Simón, another law student, also lost a parent to the war. His father, an EGP insurgent, disappeared in combat; his mother fled the country with Simón and his siblings, spending three years in exile in Costa Rica. In early 2006, Simón was invited to join the Project by its assistant director, whose brother—also a *desaparecido*—had been the very person to recruit Simón's father into the EGP decades earlier. But while Simón shared Davíd's desire to learn what had happened to his father—"of course there's a personal motivation"—he was more interested in contextualizing his father's case, in fitting it into a larger historical picture and putting the archives to diverse uses. "Sure, there's you, and there's your case, but it's just one among many other people looking for their disappeared," he said. "I work for them too." Ultimately, Simón felt, the archives' greatest impact would not be in solving individual cases or bringing war criminals to trial, but, rather, in effecting broader changes in the relationships between archives, memory, and society. "These documents will help people understand the importance that archives have to our understanding of the history of our country," he said. Simón still identified as a progressive but had abandoned the strict Marxism of his parents ("I'm no radical"), alienated by the Left's errors and its failure to regroup as an effective political force in the wake of the Peace Accords. Instead, his main political engagement, aside from his labor at the Project, was to draft a proposal for a national archives law, submitted as his law school thesis, which aimed both to protect the police archives as a special body of records with its own legal norms and to guarantee "the whole population's access to the documents."[22]

Héctor, Camilo, Rafael, Davíd, and Simón all started at the Project with well-developed ideological positions, by virtue of their childhoods, their parents' influence, and their previous work—at NGOs like the Guillermo Torriello Foundation, SEDEM, and GAM; in the effort to rescue the archives of the defunct Presidential Staff; in political parties like the Guatemalan National Revolutionary Unity (URNG) and Gathering for Guatemala (Encuentro por Guatemala); or at the PDH. With their childhoods so strongly conditioned by dislocation, they were preternaturally adaptive, motivated, political, and committed to the idea that their parents' struggles—and by extension their own experiences of instability, exile, and loss—had not been in vain. Working in the archives was, they felt, an appropriate way for them to honor that commitment. However, other young workers had far less obvious motivations. Many lacked activist pasts, did not have family connections to war participants or victims—that they knew of—and signed on for other reasons: the work seemed interesting enough, it was relevant to their academic interests, or it was simply a decent-paying job.

Amílcar, a journalism student, came from a large Kaqchikel *campesino* family who lived on a coffee plantation in western Guatemala. He was sent to Guatemala City as a teenager to make money, where he held a variety of marginal jobs that he found distasteful, including as a private security guard and a maquila worker. A twist of fate—his family's involvement in a French documentary about indigenous traditions, and the filmmaker's subsequent interest in supporting the family—allowed Amílcar to quit the maquila and attend university. Through conversations with a friend, he began to be interested in politics; the friend's mother connected them to Meoño, who offered Amílcar and his friend positions at the archives. "We thought, 'Why not?' And we never, never, never imagined that we were getting ourselves involved in something so large, so important," he remembered. Amílcar did enter the Project with a sense of partisanship; he remembered how, as a child, he and his family had had to lie down on the floor as passing bullets from guerrilla-army skirmishes punched through the walls of their modest home. He also remembered how soldiers would come to the farm and kick down the plants his father had sown, force his mother to feed them, and once pointed a gun at his little brother. "In that moment, I said, 'I hate the army. And I hate the police too,'" he recalled. But Amílcar's sense of himself as a political actor only blossomed fully at the archives, particularly when older workers shared their stories—"their living knowledge"—about the war. "We have to speak to people who lived these realities so that we can come to understand them. It's better to live and ask questions rather than moving through life dead, as a corpse," he reflected. Amílcar now hoped to spend his life asking questions of himself and others, working "to build a more just, fair country" as a journalist and filmmaker focused on issues of socioeconomic inequality.[23]

Sebastián, too, found himself asking questions about his past after beginning at the Project in early 2006. A happy-go-lucky jock, Sebastián had no background in politics. When he was assigned to read parts of the CEH report in a university class, he "just flipped through it" and "didn't really think it was that important." He was looking for work when a family friend told him about openings at the archives. Upon being shown the ropes, Sebastián thought, with trepidation, "This is very heavy work, very sensitive." But the salary was good, and so he stayed on, saying, "*Bueno*, this seems fine, this seems like any other job—you're given a task and you try to do the best you can." Later, as he gained exposure to the documents and to his fellow workers, he began to see things differently. Sebastián was clearly still uncomfortable discussing the war; he used vague phrases to describe insurgent participants (*ellos estuvieron en muchos rollos*) or the war itself (*en esos tiempos, tu sabes, los ochentas*). Only late in our interview did he reveal the greatest gift given him by the archives: knowledge of his father's past. "My mother had told me that he had been involved *en esos grupos*, and that was why he had to leave us," Sebastián recalled, though he never knew which group his father had joined, and due to the positive presence of a stepfather he never keenly felt the absence of a father figure. But, he said, "I had always felt an uncertainty. I had always wondered what had happened *con todo este rollo de aquí*." So he started to pepper older colleagues at the Project with questions about their experiences. A year and a half in, after he had earned sufficient trust, Sebastián's questions netted results: it turned out that no fewer than four of his Project counterparts knew his father from their days in the EGP. "So now I know what group he was in! It makes me want to learn even more," he exulted. "And now that's why I like the work at the Project so much, that's why I put so much effort into my work." For the first time, Sebastián was able to attach his individual experience to his country's historical context; by learning more about the EGP and the war, he felt he now had the ability to learn more about himself. Sebastián found himself returning to his once-discarded copy of the CEH report and reading it assiduously. He decided that he wanted to put his law studies to the service of antipoverty initiatives. "Now that I've come here to do this work," he said, "it's opened my eyes further about how something must be done."[24]

Others had even more tenuous connections to the war; they grew up in its midst but had nothing in their histories that could have predicted their involvement at the Project. Isabel, another USAC student in her midtwenties, had never worked a full-time job before starting at the archives via a personal recommendation. She came from a family of middle-class businesspeople; her friends were, by her description, "normal" people who worked in banks or operated small businesses, and after she started at the archives these "normal" people teased her, saying, "*Vos*, you've become a Communist!" Her interest in the archives was intellectual; she studied sociology, and she was interested in what she perceived as a lacuna in the sociological literature, an absence of human rights analyses in sociological approaches. "The connection is that Guatemalan history is a history that shows a consistent denial of human rights, and that determines social interactions," she said. "This is a fundamentally sociological theme." She was keen to explore human rights analyses "not only to arrive at prosecutions, or to reveal the truth for its own sake, but rather to involve distinct social sciences in analyzing human rights in Guatemalan history." She aspired to remain detached from her work in the documents, trying to look at the archives as an "object of study" with a dispassionate eye. In the future, she hoped to work as a political analyst; "I don't want to be a human rights promoter. I want to promote them, but I don't want to be someone working in the PDH who just reports on human rights violations. I want to work in analysis, in political and social analysis of the country." Isabel wanted to be a public intellectual—to use her experiences at the archives as a means of expanding her knowledge of Guatemalan history and one day arriving in a position of influence.[25]

Marisol was, like Isabel, a sociology student with no link to the conflict.

She heard about the Project from a friend who had volunteered there since its inception; "entering that space and meeting all the *compañeros*, I fell in love with the Project," she remembered. Though no one in her family had participated in the war, she still entered with certain preconceptions. "In my house, I was taught that the police are thieves, that you have to be careful around them, that they can kill you," she said. Tensions between Marisol and the PNC agents at the archives threatened to derail her work at various points, with the agents taking offense at her standoffish attitude. Nonetheless, Marisol rose to a leadership position at the Project, becoming a team head. Her motivations were varied: at first, what interested her was "the idea of being able to say to someone, someone who never found out the resting place of a loved one's body, where that body is." Another motivator was the possibility of understanding the conflict from the perspective of its perpetrators, rather than from that of its victims. But after several years in the archives, her goals became "more professional than personal," she said. "It ceases to be a question of, 'I want to know. I want to point fingers. I want to know who did it, who they were, why they did it, and who told them to do it.'" She conceded that the compulsion to point fingers was "always latent, that's always present in the archives," but now she had other priorities. She had come to value how the archives contained information that could be analyzed by professional researchers from a variety of perspectives—"anthropologically, sociologically, historically, psychosocially, with a gender focus"—and positioned herself within that field, choosing to write her undergraduate thesis using documents from the archives, but about a historical period predating the war. "The most important thing for me is that the Project is put to the future use of the social sciences," Marisol said.[26]

For Amílcar, Sebastián, Isabel, and Marisol, then, their work at the Project was transformative or instrumental rather than affirming. Instead of finding in the archives confirmation for their existing ideas, they found that the archives exposed them to new knowledge and approaches, providing them with new perspectives on political engagement and the responsibility of truth-telling. The work also altered their senses of themselves; in a not-so-subtle act of neoliberal subject formation, it gave them a path forward as young professionals— a way to put their academic studies to use, to advance their career aspirations, or to link the recovery of historical memory to their own experiences.

In his trilogy of works on memory in Pinochet's Chile, Steve Stern distinguishes between "emblematic memory" and "loose memory": socially influential frameworks of meaning versus raw, private personal knowledge that remains unanchored until individuals can connect these loose memories to a compelling broader experience. He writes that "memory is the meaning we attach to experience, not simply the recall of the events and emotions of experience."[27] And for these young workers, the archives indeed gave them a "memory framework"—a way to plug their half-remembered, ambient, or closely guarded childhood experiences into a deeper world of interpretive meaning and, more important, a praxis. Davíd was able to channel his grief for a father he never knew into a quest for justice. Sebastián was able to situate his uncomfortable questions about what happened "in those years" in the historical context of an intensely ideological struggle with concrete groups and goals and grievances. Isabel and Marisol were able to bring their research interests in social conflict to bear upon an initiative that offered them the chance to lead, analyze, and reflect on their society's problematics. And, just as for the older generations at the Project, young workers' process of engaging with this memory framework was an arduous one, though for different reasons.

THE LABORS OF YOUTH AND IDENTITY

One obvious tension for young workers was their charged coexistence with PNC agents. As discussed in chapter 6, older workers initially found it difficult to work on police territory because years of experience had taught them to see security forces as the enemy. It had been police agents who had dispersed their demonstrations, raided their homes, and fired into crowds of strikers with whom they had walked. And yet, the older workers were able to build peace with the PNC agents at the archives, coming to realize through conversation, sharing space, and the documents that the police had been, in a sense, victims too. But this thaw in relations did not occur to the same extent with younger workers, some of whom had to be disciplined for wearing T-shirts bearing anti-police slogans. Their hostility was occasionally based on lived experience—for example, when Davíd was once pulled over on the road by PNC agents and answered their question about his employment with "I work in human rights," one agent told the other, "Put something on his record."[28] And Camilo's activist group had seen its offices raided by the PNC on multiple occasions.[29] But there were historical dimensions to their animosity as well. If police had, in the past, harmed their parents or their parents' friends, how should they position themselves toward police agents today, most of whom were not on active duty during the war? Hoffman writes of the "post-generation" experience that, sometimes, "wrestling with shadows can be more frightening, or more confusing, than struggling with solid realities."[30] Youths at the Project struggled to interact not only with the real PNC agents at the archives but also with the ghosts of PN agents past, whose deeds they read about in the documents.[31]

Tensions between youths and the PNC agents were also related to growing pains in the Project's labor relations, and specifically to the massive expansion of the team in January 2007, composed mostly of university students. This produced the feeling of an "invasion" for the PNC agents, who often interpreted the presence of so many new people in their space "as an attack on them," and distrusted younger workers accordingly.[32] Relations worsened when the agents overheard young workers periodically making derogatory comments about the police—"that police are thieves, that they're corrupt, that sort of thing," said Ana Corado.[33] Marisol was even accused by PNC agents of tampering with documents, though the allegations were quickly dropped; "the officials argued that they couldn't work with me because I didn't respect them," she recalled. Marisol never bothered to make social niceties with the PNC agents as did the older workers, to whom the documents promised real answers about their family and friends. "I'm not going to ask them how their kids are doing," she said scornfully.[34]

The amplification of the Project, though, had farther-reaching ramifications for labor at the archives—ramifications that would strain social relations to the breaking point, generate intergenerational conflict, and change the nature of workers' engagement with the archives' recovery. As discussed in part I, the work at the Project gradually transformed from an artisanal, collaborative effort into a rationalized, assembly-line system characterized by the division of labor into discrete functions: document cleaning, scanning, description, analysis; investigating cases, writing reports, maintaining infrastructure, and keeping inventory. Organizing a group of (at its peak) more than two hundred workers required new management techniques, many of which did not sit well with a group of activists who, as Simón put it, "are not people accustomed to staying silent about what they think, or to keeping their thoughts to themselves."[35] As Amílcar said, "Before, there were only rules made when they were necessary, there was a lot more tolerance and patience. Now, everything is becoming a rule, and if you don't like the rules, too bad. We're falling into the same structure as the state, the government—employees, administrators, bosses. Bureaucracy."[36] Not only a previous era's leadership modes but also its state forms reproduced themselves at the archives, and the strong-willed twentysomethings did not approve.

In early 2007, the Project inaugurated its human resources department. Workers who formerly could just ask Meoño or Fuentes for the go-ahead to miss work for, say, a doctor's appointment now had to go through a permissions process with a human resources coordinator. While individual table teams had always had a designated head (*responsable de mesa*) who served as liaison to the leadership, relations between *responsables* and their teams had previously been horizontal and open. Now, as the Project's affairs were made more vertical, the *responsables* came to be seen as bosses, decision makers privy to information from higher-ups that they were not to share. Table teams became separated and compartmentalized, and less exchange of ideas took place across groups. Those whose labor was channeled into the more rote tasks—scanning, cleaning, or other jobs that did not involve the analysis of documents—felt devalued, no matter how often Meoño stressed in meetings that the Project was like an elaborate machine, with no task more important than another, that would grind to a halt without any individual component.[37] Work relations grew strained, and some blamed the influx of young workers, who were criticized for being less politically invested in recovering the archives and diluting the family-like atmosphere that workers had so valued at the initiative's outset.[38] "Some people aren't there to recover historical memory," Camilo complained. "They just want to build up professional experience for their careers."[39]

Discontent about the changes found a focal point, one change that particularly rankled: the introduction of a *timbre*, or bell, rung to indicate the beginning of the workday, the limits of the morning coffee break and lunch hour, and the end of the day. Workers who did not strictly obey the bell were disciplined. "It's an insult! You'd expect this kind of treatment in a bank," said Héctor.[40] Workers who joined the Project out of *conciencia* were offended to have their labor regulated as though they were working in a "regular" place of business. The bell became a stand-in for larger complaints about the growing tension between the Project-as-human-rights-initiative and the Project-as-workplace, and workers were not afraid to speak up when they perceived bad faith. When the bell was installed, recalled Amílcar, "I said, 'how terrible,' because when I worked at the maquila, they would always ring a bell when it was time to start, time to eat, time to leave."[41] Comparing the Project to a maquila became a common gripe, with younger workers in particular resisting the new technologies of labor regulation. Rafael chafed at the idea that the ex-militants running the Project were behaving like managers: "It contradicts the very principles of the revolutionaries themselves."[42]

The coordinators, for their part, were sanguine about their new role as workplace bosses. "Look, I know that the bell is unpleasant," said Fuentes, the assistant director. "But if the bell didn't ring, people would come back to work fifteen or twenty minutes late from lunch. So, *compañeros*, excuse me, but there's a schedule here."[43] In fact, the workers' opinionated nature was consciously factored in by Project leaders as an extra challenge to manage.

Transforming a ragtag collection of free thinkers into a functioning group of employees was not a task the coordinators relished, but it was one they attempted to face head-on. "You're dealing with people who are, almost by definition, contestatory—people who protest, people who demand their rights, who complain, who propose, who think, who are creative," said Meoño.[44] Coordinators valued these qualities but felt they also had to limit them. Not every decision could be made by consensus as the team became larger, the work more specialized, and the politics of the archives more complex. While the Project's early direction had been sketched out via group brainstorming, it now would instead, coordinators and international consultants argued, need to depend upon centralized strategic planning. "This is work that needs to have a clearly defined strategy, that needs to be well planned-out, work in which we each must play a specific role and in which that role must be fulfilled independently of whether our heads might be filled with a thousand ideas or a thousand suggestions," Meoño explained.[45]

While workers resented this, the coordinators absorbed their invective patiently. They saw their adoption of managerial notions like *productivity* and *discipline* not as betrayals of their principles but rather as those principles' purest enactment: only by enforcing dedication to the work would the documents be preserved for posterity. By making sure no working moment was wasted, the Project's leadership could ensure the rescue of the papers, their use in court, and the ultimate goal: their digitization, thus guaranteeing their survival and use after the PDH's fragile tenure expired. Lacking viable avenues for older modes of political struggle, coordinators focused on preserving the documents, hoping to leave a legacy for future generations that could not be crushed or erased. Each lost moment on the job was one fewer document scanned. And scanning was "the only aspect of this that is irreversible," said Meoño, "the aspect where no matter what happens, those documents will never be lost." He continued, unapologetically:

And to arrive at that point, we need to achieve of a whole series of goals. So concepts like productivity are also necessary here. Concepts like efficiency, like effectiveness. So discipline, productivity, efficiency, effectiveness— these are ideas that, many times, clash with the more liberal, open, oppositional thinking at the Project. I would prefer, a thousand times over, to be forced to confront this dynamic—regardless of who says "this son of a bitch, he's become an exploiter," or "this asshole is like a factory owner now." I know that there are people who say this, who call me "Maquila Meoño." I prefer to confront this every day than to hire a group of obedient, uncomplaining people. Why? Because that, too, comes with limitations in thinking. I think that, at the end of the day, these contradictions and conflicts are healthy—it's something we can salvage. . . . Because the other option would be to replace our thoughtful, argumentative people with obedient, submissive people who don't think.[46]

Team members had already accustomed themselves to hearing the *guerrillero* speak like an archivist; now, too, they heard him speak like management. It was uncomfortable, and it did not feel particularly revolutionary. Coordinators had to play varied roles in order to shepherd the Project along: at different points, circumstances demanded that they be colleagues, bosses, friends, archivists, historians, therapists, fund-raisers, political operators, managers, troubleshooters, diplomats, and activists. They could not please everyone, but the Project's leaders attempted to calm the waters where possible, motivated by being able to leave behind something concrete that could never be destroyed. The contribution they attempted would be not only a repository of documents preserved for posterity but also a group of engaged young leaders who would, they hoped, spend their lives fighting for social justice in one way or another.

LEADERSHIP AND THE NEXT GENERATION

One way that coordinators fused the priorities Meoño described—to get the work done while also promoting creative thinking among their young workforce—was to create spaces in which motivated younger employees could assume midlevel leadership positions. In November 2006, a group of under-thirty workers were promoted to table team leader positions, and some were invited to collaborate in the drafting of what would eventually become the initiative's first public report, released in March 2009. Young leaders were defensive, quick to point out that their new positions were no acts of charity or social engineering; instead, as Isabel put it, they were won "por puño y espada" and kept based on results.[47] But the coordinators did consciously nurture selected young workers with an eye toward their future potential; as one said, each young person occupying a leadership position was "a promise for the future."[48] "For me, it has been a beautiful experience to work alongside so many young people and to feel like an important seed has been planted," said María Elena, formerly of the EGP. "I don't want to say that these are the only young people in Guatemala with these capacities—surely there are many more. But here we have more than one hundred youths, both men and women—and many of them are women in positions of responsibility, who are doing their jobs extremely well."[49] As she pointed out, many of the students at the archives had more education than older workers like herself who had, instead, lifetimes' worth of nonacademic experience. Allowing them to take charge of aspects of the work could produce an "amalgam," in her words, of technical expertise and living history.

No amount of academic training, however, could prepare a college student to lead a team that included people decades his or her senior who had lived *la violencia* firsthand. "It's hard; it's very hard," reflected Isabel. "I've been in charge of people who know more than I do." And she knew that these wise subordinates were not always thrilled to have her calling the shots. "It's a function of age; older people will say, 'Who does this girl think she is, bossing me around? I know more than she does, I lived this history, I was a victim.'"[50] When Simón was made a team leader, he felt "bad vibes" from some other team members, who not only had been at the archives for longer but also felt that their life experiences made them more qualified to lead.[51] It was not uncommon to hear gossip about the young leaders being "upstarts," "self-important," or "disrespectful" of their elders. But though the tension between training and life experience occasionally flared up, in most cases older workers were gratified to see the next generation at work. "For the country, really, it's very satisfying to be able to count on young leaders who have tools and capabilities that are far more . . . *developed*, let's say, than ours were," María Elena said.[52] While the positions were tough, they did allow youths like Isabel, Marisol, and Simón—all, now, invested in connecting archives, history, and politics—to develop leadership skills that would serve them, and society, well. "Personally, it's helped me to develop some mediating abilities—to be directing tasks, but also to be managing personalities that are very distinct, and are very complicated in most cases," said Simón.[53] "Those of us who are young," argued Isabel, proved themselves "because we've done the work well; because we've had a positive leadership role; because we've asserted ourselves and our opinions; because we've not only listened to what we're told, but we've made our own proposals."[54]

The developing leadership of the "'post' generation" was, however, contingent—its very essence as postconflict was deeply relational, impossible to understand without consideration of what came before. At the Project, this relationship between generations took concrete form and was critical to building youth leadership. Intergenerational sharing—of war stories, experience, political opinions, wisdom, past mistakes—was cited by all the young workers with whom I spoke as fundamental to their understandings of their place in society and their dreams moving forward. Sebastián's case, in which he learned of his father's identity after conversations with his older counterparts, was the most obviously transformative. But the oral transmission of history took various forms. Intergenerational collaboration was key to the interpretation of the documents; if a young worker came across a photograph of an early-1980s demonstration, for example, she would ask the older members of her team whether they remembered the march, if they had participated, and what the political climate was like at the time. Older workers' experience was critical to younger ones' ability to situate and analyze the documents.

Working alongside their elders had impressionistic effects, too. Marisol found that "the most interesting life experience" she had had at the Project was, simply, coexisting with so many historical actors. "People have shared their stories with me, stories of survival—and that's a motivation for me, to think that when I am the same age as some of these people, that I will still be fighting for what I believe in, that I will still be fighting against injustice." She pointed out that the inequality to which the insurgency had responded with violence persisted; "there are just different ways to fight that now," she said. "So if that's still their fight, and if the archives can help accomplish that, then that's very encouraging, especially for young people like me who can't imagine living through what they lived through."[55] Working with respected ex-militants allowed Marisol to imagine for herself a life of similar dedication.

She and the other young women also took heart in the fact that the majority of Project leaders were female. "That motivates you a lot, to know that it isn't just the same old historical figure in charge of you—an old, white man— but that they're women, women who have fought, and that's why they have the positions they have," said Isabel.[56] Isabel worked closely with Esperanza, a PGT ex-militant whose process of radicalization in the mid-1970s led her to split with a longtime partner who disapproved of her political activity. "His idea was that we should just keep studying, that we should prepare ourselves academically, and that when I got my diploma we would get married, because women are meant to be in the home, and the diplomas are meant to be hung on the wall," Esperanza remembered. "I said *bueno*, this is not for me!"[57] Stories like Esperanza's, told together, presented a living portrait of struggle and social change refracted through class, race, gender, and politics. Younger workers' exposure to individuals they identified as fighters let them position themselves and their aspirations along a homegrown historical continuum of oppositional thinking.

Camilo, for his part, idolized the Left's martyrs, some of whom had been close friends of his parents: labor lawyer Mario López Larrave, student leader Robin García, and AEU president Oliverio Castañeda de León, who led the

1978 protests against Lucas García before being gunned down by security forces. When Camilo came across a report in the archives that recounted Castañeda's killing in dry, bureaucratic language, he laid down his head and wept. "It touched me very deeply [to find that document]," he remembered. "For me, and for other people in the youth movement, Oliverio is like—fuck, this guy was twenty-three years old and he had the government on its knees, and that's why they killed him. For me, he's like an icon." When Camilo had started out in activism years before, he found himself "really looking for an example, someone to look up to, someone's struggle to model my own after." Surrounded by older veterans whose actions he could assess with increasing maturity, though, he became able to balance respect for his heroes with an ability to draw inspiration from within. "After a while, you start to realize that it's inside you. I don't need these points of reference; truthfully, it depends on me, and on an incredible number of young people," he reflected. "You can't only depend on Che Guevara or Subcomandante Marcos; I can do things on my own merits." Camilo believed that the archives could empower others, too: "If organizations of young people can have access to these materials in order to understand how the interpersonal relations and social relations of today are based in their history, or if they're able to understand the historical roots of the crises in youth organizations and how that is based in past repression against the revolutionary movement, I think that will be a tool they'll be able to use to focus their struggle."[58]

However, young workers, for all their inspiration and eagerness, were keenly aware of their minority status. If the human rights sector was a small cross section of the population, then its youth contingent was smaller still.[59] Its members tended to stick together. "Most of my friends are involved in human rights in some way or another," said Héctor. "Everyone has their circles; it's natural that you have friends who see things more or less the way you do. That's your world! It's your life. You can't sit down with some airheaded girl in Zone 10 and talk about shoes and cellphones and that kind of bullshit."[60] The Project's youths tended to define themselves as distinct from what they described as "most" middle-class young people—they saw themselves, rightly or wrongly, as more enlightened, more engaged, less selfish, less materialistic. "When I talk to young people who are roughly my age, they have a totally different vision—very individualistic, seeking economic advancement, and always having this same idea about making more money, no matter what's happening to the other people around them," said Amílcar.[61] Project youths' exposure to the archives strengthened their sense of difference vis-à-vis their peers and furthered their resolve to continue political work, but they worried that the rest of society would meet their efforts with indifference. As Amílcar continued:

> What I see in these papers shows me much courage, much bravery on the part of the people who fought. And today, you don't see this bravery or courage—instead, people are living in a peaceful, conformist world, thinking of themselves and their own lives rather than of the lives of others. . . . And so this work in the archives gives me more strength with which to express myself, because how is it that people don't complain or fight for themselves now, when these people in the documents sacrificed their whole lives? It seems to me that those of us who are growing and learning about the history of our country, touching those papers—we are building consciousness about what happened, and thinking about trying to build something. That's the impact the archives have had on me.[62]

This was why older workers so valued the opportunity to share their experiences with their "post-generation" counterparts. "It isn't as though we pass them a torch and we tell them, 'Okay, it's your turn!'" said María Elena. "But I do see that, even with the great deficiencies and limitations in political development that this country's new generations face, we do find ourselves here with young people who have a lot to give, and who are committed to giving."[63] In many cases, however, ex-militants spoke of the coming generations of progressives cautiously—with optimism but also with realism, a heavy sense that the war's stifling effects on militancy and creativity would not dissipate so quickly. Young Guatemalans wishing to make a difference had the odds stacked against them; "we know perfectly well that the damage done isn't going to repair itself today, or tomorrow; that its effects will maybe last through the third, fourth, or even fifth generations," Esperanza reflected.[64]

It was true: the ripple effects of state repression had contracted or poisoned the spaces available for young people to explore, express, and work toward their visions for a more just Guatemala. Attempts at building progressive movements within the political party system had thus far failed; the URNG party was reduced to two seats in the 2007 elections, and the experiments of the Gathering for Guatemala and Winaq parties garnered even sparser support.[65] The AEU, a focal point of youth organizing during the 1970s and 1980s, fell victim to infighting by the late 1990s and was even rumored to have been infiltrated by organized crime.[66] Organized labor never recovered its 1970s-era strength. The influence of the Maya movement had waned somewhat from its high point in the aftermath of the Peace Accords. And differences of opinion regarding ideology and strategy, along with held-over resentments from the conflict, plagued efforts to reconstitute a functional Left in peacetime. "It was the army's masterwork," Camilo said. "The strategy wasn't just to win the war; it was to ultimately end the Left," using infiltration and betrayal as strategic tools to irreparably shatter activists' lifelong ties of trust.[67] The ultimate goal, therefore—for veterans and younger workers—was to be able to imagine these young leaders at the forefront of new, innovative movements for social and economic justice. Intergenerational relationship-building proved a way, for those on both ends of the exchange, to imagine the future of progressive politics. How could previous struggles be continued in a new era? How could modern youths fight for change without repeating the errors of the past? As Raúl put it, "We need to have an alternative for our current age."[68] Critically thinking young people being who they were, however, progressives across the generations did not necessarily agree on the nature of the path forward.

PROGRESSIVE POLITICS IN NEOLIBERAL GUATEMALA

It was auspicious that nobody at the Project could agree on whether or not the initiative to rescue the archives was inherently political or leftist. Was working at the archives actually part of a vision for change? Was the Project, as some claimed, a continuation of past struggles when armed conflict was no longer a thinkable option, or was it just another reminder of ideological defeat? Precisely what, in sharing experiences between generations, were both sets of individuals seeking to build? "This is a job," said Isabel. "It isn't an act of political militancy. . . . But in a country as politically polarized as ours, it is a left-wing project."[69] Most workers I asked tended to argue that although the Project included many left-wing individuals, its goals were nonpartisan. If the purpose was to uncover recent history and to ensure that human rights abusers faced punishment, then its priorities were only leftist or progressive to the extent that leftists and progressives had suffered abuses disproportionately. "The investigation is an investigation of human rights violations that were committed by the National Police, and that's not left-wing, that's just reality," said Marisol.[70]

The PDH was by no means a radical institution. Moreover, because the ombudsman Morales came, over his two terms in office, to be viewed as a corrupt political operator with ties to the political Right, neither did the Project consistently find friends on the traditional Left. "Unfortunately, the 'official' Left in Guatemala has not understood this project," said Meoño, charging that the factions emerging from the URNG were too preoccupied with their potential legal liability for the 3 percent of human rights violations (according to the CEH) committed by the guerrillas to unequivocally support justice-seeking initiatives.[71] Others saw different reasons for the Project's uneven relationship with progressive sectors: "There are people on the Left who say this project is bullshit," said Rafael. "You have to think about who these people are, and why. Maybe because psychologically, they don't want to relive that history. Maybe because they have other interests. Most of the people I know, who criticize the Project, it's because they don't want to remember this past, because they don't want to experience that loss again, and so they don't want to fight for justice."[72] Again, then, the Project was shaped by what had come before. Its young workers, endowed with educations, relevant work experience, and older mentors, were better situated than most to promote change, but they were saddled with old expectations and conflicting opinions about the path ahead. Many veterans suspected that their own ideological baggage had already dangerously constricted the space available to subsequent generations. "Let the young have their own conflicts," said Jacinto. "I think that's important, so that they learn to move past them. Our ways of thinking don't hold true anymore in a globalized world. The only thing [youths] need to figure out is how to deal with it. But we can't tell the young people to launch an agrarian reform."[73] But here, too, the defeats of the past wore heavy on members of older generations, constricting their political imaginaries. Why *not* tell young people to launch an agrarian reform, a goal toward which campesino groups like CUC and CONIC (the National Indigenous and Campesino Coordinating Council) continued to work?

Older veterans could not even agree on whether or not today's youths were the inheritors of past struggles; some were cynical about postconflict youths' ability to serve as new incarnations of their own radical selves. "In terms of continuity with these young people, I don't think there's really anything that ties us together, because the university youths of that era were clearer about what they wanted and how they wanted it," said Rosario, a former organizer with Guatemala City's municipal workers' union. "Today, I feel like there's just a little trace left behind that today's young people want to pick up—but they haven't had any experience, any experience of struggle, like that which the university students went through back then."[74] A few older workers saw their youthful counterparts as appropriating a revolutionary discourse that did not correspond to their lived experience. "I think that what's happening is that many young people on the left arrived late to the process," observed Humberto. "So they lived it, in a way. But they are romantically thinking that another moment will arrive when they too will be able to take up arms. It's romanticism, nothing more."[75] While some younger staffers at the archives, like Rafael, expressed their willingness to participate in a future armed struggle, those who had actually lived through war saw no benefit in the idea. "Arming ourselves and starting another war isn't going to solve anything," said one. "We'll just be arming the dead, arming bitterness."[76]

One of Guatemala's highest-profile youth activist groups, Sons and Daughters for Identity and Justice and Against Forgetting and Silence (HIJOS), was a flash point for the debate over revolutionary inheritance.[77] This group used bold, attention-getting tactics: staging annual counterprotests on Army Day, during military parades, that involved throwing red paint on the cadets to symbolize spilled blood; using graffiti campaigns; demonstrating at generals' homes; and, one year, marching into army barracks to confront officers they denounced as war criminals. Members of HIJOS had worked at the archives over the years, but for those who had weathered the war, such provocative actions seemed flippant, even dangerous. "For people today to stop the Politécnica students and throw red paint on them, I view that badly. I see it as a lack of respect. And at any moment, the military could make us pay for it," said Humberto. "You think that in those years, if a group of young people had tossed red paint on a bunch of soldiers, that the army would have let them go free, that they would have let them live? Not a chance."[78] And while some believed in the importance of passing the torch to the next generation, others feared for younger activists' safety, worrying that their appropriation of revolutionary discourse would invite deadly retribution. Dolores, formerly of the EGP, never told her daughters about her involvement, "because I'm scared that they'll get involved in something. When my daughter joined the AEU, I sat down with her and told her not to. Because you don't want history to repeat itself."[79] This was more than skepticism or a sense that postwar politics was only a watered-down version of battles past; it reflected a fear that counterinsurgent tactics could be reinstituted at a moment's notice, wiping out another generation of young idealists.

In the end, young workers' political decisions were theirs alone; whether their elders consecrated them as the new generation of rebels would not necessarily affect how they chose to move forward in their lives. They had been amply exposed to the history of the war and the counsel of their elders, and they would decide what to adopt and what to leave behind. What visions did they have, then, for their society's transformation? While some claimed that they would join another revolution, none seriously proposed initiating one. Instead, most of those with whom I spoke hoped, if ambivalently, to work toward social justice as professionals—journalists, educators, researchers, or lawyers. "I can't tell other people how to think, but I can act in such a way that those other people can have better opportunities in their lives," said Amílcar,

FIG. 7.1 Every 30 June, traditionally Army Day, activists hold a counterdemonstration demanding justice for the war crimes of state security forces. They call their campaign the "memory offensive." Photograph by James Rodríguez, mimundo.org. Used by permission of the photographer.

the day laborer turned aspiring filmmaker. "I still have some problems with this, because I'm still not convinced that the state and the government provide us with the space to change things in this way," he said. "I'm not sure. Sometimes I do feel that if I work with the government, all that's going to happen is the consolidation of the system we're currently living."[80]

Whether raised with Marx in the home or exposed to it later, these young activists struggled with the contradictions of capitalism. How could historical memory be rescued in an economic climate where its value seemed to diminish daily? "Youths are also the seed of capitalism," argued Camilo, who was cynical about his peers' capacity to break free. He argued that young people were products of "the system" to an even greater extent than were the older generations who modeled its hierarchies and social relations. A young student living at home while working at the Project, incurring few costs while making a decent salary, could spend his or her earnings on a life of relative leisure, all while accruing the social capital of having worked on an internationally recognized human rights initiative. "I think it's good that young people are working at the Project, but it means that the process is going to be truncated, because they are products of the system. A young person who lives at home and spends their money on clothes and CDs acts against historical memory because they're reproducing the system" instead of devoting themselves to shattering it, Camilo said.[81] A young Guatemalan could self-define as a revolutionary, but how could she live a revolutionary life?

Project youths also had mixed feelings about the archives' dependence on foreign assistance. While they appreciated other countries' support, they resented the "paternalism" and "agenda" of that aid, as well as foreign consultants' directives about how the work should be conducted.[82] "There is an attitude of conquest, the idea that they want to liberate these countries afflicted by state terror . . . because they bear some guilt or responsibility for our suffering," said Isabel.[83] On top of that, young workers wondered what they actually could build in the context of Guatemala's semifeudal economy and its place in the world capitalist system. Archival rescue would neither break up the countryside's massive agriplantations, nor force foreign mining companies to shutter their operations ravaging indigenous community lands (rural antimining activists were doing this work on the ground, at great personal risk and often with the help of other ex-guerrillas), nor stem the narco violence produced by the global North's unslakable thirst for drugs. As such, young activists were "frustrated by Guatemalan political conditions" and doubted whether their efforts would take root.[84] Everyday citizens did not have the luxury of immersion in memory and archives, many felt; instead, "they just want to be safe in the streets, they don't want to be murdered for their cellphones."[85]

But in a world of difficult questions and intractable problems, the archives did provide these young Guatemalans a means, however imperfect, of working toward something they saw as broadly positive: a deeper social engagement with the past. For all the tensions between the Project-as-human rights initiative and the Project-as-workplace, the limitations posed by inequality and a fragmented Left, and the scars of the recent past, the consensus among young workers was that their efforts mattered, that history counted, and that there was a tangible value to researching the war. And they were clear-eyed about it; these amateur historians and archivists did not, for the most part, reify "history" and "memory" as fetishes with value unto themselves. Instead, they saw the labor of engaging with history as a goal-oriented task with concrete outcomes. In the legal sphere, "if we get a single successful case out of all this work, it will all have been worth it," said Rafael.[86] In terms of recovering historical knowledge, Marisol commented, "You can go to any public list of victims and read it, you can read two hundred, five hundred, two thousand names of victims, as many as you want. But you can't open a book and find the names of two hundred perpetrators. So if you're helping to build that list of perpetrators—for me, it isn't exactly *comforting*, that wouldn't be the right word, but it is an accomplishment."[87] In matters archival, Simón attested, their work "can contribute to a change in the way that our society values archives," thus opening doors for the rescue of other bodies of documents replete with forgotten histories.[88] And in looking to the future, these young adults who spent their days poring over records of repression and resistance knew that their country could have no way forward unless it acquired the ability to look back. "I think the work is a contribution to transformation in this country. . . . Not only do we want to put people in jail, but we want to make sure this history is not repeated," said Camilo. "The fact of judging the criminals isn't going to change anything—it only guarantees that these events won't happen again."[89] Whether true or not, it was a powerful aspiration.

¿VÁMONOS PATRIA A CAMINAR?

Guatemala's statistical indicators of economic inequality, crime, and social dislocation usually made optimism a scarce commodity.[90] More than that, however, the legacies of political repression had had a powerful dampening effect on how Guatemalans expressed hope, emotion, excitement, or aspirations, from national politics all the way down to the individual and family levels.[91] As Meoño put it, "We Guatemalans are introverted, tight-lipped, and withdrawn compared to Salvadorans, Nicaraguans, Hondurans, or Mexicans. It's our way of being: reserved, introverted, but above all . . . mistrustful. We repress ourselves; we say to ourselves, 'It's better to be this way, it will keep us out of trouble.'"[92] Many remarked to me that long-term planning was an almost unheard-of modality at various levels of society—organizationally as much as personally—because the dark past served as an object lesson in the wisdom of living for the moment. Getting one's hopes up for tomorrow was a risky proposition. "These archives show us, with documentary evidence, information that can help to explain why we are the way we are," said Meoño.[93]

But this was not all the PN archives had to show, because for all the disagreements and rancor that reared their heads over the course of formulating, precisely, a long-term plan for the rescue of the documents, everyone agreed on one point: the archives, and the history they told, were critical for the future. As such, workers and those in the Project's greater orbit spoke of the archives with an enthusiasm rarely applied elsewhere. "What I think is that you always have to look for the positive," said Marisol. "We've gotten to where we are now, after two years, in spite of many blows. At first we thought the Project would only last for six months. It's always been unstable. So we think, we've been here for two years! And it might be three years!"[94] And the Project did last for three years, and then four, and beyond, even amid institutional upheaval. The personnel roster took a beating in December 2007, when the PDH refused to renew the contracts of some thirty employees as part of a power struggle between the Project's internal leadership and the ombudsman's office. But even this strike at the heart of workers' solidarity was weathered, because of the promise that the archives—and, principally, its staff and the capacity they had built—were seen to embody. "Even if the group of people left here is only forty, fifty, or sixty people," Marisol argued, "those people are going to do something great for this country."[95] This was exactly the gamble that coordinators were taking with their young staffers.

The work at the archives—the embodied experience of dealing with paper cadavers—was not easy, even for members of the "post-generation." It had the same impact on them as it did on their elders, as Amílcar attested:

> Reading for five, six hours straight is difficult—reading in the archives, I mean. You get breaks. Two straight hours are okay, with a break—but the next two hours? And the problem is that it never changes. You're reading the same things—reports of kidnappings, tortures, things like that—and you're reading it constantly. It produces a psychological fatigue—not a physical fatigue, but a psychological fatigue, which is much worse. And you're wearing a lab coat, a mask, a hood—it's depressing, it's so hot. Sometimes you just want to take it off, you feel like you're drowning in that mask. But it's tiring mainly because of the content. Sometimes you dream that you're being attacked by the police, or that there are thieves chasing after you, and these dreams are caused by the documents one reads. . . . A person who started work in January 2006 is not going to be able to work the same way as a person who starts later, because they will have an accumulation of this problem. I have this problem, it's like a disturbance—a buildup of cadavers, tortures, and all that, and the anger and frustration that produces, and then you get up the next day and you have to do it all over again. And after a while you come to accept it as a routine, which is also a problem. . . . Sometimes I dream that someone arrives and touches me, and then I am paralyzed and can't breathe. Or else someone shoots me in the head, or in the chest, and then I can't move. And these images come directly from the descriptions of crimes I read about in the archives. It is a painful feeling.[96]

But young workers were sustained through this labor by what they had in common: a sense of themselves as a generation in transition. They felt a responsibility—a sense that they needed to do memory work in order to bridge the gap between the "living history" of their mentors and the lives of those today growing up in a climate of historical amnesia. "Nothing is going to change overnight," said Sebastián. "We need a lot of time, we need to raise the consciousnesses of those who come after us."[97] As Fuentes, the Project's assistant director, put it:

> The decisions of other types will be theirs, but if they have this knowledge and these experiences from the archives, that positive and negative baggage, it can serve them well. Because this country deserves better luck. It can't be possible that Guatemala is fatally condemned to live as the victim of fourteen families who have their army, their police, their gringo and narcotrafficking friends, and who can keep the rest of the country living in subhuman conditions.[98]

Their time at the archives would galvanize these twentysomethings in a variety of ways. For young workers who saw themselves as following in their parents' footsteps, working at the archives helped them weave the loose memories of their childhoods into a socially meaningful, historically contextualized framework. "It makes a real impression to see in the documents that this was all true, that the stories I'd been hearing for my whole life weren't just stories," said Héctor.[99] For others less directly affected, the archives offered new ways of conceiving of social science research, human rights advocacy, and activism. They were interested in bringing war criminals to justice, and in writing the history of the armed conflict, to be sure. But they were also interested in writing other stories: sociological studies of crime and criminals; analyses of gender and institutions; histories of the state and of the links between bureaucracy and social control; studies of different regions and localities; examinations of the evolution of mentalities and social imaginaries across space and time; and, with a host of additional research avenues made available by the police archives, innumerable stories more.

What they wanted was to make history, in every sense of the word. They wanted to unearth history; to write history; to participate in an archival recovery initiative of indisputable historical importance; to connect the old Left to new ideas; and to evoke in their fellow citizens an awareness of history's value and of why recent history could not be repeated. This was how they would heed Otto René Castillo's call to pull up the colonels by their roots. Young Project workers saw the archives as having transformative potential, and were eager to do the necessary work. If they were to succeed at the task, however, they would need to train their eyes not only on the National Police archives but beyond, to other repositories of forgotten records elsewhere in Guatemala. And major hurdles remained in their path.

PART IV | **PASTS PRESENT AND THE FUTURE IMPERFECT**

| **CHANGING THE LAW OF WHAT**
CAN BE SAID, AND DONE

Two men are on the beach catching crabs. One of them has a bucket
with a very secure lid so the crabs won't get out, but the other one's
bucket is open. "Aren't you worried your crabs will escape?" asks the
first man. The other replies, calmly, "Oh no, these are Guatemalan
crabs. Whenever one tries to climb up and out, the other ones just
pull it back down again."
—Guatemalan joke

To extend its reach and influence, the Project for the Recovery of the
National Police Historical Archives would need to transcend its beginnings. While the emergency judicial order secured in 2005 allowed
the work to take place, it was an impossibly threadbare legal framework for an
initiative aspiring to permanently protect the PN's rich archival production.
The fact remained, too, that the Human Rights Ombudsman's Office (PDH),
still the archives' institutional host, was hardly in the business of administering state records—and for good reason. Millions of the documents had
been digitized, but many tens of millions more awaited preservation, and the
clock was ticking. And the largesse of the international community, which
had allowed the Project to evolve from a pipe dream, had sustained the effort
for some time. But would it always continue to do so? In many respects, and
despite the herculean labor to make it otherwise, several years into the Project's existence the warehoused documents were as vulnerable as they had ever
been. The Project's flanks remained exposed, and its members knew it.

Despite this tenuous state of affairs on the ground, however, the Project
became a phenomenon on the international stage. From its inception, the
idea of rescuing the archives generated tremendous enthusiasm from international NGOs and friendly foreign governments, and by 2007 the Project
had expanded to proportions that were mammoth by local standards. At its

height, it employed more than two hundred staffers, while the national archives, the AGCA, limped along with fewer than twenty-five people managing its five hundred years' worth of documentary patrimony. The Project's annual operating budget grew to 12 million quetzales, or about US$1.5 million; the AGCA's budget was 500,000 quetzales, not counting staff salaries.[1] A darling of the human rights world, the Project built relationships with such far-flung archival recovery and memory efforts as the Iraq Memory Foundation, the Documentation Center of Cambodia, Archivists without Borders, Chile's Vicariate of Solidarity, Paraguay's Archives and Documentation Center for the Defense of Human Rights, and Argentina's Provincial Commission for Memory. The archives were featured in several documentary films and even in a novel, Rodrigo Rey Rosa's *El material humano*.[2]

Importantly, however, Project leaders were not content to simply reap the rewards of international interest for their initiative's exclusive benefit. Once the Project had built its own momentum, it sought ways of sharing its state-of-the-art equipment and expertise, self-consciously attempting to provoke a sea change in how state institutions, private organizations, and the educational system conceived of archival preservation and access. For example, the Project lent its scanners for the digitizing of some 400,000 pages of adoption records from the Secretariat of Social Welfare (Secretaría de Bienestar Social [SBS]), dating from 1978 through 1986; the SBS archives documented cases of children abducted from left-wing parents by the military during the war and placed on the international adoption market.[3] Taken for forcibly disappeared, some of these children would, it was hoped, eventually be reunited with their families, as Salvadoran and Argentine children had. Other collaborations abounded: the Project accepted the Ministry of Culture's invitation to participate in drafting a proposal to develop a stronger legal foundation for documentary preservation.[4] Different municipalities, such as the city of Flores, solicited help from the Project to organize their own records, as did state dependencies like the Youth and Adolescent Appeals Court (Sala de Apelaciones de Niñez y Adolescencia) and the Property and Real Estate Registry (Registro de la Propiedad y Inmueble). The Bomberos Voluntarios, Guatemala City's firefighters, also sought assistance in grappling with their records. Here, the two efforts were naturally consonant—the Bomberos usually arrived first at crime scenes, to collect the bodies, and as such their records had the potential to shed new light on urban killings during the war. Along similar lines, the Project struck up research-sharing partnerships with the Forensic Anthropology Foundation of Guatemala (FAFG) and the National Reparations Program (PNR) in order to, respectively, help identify bodies excavated from urban mass graves and bolster victims' claims for reparations.[5] And the Project not only pitched in on like-minded initiatives and accepted others' requests for help, but creatively generated ways of making its own interventions into national archival culture. Its archivists worked with the University of San Carlos to develop a diploma program combining instruction in archival science and human rights research, to better stock the country with young professionals prepared to handle records of similar importance; its National Advisory Board worked to draft a new national archives law to replace the obsolete Decree-Law 17-68.[6] "The Project is converting itself into an archival reference point, and people are starting to ask us to help them out," said Fuentes. "We are contributing in that direction, and let's hope that this translates someday into an archival politics at the state level."[7]

Indeed, the Project came to spark, or to intersect with, a whole constellation of post-2005 initiatives surrounding citizens' access to state records, including efforts to push for the declassification of military records from the war. Two years after the appearance of the PN archives, then interior minister Adela de Torrebiarte assigned two staffers to begin the task of cleaning and organizing seventy thousand abandoned ministry files, dating from 1600 to 1983 and including penitentiary records, land distribution titles, and censuses from the days of the Central American Republic.[8] Another campaign, which began even before the signing of the Peace Accords, was won three years after the discovery of the police archives: Congress approved the Free Access to Public Information Law in September 2008.[9] It entered into force in April 2009, and though its implementation was bedeviled by official intransigence and a lack of preparation on the part of individual state dependencies, its passage nevertheless represented a major step forward in the state's archival practice.[10]

Interestingly, the push for the law was led not by human rights activists, though they were involved, but by journalists and lawyers seeking greater transparency in the management of state funds and the conduct of electoral politics.[11] This was not to say that the law did not reflect other concerns; it stipulated that "in no case can information regarding investigations of human rights violations, or crimes against humanity, be classified as confidential or restricted-access."[12] However, this relative divorce between the efforts of organizations like GAM and SEDEM to secure access to records about war crimes, and the media and anticorruption NGOs' audit-oriented focus on government accountability, spoke to a certain fragmentation of priorities among factions of civil society.[13] (And neither side, until the Project learned its lesson the hard way, showed any interest in involving archivists.) But while the protagonists may have been different, the opposition was the same: Efraín Ríos Montt's FRG party, which had long controlled Congress, and the military, which appealed again to the protection of *secreto de estado*. As Silvio René Gramajo Valdés writes, "We must not forget that the armed forces have powerful reasons for opposing the [access to information] initiative."[14]

Other post-2005 archival access initiatives were more expressly political. Much discussion in these years centered around four specific documents: Plan Ixil, Plan Sofía, Plan Victoria, and Plan Firmeza, all early-1980s military action plans for counterinsurgency operations in the province of El Quiché. The Association for Justice and Reconciliation (AJR), along with the Center for Human Rights Legal Action (CALDH), had long fought for the official release of these plans, though unofficial versions of several of them already circulated.[15] But the effort to declassify these documents faced a familiar set of obstacles: an endless succession of *amparos*, or injunctions, filed by Ríos Montt's lawyers insisting that the plans' surrender would violate Article 30 of the constitution and its *secreto de estado* provision. Each time one of Ríos Montt's injunctions was thrown out of court, his lawyers would file another to delay the case. When, finally, the AJR and CALDH won their appeal in Guatemala's highest court, army authorities argued that two of the four plans had been destroyed, and thus could not be turned over as per the court's order. Defense minister Abraham Valenzuela reported that the documents, like some of the Guatemalans whose lives were documented in them, had simply "disappeared."[16]

Supporters of the counterinsurgency plans' release had reason to be frustrated: President Colom had made an unprecedented promise a year earlier, prompted by the success of the Project, and activists wanted results, even if they knew better than to expect them. In 2008, on 25 February—the National Day of Dignity for the Victims of the Armed Conflict—Colom made the jaw-dropping announcement that he was ordering the opening of all the military's archives. "We want truth and justice," Colom indicated, acknowledging that "reconciliation" would probably prove impossible. "We will make all of the military's archives public, so that the truth can be known."[17] Colom's inspiration was clear: from day one, he indicated that the ideal approach for managing the army records would be to pass them into PDH custody, in order that PDH staffers—veterans of the Project—could commence a recovery initiative along the same lines as that of the police archives. It was a stunning reversal of the status quo.[18]

It seemed, at first, that Colom's promise might be kept. Within days, Colom asked the Project to assemble teams of its workers for deployment to the relevant military bases to begin work on the files as soon as the logistics were sorted out with army high command. Colom even visited the Project to declare his support for the plan, touring the police archives to learn about their inner workings; Meoño called the president's initiative "the most important historical opportunity to arise since the signing of the Peace Accords."[19] At the Project, workers wept and embraced upon hearing the news. "It's like Macondo," one staffer told me, referring to the fictional town in Gabriel García Márquez's *One Hundred Years of Solitude* that was transformed overnight from a sleepy backwater into a thriving modern metropolis. "It's like the whole world has changed in just a few days."[20]

In the aftermath of Colom's announcement, anticipation ran high, but so too did cynicism and doubt. As journalist Juan Luis Font wrote, "President Colom's declaration has value as another gesture, like all those we have seen from the authorities since the signing of the Peace Accords. But it is only that: a gesture." If Colom was truly serious about clarifying what had become of Guatemala's disappeared, Font suggested, opening the archives was a necessary but insufficient component of what needed to be a much larger process involving civil society consultations, efforts to secure witnesses and testimonies, the initiation of legal proceedings by the government, and forensic inspections of the relevant military and police installations—not to mention an investigation of human rights violations committed by members of insurgent groups.[21] This would beg significant judicial reform—a challenge since, in the words of former vice president Eduardo Stein, "asking the justice system to reform itself is like tying up a dog with a string of sausages."[22] Font's implication was that Colom, hoping to identify himself with the "pink wave" of leftist governments sweeping the Americas, was mouthing platitudes while lacking the muscle to truly effect change.

The bittersweet Macondo analogy was borne out, as the substantive change promised by Colom did not come to pass. First, military officials refused to accede to his request, again citing Article 30 as justification. "Even as President and commander-in-chief of the army, he is not above the law," asserted defense minister Marco Tulio García.[23] Ex-president Mejía Víctores's lawyer, Fernando Linares, called Colom's pronouncement "unconstitutional" and suggested that the president was ignorant of the constitution's stipulations. Others attempted different evasive maneuvers. General Otto Pérez Molina, who would succeed Colom as president, argued that declassification was a red herring: "In our archives, they aren't going to find that any operation to kill innocent people was designed or ordered during the armed conflict. That's not going to be found in any archives. That's not going to appear."[24] In June 2011, the army opened to the public a collection of some twelve thousand documents spanning the more than four decades between 1954 and 1996—an implausible paucity of records purporting to cover some forty years of wartime army operations. Researchers soon reported that these were little more than bureaucratic flotsam and jetsam, nothing of investigative importance.[25]

Though expectations were deflated in this instance, the fact that a civilian president had dared to even *attempt* forcing open the army's records was still significant.[26] It would not have transpired absent the paradigm-shattering precedent established by the rescue of the National Police archives. Foucault reminds us that archives determine "the law of what can be said," and the Project, through its self-conscious efforts to change the country's archival culture, did bring about a change in the law of what could be said in Guatemala. It transformed the idea of civilian access to secret military records—and the shift in the power balance between society, the state, and the army that such access would entail—into something speakable and thinkable, if not quite doable (yet). However, the Macondo episode and other aspects of the archive wars also testified to postwar Guatemala's challenges, all the more heartbreaking for the intensity of the hopes raised and dashed along the way.

MACONDO: THE LIMITATIONS OF THE POSTWAR STATE

The teams of Project workers readied for deployment to military bases were dissolved after it became clear that the army would not give in without a fight. But it was also true that Colom's commitment to archival opening was not only hot air. Colom was a nephew of the social democratic politician Manuel Colom Argueta, gunned down by the Lucas regime in 1979, and his engagement was personal as well as political. While president, Colom formally accepted responsibility on behalf of the government for the murder of his uncle, for the killings of student leaders and trade unionists, and for the state's repression of the labor movement. And within the Presidential Peace Secretariat (SEPAZ), Colom ordered the creation of a new program: the Peace Archives Directorate, which would work toward the declassification and opening of archives pertaining to the civil war. Its goals united principle and praxis: first, "to recover the historical memory of what occurred between 1954 and 1996, in order to avoid repeating this tragedy," and second, "to locate, process, preserve, and analyze the documentary heritage of the Guatemalan Army, the Secretariat of Social Welfare, the Presidential Guard, and of other related state dependencies, in order to contribute to the clarification of the events of the armed conflict and to reconciliation within Guatemalan society."[27] In May 2009, the Peace Archives effort released its first report, *The Authenticity of the Military Logbook in Light of the Historical Documents of the National Police*, which analyzed records from the National Police archives on fifty-four individuals

FIG. 8.1 President Otto Pérez Molina during his time as a military commander in the Ixil Triangle. Pérez Molina's tenure in the Ixil coincided with the bloodiest years of the scorched-earth campaign in the country's western highlands, and in the Ixil Triangle in particular. © Jean-Marie Simon/2012.

named in the "Death Squad Dossier"; other reports followed, and its documents and staff expertise were brought to bear on a number of human rights prosecutions. Many of the Peace Archives staffers were former employees of the Project, building upon their experience with the PN records to attempt a different path toward archival access. So, Colom's commitment was perhaps as real as could be expected given the political context, though in the long run it would not much matter: Otto Pérez Molina dissolved the Peace Archives Directorate within six months of assuming the presidency.

This context—citizen disenfranchisement, a woefully lacking educational system, widespread illiteracy, and a long history of hermetic, antidemocratic rule—meant that the archival battleground was not necessarily of much interest or relevance to most Guatemalans. Rescuing warehouses full of moldering Spanish-language papers would not feed or house the country's rural Maya majority, many of them living in abject poverty and desperately underserved by government. Neither would they translate directly into reparations payments, land redistribution, or bilingual schools. The fact of archives being publicly accessible in Guatemala City mattered little to those who infrequently visited the capital, could not read, or feared retribution if they were to come forward seeking information about a killed or disappeared family member.

The national conversation around access to information and archival politics was overwhelmingly an urban and elite conversation. To what extent did the archive wars resonate, then, with the population? Transparency, access, declassification—whose priorities were these?

Nearly all the efforts at securing access to state documents had been underwritten by the international community, whether by foreign governments, transnational NGOs, or research and advocacy organizations.[28] North American groups like the National Security Archive, the Washington Office on Latin America, and Human Rights First assisted activists' attempts to wrestle with the EMP archives, the police archives, the struggle to force the opening of the military archives, and the denial of military and police records to the CEH. European governments channeled funds directly to projects like the police archives and made indirect contributions to others by way of their support for human rights organizations like GAM, SEDEM, and the PDH. One of the most significant attempts to protect archives was the country's chapter of UNESCO's Memory of the World project, which published instructional manuals on archival preservation, worked toward the creation of a national inventory of documentary holdings, and lobbied government for more stringent protection of the resources housed in the country's libraries, archives, and private collections.[29] As Michael Moerth, of Switzerland's Program for the Promotion of Peace, put it, "The international community [in Guatemala] is very clear that if a country doesn't learn from its past, it won't have a future. We've always been very clear on that. . . . A country without records is a country without history. It has no memory."[30]

International donors' funding of these projects meant that they were, to some extent, inflected with donors' priorities. As discussed earlier in this book, before the PN archives were found, the donors supporting Guatemala's transition were uninterested in matters of archival preservation qua archival preservation. Their objectives were justice reform, election monitoring, socioeconomic development, promoting the rights of women and indigenous peoples, combating state corruption, and other objectives tied to liberalizing conceptions of postbellum jurisprudence, institution building, and the ever-contested idea of "reconciliation." Donors accommodated their inclination to collaborate with the Project under the rubrics of their existing programs on transitional justice; all those I spoke with agreed that their governments would never have supported an archival preservation initiative absent a human rights investigation component.[31] This was not necessarily negative; if cooperating countries had promoted different goals, then the Project might never have been adequately funded or defended, and the PN archives would have gone down in Guatemalan history as yet another lost opportunity.[32] As one Project worker told me, "International assistance is a necessary evil. The ideal would be for us to have our own state archival politics, our own state resources to care for archives. But that is the desire, not the reality."[33]

But foreign involvement in the archive wars resonated with more complex aspects of the country's politics. First, the surge of international interest in Guatemalan archival practice surrounding the Project could not help but echo a previous surge of international interest in Guatemalan archival practice: when USAID and its Office of Public Safety trained the PN in archival methods during the early years of the Cold War. While the two efforts' ends were very different, the means—professionalization, "modernization," the application of international archival standards and norms, and the streamlining and ratio-nalization of record-keeping labor—were the same. It was not the only way in which recovering the past in Guatemala at times occasioned uncomfortable acts of mimesis. Second, it was no isolated fact that international support and money served as the glue helping to hold the Project together in the face of threats to its survival. Rather, the deep involvement of international funders in the Project reflected the greater reality of foreign engagement with postwar "progress." In providing such support for Guatemala's liberal advances—by funding its NGOs, encouraging its development goals, and pressuring the state to honor its Peace Accord commitments—what, precisely, was international assistance truly fostering? Was it building Guatemalan sovereignty and inde-pendence? Or was it helping to stitch together the flimsy outward appearance of a functional free-trade partner while the domestic sphere remained hos-tage to the continued dominance of the military, foreign investors, and the drug trade?

Neither was the progressive wing of civil society that international donors hoped to nurture without its own deep divisions and conflicts. While the ar-chive wars had inspired collaborations over the course of the twenty years preceding the National Police records' appearance, those years had also been marked by the same infighting, resentments, and mistrust that characterized the postwar Left more broadly, all the more charged for the sums of foreign dollars at stake in the peace process.[34] Different victims' rights NGOs regu-larly worked separately to investigate the same cases of forced disappearance; other NGOs split asunder over procedural conflicts or interpersonal problems, not least because many of their leaders shared long and difficult histories. The weaknesses of a progressive sector that had suffered some five decades of fierce repression and infiltration would be reflected again in debates over the Project, which came to a head over the question of public access to the police records. Soon after the Project's institutionalization, it faced criticism from the very organizations whose volunteers had sparked the recovery initiative in the first place. Nongovernmental organizations like GAM and SEDEM felt as of 2007 that the Project had become too secretive, unwilling to share the fruits of its investigation with the organizations that had helped to build it.[35] Concerned parties were divided on how to attribute blame—to the Project's leaders, or to Sergio Morales and the PDH—but they all felt shut out by the one initiative that potentially promised answers to their decades-old questions, and worried that the police archives would meet the same neglected fate at the PDH's hands as the EMP images.[36] "There will come a time when our organizations are going to demand some kind of access, some kind of information, some kind of opening," a GAM staffer told me.[37] And that time did come: on the twenty-fourth anniversary of her first husband's disappearance, GAM founder and congresswoman Nineth Montenegro forced the issue by publicly demanding that the PDH open the police archives. She had inside knowledge that the PN records contained information about her lost spouse, trade unionist Edgar Fernando García, and she wanted it released.[38] Although it took longer and required more pressure than Montenegro might have hoped, documents from the PN archives about her husband's disappearance were released in 2009 and led to the successful prosecutions of multiple police officers involved in the crime. The Project's subsequent transfer out of PDH control did much to restore social organizations' goodwill, but for several years the relationships between the Project and its supposed allies were strained at best.

The tension surrounding the lag on public access to the PN records spoke to a legitimate concern about timing. No event better exemplified this than the death of General Germán Chupina in February 2008.[39] As discussed in chapter 5, Chupina served as director-general of the National Police from 1978 through 1982, overseeing one of the bloodiest periods in urban Guatemalan history. For those interested in using the PN archives as evidence against war criminals, Chupina's would have been not only one of the best-documented cases but also one of the most vindicatory emotional victories. But time ran short; the octogenarian general died peacefully of respiratory failure, a free man, in his own bed at his posh home in Boca del Monte. For activists, it was a crushing blow—to have finally gained access to hard state evidence, but for the generals to elude their grasp regardless. "Chupina is one of the bloodiest characters of this history," said one Project leader. "And for him to die in his bed, bathed in impunity. . . . For me, it hurts."[40] Indeed, of the eight military and police officials originally named in the Spanish genocide case—former heads of state Ríos Montt, Mejía Víctores, and Romeo Lucas García; former defense minister Aníbal Guevara; former interior minister Donaldo Álvarez Ruíz; former army chief of staff Benedicto Lucas García; Chupina; and former Commando Six chief Pedro García Arredondo—two were dead (Chupina and Romeo Lucas), one was hospitalized with health problems (Guevara), and one had fled into exile (Álvarez), leaving, as of 2008, just four elderly men living out their days.[41] It added an extra dimension of urgency to an already tense work pace at the Project. Perpetrators were dying before they could be charged and convicted; witnesses were dying, too, before they could testify. With these constraints in mind, the Project's staffers worked day in and day out, going years without taking vacations, mindful that their labors represented one of the last chances to see courtroom justice done. What they never suspected was that the greatest threat to the Project's survival would come from within.[42]

GUATEMALAN CRABS: AN ETHNOGRAPHIC SNAPSHOT

On first glance, the evening of 24 March 2009 seemed like it would prove a momentous historical event: the PDH threw a massive gala to commemorate the release of the Project's much-awaited investigative report, *El derecho a saber* (*The Right to Know*), and to announce the granting of public access to some ten million digitized documents from the archives.[43] Presided over by human rights ombudsman Sergio Morales, the flashy soirée was attended by the country's diplomatic and aid corps, the Project staff, representatives from nearly every human rights NGO, the Project's national and international advisory boards, Vice President Rafael Espada, and the presidents of Congress and the Supreme Court, and it was covered by every major media outlet in the country. The evening was designed to have the same sort of gravitas as had the public presentation of the CEH's report in 1999.[44] And it did turn out to be a momentous gathering—but not for its intended reasons.

Sergio Morales became a controversial figure on the Left during his 2007 efforts to secure his congressional reappointment as ombudsman. When originally named to the post in 2002, Morales was the favored candidate among left-leaning NGOS. (Installing a progressive ombudsman was important to human rights activists because, although it is popularly referred to as the Procuraduría de los Derechos Humanos, the PDH's full name is the *Institución del* Procurador de los Derechos Humanos, or IPDH. It is the *office of* the ombudsman; all revolves around the appointee, and the organization enjoys little long-term continuity independent of the official at its head.) During his first term, Morales seemed a solid pick: the PDH investigated record numbers of human rights complaints, supported the creation of the UN-backed International Commission against Impunity in Guatemala (CICIG), and worked closely with social organizations.[45] But Morales's first term was due to conclude in mid-2007, placing the future of the Project in jeopardy. Were a new ombudsman to be less interested in rescuing the archives, or to espouse a different politics, the Project would risk being ignored, muzzled, or closed down.

This was not the only stressor for Project workers surrounding Morales's exit. Wanting to leave behind a legacy, Morales tasked the Project in early 2007 with the expedited production of a major report on its findings, the release of which would coincide with his leaving office. Workers, particularly the case investigation and analysis teams, found themselves under the gun to produce the report, which was, like the REMHI report, to be organized in four volumes—another clue about how Morales sought to position himself in the historical record. ("Since Sergio was on his way out, he wanted to leave a monument," one donor told me.) Morales began speaking of his desire to build a "memory museum" at the archives, inspired by his visits to Villa Grimaldi and to Hiroshima. He envisioned "a forest of peace" with "trees for meditation, a water fountain, and rosebushes so that people could use the space as a distraction, but that they could also refresh their memories about what happened."[46] It seemed unlikely that so much could be done in the first half of 2007—the writing and release of a historic report, the construction of a memory museum, and the handing over of the Project to a new ombudsman.

Sure enough, these objectives were delayed, owing to a decisive change in the playing field: Morales ran for reappointment to an unprecedented second term as ombudsman, and won. While on its face this seemed a boon to the Project, ostensibly assuring its institutional continuity for another five years, it instead provoked deep divisions. This time around, Morales was no longer the favored candidate of the human rights community; skeptical of his ambitions, many organizations supported a more progressive contender instead. And a troubling rumor surfaced surrounding the circumstances of his reappointment: that Morales had used the archives as a bargaining chip to secure support for his candidacy from an FRG-controlled Congress.[47] The prospect was alarming: in addition to being an international-donor cash magnet, the Project also held information implicating high-level figures in human rights abuses. "As we understand it," SEDEM's Iduvina Hernández told me, "the ombudsman bargained that he would only provide public access to the documents up to a certain point, and that certain types of information would be protected or restricted. . . .What worries us is that the information [from the archives] in the ombudsman's hands is being used as a weapon for political negotiation. In service of the interests of the ombudsman as an *individual*."[48]

Gossip had it that Morales was grooming himself for a run at the presidency and planned to use the PN archives as a political commodity.[49]

Nothing could be proved, and some of the rumors seemed less like fact and more like the perennial accusations of duplicity and *engaño* that, as Diane Nelson points out, haunt postconflict Guatemala.[50] But with Morales's reappointment, conditions at the Project deteriorated markedly. The publication of the report, over which researchers had been feverishly laboring, was postponed indefinitely, to the consternation of donors and the workers who had spent months desperately trying to complete it. In December 2007, the PDH ordered the firings of more than thirty Project employees, chosen seemingly at random, in an overnight decision remembered by those left behind as *el golpe* (the blow, or the coup).[51] At the same time, the PDH appointed an administrative coordinator to be the Project's titular head—a way to strip autonomy, and power over funds and information, from Meoño and his team.[52] Donors began to wonder if the PDH was playing fast and loose with the funds earmarked for the Project. Most distasteful was the suspicion that the Project had been forced to hire FRG loyalists into its team of workers, which raised the threat not only of fraud but of surveillance and infiltration—dynamics that harkened back to the very war years the Project was investigating.

This turmoil eroded Project workers' morale. From late 2007 through mid-2008, the archives were a rat's nest of gossip, fear, and cynicism, with everyone waiting for the next ax to fall and many angry at the lack of transparency behind the changes to their workplace. As one worker, among the Project's first hires but who was fired in *el golpe*, told me, "I was frustrated, because after three years, they haven't published the report. They told us we had to do all this work on the report and it never came out; it was a lie. They don't want anyone to talk. They snuck people from the FRG into the groups. . . . And then Gustavo [Meoño] came to tell me I was fired, and nobody will take responsibility for it."[53] His wife, who survived *el golpe*, spoke sadly of how a new hire at the archives showed up bearing a photograph of her disappeared spouse, saying that she wanted to learn her husband's fate. "And today, what are you going to tell that woman?" she asked. "That the ombudsman wanted to secure his reelection and so the archives got screwed because of it? No. It can't be that way."[54]

Though the circumstances were dispiriting, workers attempted to maintain some optimism. Moods were lifted by the fact by early 2009, Project employees enjoyed the security of six-month contracts—in the past, they had worked under two-month contracts, or without contracts at all—and by the fact that they had just returned from a twenty-day vacation, the first substantial break in the Project's nearly four years of existence.[55] Additionally, the idea of building a memory museum, bandied about since the Project's earliest days, continued to inspire. "From the outset, the idea of a museum was talked about," said Dolores, a case investigator. "It came up in December 2005, when we were working on a progress report. In that moment, [another coworker] said, 'We just need to bring a little tree and give it water,' and right then I visualized it, I visualized the whole thing." She continued, bursting into tears. "In Europe, they have those huge monuments to the fallen; I imagine it as a symbol of peace, one hundred percent. . . . A monument would create the space that our fallen ones deserve."[56] But the idea of a memory museum did not escape the corrosive effects of power struggles at PDH headquarters. Amid the gossip regarding Morales's political compromises, other workers worried that the monument initiative would prove an empty gesture—a totem disguising a lack of commitment to access and justice. "If there is a museum without justice," one argued, "then it will be nothing more than kitsch."[57]

Though the ombudsman's ambitions ran high, so did the expectations of domestic and international Project allies. The PDH could not stall indefinitely on granting public access to the scanned documents or releasing the report. Pressure mounted from all sides—from human rights groups, victims' families, donors, and Project advisers—counterbalancing the message the PDH was likely receiving from conservative sectors to silence the Project's findings. As a result, and suddenly it seemed at the time, the PDH announced that during the week of 23 March 2009, it would make a number of advances. First, Morales would inaugurate a *rosalera*, or rose garden, in honor of the women disappeared during the armed conflict. The next day, he would release *El derecho a saber*, the report that had been some three years in the making. The following day, public access to the scanned documents—some eight million images at that point—would be granted, its access norms regulated by the newly generated Regulation for the Reference Service on Human Rights Violations (SEREVIDH).[58] A public documentation center, just adjacent to the *rosalera*, would open on 25 March, while the finishing touches were being put on a "memory museum" next door. And though the paint was still fresh on the walls, the documentation center successfully received its first petitioner that very day.

The rose garden and museum were underwhelming and poorly executed. But the week's hallmark event was to be the release of *El derecho a saber* on 24 March. The atmosphere at the Project had been tense for the weeks leading up to the release. In early March, the Public Ministry had made the first arrests based on information from the archives, of two of the rank-and-file agents accused in the forced disappearance of Fernando García. But immediately after the arrests, the head of the PDH's Special Investigations Unit was ambushed and badly beaten, and Project staffers began to notice unfamiliar cars parked outside the archives, whose occupants photographed them as they left work.[59] On the morning of 24 March, this localized uneasiness spread throughout the city. Capital dwellers were accustomed to everyday violence, but that day was different. Early in the morning, armed attacks on buses at high-volume transit arteries—along the Periférico highway in Zone 2, on Castellana Avenue in Zone 9—left five dead, seven wounded, and traffic paralyzed for hours. After the morning's deaths, bus drivers blockaded the Periférico and Petapa Avenue, near the USAC, to protest the state's failure to protect them from gangland-style assassinations.[60] This jammed traffic further, impelling businesses to close early so that employees could get home before nightfall, giving the city center the feel of a ghost town by midafternoon. Rumors circulated via radio that the government had declared a state of siege, abetted by the fact that "an unusually high military presence" began patrols after dusk.[61] President Colom gave a defensive radio address that evening refuting the state-of-siege gossip and arguing that the violence represented an effort by organized crime to destabilize his government.[62] There was no hard evidence linking any of this to the release of the PDH's report, but as Project advisory board member Antonio González Quintana later wrote, "None of us who attended the release ceremony could avoid thinking that all this bore some relation to the presentation of the report and the opening of the archives to the public."[63]

The mood at the gala, then, was anything but relaxed, with clusters of guests huddled and whispering about the day's events.[64] Nonetheless, nearly a thousand attendees, after passing through metal detectors, assembled in the hotel's chandeliered ballroom for the presentation of El derecho a saber. The hushed conversations taking place included speculations as to just how watered-down the report would be: the Project's investigative team had had to submit its final version to the PDH for "editing," and several expressed fears that, because of Morales's rumored political compromises, perpetrators' names would be excised. Nonetheless, the event showed promise early on. Project director Gustavo Meoño cut a surreal figure in his brown 1970s-style suit: a former guerrilla commander lecturing a banquet hall full of dignitaries about the marvels of archival science. Meoño praised the work of the Project staff, accused the state of concealing information about war-era abuses, and argued that Guatemalans were "a fearful and fragmented people" afflicted by the country's failure to right the war's wrongs. He called the goal of giving victims' families access to the archives the Project's "moral heart." But, standing at the lectern, he looked both weary and wary.

The rest of the event had a schizophrenic character, uneven and charged with intensity. Control of the lectern alternated between government functionaries making vague remarks about the importance of "knowing the truth," and children of prominent Guatemalans disappeared or killed during the war speaking forcefully to the need for justice. First to speak was the daughter of the poet Luis de Lión, a PGT activist who was disappeared in 1984.[65] She told the crowd of the emotional torture inflicted upon her family, and thousands of families more, by the unending crime of forced disappearance. Her gripping testimony was followed, however, by a dry description of the report by a PDH official who pointedly failed to mention specific perpetrators or cases in his exposition. It then became clear to Project staff that their report's conclusions had been bowdlerized, and whispers of dissatisfaction began to bubble forth from the audience. This splitting, between victims' penetrating accusations and state representatives' reiterations of the value of historical knowledge for its own sake, caused the room's collective frustration to mount with each subsequent speaker. Next at the podium was Julio Solórzano Foppa, the son of feminist intellectual Alaíde Foppa, who was disappeared by the Lucas García government in 1980. Where de Lión's daughter's words had been elegiac, those of Foppa's son were angry. "Who were those responsible," he thundered, "and how will they be brought to justice?" He turned to the head table, where Vice President Espada and the other dignitaries sat, and, addressing Espada directly, demanded that the government tell victims exactly when they would be given access to the still-closed military archives. In a country with such a hierarchical political culture, this bold statement to a sitting official was shocking, and it was met with wild applause by the activists at the back of the ballroom. Solórzano was followed by another PDH functionary who provided information about the documents' access norms. Next to speak was Mayra Alvarado, the daughter of PGT leader Bernardo Alvarado Monzón—killed by security forces alongside other PGT activists in 1972—and her testimony shook the event's foundations. She never knew her father, who was detained seventeen days after her birth, and in tears, she read aloud a tender letter he had written to her immediately after she was born. Still crying but now defiant, the younger Alvarado proclaimed that she both affirmed her father's right to rebellion and defended his struggle for all Guatemalans to be able to think differently about their country. By this point, dozens of audience members were in tears themselves; they gave Alvarado a standing ovation.

The evening's charged tone had now become electric. Sergio Morales got up to present the report to Espada. Upon receiving the report and taking the podium, Espada found his prepared statement interrupted by the cries of a well-known activist in the front row, who screamed a demand that Congress approve the proposed Law 35-90 ratifying the International Convention on Forced Disappearance. She cried that if Espada's government failed to do so, it would be complicit in the crimes of its predecessors. Again, it was a breach of protocol that set the room abuzz. When Espada continued with his remarks, which focused on the abstract importance of "truth" without mentioning criminal justice, the room's center could no longer hold. "¡QUEREMOS JUSTICIA!" yelled an audience member. When Roberto Alejos, the president of Congress, rose to take the microphone from Espada, he was drowned out by hundreds of audience members chanting "¿Qué queremos?" followed by "¡JUSTICIA!" The president of the judiciary and the attorney general faced similar reactions, contrasting sharply with the sense of jubilation that rippled through the hall when those giving testimony spoke.

Even before the speeches concluded, attendees began flooding out to the foyer in search of an answer to the great hanging question of the evening: What, exactly, did *El derecho a saber* actually say? Print copies were available only to elite guests, mainly the foreigners, while others received a compact disc copy to read later. Nonetheless, the print copies made it around the room, and even a cursory flip through the volume confirmed suspicions: while the report contained interesting information about the archives themselves and the police's history, its investigations of specific human rights violations and harder-hitting conclusions had been stripped. Milling about and discussing the report, young Project workers joked around, mocking Morales and the PDH. But older workers were somber, feeling that the report's "editing" represented yet another defeat. "We've been crushed and beaten down a thousand times," one told me. "And a thousand times we stand up and keep on fighting." At her side her husband, a Project case investigator, simply shook his head in disbelief.

The next morning at the archives, anger and disappointment crackled through the air. Few had slept. Meoño, nearly in tears, told me that the report had been "censored" and "mutilated," its heart removed. Although many had seen this coming, it was still painful; they had hoped, against the odds, for better. After nearly four years of exhausting labor, the limitations of their post-war, post-peace state still reigned: corruption, shady power brokering, and a lack of political will to attempt redress for state crimes against humanity. "It's as though they're making fun of us" and "They're mocking us" were comments I heard from many rank and filers at the archives that day, who felt *engañado* yet again. Many wondered about the future; perhaps, some speculated, the takeaway message was that the Project would not be permitted to keep going at all. The members of the international advisory board (CCI), for their part—some of whom had had access to the unedited, complete report, and knew exactly how much of it had been excised—met that day to craft a public response sharply critical of the PDH.

They would never release it, however, because of the next day's news: Morales's wife, the lawyer and politician Gladys Monterroso, had been kidnapped. At seven in the morning, as Morales reported upon her release twelve hours later, she was eating breakfast in a restaurant when she received a phone call instructing her to step outside. When she did, three armed men wearing hoods forced her into an SUV for an ordeal that she thought would be "the last day of [her] life."[66] As a sobbing Morales told reporters the next day, during Monterroso's captivity she was burned with cigarettes, threatened at gunpoint, raped, beaten, and drugged before being dumped at the side of a road in Zone 18, where she was rescued. "This barbarity must end," Morales wept at his press conference. "We must continue on with our work," he affirmed, theorizing that the attack was an act of retribution for the release of *El derecho a saber*—much as Bishop Juan Gerardi had been assassinated following the release of *Guatemala: Nunca Más!* in 1998.[67] Given the news, the CCI opted to shelve its critique. Civil society groups called for Monterroso's case to be investigated by the UN-overseen CICIG. Soon after, the PDH detained one Oscar Gutiérrez Valle as a suspect in Monterroso's case.

The commission began to look into the case in collaboration with the Public Ministry (MP), but within three months it withdrew from its investigation of Gutiérrez Valle, and CICIG director Carlos Castresana began advocating for the detainee's release, arguing, "There is no greater injustice than an innocent person being sent to prison." Cynical rumors had abounded in the days following Monterroso's kidnapping that the incident had been an *auto-secuestro*, or self-kidnapping—a publicity move with some precedent in Guatemalan political history. Yet there was no doubt that Monterroso had been savagely assaulted; photographs of her arms, scored with cigarette burns, and her blackened eyes were published widely. So what had taken place? In August 2009, journalist Claudia Méndez Arriaza published a withering exposé of the circumstances behind Gutiérrez Valle's arrest, suggesting that the PDH had trumped up the charges and conducted a slipshod investigation of the case.[68] Around the same time, word spread that the MP had obtained video footage contradicting Monterroso's testimony, by way of the security cameras at a bank adjacent to the restaurant from which Morales said Monterroso was kidnapped.[69] As well, blood tests performed by the MP indicated that Gutiérrez Valle "very probably could not have been the author of the sexual violation of Ms. Monterroso."[70] All that the alleged video could suggest was that Monterroso had not been abducted from outside the Zone 9 restaurant, and the blood tests only demonstrated that Gutiérrez Valle was not the primary assailant. This did not prove that she had not been attacked later. However, it was enough to raise doubts.

The competing versions of the Monterroso story—and, by extension, of Morales's credibility—came to a head in June 2009, three months after the report's release. On 20 June, Morales announced that the PDH could no longer afford to pay its staff at the archives and so it would be forced to shut the Project down, effective 30 June. This came as a surprise to the donors, whose financial support for the Project had been unwavering during the preceding four years and who had no intention of abandoning it.[71] It also came as a shock to Project workers, who were informed of the decision by internal memo. Donors, along with the Project's workers and leaders, interpreted the move for what it was: a move to shut the initiative down once and for all, as predicted in the aftermath of the 24 March gala, and the culmination of the slow internal move, dating back to Morales's 2007 reappointment, to silence the archives' revelations. While Morales feigned displeasure at the situation, his message was clear: the Project had lost the backing of the PDH.[72]

This now being clear not only to insiders but also to the general public, Meoño and his colleagues decided to reveal what they had known for years but which, hoping to protect the archives, they had not previously disclosed: that the PDH was diverting Project-earmarked funds elsewhere; that the PDH was burning through some 10 percent of the Project's payroll budget to fund individuals in "ghost positions" who were not actually working at the archives; and that the PDH had stripped the Project's control over human resources in order to make nepotistic hires. Meoño made two additional, weightier accusations. First, he attested that Morales had "mutilated and censored" *El derecho a saber*, removing any discussion of the army's role in the counterinsurgency or naming of names from the police's chain of command. Second, and more damning, Meoño argued that Morales had protected the intellectual authors of Edgar Fernando García's forced disappearance. Though the archives had revealed both the names of the crime's low-ranking material authors *and* of the Fourth Corps chief (Jorge Alberto Gómez) who ordered it, the PDH only moved to prosecute the rank-and-file agents who had carried out Gómez's orders, not naming their superior officer in the suit. Meoño told reporters that while the Project had presented the PDH with more than two hundred documents on the Fernando García case, including full documentation of the chain of command behind it, Morales had ignored the higher-ups in the

Fourth Corps and the layer of military authority above them. Ultimately, Gó-mez's name was first disclosed not by Meoño or human rights activists but by the lawyer representing the detained agents, who questioned why his clients were being punished for a kidnapping ordered by their boss.[73]

After Meoño's revelations, NGOs and research organizations came together to demand that the Colom administration step in and assume responsibility for the archives. In a joint statement, more than forty groups asked that Colom oversee the archives' transfer to the Archivo General de Centroamérica, guarantee unobstructed access to them, publish the unedited original version of *El derecho a saber*, ensure that Project staffers' jobs were protected, and create a National Commission on Historical Memory to coordinate access to various bodies of documentation pertaining to the armed conflict.[74] Colom acceded, announcing that custody of the archives would be transferred to the Ministry of Culture and Sports, the parent ministry of the AGCA, a move some had argued for since the outset. All of the staff would keep their jobs, and the donors would continue funding the archives in their new home. According to Colom, this shift would form the foundation for the building of a new national archives system, one that would one day include the military's historical records as well.[75] Human rights organizations were thrilled, both at the short-term transfer of the PN records and at the long-term shift it portended for state archival practice.[76] It was, finally, the opportunity at institution building that had been impossible to pursue in 2005 when the records were first located. The state had mustered the political will (if not the cash) to take on its archival responsibilities. And while this was partially due to Colom's intervention, the truth was that the Project would not have lasted until Colom took power had its workers and allies not worked tirelessly for four long years to protect it. The Project had not only successfully changed the law of what could be said in Guatemala—it had changed the law of what could be done.

On 1 July, formal custody of Guatemala's National Police Historical Archives was transferred to the AGCA. "A new phase of the Project has begun," read a communiqué from Meoño, "characterized by the institutionalization of the archives."[77] Next, the Project would work on securing the archives' legal foundations by promoting the passage of a new national archives law, further developing the records' access norms, and continuing to process and scan millions more documents. A new chapter had begun, one remaining in its infancy at the time of this writing; it remains to be seen how the Project will handle the obstacles sure to present themselves in the future. Come what might, however, the Project had achieved its major victory, having created and saved an unprecedented initiative that, a scant few years before, would never have even been imaginable. The transition was marked by a change in the effort's name: from the Project for the Recovery of the National Police Historical Archive (PRAHPN) to, simply, the National Police Historical Archive (AHPN). The archives had thus concluded their period of *becoming*—their malleable, shape-shifting phase, their years of improvisation and missteps and raw struggles with the production of knowledge—and had undergone an ontological shift into a new, more stable state, that of *being*.

THE LAW OF WHAT CAN BE DONE

In one of his most frequently cited commentaries on the subject, Michel Foucault writes, "The archive is first the law of what can be said, the system that governs the appearance of statements as unique events."[78] Foucault's archive, which he describes as "the general system of the formation and transformation of statements," polices the parameters of discourse. It is the elephant in every room, the ur-notion defining the very boundaries of enunciability, reminding us that however enthusiastically we might seek to investigate the past, our forays into the archive ultimately only underscore the past's unattainability, its distance from ourselves. The archive, Foucault tells us, "is the border of time that surrounds our presence, which overhangs it, and which indicates it in its otherness; it is that which, outside ourselves, delimits us . . . its threshold of existence is established by the discontinuity that separates us from what we can no longer say."[79] The poetics of applying Foucault's framework to the real-world context of the PN archives certainly tempt a writer's imagination, and elements of his analysis ring true. Surely the specters of the country's *desaparecidos*, who survive only in memories and in state documents, can be said to "surround" and "overhang" the lives of surviving family members, reminding them daily that they will never be reunited. But one must not confuse the rich life of a person with its thin archival record—its paper cadaver—nor confuse state security forces' purposeful political repression with the depersonalized exercise of power Foucault describes. In the Guatemalan case, the police archives have at different points in time bounded speech and action, it is true—but only to the extent that their records were used by actual, living police officers to locate suspicious individuals for interrogation or worse. Student leader Oliverio Castañeda regularly gave speeches during his too-short life, and he must have known that the military state was keeping track of his words; but Castañeda gave the speeches regardless, and in them, he dared the army to come after him. Counterinsurgency archives did not constrain him discursively; they did so corporeally and bloodily in their use by his assassins.

As historian Craig Robertson observes, "Archives do not neutrally store documents; rather, objects captured through archival practices are transformed into knowledge."[80] This is true both of the surveillance data captured through counterinsurgent archival practices *and* of the criminal evidence captured through memory-oriented, recuperative archival practices. Such knowledge, produced by way of the contact between police officer and document, once informed actions including abduction, torture, and murder. Now, the archives' use by a mobilized group of activists—even in spite of the internal divisions and dangers threatening their progress—redefined the law of what could be said about the past in Guatemala, making possible new worlds of expression and interpretation. And this was not all: the Project also changed the law of what could be *done* about the past in Guatemala. Subsequent developments in the treatment of state records, including Colom's 2008 attempt to force the opening of military archives and the creation of the Peace Archives initiative, owed their thinkability to the Project's work on changing archival culture—assigning new value to state documents, transfiguring them from garbage into treasure by putting them at the service of new objectives.[81] The Project redefined archival preservation in Guatemala as a political act. In the process, the initiative ceased to be a "project" at all, transcending its benighted origins and turning the police's archives into the people's archives.

The actual conditions delimiting the Project's field of possibility were structural. For all its utility in the struggle against impunity, increased archival access would not repair the broken justice system, repel the corrupting influence of foreign aid dollars, redistribute land and wealth, or bring back the dead. On the other hand, however, veterans of political struggle knew that every glimmer of opportunity had to be seized upon and fought for. A convergence of propitious factors—international interest, Colom's desire to legitimate himself as a social democrat, and the experience gained over the course of the archive wars—presented survivors and activists with a chance, however beset by challenges it was, to effect a small shift in the country's balance of power. Archival access did not *equal* socioeconomic change, but it did complement it. "In one way or another, knowing *what happened* makes an important difference, at least to be able to end these cycles of grief," said Esteban, a Project worker. "Even better, to learn that there was an intellectual author to these acts and that there exists a log or register of where the disappeared were buried. So, even the minimum provided by the archives can at least form the base for changes—for an end to impunity, for the birth of a certain respect for human rights."[82] The hope was that advances on the archival front would impact other spheres of social and political life. If archival practice served as a metonym for governance, or as a microcosm of it, then successful attempts to change a country's archival practice would alter the way it governed, and expand the nature of political possibility. Sonia Combe writes that the "'repressed' archive" represents the "power . . . of the state over the historian."[83] What activists learned during the archive wars was that fighting archival repression, whether sponsored by past military regimes or by corrupt politicians in the present day, was a way to assert the power of the amateur historian—the witness—over the state. This was not everything. But it was certainly something.

NINE

CONCLUSION

THE POSSIBILITIES AND LIMITATIONS
OF ARCHIVAL THINKING

Archiving is not about history looking backward, but about stor-
ing and securing for the future. Archiving—all the activities from
creation and management to the use of records and archives—has
always been directed towards transmitting human activity and
experience through time and, secondly, through space. . . . It is the
quality of the archive as a time machine.

—Eric Ketelaar, "Archival Temples, Archival Prisons"

Archives, or the truths we imagine them to contain, fascinate us. They speak to us of the most elemental human preoccupations: birth, death, identity, history. They attract us, and we fetishize them, hoping they will provide proof points—trustworthy signposts of fixity—to help guide us through the "epistemic murk" of modern life.[1] As archivists Terry Cook and Joan M. Schwartz write, archives "are the basis for and the validation of the stories we tell ourselves, the story-telling narratives that give cohesion and meaning to individuals, groups, and societies."[2] They are the stuff of which our histories are made and remade, the places where voices once silenced can be resurrected and where truth-claims might be substantiated. They are sites of hope and aspiration.

But at the same time, archives also intimidate us; we want access to them, but we fear what we might learn in the process of looking. Archives are the treasure houses, the cornerstones, of modernity's most powerful institutions: banks, states, police forces, corporations, employers. Their archives remind us that we are small, and when we are denied access to them, it makes us feel smaller still. Moreover, we are uncomfortable with archives because we know that their flat, bureaucratic representations of our rich, full lives will outlive us, and outlive the memory of us. We know all the things the archives can never record, and we know that even being archived does not guarantee that we will be remembered. No one likes to think that she can, and will, be reduced to a file in the end, even if, as Milan Kundera writes, "police files are our only claim to immortality."[3]

In a postconflict or postcolonial setting, this archival thrall—the simultaneous push and pull, the twinned promise and peril of institutional archives—takes on outsize proportions, mirroring the outsize proportions of those past (and/or present) regimes' carceral, punitive institutions. On the one hand, the archives of bygone governments are great gifts to those tasked with rebuilding shattered societies; they can be used to locate missing persons, lustrate state dependencies, rewrite histories, and design programs of reparation and healing. As such, reformers and victims understandably clamor for the records, demanding their accessibility and preservation. On the other hand, opening the archives presents real risks, the most dramatic being the danger of finding unwanted information. For example, East German dissident Vera Wollenberger was among the throngs of citizens who flocked to consult the records of the Stasi after Germany's reunification. In the archives, she learned to her horror that her husband had been informing on her for years, feeding intimate details about her political and personal life to his Stasi handler; it destroyed their marriage, and her world as she had known it. "What I have had to go through," she wrote of what her file revealed, "I wouldn't wish on anyone, not even my worst enemy."[4] Yet while the appearance of unbidden truths is a hazard of the process, worse still is information's absence. What if, after thirty years of waiting for a spouse or child to reappear, new state security archives are opened to great expectations but contain no mention of that particular *desaparecido*? What happens if, and when, the archives do not speak? Archives can liberate, but they can also enclose, silence, or disappoint.

This book has outlined a dialectical analysis of archival recovery in contexts of political transition. Records once used in the service of state terror are repurposed by surviving reformers as building blocks for the rule of law and tools of social reckoning. Archivist Eric Ketelaar highlights this "essential connection between archives and human rights: the violation of these rights has been documented in the archives and citizens who defend themselves appeal to the archives. . . . If the fact of oppression appears in records originally inscribed for surveillance and tyranny, they can also be used for reclaiming human rights and regaining freedom."[5] This is, of course, a well-established dynamic, familiar to activists and activist-scholars who have made use of Soviet, Nazi, Spanish Civil War, or other documentary collections for the purposes of historical, moral, or legal repair. But far less understood are the *processes* by which such a transformation—from terror archive to people's archive—is made to come about, and the shifting, volatile synthesis resulting from that transformation. I hope to have addressed this lacuna by detailing the interiorities of this process as it unfolded in Guatemala and by advancing a series of interrelated, yet distinct arguments: that how a state deals with its past bureaucratic production, and how citizens respond in turn, reveals much about the present and perhaps the future contours of that society; that the National Police and the urban theater of the war need to be written back into Guatemalan history; that documentary production and preservation are always functions of power relations; that human interactions with terror archives strongly impact individual and collective subjectivities in ways that cannot always be foreseen or comfortably managed; that what matters most about such archives is not their supposedly depersonalized, abstracted exercise of panoptical control but rather their use-value by real humans, whether police officers or peacemakers, engaged in real political struggles; and that in a country where legal justice is for the most part impossible, and where the notion that national social solidarity ("reconciliation") could ever be born out of catharsis or peace treaties or reparations programs rings hollow, history and historical narratives matter—intensely so.

Yet for all the ways in which this is a story about Guatemala, informed by the country's sobering specificities and determined by the contingencies of its uniquely stygian history, it is not Guatemala's story alone. No transition out of authoritarian or military rule has failed to include significant debate about how to deal with the surviving records of past regimes. In Latin America and beyond, the trend toward privileging, protecting, and opening state records as vital elements of transitional justice has escalated significantly in recent years, making these dynamics near universal—challenges confronted from Russia to Rwanda by activists who have been transformed by necessity into amateur historians and amateur archivists. (Importantly, these are not only dynamics of the global South, or of settings conventionally labeled as "postconflict." Watchdog groups like Wikileaks or the National Security Archive in the United States can attest all too well to the challenges of forcing governments that are, in the main, considered "democratic"—to say nothing of private corporations—to relinquish records documenting abuses of power both past and present.)

As archival rescue and preservation have come to be considered fundamental to dismantling authoritarian state apparatuses alongside more traditional approaches like reparations payments or police reform, however, the nexus between the worlds of archivists and human rights activists and lawyers has grown, producing several new precedents in international human rights law.

The first is the writ of habeas data, discussed in this book and implemented throughout the Americas over the course of the past two decades; habeas data allows an individual to petition her government for any information it holds about her, and obliges that government to furnish it.[6] Another is the notion that a state's violence against its documents, whether via willful destruction or negligence, is a form of violence against its citizens. This is particularly relevant in a country like Guatemala, because of its high number of *desaparecidos*; if the state withholds or destroys documentation confirming that someone considered to have disappeared is actually dead, it subjects that person's surviving family members to decades of torturous searching for someone they believe might still be alive. The evolving legal concept has now been enshrined by both the Organization of American States and the UN as the "right to truth," with the UN naming 24 March, the anniversary of Salvadoran archbishop Oscar Romero's 1980 assassination, the International Day for the Right to the Truth Concerning Gross Human Rights Violations and for the Dignity of Victims.[7]

Perhaps the most important innovation on this front has been the landmark *Gomes Lund v. Brazil* (2010) ruling by the Inter-American Court on Human Rights (IACHR). The case concerned a small guerrilla movement in Brazil's Araguaia River region, formed in 1972 to oppose the military dictatorship. The Brazilian army's counteroffensive destroyed the movement and disappeared more than seventy people, forcing their families into a long crusade to learn the fates of their loved ones. Culminating a legal battle lasting more than twenty years, the IACHR ruled against Brazil and its long-standing refusal to turn over documentation pertaining to the resting places of the Communist Party and guerrilla members. The court rejected Brazil's amnesty law, held the state liable for the deaths of the guerrillas, and mandated broad reparatory measures. It also ruled that the *secreto de estado*, or the national security argument for preserving state secrets, could not be used to deny access to documentation of crimes against humanity. And it included an extraordinary provision obliging the Brazilian government, if it claimed that the relevant archives detailing the murders of the guerrillas had been destroyed and could therefore not be furnished to survivors, to investigate and prosecute those responsible for their unlawful destruction.[8] Archival thinking, it appears, has taken hold.

This global phenomenon represents the archival dimension of what political scientist Kathryn Sikkink terms the "justice cascade," the domino or ripple effect of individual societies' juridical reckonings with authoritarian or bloody pasts.[9] As early adopters like Portugal, Greece, and Argentina moved first to prosecute their respective ancien régime officials, Sikkink argues, they built a growing body of international legal precedent making it increasingly difficult for perpetrators elsewhere to evade accounting. The archive and the courtroom are closely linked, as this study has demonstrated; the "justice cascade," which has seen countries like Peru, Cambodia, Argentina, Colombia, the former Yugoslavia, Rwanda, and Sierra Leone explore forms of redress ranging from state apologies to community justice (most famously, Rwanda's *gacaca* courts) to international tribunals, has unfolded contemporaneously with what one might call the "archival cascade."[10] However, Sikkink's terminology, in which justice "diffuses" across space and time, or moves in "streams" via its own momentum, risks eliding the all-too-material struggles over politics and power that yielded those trials or acts of official contrition, and the backlash that often ensues. Moreover, what of the effects of strengthening a liberal jurisprudence whereby positive verdicts in the cases of single individuals or aggrieved parties are prioritized over any meaningful recognition or redress of *collective* repression—say, by way of concrete educational reform, demanded in Guatemala's Peace Accords but only unevenly implemented, or institutional reparations, or agrarian reform and other means of economic redistribution? Transitional justice in Guatemala may be beginning to take root, but it is because Guatemalans and their allies have fought on the ground for the few victories they have won, often at great personal cost. The transfiguration of the country's terror archives has reflected larger asymmetries of power and politics, and rather than occurring at the flip of a switch, the transition from one archival logic to another has more closely resembled a hard-fought war by other means.

BACKLASH, OR "YES, IT'S POLITICAL, FOR THE LOVE OF GOD"

It took fifteen years after the signing of the Peace Accords for Guatemalans to begin to see a shift: an uptick, from zero, in the number of prosecutions for wartime human rights violations, and the increased institutionalization of efforts to reckon with the past. The recovery of the PN archives was but one element of a larger constellation of projects, including exhumations, court cases, memorials, truth commissions, and social movement campaigns, all seeking to implement both the spirit and the letter of the accords. These initiatives nourished one another and were extensively cross-pollinated, making it impossible for any organization or individual to claim sole credit for progress made. That said, some of the most notable advances in the struggle against impunity in the years following the police records' rediscovery bore the imprimatur of the Project's contributions.

For example, in 2010 and 2011, evidence collected and analyzed by the Project secured the first-ever convictions for a forced disappearance committed in the capital city by the police.[11] The verdict came in the case of Edgar Fernando García—the trade unionist, PGT activist, and young father who was abducted by four rank-and-file agents of the National Police's Fourth Corps in 1984 and never heard from again. In October 2010, based almost entirely on evidence from the police archives, two of those four agents were tried and given the maximum sentence of forty years in prison.[12] At the trial, García's daughter Alejandra, a young lawyer who helped prosecute the case, gave powerful testimony:

> I do not seek revenge, neither would my dad have, but I do seek the truth, I want to know where he was taken, I want to know why he wasn't formally charged, I want to know who gave the order, I want to know where he was taken and who he was handed over to, I want to know what happened to him. My heart cannot rest and be at peace without the truth; as harsh as it may be, the truth always heals the soul. If my father is dead, he deserves to be buried like the beloved man that he was and still is, his name deserves dignity. He was not a sewer rat that can be killed with impunity; he was a human being.[13]

As we should be able to surmise by now, there was no smoking-gun document in the archives that spoke directly of García's abduction. Rather, investigators happened upon an announcement in the police's daily reports that the head of the Fourth Corps, Jorge Alberto Gómez (whom the ombudsman Morales had tried, in 2009, to protect), had awarded medals of distinction to four agents for their work in carrying out an operation against "two subversives" on the very date, at the very time, and in the precise location where witnesses saw García and his companion, Danilo Chinchilla, forced into separate vehicles and taken away.[14] To make their case, Project researchers had to triangulate this information with that yielded by dozens of other documents and testimonies, in collaboration with a Public Ministry led, as of late 2010, by a dogged crusader for transitional justice, attorney general Claudia Paz y Paz.

Shortly after the agents' sentencing, the intellectual authors of García's disappearance—Gómez's disappearance—Gómez and former police director-general Héctor Bol de la Cruz, who commanded Gómez—were also taken into custody. In 2013, both were convicted. Another arrest based on the Project's work came in July 2011: that of Pedro García Arredondo, the reviled former head of the police's Detective Corps and its Commando Six death squad, for his role in the 1981 disappearance of agronomist Edgar Saénz Calito and the 1980

FIG. 9.1 Former army chief of staff Héctor López Fuentes, behind bars at his 2011 arraignment for the crime of genocide. Photograph by James Rodríguez, mimundo.org. Used by permission of the photographer.

Spanish embassy fire; in 2012, García Arredondo was sentenced to seventy years in prison.[15] More indictments are anticipated in other cases involving PN officials, building on the momentum of these initial successes. As well, hundreds of documents from the police archives are being used in a case before the Inter-American Court on Human Rights by family members of the victims profiled in the Diario Militar. Meanwhile, parallel efforts secured the 2011 arrests of the former army chief of staff Héctor López Fuentes, who served under Romeo Lucas García, and ex-dictator Oscar Humberto Mejía Víctores, who pled health problems to have the charges against him suspended. But it was January 2013 that saw the most stunning advance: the opening of judicial proceedings against ex-dictator Efraín Ríos Montt, the first-ever former head of state to be prosecuted for genocide in his home country's domestic court system.

The indictments were an absolute watershed, something inconceivable just a scant few years earlier. But such impertinence on the part of activists did not pass unnoticed. As discussed earlier in this book, the Project, like other human rights groups, confronted at various points an array of warnings including verbal threats, at least five Molotov cocktail attacks at the archive installations, the periodic harassment of archive workers, and political pressure to not publish perpetrators' names or high-impact case files. But in late

2010 and 2011, on the heels of the aforementioned arrests and in the lead-up to presidential elections favoring powerful military candidate Otto Pérez Molina, the tenor of establishment disapproval rose. A July 2011 article in the conservative *Prensa Libre* quoted retired general Mario Mérida disputing the "juridical character," or legal integrity, of the Peace Accords—a clear attempt at intimidation, implying that security forces might no longer feel bound by the agreement to demobilize. Right-wing members of the press corps moved to ratchet up the tension. Polemicist and *el Periódico* columnist Raúl Minondo Ayau wrote:

> If [activists] continue in this way, peace will never arrive. The armed conflict should stay where it belongs, in the past. The future is today. This business of locking up ex-officials who simply did their constitutional duty is embarrassing. . . . These people who continue to make their living off the war and off spilled blood have neither father nor mother! The capture of ex-officials is nothing more than a ticket for them to get euros from the same governments who financed the armed conflict. . . . Pathetic.[16]

Shortly after, in a paid newspaper advertisement, the Association of Military Veterans (AVEMILGUA) all but declared war:

> During 36 long years, the Guatemalan population was subjected to the most cowardly and serious acts of armed aggression by delinquent organizations organized in four terrorist factions. . . . Given the persecutory actions being carried out against military personnel who, in compliance with their constitutional mandate and in obedience of their orders, prevented Guatemala from being converted into a communist state . . . [AVEMILGUA], in light of the capture of Colonel Héctor Rafael Bol de la Cruz and General Héctor Mario López Fuentes . . . expresses its strenuous opposition and asks that the Rule of Law be respected. . . . Until today, we have maintained our respect for the dominion of law, but we lament the acceptance and interference of "extrajudicial" factors, who, hypocritically shielded by the "search for justice," misinterpret [military documents] at their convenience. . . . *This is why our patriotic spirit remains high and our honor unassailable and why, for those very reasons, we warn that we are willing to fight anew if the circumstances thusly demand it.* . . . Peaceful coexistence will be impossible if society continues to be confronted in this way.[17]

AVEMILGUA's communiqué, in addition to threatening renewed violence, made two interventions. First, it conveyed official hostility toward war crimes prosecutions, accusing their proponents of being "fools trapped in the ideological past" who had "continued the conflict by other means" and "penetrated the institutions of the State and the key structures of the justice system" in order to run a witch hunt against police and military officers. (The wording appropriated the terms with which progressives typically decried military or narco infiltration of state institutions.) Second, it prominently reiterated the army's version of history, in which its cadres had loyally rescued the nation from the dangers of subversion.[18] Soon after, AVEMILGUA and other conservative groups—associations of military officers, widows, and wives, and marginal groups with names like the Movement for Equality in Justice—began holding marches to, as they put it, "break the silence" surrounding what they saw as the unjust persecution of the arrested generals. Marchers wore white and carried banners bearing slogans such as "We Can Speak Freely Thanks to Soldiers, Not Poets," "We Have Freedom of Religion Thanks to Soldiers, Not Priests," and "We Have the Right to a Fair Trial Thanks to Soldiers, Not Lawyers." As one such protester complained to a journalist, "Justice is in the hands of the radicalized left. And it is being used as a political tool, for vengeance."[19]

Also in late 2011, military groups began a legal counterinsurgency with, they proclaimed, the goal of deposing the crusading Attorney General Paz y Paz. Ricardo Méndez Ruiz, a politician from Ríos Montt's FRG party, fired the first salvo: a lawsuit against twenty-six ex-guerrilla leaders, including Gustavo Meoño, director of the archival recovery project. "The lawsuit I presented is simply the beginning of the military's counteroffensive in this third stage of the war that has already been started, the counteroffensive to the offensive that the guerrilla launched with the arrests of the generals," Méndez attested. "What you are seeing now is our response, the response of the army."[20] Two of those named in Méndez's suit were immediate family members of the attorney general. "This is in order to get rid of Claudia Paz y Paz; she decided to start this witch-hunt against the soldiers," Méndez told the media. "This is not something improvised; we are working closely on it with retired and active intelligence officers. . . . Yes, it's political, for the love of God, I'm going after the Attorney General."[21] Soon, more lawsuits of a similar character were filed, each including lists of alleged ex-guerrillas. Some of those named were indeed former militants—several lists included Meoño—but others still were journalists, activists, and authors whose connection to the events in question were dubious at best. Interestingly, one such list of suspects included each individual's supposed guerrilla pseudonym, a level of detail possible only with the help of the high-impact military archives for which leftist activists had long clamored. The placards hoisted by conservative protesters at their marches, which featured the faces of these accused individuals, made this point manifest by including file numbers beneath each person's image, offering confirmation of the secret archives' existence as a tease.

Méndez and the rest sought, through their lawsuits, to generate a sense of equivalency between their cases and those against Bol de la Cruz, López Fuentes, García Arredondo, and Ríos Montt. In launching legal attacks, the military old guard hoped to delegitimize the lawsuits of their adversaries; in threatening a "return to an armed struggle," they hoped to scare civil society away from the country's courtrooms. "What has been seen thus far is only the tip of an enormous iceberg," Méndez warned.[22] He and members of AVEMILGUA went on to found the so-called Foundation against Terrorism, which published online screeds and expensive glossy inserts in the country's major dailies attacking the Catholic Church and Guatemalan progressives, most memorably in a long photo blacklist titled "The Faces of Infamy"; its logo featured the scales of justice hanging from either side of a sword's cross-guard. Méndez's positions were echoed both by powerful institutions, such as the business association CACIF, and by powerful individuals like the president. In his initial months in office, Pérez Molina vowed not to interfere with the attorney general's work, but on the day following Ríos Montt's indictment, Pérez Molina used the presidential bully pulpit to argue that "in Guatemala, there was no genocide"—a claim that sought to exculpate not only Ríos Montt but himself too, as he had commanded troops in the Ixil region, the focus of Ríos Montt's trial.[23] It remains to be seen how this story will unfold over the course of Pérez Molina's term and beyond, but what is clear is that the struggle over criminal justice—a war waged by other means—will be fought out over many years.

In one sense, this evolving conflict was a matter of specific cases and individual victims—provable facts, incontestable evidence, objective court rulings, particular and knowable historical moments. But more broadly, this was a battle over historical interpretation, waged in the fungible and subjective territory of memory. The arrests of army and police officials so enraged the conservative Right not because of the fine points of their cases or any personal loyalties to the perpetrators in question—the military's legal countercrusade was an institutional, not personal, defense—but because they were incompatible with the Right's conception of history. In this interpretation, the military had saved the country from communism, with its soldiers having been the true patriots of the Guatemalan Cold War. Hard-liners' ideological model had been not the United States' domestic anticommunism, or even its international policy of containment, but rather the epic destruction of the Spanish Popular Front by Francisco Franco, after whose methods influential wartime groups like Guatemala's Movement for National Liberation (MLN) expressly modeled their own. It was no coincidence that the bitter back-and-forth over Guatemalan historical memory so resembled Spain's own tortured attempts at reckoning with the Spanish Civil War. As one banner, hung outside the courtroom by Ríos Montt's supporters as the general's genocide trial unfolded, argued, the fact that "terrorists, extortionists, assassins, and criminals" (human rights activists) were now prosecuting "the defenders of your liberty" (the military) represented nothing less than "the world turned upside-down."

Meanwhile, human rights activists had their own interpretation of history—one supported, it bears mentioning, by a supermajority of scholarly analyses—and goals that went beyond simply locating and tallying the dead. They sought, through their legal and memorial efforts, the *reivindicación* of the war's students, trade unionists, community organizers, progressive priests and teachers, and even its insurgents—to prove that these people were not terrorists or felons but rather idealists radicalized by the absence of democratic political spaces. As the CEH's final report observed, the wartime criminalization of victims had formed part of the military state's overall strategy: "The State also tried to stigmatize and blame the victims and the country's social organizations, making them into criminals in the public eye and thus into 'legitimate' targets for repression. This was done by stripping them of their dignity as individuals, using fire and sword to teach them the lesson that the exercise of their rights as citizens could mean death." The commissioners went on to describe how "this systematic indoctrination," not only against socialism but against independent thought, youth culture, contrarianism, civil society, and political agency, "has profoundly marked the collective consciousness of Guatemalan society. Fear, silence, apathy and lack of political participation are some of the most important effects of having criminalized the victims, and present a serious obstacle to the active participation of all citizens in the construction of democracy."[24]

It was the position of many Project workers that the only way new ideas and leaders would be able to emerge in the future—the only way such pervasive "fear, silence, apathy, and lack of political participation" could be overcome—was to *reivindicar* or redeem the dissenters, oppositional thinkers, and rebels of the past.[25] This had occurred, for example, in South Africa, where no present-day public figure would dare hazard a defense of apartheid and where antiapartheid activists are rightly hailed as national heroes.[26] The critical difference between South Africa and Guatemala, of course, was that apartheid rule was terminated and discredited, while in Guatemala those trying to force open their society had lost, and badly, making their postconflict journey toward historical redemption steeply uphill. In amassing documentary proof of the terror state's atrocities, ex-militants at the Project hoped not only to see justice done but also to "give value to people's struggle," to prove that their fight against dictatorship and social exclusion had been commendable, not criminal.[27]

But could the National Police archives really shoulder such a weighty burden of proof? The history of the war would and should never be written from the police records alone, incomplete, imperfect and bureaucratically turgid as they were.[28] Nor would the disputes over that history be settled by a few victories in court cases, however powerful those victories might be for survivors. (Cambodia's genocide tribunal, for example, was ten years and many millions of dollars in the making but secured just one criminal conviction; some argued that the resources would have been better spent elsewhere.) Moreover, the whole notion of "recovering historical memory" ran the risk of conflating history and memory, of collapsing history's gray areas and complexities into a narrative of morality and immorality, of simply reversing the military's official story without deconstructing its stark binaries.[29] (For example, what of the guerrillas' own killings and internal purges?) To put Ríos Montt behind bars for his war crimes—to "nail a dictator," as one U.S. documentary film cavalierly put it—would be a critical contribution to the country's future, a testament to the indefatigability of justice advocates, and a relief for many families. But not even Ríos Montt's conviction would salve the wounds of an internal armed conflict that was waged, at the rank-and-file level, by forcibly recruited soldiers, near-destitute police agents, and guerrilla cadres who resembled each other (in poverty, ethnicity, and educational attainment) far more than they would have suspected at the time, something Project workers and PNC agents discovered upon sharing space at the archives. Putting Ríos Montt in jail would not change the fact that victims and victimizers still lived cheek by jowl both in rural villages and in the city, and it would neither bring those groups closer together nor solve the problem of how they, in certain instances, blurred. Criminal justice mattered, but it would not address the socioeconomic divides that gave rise to the war in the first place, or resolve the incompatibility of different historical interpretations. This left hanging the question of what could be done with the archives and how much of an impact they could make.

"WHAT IS NO LONGER ARCHIVED IN THE SAME WAY
IS NO LONGER LIVED IN THE SAME WAY"

As we have seen, archival access became a central focus of the struggles accompanying Guatemala's "transition to democracy." Derrida reminds us that "there is no political power without control of the archive," and Guatemala's counterinsurgent state grasped this reality, with assistance from the United States, as early as the 1950s.[30] The state was thereafter strongly resistant to any form of archival opening, and it abetted an official culture that held documents to be garbage, memory and victimhood to be sicknesses, and postwar reconciliation to be a fait accompli.[31] But as war survivors and victims' families began to demand answers about the dead and disappeared, they came to comprehend the power of archives—and to assert their right to consult state records. The ensuing archival tug-of-war between civil society organizations and the state would last more than twenty-five years, comprising a variety of individual conflicts that I have dubbed "archive wars." Tracing the archive wars through their thorny evolution, in which advocates of access faced seemingly insurmountable barriers and sharp technical learning curves, demonstrates the slow, difficult, and often excruciating nature of postconflict political change. No governmental accord affirming citizens' right to information, in the context of a deeply authoritarian tradition of rule and a largely disenfranchised population, could dismantle old structures or erase old habits; instead, real transition required blood, sweat, and tears, as it always does, and in the Guatemalan case, the herculean effort devoted to archival opening was contributed by a small human rights community that had already made more than its fair share of sacrifices for the sake of social democracy. Over the course of the archive wars, citizens' fight for archival access became a key means of making claims upon the postwar state, especially once making arguments overtly about capitalism and class became a death sentence. The concept of "archives" became bound up in a whole host of demands—for justice, for truth, and for a new kind of relationship between state and society.[32] In coming to frame their objectives in terms of archival access, these activists made a strategic decision—to focus on old papers commonly considered trash, a seemingly innocuous crusade, as a way of forcing the military to relinquish some measure of power vis-à-vis the civilian government. They took the abstract concepts of justice and power and made them concrete, physical, material: papers, documents, files. In so doing, they established that to commit violence against documents was also to commit violence against people, and against their rights.

It was only with the work of the Project for the Recovery of the National Police Historical Archive that the wars of position over archives became not simply a way of articulating calls for redress and reparations but also a vision for a new kind of postconflict politics. Not content to simply sift through the ghosts of the past, the Project deliberately moved to change Guatemalan archival culture at its core. By working toward the passage of a national ar-

FIG. 9.2 The Project collaborated with the Forensic Anthropology Foundation of Guatemala in the first-ever exhumations of mass graves from La Verbena, the main cemetery in Guatemala City. Investigators hoped that by triangulating DNA evidence with the National Police archives' extensive documentation on cadavers buried as "XX" or "unidentified," they would be able to establish the identities of deceased individuals previously considered to be disappeared. Photograph by James Rodríguez, mimundo.org. Used by permission of the photographer.

chives system law, building new diploma programs in archival science and human rights at the national university, sharing its expertise with arms of government seeking to preserve their own records, and collaborating with other NGOs on standing legal cases and efforts to identify war dead, the Project was arguing for archives to occupy a new and different role in national culture—and, hence, pushing to establish a different and more equitable relationship between the government and its citizens. By changing the way Guatemala archived, the Project sought to change the way Guatemalans lived.[33]

In a strange and still hypothetical sense, the Project's greatest accomplishment would be, in the future, its own banalization—to arrive at a point at which the archives' most common use would be not for hot-button prosecutions but for quiet consultation by scholars, genealogists, and curious members of the public. In short, the records would become normalized like any other archival repository, once justice was done. Many of the histories written from these archives would still look at the civil war because of its obvious historical import, but many others would not. They would include examinations of crime and punishment in the capital city, or social histories of urban life in, say, the Ubíco or Barrios years. They would involve reading along and against the archival grain to recover the voices of rural migrants driven to seek urban employment, rank-and-file police agents, squatters, sex workers, civil society activists, or municipal workers; they would analyze the categories of information recorded by the PN in order to shed light on changing societal attitudes regarding race and ethnicity (for example, the early twentieth-century use of *sin calzado*, "shoeless," as a way to denote indigeneity). They would illuminate the relationship between the police and other institutions, including the military, over the *longue durée*. Such histories not only would focus on what police agents did but also would seek to understand why they did it, and what it meant. Their production will take time.

It was true that the declassification of military records, or the release of information from the police archives, would not feed the country's hungry or educate the country's children, absent any governmental will to integrate the new knowledge afforded by the archives into its school curricula. Neither could these victories expunge so-called parallel powers from government or stanch narcotrafficking violence. Ultimately, the Project's archival triumphs served, above all, to highlight how much work remained to be done, how shallow the country's transition had been. More than fifteen years after the Peace Accords, Guatemala had a weak procedural form of political democracy; it did not enjoy anything approaching economic or social democracy. Existing in a state of what I have called post-peace, most Guatemalans struggled to eke out a living in the midst of appalling violence, impunity, and state institutions that were either totally ineffectual or deeply enmeshed in organized crime, calling to mind Tacitus's admonition that a bad peace is worse than war. And the new avenues opened by the Project were not uncomplicated ones. Dependent upon international funding and political capital, as were other transitional justice initiatives in Guatemala, the Project labored to meet its donors' and allies' expectations while always anxious that those donors' attentions would turn elsewhere.

Despite these pressures, the Project succeeded at placing archives at the center of national conversation for the first time. This conversation was necessarily urban and elite and largely *ladino*, mainly limited to literate Spanish speakers who were, for the most part, both educated and already keyed into the human rights sphere. However, the Project symbolized something larger than itself: reconstitution and reconstruction, or else constitution and construction. The efforts to gain ground on the archival battlefield ultimately tell the story of a battered progressive sector attempting not only to breathe life into past struggles but also to build something new in the face of great obstacles; among their innovations was a freely accessible digital archive of nearly twenty million National Police records, preserved and protected forever, along with an unprecedented new set of human relationships spanning generations, old battle lines, and the slippery space between war and not-war.[34] The activists leading this charge had lost the revolution; they had lost family and friends, their youth, their dreams. They knew that the police archives' greatest impact might come not from the actual *content* of the files but, rather, from the unprecedented convergence and energy of the nearly two hundred Guatemalans trained in archival methods and committed to history's ongoing political relevance, and from the new thinkability of similarly ambitious initiatives. "For the purpose of building a different mentality, for the people who still think that this country can move toward a place of social solidarity and deep change, the archive can bring us a lot," said Gregorio, a Project worker and PGT veteran. "The archives can be very beneficial—so that we don't forget. Let's try to build a different society, without forgetting what came before. It's a possibility—because what other spaces do we have?"[35]

The instructive lesson of this tale, from the archives' accidental discovery through the Project's split with the PDH and beyond, was not that the postwar period saw Guatemala become the kind of society others might aspire to emulate. It was, instead, a parable that spoke to the difficulties of carving out oppositional political spaces in a country deeply divided along economic, social, and ethnic fault lines. Because the AGCA was kept desperately underfunded and understaffed, it enjoyed neither the political clout nor the financial means to carry out its mandate to care for the police archives when they first came to light. Instead, the task of recovering the PN documents was supported, like so many other essentials, by foreign dollars, propelled transnationally by their own logics of neoliberal state formation and polyarchy promotion. The national archives system's deficiencies were mirrored in most other arms of the state tasked with protecting citizens' rights: agencies charged with providing food, health care, sustainable development, safety, or justice operated, more often than not, in name only. And this was no accident. With taxation rates the lowest in the hemisphere after Haiti—and with a small elite deeply invested in maintaining a weak state from which it could derive the greatest gain—Guatemalans were left with a government that could barely fulfill its basic functions. No single archives project could change this reality. In a corrupt narco-state long structured by, of, and for a tiny oligarchy, even the hardest-won liberalizing efforts made but small dents in a larger system of power and exclusion. The Project's circumstances spoke all too eloquently to the adaptability and strength of that larger system.

As such, the Project revealed, over the course of its struggle to survive, both the possibilities and the limitations of archival thinking. The ferocity of the efforts to derail the Project and its sister initiatives spoke to the persistence of a counterinsurgent mentality in the halls of power, and no amount of international support, archival norms, or technocratic knowledge production could break this dynamic overnight—just as no amount of auditing, reparations, or symbolic apologies could heal a society so pervasively scarred. As in other Latin American post–Dirty War contexts, the military was willing to permit "truth," up to a point, but for the most part intervened to forestall efforts at formal legal justice.[36] The low-ranking agents who carried out the forced disappearance of Edgar Fernando García could be sacrificed to mollify what right-wing columnist Raúl Minondo Ayau derisively called "la suciedad civil," but the president who presided over that disappearance would live out his days peacefully in his home.[37]

Knowing all too intimately what they were up against, and that the historical wounds they were investigating could never be healed, the coordinators and workers of the Project took a page from the CEH in their approach to the PN archives. When Guatemala's truth commission was convened in the mid-1990s, it was evident to the jurists leading it that the country had been too damaged for any simple accounting of deeds done to produce reconciliation. Aware of the implausibility of legal justice or achieving consensus on what had happened during the war, the CEH attempted neither, opting instead for a novel strategy among Latin American truth commissions: providing a deep historical analysis, stretching back five hundred years, of the structural causes of civil war violence.[38] In a country without other avenues for redress, telling and substantiating this history was critically important, and the CEH's exegesis of Guatemala's unequal, racist socioeconomic structures galvanized survivors and victims' families. The Project, then, in many ways carried the spirit of the CEH to a new level: by fighting for and demanding access to archives and history writing, its activists believed, they were resisting ahistorical discourses of "reconciliation" by carving out their own narratives, page by rescued page. They sought to use history as a moral language.

In doing so, the Project's amateur archivists and historians had a new tool at their disposal, one the CEH had never enjoyed: terror archives, or evidence reflecting perpetrators' perspectives. The National Police records certainly did not contain all the answers that survivors sought; neither could any archives. Nonetheless, the Project represented a formerly unimaginable victory, in which the survivors of state repression now wielded some measure of their repressors' archival power. Archival thinking was historical thinking, and historical thinking was Guatemalans' best hope for creating new mentalities and political spaces—especially because the type of victory the Project embodied was the sort that would beget others, by having incrementally changed the laws of what could be said and done. "Without the police archives, it would have been unthinkable, the idea that we could have access to the military archives!" exulted one young Project *compañero*, and indeed, it was true.[39] Many histories of the armed conflict remain to be written, and many more obstacles to their writing will present themselves. The personal and political losses suffered over the course of activists' attempts to take ownership of their histories, whether by gun or by pen, were staggering. But as a Guatemalan colleague once quipped, riffing off Ríos Montt's scorched-earth strategy of *quitar el agua al pez* (taking the water from the fish), the true goal of the counterinsurgency had been to *quitar al pez la cabeza*, to decapitate Guatemalans' future capacity for critical, oppositional thinking. And the Project's labor and spirit proved that the army had failed at this goal, calling to mind Hannah Arendt's observation that while a state's repression aims to consign memory to "holes of oblivion," its efforts to make its opponents "disappear in silent anonymity" are necessarily doomed to failure.[40] The road ahead would be arduous, but there were still Guatemalans willing to walk it. "What we cannot expect, because nowhere in the world and in no society has it ever taken place, is for social victories to be handed out for free," reflected Maria Elena, who was among those who referred to her work at the archives as *un regalo de vida* (the gift of a lifetime). "Social victories are the fruit of the people's struggle, always. Nothing is easy, and it all represents a lot of work, no?"[41]

ARIADNE'S THREAD

In recent years, humanities scholars have taken an "archival turn" best characterized by, as Ann Stoler puts it, the "move from archive-as-source to archive-as-subject."[42] Putting the archive itself under the magnifying glass, as I have done in this book, refracts one line of inquiry into a series of rays, or beams, that extend in different directions—forward and backward in time, through stacked layers of analysis, looking not only at "what history is" but also at "how history works," examining how societies think through, record, substantiate, engage with, and create the past.[43] But while we have long known that writing history is hardly the unique preserve of professional historians, we now see that archival thinking, too, derives its vitality from outside the ivory tower. Indeed, its keenest innovators have been the amateur historians and amateur archivists for whom access to documentation can be, quite literally, a matter of life and death.

This is reflected most clearly at the police archives, which remain at the base where human rights activists first encountered them in 2005. This book's early chapters chronicled the dire conditions of the archival depot upon its rediscovery. But by 2011 the site was transformed, most powerfully by the repurposing of the pitted, barbed wire–topped concrete perimeter walls into canvases for dozens of brightly painted murals. The murals, designed and rendered by representatives of human rights organizations, championed the values of truth and memory and quoted progressives' best-loved poets, among them Otto René Castillo and Humberto Ak'abal. But two murals in particular spoke eloquently to how the Project has inextricably linked the subject of archives to the concept of justice in Guatemala. The first, bearing the words "From Silence to Hope," depicted a sun rising over a verdant highland village, with several shadowed graves set back from an otherwise bucolic pastoral scene of a church, homestead, and field of crops and flowers. Above the scene flew a dove composed, in lieu of feathers, of pages from the archives; from its tail, additional pages fluttered down to blanket the graves. The second featured a Lady Justice figure, blindfolded and holding the traditional balance scale in her left hand, wading through a sea of scattered documents framed by archival storage boxes, from which a bright green shoot sprouted skyward. In her right hand, in place of her customary sword, Justitia held a bundle, or *legajo*, of police documents.

Archives and graves; archives as weapons and tools; archives as prisons and temples; archives in opposition to silence; archives, peace, and justice. Archives were perhaps a curious and inadequate repository for such lofty hopes and aspirations, but Guatemalan history, the archive wars, and the Project had made it thus, in a country so unsparing and pained that the poet Castillo once called it "God's tomb."[44] As Howard Zinn writes, "To refuse to be instruments of social control in an essentially undemocratic society, to begin to play some small part in the creation of a real democracy: these are worthy jobs for historians, for archivists, for us all."[45] If the path out of Guatemala's "eternal tyranny" was labyrinthine, then historical knowledge and the archives might serve as an Ariadne's thread, guiding a way forward that would necessarily be marked by trials and errors.[46] In any event, the hard work would still fall, as it always does, to the idealists: those who worked to recover the past not for its own sake but as a way to imagine more felicitous—even beautiful—possibilities for the future. This was more than sufficient motivation for Guatemalan activists to learn international archival standards, to dig through history for signposts and lessons, to plumb the depths of rotting archives—and to endure

FIG. 9.3 A mural at the Project depicts a dove with feathers made of pages from the archives, shedding documents down to the earth in order to blanket rural graves. Photograph by James Rodríguez, mimundo.org. Used by permission of the photographer.

FIG. 9.4 A mural at the Project depicts Lady Justice wading through a sea of archival documents with a file folder in her hand in lieu of the traditional sword. Photograph by James Rodríguez, mimundo.org. Used by permission of the photographer.

the profoundly unsettling, dangerous, ambivalent, and human experience of reckoning with paper cadavers.

This is why history and archives matter. To exhume a paper cadaver or rescue a document is to stave off oblivion, to look backward, to prevent stories and lives and traumas from being forgotten, and to accord dignity to the dead, disappeared, and displaced. But while to delve deeply into dark pasts is an act of remembering, it is also a constructive act, one of imagination. The activists seeking to save the Guatemalan historical record from itself did so, and continue to do so, with regret and sadness—but also with inspiration. They had nightmares about the violence of the war and the postwar period, but they had dreams, too. Raúl, the former trade unionist turned amateur archivist at the Project, had quite literally dreamed of entering the fearsome National Police archives decades before it ever came to pass. And he and other workers at the Project, despite everything they had lived, still envisaged a better Guatemala—one in which they might, at the very least, be the last and final generation charged with exhuming the massive archives of the dead. "Justice should mean that if someone commits an error they should be brought to justice, whether today or tomorrow," Raúl reflected. "We have to keep insisting, and bit by bit, perhaps, we will advance."[47]

NOTES

ACKNOWLEDGMENTS

1. Saramago, *All the Names*, 4–5.

INTRODUCTION

1. The National Police (PN) was disbanded under the Peace Accords and replaced with the National Civil Police (PNC).

2. Interview, PRAHPN024, 5 December 2007.

3. The archives contain an estimated seventy-five to eighty million pages. See Procuraduría de los Derechos Humanos (PDH), "Informe Archivo Histórico de la Policía Nacional—por el derecho a la verdad" (2 March 2006).

4. Comisión para el Esclarecimiento Histórico (CEH), *Guatemala: Memoria del silencio*.

5. "Discurso del Profesor Julio Alberto Martí," in Ministerio de Gobernación, *Boletín del Archivo General de la Nación* (1967).

6. As of this writing, the cases of Julian Assange and Chelsea Manning are paramount in the public eye, but there have been others, and there will be many more.

7. Thompson, *The Poverty of Theory*, 11.

8. Trouillot, *Silencing the Past*, 150.

9. On the war, see Proyecto Interdiocesano de Recuperación de la Memoria Histórica (REMHI), *Guatemala: Nunca Más!*; Rosada Granados, *Soldados en el poder*; McAllister, *The Good Road*; Simon, *Eternal Spring, Eternal Tyranny*; Falla, *Masacres en la selva* and *Quiché Rebelde*; Jonas, *The Battle for Guatemala*; Flores, *Los compañeros*; Ramírez, *La guerra de los 36 años*; Schirmer, *The Guatemalan Military Project*; Grandin, *The Last Colonial Massacre*; Payeras, *Los días de la selva*; Manz, *Refugees of a Hidden War*; Bastos and Camus, *Sombras de una batalla*; Moller and Menchú Tum, *Our Culture Is Our Resistance*; Filóchofo, *La otra historia*; Gallardo Flores, *La utopia de la rosa*; Centro de Investigación y Documentación Centroamericana (CIDC), *Violencia y contraviolencia*; Sánchez del Valle, ed., *Por el delito de pensar*; Sichar Moreno, *Guatemala*; García, *El genocidio de Guatemala*.

10. Tomuschat, "Clarification Commission in Guatemala," 233–58. Investigators for the CEH were allowed into the Center for Military Studies to hand-transcribe four key military action plans; no access was provided to PN documents.

11. Alberti, "Archives of Pain."

12. Jelin, *State Repression*, 27.

13. For example, the 1968 poster "Red Wall" displayed the photographs of fifteen accused guerrillas along with these words: "People of Guatemala! Here are your *vendepatria* [sellout] enemies, Communists from the PGT and the FAR, who with their crimes

daily bring mourning to the hearths of the Homeland. Know them and denounce them wherever they are found!" CEH, *Guatemala: Memoria del silencio*, vol. 1, appendix 18, 285.

14. In his "Theses on the Philosophy of History," Benjamin writes, "The tradition of the oppressed teaches us that the 'emergency situation' in which we live is the rule. We must arrive at a concept of history which corresponds to this. Then it will become clear that the task before us is the introduction of a real state of emergency; and our position in the struggle against Fascism will thereby improve." In Benjamin, *Illuminations*, 253–64.

15. See Centro Internacional de Investigaciones en Derechos Humanos (CIIDH), *Situación de los derechos económicos, sociales, y culturales en Guatemala, 2006*; Impunity Watch, *Recognising the Past*; Programa de Seguridad Ciudadana y Prevención de la Violencia, *Informe estadístico de la violencia en Guatemala*.

16. International Crisis Group, "Learning to Walk without a Crutch."

17. Nelson, *A Finger in the Wound*; Sánchez del Valle, ed., *Por el delito de pensar*; Amnesty International, *Persecution and Resistance*; United Nations Office of the High Commission for Human Rights, "Report of the High Commissioner for Human Rights on the Situation of Human Rights in Guatemala," 1–21; Coalición para la Comisión de Investigación de Cuerpos Ilegales y Aparatos Clandestinos y de Seguridad, "El rostro del terror"; Goldman, *The Art of Political Murder*; Oglesby, "Educating Citizens in Postwar Guatemala."

18. The United Nations' International Commission against Impunity in Guatemala (CICIG) has taken up this question, but the intractability of corruption and "parallel powers" has made its progress slower than hoped. Carlos Castresana, the CICIG's first director, admitted the occasional temptation to throw in the towel. "For these kinds of missions," he told reporters, "you just have to come without a towel." Coralia Orantes, "Critica falta de atención a propuesta," *Prensa Libre* (19 February 2010). Also see Peacock and Beltrán, *Poderes ocultos*; United Nations Development Program, *El costo económico*.

19. McCleary, *Dictating Democracy*.

20. CIIDH, *Situación de los Derechos, 2006*; State Department, Bureau of Democracy, Human Rights, and Labor, *2008 Country Reports on Human Rights Practices: Guatemala*.

21. In speaking of two distinct historical "moments" or periods, I do not mean to draw an artificial boundary between them or suggest that the archives' uses were static in those moments. Rather, I use the continuity and change in the conditions of the archives as an analytical entry point to studying continuity and change in the broader Guatemalan context. As E. P. Thompson writes, "In investigating history we are not flicking through a series of 'stills,' each of which shows us a moment of social time transfixed into a single eternal pose: for each one of these 'stills' is not only a moment of being but also a moment of becoming: and even within each seemingly-static section there will be found contradictions and liaisons, dominant and subordinate elements, declining or ascending energies. Any historical moment is both a result of prior process and an index toward the direction of its future flow." Thompson, *The Poverty of Theory*, 64.

22. Trouillot calls these two meanings "historicity 1" and "historicity 2." Trouillot, *Silencing the Past*, 29.

23. See www.avemilgua.org.

24. Fujino, ed., *Winds of Resistance*.

25. These observations come from my visit to the festival in 2007.

26. McCreery, *Rural Guatemala 1760–1940*; McCreery, "Wage Labor, Free Labor"; Handy, *Gift of the Devil*; Casaús Arzú, *Guatemala*; Smith, ed., *Guatemalan Indians and the State*; Grandin, *The Blood of Guatemala*; Lovell, *A Beauty That Hurts*; Martínez Peláez, *La patria del criollo*; Arenas Bianchi, Hale, and Palma Murga, eds., *Racismo en Guatemala?*

27. On the 1944 Revolution and the Revolutionary Spring, see Galich, *Del panico al ataque*; Flores, *Fortuny*; Handy, *Revolution in the Countryside*; Grandin, *The Last Colonial Massacre*; Cardoza y Aragón, *La revolución guatemalteca*; García Laguardia, *La revolución*.

28. On the coup, see Cullather, *Secret History*; Gleijeses, *Shattered Hope*; Immerman, *The CIA in Guatemala*; Kinzer and Schlesinger, *Bitter Fruit*.

29. Sabino, *Guatemala*; CEH, "Orígenes del enfrentamiento armado, 1962–1970," in *Guatemala: Memoria del silencio*, vol. 1, 123–146; Rosada Granados, *Soldados en el poder*; Ramírez, *La guerra de los 36 años*; Sandoval, *Los días de la resistencia*; Maldonado, "Marzo y abril de 1962"; Toriello Garrido, *Guatemala*.

30. Many of the insurgency's surviving leaders wrote memoirs about the war and the ideological divides within the revolutionary movements. See Payeras, *Los días de la selva* and *Los fusiles de octubre*; Morán (Ramírez de León), *Saludos revolucionarios*; Macías, *La guerrilla fue mi camino*; Colom, *Mujeres en la alborada*.

31. URNG, *Línea política de los revolucionarios guatemaltecos*.

32. Kobrak, *Organizing and Repression*; Aguilera Peralta and Romero Imery, *Dialéctica del terror*; Levenson-Estrada, *Trade Unionists*; Asociación de Investigación y Estudios Sociales en Guatemala (ASIES), *Más de cien años*, vol. 2; Figueroa Ibarra, *El recurso del miedo*; McClintock, *The American Connection*.

33. CEH, *Guatemala: Memoria del silencio*; REMHI, *Guatemala: Nunca Más!*; Figueroa Ibarra, *Los que siempre estarán en ninguna parte*.

34. Hernández Pico, *Terminar la guerra*; Sáenz de Tejada, *Revolucionarios*; Armon et al., *Guatemala 1983–1997*; Rosada Granados, *El lado oculto*; Aguilera Peralta, *Las propuestas para la paz*; Jonas, *Of Centaurs and Doves*; Stanley and Holiday, "Broad Participation, Diffuse Responsibility"; Sieder et al., *Who Governs*; Schirmer, "The Guatemalan Politico-Military Project."

35. On the solidarity movement, see Smith, *Resisting Reagan*; Erickson Nepstad, *Convictions of the Soul*; Gosse, "Active Engagement"; Perla, "Si Nicaragua Venció."

36. Despite anthropologist David Stoll's efforts to undermine the narrative that Rigoberta Menchú Tum recounted to Elisabeth Burgos-Debray and published as *Me llamo Rigoberta Menchú y así me nació la conciencia*, Menchú's account remains the most influential account of the war. Her book was used as an advocacy tool to draw attention to the Guatemalan state's mass killings of Mayas; Menchú was awarded the Nobel Peace Prize in 1992. See Arias, ed., *The Rigoberta Menchú Controversy*; Stoll, *Rigoberta Menchú and the Story of All Poor Guatemalans*.

37. As Greg Grandin asks, "Does labeling the massacres *genocide* overshadow the fact that the state was being challenged by a powerful, multiethnic coalition demanding economic and political reform? Does the charge of genocide eclipse the destruction and violence inflicted on *ladinos* (Guatemalans not considered indigenous), who until 1981 constituted the majority of the victims of state repression? Likewise, does it overstate the racial dimensions of the insurgency while downplaying its class component? Does it deny indigenous participation in the popular movement and reduce the repression to a

simplified tale of *ladino* violence heaped on defenseless Indians?" Grandin, "Chronicles," 399. For more on the "genocide" label's complexities, see Garrard-Burnett, *Terror in the Land of the Holy Spirit*, 13–18.

38. For an incisive exegesis of these politics, see McAllister, "Good People."

39. These scholars include (but are not limited to) McAllister, Konefal, Oglesby, Garrard-Burnett, Manz, Falla, Schirmer, Nelson, Grandin, and Vela Castañeda, as well as the many Guatemalans at research organizations like AVANCSO (Asociación para el Avance de las Ciencias Sociales de Guatemala), ICCPG (Instituto de Estudios Comparados en Ciencias Penales de Guatemala) and FLACSO (Facultad Latinoamericana de Ciencias Sociales de Guatemala).

40. Notable exceptions are Kobrak, *Organizing and Repression*; Levenson-Estrada, *Trade Unionists*; and McClintock, *The American Connection*.

41. On the Pan-Maya movement, its advances, and the "neoliberal multiculturalism" that has been its unexpected result, see Hale, *Más Que Un Indio*; Warren, *Indigenous Movements*; Fischer and Brown, eds., *Maya Cultural Activism*; Bastos and Camus, *El movimiento maya*; Cojtí Cuxil, *El movimiento maya*.

42. See, for example, Payeras, *El trueno en la ciudad*.

43. Kobrak, *Organizing and Repression*, 68–69.

44. I borrow this formulation from Derrida, who writes in *Archive Fever* that "what is no longer archived in the same way is no longer lived in the same way."

45. The phrase "archival thinking" finds use mainly by professional archivists as a way of describing current trends in their field, such as in the journal *Currents of Archival Thinking*. Here, however, I borrow and adapt the phrase to analytical ends. The phrase also appears in Strobel's 1999 article "Becoming a Historian," as a way for Strobel to describe how crucial it is that activists keep records of their work. Archival thinking is not developed conceptually in her piece; her point that activists must self-archive is taken up by Bickford in "The Archival Imperative."

46. See, for example, Stoler, "Colonial Archives"; Trouillot, *Silencing the Past*; Ketelaar, "Muniments and Monuments"; Ketelaar, "Tacit Narratives"; Bickford, "The Archival Imperative"; Huskamp Peterson, "The Role of Archives in Strengthening Democracy"; Fredriksson, "Postmodernistic Archival Science."

47. See the essays in the special issues of *Archival Science* devoted to the theme "Archives, Records, and Power," including Cook and Schwartz, "Archives, Records, and Power"; Trace, "What Is Recorded Is Never Simply 'What Happened'"; Hedstrom, "Archives, Memory, and Interfaces with the Past"; Ketelaar, "Archival Temples, Archival Prisons"; and O'Toole, "Cortes's Notary."

48. Huskamp Peterson, "The Nasty Truth about Nationalism"; also see Lowenthal, *The Heritage Crusade*; O'Toole, "Between Veneration and Loathing"; Cook, "What Is Past Is Prologue"; Duchein, "The History of European Archives"; Lowenthal, *The Past Is a Foreign Country*; Brown and Davis-Brown, "The Making of Memory."

49. See Nelson, *Reckoning*, 27; Strathern, *Audit Cultures*; Power, *The Audit Society*; Hetherington, *Guerrilla Auditors*.

50. On the Guatemalan case, see chapter 4; also see Huggins, *Political Policing*; and Kuzmarov, *Modernizing Repression*.

51. Stoler, *Along the Archival Grain*, 33.

52. See Stoler, *Along the Archival Grain*; McCoy, *Policing America's Empire*; Richards, *The Imperial Archive*; and Burton, *Dwelling in the Archive*.

53. Derrida, *Archive Fever*, 4. Derrida's work has proved a stimulating and controversial departure point for archival thinkers. See Steedman, *Dust*, 77; Ferreira-Buckley, "Rescuing the Archives"; Shetty and Bellamy, "Postcolonialism's Archive Fever"; Van Zyl, "Psychoanalysis and the Archive"; Harris, "A Shaft of Darkness"; in a truth commission context, Harris, "The Archive, Public History, and the Essential Truth"; and Manoff, "Theories of the Archive."

54. Mario Castañeda, "De memoria y justicia," *Plaza Pública* (19 June 2011).

55. On *escrache* protests in Argentina, see Taylor, "You Are Here."

56. On the Diario Militar, see Doyle, "Death Squad Diary."

57. Bickford, "The Archival Imperative," 1097.

58. See Huskamp Peterson, "The Nasty Truth about Nationalism," 5; Stephen Kinzer, "East Germans Face Their Accusers," *New York Times* (12 April 1992); and McAdams, *Judging the Past*; also, for a more *longue durée* perspective, see part V of Blouin and Rosenberg, eds., *Archives, Documentation, and Institutions*, 379–496.

59. See Huskamp Peterson, "Privacy Is Not a Rose."

60. Martín Almada, "The Man Who Discovered the Archives of Terror," *The* UNESCO *Courier* 9 (2009); Mike Ceasar, "Paraguay's Archives of Terror," BBC News (11 March 2002).

61. UNESCO, "Memory of the World Programme," www.unesco.org/webworld/en /mow.

62. "Tendremos Archivo de la Memoria," *La República*, Uruguay (12 November 2008).

63. The online service, "Memorias Reveladas," is maintained by Brazil's Arquivo Nacional.

64. Osorio, "Argentina."

65. "Inauguración museo de la memoria en Chile," *Los Andes* (8 January 2010).

66. Aguilar, "Transitional or Post-transitional Justice"; José Andrés Rojo, "Conflict That Never Ends: Civil War Oral Testimony on Trial," *El País* (4 August 2008).

67. Iraq Memory Foundation Documentation Project, www.iraqmemory.org/EN /Projects_Documentation.asp; on the U.S. military's seizure of Iraqi records, see Huskamp Peterson, "Archives in Service to the State."

68. The work of the National Security Archive merits particular recognition (discussed in Blanton, "Recovering the Memory"), as does that of Germany's federal commissioner for the Stasi archives, which has worked with former Soviet bloc countries on the handling of their secret service records.

69. Borzou Daragahi, "In Tunisia, Where Record Keeping Is Good, Some Seek to Preserve Documents of Tyranny," *Los Angeles Times* (16 April 2011).

70. Interview, Estuardo Galeano, 6 February 2008.

71. Ketelaar, "Archival Temples, Archival Prisons"; Ketelaar, "Recordkeeping and Societal Power."

72. Benjamin, *Illuminations*.

73. For meditations on this, see Steedman, *Dust*; Felman, *The Juridical Unconscious*.

74. On "archival truth claims," see Stoler, "Colonial Archives"; see also Huskamp Peterson, "The Probative Value."

75. Jelin, *State Repression*.

76. Years later, now that the digitized documents are accessible online thanks to the Project's partnership with UT Austin, more traditional historical studies can be conducted using the PN records.

77. Interview, PRAHPN010, 16 October 2007.

78. Interview, PRAHPN007, 10 October 2007.

ONE. EXCAVATING BABYLON

1. Interview, PRAHPN005, 8 October 2007.

2. Interview, Alberto Fuentes, 21 February 2008.

3. For the denial of the archives as a matter of state policy, see the more than one hundred pages' worth of correspondence between the truth commissioners and Arzú government functionaries appended to the CEH report, *Guatemala: Memoria del silencio*, vol. 12, annex 3, 31–196; also see Tomuschat, "Clarification Commission in Guatemala."

4. Trouillot, *Silencing the Past*, 20–23.

5. On archival description as the control of information and the construction of meaning, see Duff and Harris, "Stories and Names."

6. Ketelaar writes, "Here we see an essential connection between archives and human rights: the violation of those rights has been documented in the archives, and citizens who defend themselves appeal to the archives. The archives have a twofold power: being evidence of oppression and containing evidence required to gain freedom, evidence of wrongdoing and evidence for undoing the wrong." Ketelaar, "The Panoptical Archive," 146.

7. Guha, "The Prose of Counter-insurgency."

8. Trouillot, *Silencing the Past*, 28.

9. Nancy Arroyave, "Vuelve la calma tras explosión en brigada Mariscal Zavala," *Prensa Libre* (18 June 2005).

10. Interview, Edeliberto Cifuentes, 10 November 2007.

11. Grandin writes that "Latin America's move away from military dictatorships in the 1980s was less a transition than it was a conversion to a particular definition of democracy . . . by abandoning social-democratic principles of development and welfare, opening up their economies to the world market, and narrowing their conception of democracy to focus more precisely on political and legal rights rather than on social ones." Grandin, "The Instruction of Great Catastrophe."

12. Morales would fall from progressives' good graces as he maneuvered to secure his 2007 reelection.

13. Corte Interamericana de Derechos Humanos, *Molina Thiessen v. Guatemala*.

14. Interview, Sergio Morales, 12 February 2008.

15. See Amnesty International, "Persecution and Resistance." The NGO National Movement for Human Rights reported almost two hundred attacks against human rights defenders in 2007. See Human Rights First, "Human Rights Defenders in Guatemala."

16. Cited in Doyle, "The Atrocity Files," 54.

17. Interview, Ana Corado, 23 January 2008.

18. Interview, Ana Corado.

19. Interview, Anna Carla Ericastilla, 29 November 2007.

20. The CEH did not enjoy subpoena powers, nor could it search any premises for records, nor could it order the seizure of evidence in the possession of state institutions. When the CEH requested documentation from the Arzú administration related to four "test cases" under investigation, it "failed to receive any substantial response to its request for information"—the CEH was informed that the president had transmitted the letter to the minister of defense, where it "got lost," and when the minister of defense finally retrieved it, he chose to transmit it to the interior minister, who sent it to the head of police, which yielded nothing. The armed forces pursued "a deliberate strategy of obstruction" regarding documentary disclosure; Tomuschat writes that President Arzú's failure to assist the CEH was a "black stain" upon his presidency. Tomuschat, "Clarification Commission in Guatemala," 246–51.

21. Interview, Alberto Fuentes.

22. Interview, Ingrid Molina, 11 November 2007. For *gente de confianza*, see chapter 6; interview, PRAHPN003, 1 October 2007.

23. Interview, Iduvina Hernández, 26 November 2007; interview, Mario Polanco, 20 February 2008. The EMP records will be discussed in detail in chapter 2.

24. Interview, PRAHPN028, 22 January 2008.

25. On "studied indifference" and why a society plagued by authoritarianism and impunity might find itself the victim of poor "archival culture," see chapter 2 and Ingrid Roldán Martínez, "Guardián de la memoria escrita," *Revista D (Prensa Libre)*, 20 January 2008.

26. Letter, Anna Carla Ericastilla to Julio Galicia Díaz, 24 August 2005; copy in author's files.

27. Only in 2009 was custody of the archives transferred from the PDH to the Ministry of Culture and the AGCA.

28. Interview, Frank La Rue, 7 February 2008.

29. Interview, Frank La Rue.

30. Interview, Carla Villagrán, 12 October 2007.

31. Interview, Anna Carla Ericastilla.

32. As Ericastilla told me, "The PDH has enough social capital to make the contacts with the necessary institutions around the world and to win the support and connections that they have so far. If this had been under the purview of the Ministry of Culture and thus the AGCA, we simply don't have the same kind of social capital, connections. I can't just show up at different institutions, places, or embassies like the PDH can. . . . We have to recognize this, the fact that the PDH's taking control of these archives has gotten a lot of attention, which has in turn sparked a lot of donations, which is very positive." Interview, Anna Carla Ericastilla.

33. Interview, Åsa Wallton, 28 November 2007.

34. Interview, Michael Moerth, 8 February 2008.

35. Interview, Christina Elich, 4 December 2007.

36. Interview, Christina Elich.

37. Confidential interview, 15 November 2007.

38. Bickford, "The Archival Imperative."

39. Interview, Åsa Wallton.

40. Interview, Agnes Bernzen, 12 February 2008.

41. Comisión Provincial por la Memoria, www.comisionporlamemoria.org.

42. UNESCO information officer Gloria Alberti distinguishes between "archives of terror," records produced by repressive state agencies, and "archives of pain," records produced by human rights groups gathering information about human rights violations. Alberti, "Archives of Pain."

43. The best English-language account of the challenges presented by the Stasi archives is McAdams, *Judging the Past*. Reconstructing the shredded files will be accelerated with the introduction of a specialized computer/scanner machine, known as the E-puzzler, that is currently in development in Berlin.

44. Stephen Kinzer, "East Germans Face Their Accusers," *New York Times* (12 April 1992).

45. Wolf Biermann's file, for example, held forty thousand pages; writer Jürgen Fuchs merited thirty binders' worth. Garton Ash expresses disappointment that his own file fit into a single binder, exhibiting the desire to have been a more "worthy" archival subject and thus a more influential dissident. Garton Ash, *The File*, 20–23.

46. González Quintana, "Archives of the Security Services."

47. Mike Ceaser, "Paraguay's Archive of Terror," *BBC News*, 11 March 2002.

48. Blanco-Rivera, "Transitional Justice," 5.

49. Archives, history, and impunity are closely linked; one Impunity Watch report identifies the three major obstacles to truth-seeking in Guatemala as (1) the lack of political acknowledgment or adequate dissemination of the CEH report, (2) minimal state support for exhumations and efforts to locate victims of forced disappearance, and (3) state reluctance to open archives bearing information about the armed conflict. Impunity Watch, *Recognising the Past*.

50. Louis Bickford writes that the English word "impunity" "does not capture the richness of meaning that the word *impunidad* confers in Spanish. In Spanish, this term encompasses more than simply exemption from punishment for evil deeds. It also implies systemic corruption, the fundamental absence of the rule of law (especially as it applies to those in positions of power), distorted norms of justice and fairness, and the constant sabotaging of democracy through the erosion of democratic institutions." Bickford, "The Archival Imperative."

51. Interview, Gustavo Meoño, 3 December 2007. Scattered details about Meoño's life appear in Konefal, *For Every Indio*; Saxon, *To Save Her Life*; Figueroa Ibarra, *Los que siempre estarán en ninguna parte*; Ludec, "Voces del exilio guatemalteco"; McAllister, "Good People."

52. Interview, Gustavo Meoño.

53. Interview, Gustavo Meoño.

54. Cited in Anne Marie O'Connor, "Payments and Apologies for Victims of Guatemala's Civil War," *Washington Post* (6 May 2009).

55. Interview, Carla Villagrán.

56. Interview, Carla Villagrán.

57. The account par excellence of this dynamic is Goldman's *Art of Political Murder*.

58. Interview, Carla Villagrán.

59. Coralia Orantes, "Juez denuncia intimidaciones: Ordenó traslado de archivos de Policía a la PDH," *Prensa Libre* (11 May 2006).

60. Juan García, "Tratan de quemar archivos policiales," *La Hora* (11 May 2006). By February 2008, there had been five suspicious fires at the archives site and two Molotov cocktail incidents. Leonardo Cereser, "Intentan quemar archivos de PN," *Prensa Libre* (9 February 2008).

61. Interview, PRAHPN006, 9 October 2007.

62. Interview, PRAHPN008, 11 October 2007.

63. For literary-minded discussions of "archivist's lung," see Steedman, *Dust*; also Lowenthal, "Archives, Heritage, and History."

64. Reuters, "Hole opens in Guatemala neighborhood, 3 missing," 23 February 2007.

65. Interview, PRAHPN010.

66. Interview, PRAHPN004, 3 October 2007.

67. Interview, PRAHPN004.

68. The experts were Jean-Marc Comment and Erwin Oberholzer, sent by Switzerland to advise the Project in digital preservation and archival fumigation.

69. On Spain's efforts to prosecute human rights abusers under the principle of universal jurisdiction, see Roht-Arriaza, *The Pinochet Effect*.

70. See Coralia Orantes, "Llega comisión española," *Prensa Libre* (25 June 2006).

71. Field notes, June 2006.

72. Interview, PRAHPN022, 29 November 2007.

73. Stoler, *Along the Archival Grain*, 20.

74. Hetherington discusses related dynamics in his *Guerrilla Auditors*.

TWO. ARCHIVAL CULTURE, STATE SECRETS, AND THE ARCHIVE WARS

1. "Urinate with contentment, urinate happily, but please, urinate neatly!"

2. Interview, Lizbeth Barrientos, 29 January 2008.

3. Field notes, 2008.

4. See chapter 1; interview, Alberto Fuentes; interview, Ana Corado.

5. Mario Cordero, "La situación de los archivos históricos en el país," *La Hora* (17 May 2008).

6. Stoler, "Colonial Archives and the Arts of Governance," 100.

7. Stoler, *Along the Archival Grain*; Riles, ed., *Documents*.

8. Cordero, "La situación de los archivos históricos."

9. Trouillot, *Silencing the Past*.

10. I thank Gustavo Palma for his turn of phrase about how "memory is a sickness" in official Guatemala; interview, 14 November 2007.

11. Constitution of Guatemala, 1985 with 1993 reforms. On the *secreto de estado* defense, see Delgado Duarte, *Aproximación al secreto de estado*; Garrido, ed., *Secreto de estado*; Gramajo Valdés, *El derecho de acceso*.

12. See Stoler on the state secret as state fetish: *Along the Archival Grain*, 26.

13. For "war of position" see Gramsci, *Selections from the Prison Notebooks*.

14. See, for example, Stern, *Peru's Indian Peoples*; Burns, *Into the Archive*; Rama, *La ciudad letrada*; González Echeverria, *Myth and Archive*; Sellers-García, "Distant Guatemala."

15. John Sullivan, "Guatemalan Held in Document Sale in New York," *New York Times* (28 June 1995). The stolen documents were eventually returned.

16. I do not include the archives held at CIRMA because they are not a state collection.

17. Ingrid Roldán Martínez, "Guardián de la memoria escrita," *Revista D, Prensa Libre* (28 January 2008).

18. Roldán Martínez, "Guardián de la memoria escrita."

19. The colonial *ayuntamiento* of Guatemala of course kept an archive, though it was less centralized than its modern iterations; many of its documents would later be housed in the AGCA. Sellers-García, "Distant Guatemala."

20. Chinchilla Aguilar, "La clasificación"; italics mine.

21. "Reconocen al archivo nacional su categoría centroamericana," *La Hora* (26 February 1968); "Directores de archivos subscribieron resolución," *Prensa Libre* (26 February 1968).

22. For more on the AGCA see Roldán Martínez, "Guardián de la memoria escrita."

23. "Discurso del Licenciado Héctor Mansilla Pinto, Ministro de Gobernación," in *Boletín del Archivo General de la Nación*, Segunda Epoca (1967).

24. Interview, Ingrid Molina.

25. Interview, Ingrid Molina.

26. Interview, Alberto Fuentes.

27. Interview, Anna Carla Ericastilla.

28. Barrientos, "Importancia de la conservación," 2.

29. Interview, Ingrid Molina.

30. See *Compendio de leyes sobre la protección del patrimonio cultural guatemalteco* (Guatemala City: UNESCO, 2006). For a probing analysis of the concept of patrimony, see Ferry, *Not Ours Alone.*

31. Ministerio de Cultura y Deportes, *Ley para la protección del patrimonio cultural de la nación*, 19. See also Ministerio de Cultura y Deportes, *Políticas culturales y deportivas nacionales.* For more on the techniques of cultural genocide deployed during the war, see Arriaza and Arias, "Claiming Collective Memory"; Schirmer, *The Guatemalan Military Project*; Nelson, *A Finger in the Wound*; Montejo, *Voices from Exile*; and the CEH and REMHI reports.

32. Interview, Anna Carla Ericastilla; Leonardo Cereser, "Historia del país se pierde entre miles de papeles," *Prensa Libre* (14 May 2009). The UNESCO Memoria del Mundo project is generating a central Guatemalan archival registry. Interview, Lizbeth Barrientos.

33. Gramajo Valdés, *El derecho de acceso*, 28.

34. Robinson, *Promoting Polyarchy.*

35. González Quintana, "Archives of the Security Services"; Huskamp Peterson, *Final Acts*; Huskamp Peterson, "The Nasty Truth about Nationalism."

36. Bickford, "The Archival Imperative"; Agamben, *State of Exception*; Gramajo Valdés, *El derecho de acceso*; Bobbio, *The Future of Democracy*; Weber, "Bureaucracy."

37. Bickford, "Human Rights Archives and Research on Historical Memory."

38. Interview, Mario Polanco.

39. Organizations with similar objectives, like CONAVIGUA (National Coordination of Widows of Guatemala), FAMDEGUA (Families of the Detained-Disappeared of Guatemala), and CERJ (Council for Ethnic Communities "We Are All Equal"), came into being slightly later, during the late 1980s and early 1990s.

40. Departamento de Información y Divulgación del Ejército, "El Ejército de Gua-

temala Remite al GAM ante la Opinión Pública," Guatemala City, 17 September 1986, CIRMA: Colección de Documentos, 2807.

41. Interview, Mario Polanco.

42. Archivo Histórico de la Policía Nacional, *Del silencio a la memoria*, 18.

43. "Denuncian propósitos para destruir archivos de Investigaciones Técnicas," *Prensa Libre* (1 March 1993).

44. "Denuncian propósitos para destruir archivos de Investigaciones Técnicas."

45. "Archivos del Gabinete de Identificación no serán destruidos, dice Guerra," *Siglo Veintiuno* (2 March 1993).

46. "Otorgan virtual amnistía a millares de delincuentes," *Prensa Libre* (1 July 1993).

47. See Guadamuz, "Habeas Data."

48. González Quintana, "Archives of the Security Services." It was Brazil that first incorporated habeas data into its constitution; Argentina, Brazil, Ecuador, Paraguay, and the Philippines followed suit. See Guadamuz, "Habeas Data."

49. Roht-Arriaza, *The Pinochet Effect*, 102. Of course, securing habeas data rights was more difficult in cases like that of the National Intelligence Directorate, or DINA, in Chile, in which security forces argued that they had destroyed their archives before the establishment of civilian government. See Rzeplinski, "Habeas Data."

50. Interview, Mario Polanco.

51. Cited in Higonnet, *Quiet Genocide*, 214.

52. Letter, Jean Arnault (MINUGUA) to Eduardo Stein Barillas, 12 December 1997; reprinted in CEH, *Guatemala: Memoria del silencio*, vol. 12, annex 3, 15.

53. Letter CT008-97/sp, Christian Tomuschat to Alvaro Arzú Irigoyen, 9 September 1997; reprinted in CEH, *Guatemala: Memoria del silencio*, vol. 12, annex 3, 37–45.

54. Letter No. 002-MDN-acom/98, Héctor Mario Barrios Celada to Christian Tomuschat, 5 January 1998; reprinted in CEH, *Guatemala: Memoria del silencio*, vol. 12, annex 3, 109–11.

55. Letter, Christian Tomuschat et al. to Alvaro Arzú Irigoyen, 19 February 1998; reprinted in CEH, *Guatemala: Memoria del silencio*, vol. 12, annex 3, 136–39.

56. Interview, Sergio Morales.

57. All Tomuschat citations from his "Clarification Commission in Guatemala."

58. Gobierno de la República de Guatemala, URNG, and Naciones Unidas, *Acuerdo Sobre el Fortalecimiento y Función del Ejército en una Sociedad Democrática*, 30–31. More on the passage of the access to information law is found in Gramajo Valdés's *El derecho de acceso*. On the spotty implementation of the Peace Accords by postwar governments, see Spence et al., eds., *Promise and Reality*; Sieder et al., *Who Governs?*; Montejo, "Convention 169"; Jonas, *Of Centaurs and Doves*; Sieder, *Guatemala after the Peace Accords*; and Stanley and Holiday, "Broad Participation, Diffuse Responsibility."

59. Personal communication, Trudy Huskamp Peterson.

60. Four organizations co-published the document: the National Security Archive, Human Rights Watch, the Washington Office on Latin America, and the American Association for the Advancement of Science. They obtained the document from unidentified individuals, who paid the smuggler two thousand dollars for it. See Doyle, "Death Squad Diary," 52–53, and Blanton, "Recovering the Memory," 61.

61. Pavel Arellano, "Sin golpes de Estado," *Prensa Libre* (20 July 1999); Olga López

Ovando, "Aumentan denuncias," *Prensa Libre* (20 June 1999); Pavel Arellano and Olga López, "Ejército rechaza el 'diario militar,'" *Prensa Libre* (26 May 1999).

62. Arellano and López, "Ejército rechaza el 'diario militar.'" Mejía Víctores made the same appeal to absent markers of archival provenance—military seals, signatures, and letterhead—to justify his rejection of the Diario's authenticity. Carlos Arrazola, "Entrevista con Oscar Humberto Mejía Víctores," *El Periódico* (21 May 1999).

63. "'Ni lo aceptamos, ni lo rechazamos,'" *Prensa Libre* (22 May 1999).

64. Ramón Hernández S., "'Yo no ordené matar a nadie,'" *Prensa Libre* (21 May 1999).

65. Marco Tulio Trejo, "Ejército reitera que no ha destruido documentos," *Siglo Veintiuno* (12 August 1999).

66. Ronaldo Robles, "Ejército no lo niega, solo lo pone en duda," *El Periódico* (22 May 1999).

67. "PDH actuará como querellante adhesivo," *Prensa Libre* (26 May 1999).

68. Ramón Hernández S., "Se abre gran polémica," *Prensa Libre* (21 May 1999); "Piden abrir expedientes secretos del Ejército," *El Periódico* (2 June 1999).

69. "Exigen esclarecer desapariciones," *El Periódico* (29 May 1999).

70. Interview, PRAHPNO23, 3 December 2007.

71. Marta Sandoval, "El diario militar y su relación con los archivos de la Policía," *El Periódico* (24 May 2009).

72. On dissolving the EMP, see Gutiérrez, *Hacia un paradigma democrático*; Garst, *Military Intelligence and Human Rights*; Hernández, "A Long Road."

73. See Goldman, *The Art of Political Murder*.

74. Interview, PRAHPNO15, 2 November 2007; interview, PRAHPNO23.

75. Interview, PRAHPNO15; interview, PRAHPNO23.

76. Interview, PRAHPNO12, 30 October 2007.

77. Interview, PRAHPNO23.

78. Interview, Estuardo Galeano.

79. Interview, Iduvina Hernández.

80. Interview, Iduvina Hernández.

81. Interview, Estuardo Galeano.

82. Interview, Iduvina Hernández.

83. Interview, Lizbeth Barrientos.

84. Interview, Iduvina Hernández.

85. Interview, Estuardo Galeano.

THREE. HOW THE *GUERRILLERO* BECAME AN ARCHIVIST

1. See AHPN, *El Archivo en cifras*.

2. Huskamp Peterson, "Records of the Policía Nacional de Guatemala." The *Provenienzprinzip*, or principle of provenance (PP), was first introduced by the Privy State Archive in Berlin, in 1881; for more, see Spieker, *The Big Archive*, 17–18.

3. See Douglas, *How Institutions Think*.

4. See Stoler, *Along the Archival Grain*, 25; and Douglas, *How Institutions Think*.

5. Interview, Lizbeth Barrientos.

6. Morán and Samayoa, "Evolución de las estructuras."

7. Interview, PRAHPN008.

8. Morán and Samayoa, "Evolución de las estructuras," 61.

9. War and crisis affect archival production and description; as Ketelaar notes, "Files created under unprecedented circumstances or in an extraordinary era—for example, during or after war, revolution, natural or man-made disasters, or political or economic crises—have to be appraised differently from those created in the course of 'normal' human business." Ketelaar, "The Panoptical Archive," 145.

10. Field notes, August 2006.

11. PRAHPN, "Informe de Avances—Diciembre 2006," 17.

12. Interview, PRAHPN022.

13. Field notes, May 2006.

14. Interview, PRAHPN022.

15. Doyle discusses this case in "The Atrocity Files."

16. Interview, PRAHPN028.

17. Interview, PRAHPN007.

18. In 2007, the Project initiated a mental health program featuring monthly group meetings where workers could process the emotional strains of their labor. PRAHPN, "Informe de Avances—Marzo 2008," 8–10.

19. See Cereser, "Capturaban sin orden de juez," *Prensa Libre* (19 January 2008); interview, Anna Carla Ericastilla.

20. Interview, Jorge Villagrán, 21 February 2008.

21. HRDAG subsequently become independent from Benetech.

22. Interview, Iduvina Hernández. For a previous statistical analysis of Guatemalan state terror, see Davenport and Ball, "Views to a Kill." The utility of statistical instruments for human rights research is also seen in Steinberg et al., "Mapping Massacres," 62–68.

23. On Benetech's involvement, see Harrison, "Guatemalan National Police Archive Project."

24. Interview, Jorge Villagrán.

25. Interview, Jorge Villagrán; Ana Miza, "Críticas contra justicia por deceso en impunidad," *La Hora* (19 February 2008).

26. Interview, Jorge Villagrán.

27. Interview, Gustavo Meoño.

28. Interview, PRAHPN007, and field notes.

29. Its members included Patrick Ball, director of Benetech's Human Rights Program; Ana Cacopardo, executive director of Argentina's Comisión Provincial para la Memoria; Wynne Cougill, of the Documentation Center of Cambodia; Kate Doyle, senior analyst at the National Security Archives; archivist Antonio González Quintana; Hassan Mneimneh, director of the Iraq Memory Foundation; Manfred Nowak, UN special rapporteur on torture; Nobel Prize winner Adolfo Pérez Esquivel; Fina Solà, international secretary of Archivists without Borders; and Maria Paz Vergara, director of the Documentation Foundation and Archive of the Vicariate of Solidarity in Chile.

30. Interview, Jorge Villagrán; PRAHPN, "Informe de Avances—Marzo 2008," 8–10.

31. The ISAD(G) and the International Standard Archival Authority Record (ISAAR) are the general descriptive frameworks endorsed by archivists' professional associations.

The ISAD(G) is used to describe records' contents; the ISAAR is used to describe the organizational unit that created the records. They outline standard formats for the establishment of archival reference codes and for describing documents' dates, creators, archival histories, contents, cross-references, relationships to other documentary fonds, sources of acquisition, systems of arrangement, and access conditions.

32. Interview, Lizbeth Barrientos.

33. The Project's first archivist, Ingrid Molina, was the first archivist to graduate in Guatemala; Barrientos, its second, was the second.

34. E-mail to author, 28 August 2006.

35. Interview, Lizbeth Barrientos.

36. Interview, Ingrid Molina.

37. Interview, Anna Carla Ericastilla.

38. Not infrequently, when I was at the Project, I served as her translator.

39. Interview, Anna Carla Ericastilla.

40. Interview, Ingrid Molina.

41. PRAHPN, "Informe de Avances—Agosto 2007," 2.

42. The damage was not irreversible; it simply signified more work down the line, when keen archival thinkers would need to reopen the boxes and integrate the documents into their proper archival fonds and subfonds.

43. Interview, PRAHPN018, 9 November 2007.

44. Interview, PRAHPN022.

45. Interview, PRAHPN028.

46. Interview, PRAHPN027, 22 January 2008; interview, PRAHPN028; interview, PRAHPN006; interview, PRAHPN002, 28 September 2007; field notes. By August 2007, some 65 percent of the Project's more than two hundred personnel were under the age of thirty. PRAHPN, "Informe de Avances—Agosto 2007," 1.

47. Interview, PRAHPN002.

48. Interview, Alberto Fuentes.

49. Interview, Christina Elich.

50. Huskamp Peterson, "The End of the Beginning."

51. Interview, Lizbeth Barrientos.

52. Interview, Carla Villagrán.

53. Interview, Åsa Wallton; interview, Michael Moerth; interview, Agnes Bernzen.

54. PRAHPN, "Informe de Avances—Agosto 2007," 4.

55. As one archivist writes, "All fonds are not created equal." Millar, "Creating a National Information System," 182–92. For a summary of archivists' thinking on this tension between objectivity and subjectivity, dating back to the Dutch Manual, see Ridener, *From Polders to Postmodernism.*

56. Interview, Ingrid Molina.

57. Huskamp Peterson, "Records of the Policía Nacional de Guatemala," 12.

58. Interview, Gustavo Meoño.

59. The qualitative investigation focused on three main areas: the PN's structural history, its role in the counterinsurgency, and particular cases of death and forced disappearance attributed to state security forces, including the PDH's *casos de averiguación especial.* PRAHPN, "Informe de Avances—Agosto 2007," 8.

60. Huskamp Peterson, "Records of the Policía Nacional de Guatemala," 10.

61. Interview, PRAHPN022.

62. Interview, PRAHPN003.

63. Rachel Donadio writes, "Access to archives is a barometer of any government's commitment to transparency." Rachel Donadio, "The Iron Archives," *New York Times* (22 April 2007).

64. Interview, PRAHPN004.

65. Interview, Estuardo Galeano.

66. On impunity in Guatemala, see Impunity Watch, *Recognising the Past*.

67. Interview, PRAHPN007.

68. Cited in Paul Jeffrey, "Secret Files Open Window on Guatemala's Violent Past," *National Catholic Reporter* (3 August 2007).

69. Cited in Ginger Thompson, "Mildewed Police Files May Hold Clues to Atrocities in Guatemala," *New York Times* (21 November 2005).

70. On this, see Ketelaar, "Recordkeeping and Societal Power."

71. Interview, PRAHPN010.

72. For "parallel powers," see Peacock and Beltrán, *Poderes ocultos*.

73. As Andrzej Rzeplinski writes, "One should realize that the temptation to use archival resources of the [defunct] security services for further repressive purposes may emerge any time, should the rule of law ever get overthrown. . . . such documents may always turn up as instruments of blackmail or other lawlessness." Rzeplinski, "Habeas Data."

FOUR. BUILDING COUNTERINSURGENCY ARCHIVES

1. On Arbenz's fall, see Gleijeses, *Shattered Hope*; Cullather, *Secret History*; Kinzer and Schlesinger, *Bitter Fruit*.

2. International Cooperation Administration (ICA), "Report on the National Police of Guatemala," Washington, DC, 9 April 1956, DNSA, GU00019.

3. ICA, "Report on the National Police of Guatemala." In fact, Castillo Armas's envoy to the ICA had already lamented the "absence of a central filing system to which the Government could turn for rapid information." U.S. Embassy in Guatemala (USE/G) to U.S. Secretary of State (SecState), "Guatemalan Request for Technical Assistance in Intelligence," 18 August 1955, NACP, RG 286, Office of Public Safety (OPS), Latin America Branch (LAB), Country File: Guatemala (CF:G), Box 65, Folder IPS 1/General/Guatemala.

4. ICA, "Report on the National Police of Guatemala."

5. ICA, "Report on the National Police of Guatemala." He notes that the Sección de Defensa Contra el Comunismo had processed 600,000 records without a single lost file—this after only two years in existence, and in a country with a population of only 3.2 million.

6. ICA, "Report on the National Police of Guatemala."

7. ICA, "Reply to November and December Public Safety Reports," Washington, DC, 13 January 1959, NACP, RG 286, OPS, LAB, CF:G, Box 68, Folder IPS 2–2/Monthly Reports /Guatemala.

8. United States Operations Mission to Guatemala (USOM/G), "Recent Activities of Public Safety Program, Guatemala," 8 September 1958, NACP, RG 286, OPS, LAB, CF:G, Box 69, Folder IPS 2–3/Programs/Guatemala 2.

9. ICA, "Reply to November and December Public Safety Reports."

10. Rubottom to Atwood, "Overseas Internal Security Program," 3 June 1957, NACP, RG 286, OPS, LAB, CF:G, Box 69, Folder IPS 2–3/Programs/Guatemala 2.

11. There is but one substantive account of the U.S. role in shaping the ragtag PN into a counterinsurgent force; though excellent, it is more than twenty-five years old, and many government documents have been declassified since. McClintock, *The American Connection*.

12. The CEH ruled that only the 1981–1983 period, in four rural departments, could be termed "genocide." CEH, *Guatemala: Memoria del silencio*.

13. USAID Bureau on Latin America, "Use of Firearms by the National Police of Guatemala," 28 March 1962, DNSA, GU00077.

14. For the United States' use of similar tactics in the Philippines, see McCoy, *Policing America's Empire*, 61.

15. Kuzmarov, "Modernizing Repression." See also Langguth, *Hidden Terrors*; McCoy, *Policing America's Empire*; and Huggins, "U.S. Supported State Terror."

16. Huggins, *Political Policing*, 60.

17. Lobe, "The Rise and Demise," 190. On the institutional evolution that led to the creation of USAID, see Huggins, *Political Policing*.

18. REA/Williams to U/NSA/Mr. de Lima, "Overseas Internal Security Program—Guatemala," 26 April 1957, NACP, RG 286, OPS, LAB, CF:G, Box 69, Folder IPS 2–3/Programs /Guatemala 2.

19. USOM/G, "Recent Activities of Public Safety Program, Guatemala," 8 September 1958, NACP, RG 286, OPS, LAB, CF:G, Box 69, Folder: IPS 2–3/Programs/Guatemala 2.

20. Huggins, *Political Policing*, 79.

21. Huggins, *Political Policing*, 81.

22. For "exotic horrors," see *Orden—Organo de la Policía Nacional de la República de Guatemala, C.A.* (24 September 1955), CIRMA. Siekmeier notes that communism, "in the argot of U.S. officialdom, clearly was a more inclusive term than simply rule by a Marxist-Leninist regime or a Soviet-backed or Soviet-dominated government," and suggests that the primary U.S. objective in the Americas was the containment of all forms of economic nationalism. Siekmeier, *Aid*, 164.

23. USE/G to SecState, "Guatemalan Request for Technical Assistance in Intelligence," 18 August 1955, NACP, RG 286, OPS, LAB, CF:G, Box 65, Folder: IPS 1/General/Guatemala.

24. McClintock, *The American Connection*, 29. McClintock notes that although many were detained, probably only three hundred leftists were killed in the aftermath of the coup, and that such relative "softness" compared to the post-1960s can be explained by the fact that "in 1954 there was neither an apparatus, nor a counter-insurgency orientation encouraging wholesale murder along modern lines" (30).

25. McClintock, *The American Connection*, 35; and Doyle, "The Art of the Coup."

26. USE/G to SecState, "Guatemalan Request for Technical Assistance in Intelligence," 18 August 1955, NACP, RG 286, OPS, LAB, CF:G, Box 65, Folder: IPS 1/General/Guatemala.

27. Decree-Law 553, cited in Contreras Cruz and Sinay Álvarez, "Historia de la Policía Nacional de Guatemala 1881–1997," 65. The General Directorate of National Security was created because the Committee against Communism's mandate put it into conflict with the new 1956 Constitution, particularly concerning the permitted length of preven-

tive detentions. The committee had come under fire from labor unions, who asserted that the workers being arrested by the committee were innocents being denounced by employers for engaging in legal union activities. The Committee against Communism's name switch was only one of many such cosmetic changes by security forces during the war; any time that a group's extralegal methods attracted excessive attention, its agents were recycled into a new group with a new moniker. See William B. Connett Jr. to State Department (DOS), "Establishment of General Office of National Security," Guatemala City, 6 March 1956, DNSA, GU00018.

28. AHPN, *Del silencio a la memoria*, 47.

29. ICA, "Report on the National Police of Guatemala."

30. D. L. Crisostomo, "Briefing Report for the Washington Evaluation Team on the Public Safety Program in Guatemala," 23 October 1964, NSA, McClintock Collection, Box 4, Folder: Guatemala Evaluation of OPS 1961–69.

31. AHPN, *Del silencio a la memoria*, 479–505.

32. USOM/G, "Recent Activities of Public Safety Program, Guatemala," 8 September 1958, NACP, RG 286, OPS, LAB, CF:G, Box 69, Folder: IPS 2–3/Programs/Guatemala 2. On Piloña's comments, see "Hoy Asume Casado la Policía," *El Imparcial*, 17 July 1958.

33. ICA to USE/G, "Reply to August Public Safety Report," Washington, DC, 29 September 1959, NACP, RG 286, OPS, LAB, CF:G, Box 68, Folder: IPS 2–2/Monthly Reports /Guatemala.

34. USOM/G to ICA, "Special Police Investigation Services," Guatemala City, 25 August 1960, DNSA, GU00032.

35. This dovetailed with Kennedy's expansion of the USAID police assistance program worldwide; see Rabe, *The Most Dangerous Area in the World.*

36. USOM/G to ICA, "Special Police Investigation Services."

37. USOM/G to ICA, "Special Police Investigation Services."

38. AHPN, *Del silencio a la memoria*, 51.

39. AHPN, *Del silencio a la memoria*, 280.

40. AHPN, *Del silencio a la memoria*, 50–52.

41. For Ubico's "auxiliary army," see Crisostomo, "Briefing Report," 23 October 1964. McClintock notes that Ubico's secret police were by far the most effective state security force at the time—more so than the military, which played a secondary role in internal security until the 1960s. See McClintock, *The American Connection*, 18.

42. Interview, PRAHPN018.

43. USE/G to DOS, 24 August 1966, NACP, RG 59, Central Foreign Policy Files 1964–1966, Box 2253, Folder: POL 23—Guat—1/1/66.

44. For "common thug and assassin," see AID Bureau on Latin America, "Use of Firearms by the National Police of Guatemala."

45. "Ningún vestigio: Judiciales se llevaron instrumentos de tortura," *El Imparcial*, 7 July 1966. *Gamexán* (alternately spelled as *gamesán* or gamezan) was an insecticide used in the torture practice of "hooding," in which interrogators covered victims' heads with a rubber hood impregnated with the poison. McClintock, *The American Connection*, 119n105.

46. Crisostomo, "Briefing Report," 23 October 1964.

47. Schirmer, *The Guatemalan Military Project*, 157.

48. "Policía: Gobierno elimina el departamento judicial," *El Imparcial*, 1 November 1966.

49. All citations in this paragraph from AID Bureau on Latin America, "Use of Firearms by the National Police of Guatemala."

50. The Days of March and April reflected momentum built up by strikes in 1960 and 1961, and absent brutal repression could well have resulted in Ydígoras's overthrow. See Ramírez, *La guerra de los 36 años*; and Rosada Granados, *Soldados en el poder*.

51. "Academia de la Guardia Judicial," *Orden: Organo de la Policía Nacional de Guatemala*, Tomo II, Segunda Epoca, No. 2 (Guatemala City: 1960), 18, CIRMA: Colección de Documentos.

52. Jonas, "Dangerous Liaisons," 146.

53. CIA Directorate of Intelligence (CIA/DOI), "Intelligence Handbook for Special Operations: Guatemala," Washington, DC (June 1967), 166, NACP, CIA-CREST Database.

54. USE/G to SecState, 24 September 1963, NACP, RG 286, OPS, LAB, CF:G, Box 65, Folder: IPS 1/General/Guatemala.

55. Byron Engle to David Laughlin, "Program Adequacy Bolivia, Colombia, Ecuador, Guatemala, and Venezuela," 1 April 1964, DNSA, GU00170.

56. D. L. Crisostomo, "Report on Police Progress and Development in Guatemala," Guatemala City, January 1965, NSA/GDP.

57. CIA/DOI, "Guatemala—A Current Appraisal," 8 October 1966, DDRS.

58. Grandin, *The Last Colonial Massacre*, 76.

59. McClintock, *The American Connection*, 71.

60. AHPN, *Del silencio a la memoria*, 438.

61. McClintock, *The American Connection*, 72–73.

62. See Grandin's book *The Last Colonial Massacre* for the best account of the 1966 disappearances.

63. For "Communist big-leaguers," see USE/G to SecState, "Internal Security Situation and Needs," Guatemala City, 22 May 1961, DNSA, GU00047.

64. John P. Longan to Byron Engle, "TDY Guatemala: November 7 through December 27, 1965," 4 January 1966, DNSA, GU00244.

65. Grandin, *The Last Colonial Massacre*, 95–96.

66. For "unconfirmed rumors" and "a considerable success," see Mein/USE/G to AID/Washington, "Public Safety Monthly Report, March 1966," 13 April 1966, DNSA, GU00279. For increased Public Safety engagement after Mein's death, see "Summary Statement of AID Program in Guatemala," 1971, NACP, OPS, Office of the Director, Numerical File 1956–74, Box 1, Folder: History of PS Program—Guatemala FY 70–72.

67. Jennifer Schirmer dates the birth of the G-2 to this period and identifies U.S. military assistance as its key architect. See Schirmer, *The Guatemalan Military Project*, 6.

68. The Ford Bronco was routinely used by special police squads for arrests and disappearances. In this case, the fifty-four vehicles in question were purchased by the Guatemalan military and given to the PN as a gift to help them "guarantee the security and tranquility the Guatemalan people need in order to dedicate themselves to honorable activities"; see "54 Radiopatrullas entrega el Ejército a la Policía Nacional," *El Imparcial* (1 March 1967). The gift shows how aid to the military sometimes was, by extension, aid to the police, because of resource sharing between the forces, their special-ops collabo-

rations, and the fact that army colonels, usually trained by the United States, ran the PN for almost the entire conflict.

69. "Arzobispo bendijo nuevos vehículos de la policía," *El Imparcial* (14 March 1967). For the relationship between Ponce Nitsch and Ríos Montt, see USE/G to SecState, "Guatemalan Coup Developments: Thunder on the Right, Dissatisfaction by Young Officers," Guatemala City, 25 March 1982, DDRS.

70. AHPN, *Del silencio a la memoria*, 160.

71. For "counterinsurgency coordinator," see USE/G to SecState, "Police Vehicles," 28 October 1966, NACP, Record Group 286, OPS, Technical Services Division, General Correspondence Relating to Geographic Areas, 1965–71, Guatemala–Ivory Coast, Box 4, Folder: Guatemala Chron 3/25/66–12/27/68. Sosa was a close ally of defense minister Rafael Arriaga Bosque, a powerful political actor who had directed the execution of Operación Limpieza.

72. Ted Brown, "Meeting with Colonel Manuel Francisco Sosa, Director General of the National Police," 17 July 1967, NACP, RG 286, OPS, LAB, CF:G, Box 71, Folder IPS 3/Meetings/Guatemala.

73. CIA/DOI, "Intelligence Handbook for Special Operations: Guatemala."

74. Additional corps were added later, as both the city and its police force expanded.

75. USE/G to DOS, "Students Sight in on New Minister of Government," 30 June 1969, NACP, RG 59, Central Foreign Policy Files, 1967–1969, Political and Defense, Box 2160, Folder POL 13—Guat—1/1/67.

76. Thomas L. Hughes/INR to SecState, "Guatemala: A Counterinsurgency Running Wild?," 23 October 1967, DNSA, GU00348.

77. CIA, February 1968, DNSA, GU00355.

78. USE/G to DOS, "Weeka No. 42," Guatemala City (22 October 1967), NACP, RG 59, Central Foreign Policy Files, 1967–69; Political and Defense; Box 2158 Folder POL 2–1—Guat—7/1/67.

79. Reprinted in CIDC, *Violencia y contraviolencia*, 103.

80. CIA/DOI, "Intelligence Handbook for Special Operations: Guatemala."

81. Really, it was not much of a bet at all, since during this period AID sent hefty shipments of weapons to both the PN and the Judicial Police. In June 1967, Peter Costello announced to delighted police chiefs that among AID's partner countries, Guatemala had been identified as the highest-priority recipient for a major delivery of "the most modern weapons available on the market." See "Armamentos entregará la AID la la Policía Nacional," *El Imparcial* (27 June 1967).

82. Interview, PRAHPN018; and Ramírez, *La guerra de los 36 años*, 92.

83. "Medidas policíacas," *Prensa Libre* (June 1967).

84. AHPN, *Del silencio a la memoria*, 290.

85. "Medidas policíacas."

86. "Ciento cuarenta policías adiestrados en nuevo plan," *El Imparcial* (28 June 1967).

87. Streeter, "Nation-Building."

88. McClintock, *The American Connection*, 95; and Krujit, *Sociedades de terror*, 36.

89. Cited in USE/G to DOS, "Students Sight in on New Minister of Government."

90. CIA, "Back-Up Material for DCI's June Briefing," 6 June 1969, NACP, CIA—CREST database.

91. USE/G to DOS, "Students Sight in on New Minister of Government."

92. "Una policía en la fusión desde mañana," *El Imparcial* (30 November 1970).

93. "Ocho jefes y ex-jefes de la Policía Secreta han sido muertos a tiros," *El Imparcial* (2 May 1974).

94. CIA/DOI, "Guatemala's Political Transition," 11 March 1970, NACP, CIA-CREST database.

95. For "civilian extremists" and "history of violent, irrational activity," see CIA/DOI, "Guatemala's Political Transition."

96. See *Discursos del Presidente Arana Osorio*, as well as USE/G to DOS, "Biweekly Political Review: November 14–27, 1970," 27 November 1970, NACP, RG 286, OPS, LAB, CF:G, Box 68, unlabeled folder.

97. USAC students' nicknames for Arana are documented in the satirical Huelga de Dolores publication *No Nos Tientes* (Don't Tempt Us) through the 1970s and 1980s.

98. Cited in CIDC, *Violencia y contraviolencia*, 108.

99. From "Mensaje de paz y esperanza dirigido al pueblo en la vigilia de Navidad," reprinted in *Discursos del Presidente Arana*.

100. State Department, "FY 72 Program Review," 27 July 1970, NSA/GDP.

101. For the spike in violence after Arana took office, see CIDC, *Violencia y contraviolencia*, 105.

102. Viron P. Vaky to Covey T. Oliver, "Guatemala and Counter-terror," 29 March 1968, DNSA, GU00367.

103. U.S. Embassy/Guatemala to State Department, "Debriefing of Sean M. Holly," Guatemala City, 16 March 1970, NACP, RG 286, OPS, LAB, CF:G; Box 73, Folder: IPS 14/Kidnapping/Guatemala. In his statement, Holly noted with surprise that his captors did not seem to view Arana with any particular rancor, seeing him merely as a "puppet" of the far right; they did, however, single out Colonel Sosa as a "butcher."

104. USE/G to SecState, "Ojo Por Ojo," 19 May 1970, NACP, RG 286, OPS, LAB, CF:G, Box 73, Folder: IPS-8/Narcotics Training/Guatemala.

105. Mario Ramírez Ruiz, "Experiencias que deben aprovecharse dentro de la organización policial," *Revista de la Policía Nacional* 4, no. 7 (September–October 1970): 12, HN.

106. "Escuela de Capacitación de la Policía Nacional," *Revista de la Policía Nacional* 5, no. 8 (February–April 1971): 8, HN.

107. Héctor René Rivera Méndez, "La instrucción como medio de superación en el servicio policial," *Revista de la Policía Nacional* 5, no. 8 (February–April 1971): 40, HN. As of 1971, the PN required all applicants for new or renewed driver's licenses to register their fingerprints in the archives, thus tightening control over everyday Guatemalans. See PDH, *El derecho a saber*, 178.

108. AHPN, *Del silencio a la memoria*, 288. Applying for the new *cedula* cards required Guatemalans to provide photographs along with their birthplace, birth date, sex, civil state, nationality, age, skin color, height, weight, hair color, hair texture, general state of health, eye and nose shape, profession, address, parents' names, and any other physical or psychological data deemed necessary by the intake official. See AHPN, *Del silencio a la memoria*, 470, for a representative *cedula* application in the name of Anastacio Sotz Coy, who headed a campesino organization in 1980 when he was captured, tortured, and executed, allegedly by the military. Though the PN had documented Sotz Coy's death and

mutilation, it never released this information to his family or to lawyers investigating his case, such that the murdered Sotz Coy remained "disappeared" for more than thirty years before the Project's research revealed his fate.

109. Joseph Sobotta, "Survey of the Guatemala Police Forces Weapons System," 9 October 1970, Courtesy NSA/GDP.

110. David R. Powell to DOS, "Review of FY 72 Country Field Submission (CFS) Guatemala," 10 August 1970, Courtesy NSA/GDP.

111. Grandin points out this argument's recurrence in declassified U.S. documents in his *Denegado en su totalidad*.

112. USE/G to SecState, "University Rector's Life Threatened by 'Ojo Por Ojo,'" 6 October 1971, NACP, RG 59, SNF 1970–1973, Political and Defense, Box 2337, Folder: POL 23—Guat—1/1/71.

113. For "unscrupulous persons," see USE/G to SecState, "Disappearance of Communist Leaders," 29 September 1972, NACP, RG 59, SNF 1970–1973, Political and Defense, Box 2336, Folder: POL 12—Guat. For "police sources," see USE/G to DOS, "Internal Security: Monthly Report of Incidents, November 1972," 19 December 1972, NACP, RG 59, SNF 1970–1973, Political and Defense, Box 2337, Folder: POL 23—Guat—1/1/70.

114. USE/G to SecState, "Internal Security: Monthly Report of Incidents, January 1973," 9 February 1973, NACP, RG 59, SNF 1970–1973, Political and Defense, Box 2337, folder POL 23—Guat—1/1/70.

115. Byron Engle to Robert A. Hurwitch, "Creation of a Special Action Unit within the National Police to Assume Death Squad Functions," 11 October 1972, NACP, RG 286, OPS, LAB, CF:G, Box 72, Folder: IPS-8/Telegrams/Guatemala. The memorandum, recently declassified, is heavily redacted.

116. John H. Caldwell, "Guatemala CASP, FY 73–74," 9 March 1972, NACP, RG 286, OPS, LAB, CF:G, Box 4, Folder: IPS 1–1.

117. NSC, "Country Analysis and Strategy Paper—FY 73–74—Guatemala," 4 May 1972, NSA/GDP.

118. NSC, "Country Analysis and Strategy Paper."

119. McClintock, *The American Connection*, 101.

120. Senate Committee on Foreign Relations, Subcommittee on Western Hemisphere Affairs, *Guatemala and the Dominican Republic*, staff memorandum, Pat Holt (Washington, DC: Government Printing Office, 1971); cited in McClintock, *The American Connection*, 101.

121. See Lobe, "The Rise and Demise," 192; also Langguth, *Hidden Terrors*; Kuzmarov, "Modernizing Repression."

122. Cited in Huggins, *Political Policing*, 187.

123. Huggins, *Political Policing*, 187.

124. Kuzmarov's account of OPS trainees' abuses in South Vietnam is chilling. Kuzmarov, "Modernizing Repression," 209–19.

125. Huggins, *Political Policing*, 192.

126. Huggins, *Political Policing*, 195.

127. See Abourezk's statement on the Amendment to the Foreign Assistance Act before the Senate Committee on Foreign Relations, 21 June 1974, NACP, CIA-CREST database.

128. Kuzmarov, "Modernizing Repression," 220.

129. Caesar P. Bernal et al., "Termination Phase-Out Study—Public Safety Project Guatemala," 1 July 1974, DNSA, GU00486.

130. "Summary Statement of AID Program in Guatemala," 1971.

131. McClintock, *The American Connection*, 54.

132. ICA, "Report on the National Police of Guatemala."

133. Lobe, "The Rise and Demise," 187.

134. Vaky to Oliver, "Guatemala and Counter-terror."

135. Streeter, "Nation-Building," 65.

136. John P. Longan to Byron Engle, 12 April 1968, DNSA, GU00369.

137. CEH, *Guatemala: Memoria del silencio*, vol. 1, annex 1.

138. Doyle, "The Atrocity Files."

139. In 1958, during the height of U.S. archival assistance, the PN switched from the five-by-eight-inch *fichas* in use since 1943 to the three-by-five-inch *fichas* it would use thereafter. See César Edgar Yon García, "Cronología de una ficha de antecedentes policíacos," *Revista de la Policía Nacional* 13, no. 27 (1979): 37–38.

FIVE. RECYCLING THE NATIONAL POLICE IN WAR, PEACE, AND POST-PEACE

1. See United Nations Commission on the Truth for El Salvador, *De La Locura a La Esperanza*.

2. Mirna Jiménez, "Asesinatos fueron premeditados, asegura Presidente Saca," *Diario Co Latino* (San Salvador), 20 February 2007.

3. Lorena Seijo, "Matan a los 4 policías implicados en crimen de diputados salvadoreños," *Prensa Libre*, 26 February 2007.

4. M. A. Bastenier, "Guatemala, ¿Estado fallido?," *El País*, 21 January 2008; Sonia Pérez, "Impunidad afecta funciones del Estado," *Prensa Libre*, 3 March 2007.

5. Sonia Pérez, "Iglesia, PDH y la Usac demandan clausura de Dinc," *Prensa Libre*, 14 March 2007; "Impunidad uniformada," *el Periódico*, 23 February 2007.

6. Lorena Seijo, "Nuevo jefe depurará el Dinc," *Prensa Libre*, 12 April 2007.

7. Julio Caballeros Seigné cited in *Human Rights in Guatemala: Delegation Report*, the Human Rights Project, 1991, NSA, box labeled "Guatemala Incoming FOIAS."

8. Byrne, Stanley, and Garst, *Rescuing Police Reform*.

9. Lorena Seijo and Leonardo Cereser, "Depuración afecta a la Dinc," *Prensa Libre*, 28 August 2007; and CEH, *Guatemala: Memoria del silencio*, vol 1.

10. CEH, *Guatemala: Memoria del silencio*, vol. 2, 93.

11. William Robinson adapts the term "polyarchy," originally defined by Robert Dahl, to describe political contexts in which electoral democracy does exist, but in which mass participation is limited to casting votes only for members of a tiny power-holding elite. Robinson, *Promoting Polyarchy*.

12. See, for example, Nelson, "Maleficium Jingle."

13. Call and Stanley, "Protecting the People."

14. "Informe señala que Guatemala es uno de los países más violentos del mundo," *Prensa Libre* (25 March 2009); PDH, *Informe Anual 2008*; C. Méndez Villaseñor and M. Marroquín Cabrera, "Crimen deteriora salud mental de guatemaltecos," *Prensa Libre* (29 March 2009); "Impunidad alcanza el 98% en el país," *Prensa Libre* (27 November 2007).

15. "Ante la inseguridad los policías se encomiendan a Dios," *Prensa Libre* (24 March 2009).

16. "Texto del discurso del Ministro de la Defensa General Vassaux," reprinted in *El Imparcial* (17 February 1975).

17. U.S. documents identify Laugerud's victory as "the most blatant electoral fraud in modern Guatemalan history." See U.S. Southern Command, "Brigadier-General (ret.) Kjell Laugerud García," February 1976, DNSA, GU00498.

18. Cited in McClintock, *The American Connection*, 127.

19. Kobrak, *Organizing and Repression*, 43–51.

20. McClintock, *The American Connection*, 126.

21. See CIDC, *Violencia y contraviolencia*, 96; and Levenson-Estrada, *Trade Unionists*, 106. On Guatemalan trade unionism, see Levenson-Estrada, *Trade Unionists*; ASIES, *Más de cien años*; Obando Sánchez, *Memorias*; and Albizures, *Tiempo de sudor y lucha*.

22. For the "waves" to "system" transition, see CIDC, *Violencia y contraviolencia*, 109.

23. Levenson-Estrada, *Trade Unionists*, 124–25.

24. See Walker, "Economic Fault Lines"; Buchenau and Johnson, eds., *Aftershocks*; and Davis, *Planet of Slums*. On the quake's impact amid a larger reconfiguring of society, particularly youth culture, see Castañeda, "Historia del rock," 66.

25. EGP, "Boletín Interno de Noticias," no. 1 (May 1976), CIRMA: Colección Payeras-Colom. On the EGP's inception, see Ricardo Ramírez de León's (or "Rolando Morán's") chapter "Interpretando la historia del EGP," in his *Saludos revolucionarios*, as well as Payeras's *Los días de la selva*.

26. EGP, *Compañero: Boletín Internacional*, no. 2 (February 1976), CIRMA; Colección Payeras-Colom.

27. Levenson-Estrada, *Trade Unionists*, 122.

28. Kobrak, *Organizing and Repression*, 46–47.

29. Arias, "After the Rigoberta Menchú Controversy," 489. On the Maya movement, see Konefal, *For Every Indio Who Falls*; Fischer and Brown, eds., *Maya Cultural Activism*; Montejo, *Voices from Exile*; Wilson, *Maya Resurgence*; Warren, "Interpreting *La Violencia*"; Smith, ed., *Guatemalan Indians and the State*.

30. One example of how the PN's reach extended beyond the capital: in January 1977, three campesinos from Nebaj, suspected of being EGP sympathizers, were dragged from their homes by individuals identified by U.S. documents as "'plain-clothes policemen' (probably from the Corps of Detectives)." The campesinos' corpses appeared days later with signs of torture. USE/G to DOS, "Monthly Report on Political Violence and Human Rights: January 1977," 1 March 1977, DNSA, GU00507.

31. AHPN, *Del silencio a la memoria*, 285.

32. AEU, *Jornadas de Agosto de 1977*, 21 September 1977, CIRMA: Colección de Documentos.

33. Paola Hurtado, "Los archivos de la Policía Nacional," *El Periódico* (29 January 2006).

34. Hurtado, "Los archivos de la Policía Nacional."

35. Cohen, *States of Denial*, 82–85.

36. Cifuentes Cano would later direct the Special Operations Commando (COE), also known as BROE (Special Operations and Reaction Brigade), one of the PN's shadowiest

counterinsurgency units. In 1982 its existence was made official as the Fifth Corps. See Juan Francisco Cifuentes Cano, "La Institución Policíaca Ante Sus Difamantes," *Revista de la Policía Nacional* 11, no. 21 (February–April 1977): 18–19, HN.

37. Capitalization his. All quotations in this paragraph from Cifuentes Cano, "La Institución Policíaca Ante Sus Difamantes."

38. Cifuentes Cano, "La Institución Policíaca Ante Sus Difamantes."

39. EGP, "Boletín Interno de Noticias," no. 1 (May 1976), CIRMA: Colección Payeras-Colom. Ramírez had run the Regional Telecommunications Center since at least the early 1970s, according to one heavily redacted U.S. document indicating that U.S. advisers were kept well informed about the center's activities. Department of State (DOS), "Guatemalan Security Force Activities," 22 September 1971, DNSA, GU00460.

40. For Panzós as moment of rupture, see Grandin, *The Last Colonial Massacre*.

41. Cited in Schirmer, *The Guatemalan Military Project*, 18.

42. For "neither sloppy ones nor lazy ones," see "Entrega de despachos en la policía," *El Imparcial* (7 July 1978). For "civilian corps," see "Será depurado el Cuerpo de Detectives," *El Imparcial* (12 July 1978).

43. The term "Special Agents" was, after the structural transition within the PN that saw the Detective Corps replaced by the DIT, superseded by "Collaborators." PDH, *El derecho a saber*, 113. *Orejas* had always been used, though never as a matter of official protocol.

44. GT PN 51-01-S002 28.10.1981, reproduced in AHPN, *Del silencio a la memoria*, 90.

45. GT PN 51-01-S002, cited in AHPN, *Del silencio a la memoria*, 256–57.

46. PDH, *El derecho a saber*, 22.

47. "Será depurado el Cuerpo de Detectives," *El Imparcial* (12 July 1978).

48. CEH, *Guatemala: Memoria del silencio*, vol. 2, chap. 2.

49. For example, "Movilización ante el crimen recrudecido," *El Imparcial* (28 July 1978).

50. "Gobierno llama a los ciudadanos a abstenerse de los actos ilegales," *El Imparcial* (5 August 1978); "15 heridos de bala hubo hoy," *El Imparcial* (10 October 1978); "10 heridos de bala hoy," *El Imparcial* (11 October 1978).

51. Kobrak, *Organizing and Repression*, 58.

52. Kobrak, *Organizing and Repression*, 59.

53. "DC investigará la actuación del nominado Batallón de la Muerte," *El Imparcial* (7 August 1978).

54. "Organización Cero elimina a tres bajo el lema: 'Matar por justicia,'" *El Imparcial* (5 March 1979).

55. "600 guatemaltecos muertos en 28 días," *El Imparcial* (12 March 1979). The Escuadrón de la Muerte was likely a front for police-perpetrated social cleansing of urban "undesirables," such as street children—a practice that continues to this day. See Tierney, *Robbed of Humanity*. The EGP, for its part, believed that the "Escuadrón de la Muerte" was an appendage of the National Police's Second Corps; they may have been confusing it with Commando Six. EGP, "Boletín de prensa: El Ejército Guatemalteco de los Pobres golpea a los cabecillos del terror reaccionario," 2 January 1978, CIRMA: Colección de Documentos. As Schirmer points out, the police were also used by the military leadership of CRIO/La Regional to carry out killings. See Schirmer, *The Guatemalan Military Project*, 159.

56. For example, see "Hallan cadáveres posible de dos que fueron escuadronados," *El Imparcial* (14 March 1979); "Cadáver de un escuadronado al parecer," *El Imparcial* (16 March 1979); "Otro delincuente escuadronado," *El Imparcial* (21 March 1979); "Siete escuadronados más aparecieron," *El Imparcial* (22 March 1979).

57. See Rebeca Alonso's essay in Sánchez del Valle, ed., *Por el delito de pensar*.

58. AHPN, *Del silencio a la memoria*, 397–423.

59. The National Police had been surveilling Colom Argueta for more than twenty years; Leonardo Cereser, "Policía controló 22 años a líder Colom Argueta," *Prensa Libre* (19 October 2008).

60. Secret untitled cable, CIA, March 1980, DNSA, GU00634.

61. In 1980, more than 125 USAC students and professors were killed or disappeared. Kobrak, *Organizing and Repression*, 70.

62. See PDH, *El derecho a saber*; Kobrak, *Organizing and Repression*, 63.

63. For U.S. knowledge of the Guatemalan government's role in running death squads, see USE/G to DOS, "Right-Wing Terrorism," 11 April 1979, DNSA, GU00574. For "part of the Cold War," see McAllister, "Rural Markets," 350.

64. "Decapitan busto de Castillo Armas," *El Imparcial* (24 March 1979).

65. Figueroa Ibarra, *Los que siempre estarán en ninguna parte*, 142.

66. Figueroa Ibarra, *Los que siempre estarán en ninguna parte*, 152.

67. CIA, "Clandestine Mass Grave Near Comalapa," April 1980, DNSA, GU00640. When the clandestine cemetery was made public, Guatemalan officials pled ignorance; see "Exhaustiva investigación sobre el aparecido cementerio clandestino, ordenó Lucas," *El Imparcial*, 21 March 1980. The corpse of USAC student Liliana Negreros, kidnapped by police after the funeral procession for those killed in the Spanish embassy fire, was among the dozens exhumed from the Comalapa cemetery. Kobrak, *Organizing and Repression*, 67–68.

68. Doyle, "Remains of Two of Guatemala's Death Squad Diary's Victims Found"; Doyle and Willard, "Remains of Three Death Squad Diary Victims Identified."

69. CEH, *Guatemala: Memoria del silencio*, vol. 2, chap. 2, para. 437. For more on the Frozen Area Plan, see chapter 4, as well as Grandin's *The Last Colonial Massacre* and *Denegado en su totalidad*.

70. CEH, *Guatemala: Memoria del silencio*, vol. 1, annex 1, illustrative case no. 51.

71. USE/G to DOS, "Guatemala: Trade Union Leaders Abducted," 23 February 1984, DNSA, GU1001.

72. On the embassy fire, see Cajal, *Saber quién puso fuego ahí!*; for the "official" (government) position, see Luján Muñoz, *La tragedia de la Embajada de España en Guatemala*; also see Amézquita, *Guatemala*; REMHI, *Guatemala: Nunca Más!*; and frequent references in Arias, ed., *The Rigoberta Menchú Controversy*. What I cite as the "consensus" explanation is Kobrak's in *Organizing and Repression*, supported in the CEH's Illustrative Case No. 79.

73. Cited in Stoll, *Rigoberta Menchú*.

74. *Siete Días en la* USAC, Epoca I, Año 3, no. 67 (10–16 March 1980).

75. For example, "Policía muere tras ataque a tiros por desconocidos," *El Imparcial* (30 January 1980), or "Tiroteo en la zona 5: Uno perece," *El Imparcial* (28 January 1980).

76. It was rumored that "El Chino" Lima bore responsibility for Oliverio Castañeda de León's assassination. AHPN, *Del silencio a la memoria*, 417.

77. "Ametrallado 2do. jefe del Comando 6 de la PN," *El Imparcial* (15 January 1980); for "El Chino" Lima as torturer, see McClintock, *The American Connection,* as well as "Siguen pista a quienes dieron muerte al 2do jefe del Comando 6," *El Imparcial* (16 January 1980).

78. "Policía muere, señorita de gravedad en atentado armado," *El Imparcial* (6 February 1980); EGP, *Guerra Popular,* no. 10 (April 1980), CIRMA: Colección Luis Pedro Taracena.

79. EGP, "Comunicado de prensa" (15 July 1980), CIRMA: Colección Luis Pedro Taracena.

80. For the EGP's attempts on Álvarez and Chupina's lives, see EGP, "Boletin de prensa: A Donaldo Álvarez y a Hermán [sic] Chupina tratamos de ajusticiarlos por criminals, represores y terroristas," February 1980, CIRMA: Colección Luis Pedro Taracena. Also see "Álvarez Ruiz escapa de atentado," *El Imparcial* (11 February 1980). For the FAR's plans to assassinate Chupina and Valiente Téllez, see CIA, "National Workers Central Hostages and Guatemalan Government Forces," 6 July 1980, DNSA, GU00659.

81. EGP, "Boletin de prensa: A Donaldo Álvarez y a Hermán [sic] Chupina."

82. USE/G to DOS, "Political Violence and Inter-agency Rivalry within Guatemalan Police Forces," 29 December 1980, NSA/GDP.

83. In one incident that demonstrated military intelligence's authority over the PN, Valiente ordered the execution of a navy captain in Escuintla who had been investigating cattle thefts in the area; one of the thieves was a relative of Valiente's who had asked his powerful family member for help. Valiente dispatched three detectives to the area and eliminated the inquisitive captain. When military intelligence traced the killing back to Valiente, they offered him two choices: kill the detectives who carried out the hit and the matter would be dropped, or else resign from the corps. The cadavers of the three detectives were found shortly thereafter, on the old road to Lake Atitlán. Secret untitled cable, CIA, March 1980, DNSA, GU00634.

84. For "bad blood," see USE/G to DOS, "Political Violence and Inter-agency Rivalry." For attacks on Los Vigilantes, see "Gobierno investigará las denuncias del ex-jefe del cuerpo de detectives," *Prensa Libre* (9 July 1981). For attacks on García Arredondo, see "Jefe policíaco emboscan," *El Imparcial* (3 June 1980).

85. "Despido masivo en Cuerpo de Detectives," *El Imparcial* (2 September 1980); "10 muertos, 6 heridos: Ataque a Vigilantes," *El Imparcial* (6 July 1981).

86. "Valiente se repone de heridas," *El Imparcial* (11 December 1981); "Valiente Téllez acusa al jefe de detectives," *Prensa Libre* (8 July 1981); "Atacada con morteros la casa de Valiente Téllez," *El Imparcial* (29 December 1981); "Valiente en proceso de recuperación," *El Imparcial* (30 December 1981); "Valiente Téllez abandonará el país," *El Imparcial* (31 December 1981).

87. McClintock, *The American Connection,* 159.

88. PDH, *El derecho a saber,* 37; USE/G to DOS, "Political Violence and Inter-agency Rivalry."

89. Carlos Díaz, "Detectives: Un dinámico cuerpo de la Policía Nacional," *Revista de la Policía Nacional* 15, no. 29 (1981): 39–40, HN.

90. USE/G to DOS, "Political Violence and Inter-agency Rivalry."

91. On the 1981 urban offensive, see Payeras, *El trueno en la ciudad.* It was hard-fought; from mid-December 1981 to mid-January 1982, the EGP reported that it had

undertaken forty-one successful "guerrilla actions" in the department of Guatemala, compared with just nine in El Quiché, eleven in Chimaltenango, and eleven in Alta Verapaz. EGP, "Número de acciones guerrilleras realizadas por las organizaciones politico-militares del 16 de diciembre de 1981 al 15 de enero de 1982," *Informador Guerrillero* (15 December 1981–15 January 1982): 1.

92. Ríos Montt's words to a Reuters journalist in December 1982 were "We have no scorched-earth policy. We have a policy of scorched Communists." Americas Watch Committee, "Guatemala Revised: How the Reagan Administration Finds 'Improvements' in Human Rights in Guatemala," September 1985, CIRMA: Colección Infostelle.

93. McClintock notes that Argentine and Israeli intelligence assistance was instrumental in the government's final rout of the urban insurgency, playing a decisive role in training the Guatemalans in "network analysis"—the computerized review of telephone calls and utility bills for suspect houses, which allowed the state to identify safe houses by their unusually high electricity consumption. McClintock, *The American Connection*, 219.

94. Garrard-Burnett, *Terror in the Land of the Holy Spirit*.

95. "No habrá más asesinatos, ni más corrupción en Guatemala," *El Imparcial* (24 March 1982).

96. Albizures, *El movimiento sindical*; Garrard-Burnett, *Terror in the Land of the Holy Spirit*.

97. USE/G to DOS, "Guatemalan Coup Developments: Thunder on the Right, Dissatisfaction by Young Officers," 25 March 1982, DNSA, GU00785. For School of the Americas, see "Hernán Orestes Ponce Nitsch," 12 January 1983, NSA/GDP, Box 13, Folder: Military Bios #4—950118DIA011.

98. For Álvarez's arsenal, see "Catearán casas de otros ex-funcionarios," *El Imparcial* (27 March 1982).

99. PDH, *El derecho a saber*, 39.

100. Schirmer, *The Guatemalan Military Project*, 167.

101. "Ningun asesinado a tiros, hoy," *El Imparcial* (27 March 1982).

102. Asociación de Estudiantes Universitarios, *No Nos Tientes* (1982), HN.

103. Cited in McClintock, *The American Connection*, 230; also see Schirmer, *The Guatemalan Military Project*, 291.

104. Secret cable, CIA, February 1983, DNSA, GU00897.

105. The process was interrupted by Mejía Víctores's coup.

106. For "often unruly," see CIA/DOI, "Latin America Review," 23 May 1983, DNSA, GU00919. For "corrupt Lucas García-Álvarez-Chupina model," see Schirmer, *The Guatemalan Military Project*, 32.

107. "Los generales no quieren que el pueblo piense," *Claridad: Organo Periodístico del* PGT-CC no. 7 (1–15 March 1983), CIRMA: Colección Holandés.

108. Kobrak, *Organizing and Repression*, 90.

109. For example, "2 muertos, 14 heridos por bombazo," *El Imparcial* (11 April 1983); "Operativo de registro de carros siguió en la ciudad," *El Imparcial* (8 April 1983); "Radio fue intervenido para pasar propaganda subversiva," *El Imparcial* (23 May 1983). The FAR carried out several high-profile kidnappings in the second half of 1983, capturing the sisters of both Ríos Montt and Mejía Víctores in an attempt to force the release of kidnapped activists. FAR, "Declaración de las Fuerzas Armadas Rebeldes (FAR) ante la

escalada intervencionista del gobierno de Ronald Reagan en Centroamérica," printed in *El País* (24 October 1983).

110. McClintock, *The American Connection*, 260n50.

111. A sampling of Ríos Montt's messianic rhetoric can be found in his weekly Sunday night radio addresses, compiled in *Mensajes del Presidente de la República*. Ríos Montt's evangelical connections did net him certain benefits; for example, his embargoed government was able to privately purchase cut-rate helicopter parts from Canadian "religious fundamentalists." NSC/Alfonso Sapia-Bosch, "Message from Guatemalan President Ríos Montt," 31 May 1983, DDRS.

112. "De Guatemala salen informes interesados," *El Imparcial* (21 September 1983).

113. Alonso, *15 fusilados al alba*.

114. "Guatemala no da importancia mayor a resolución de la ONU sobre derechos humanos," *El Imparcial* (14 December 1983).

115. "Alrededor de 50 universitarios han desaparecido ultimamente," *El Imparcial* (7 November 1983).

116. Kobrak, *Organizing and Repression*, 95.

117. Levenson-Estrada, *Trade Unionists*, chap. 6.

118. CIA/DOI, "Recent Kidnappings: Signs Point to Government Security Forces," 2 February 1984, DNSA, GU00995.

119. DOS Bureau of Intelligence and Research, "Central American Highlights—Guatemala: Political Violence Up," 23 February 1984, DNSA, GU01000.

120. Amézquita, *Guatemala*, 63.

121. Mejía Víctores cited in USE/G to SecState, "Mutual Support Group (GAM) Update," June 1985, NSA/GDP/Box 7; Americas Watch Committee, "Guatemala Revised," September 1985.

122. USE/G to SecState, "Background on Case of Héctor Orlando Gómez Calito, Murdered 'Mutual Support Group' (GAM) Member: Embassy Discussions with Two Sources," 3 April 1985, DNSA, GU01037.

123. On the Cuevas case, see Figueroa Ibarra, *Los que siempre estarán en ninguna parte*, 165–169; and Amézquita, *Guatemala*, 61–66.

124. See Amézquita, *Guatemala*, 59–65; and CEH, *Guatemala: Memoria del silencio*, vol. 1, annex 1, Illustrative Case No. 35.

125. In 1987, GAM activists led by Nineth Montenegro presented a legal brief naming seventeen military and ex-DIT officers as responsible for the Holy Week murders. USE/G to DOS, "The Mutual Support Group (GAM) Asks for Justice," 20 October 1987, NSA/GDP, Box 13, Folder 950114DIA010.

126. Letter, Ronald Reagan to Oscar Mejía Víctores, 30 October 1985, DDRS.

127. Letter, Ronald Reagan to Oscar Mejía Víctores.

128. McCleary, *Dictating Democracy*, 27–28; Schirmer, *The Guatemalan Military Project*, 22.

129. CIA, "National Intelligence Estimate: Guatemala: Prospects for the New Government," NIE 82-86, 30 January 1986, CIA/F. Also see McCleary, *Dictating Democracy*, 6.

130. The most prosaic example of this strategy was Ríos Montt's "frijoles y fusiles" campaign in the highlands; Schirmer, *The Guatemalan Military Project*, 22–25.

131. CIA, "National Intelligence Estimate: Guatemala: Prospects for the New Government."

132. CIA, "National Intelligence Estimate: Guatemala: Prospects for the New Government."

133. McCleary, *Dictating Democracy*, 29.

134. Schirmer, *The Guatemalan Military Project*, 1.

135. PGT, "La democratización forma parte del proyecto contrainsurgente," *Verdad*, 1984, CIRMA: Colección de Documentos.

136. Abrams, "An End to Tyranny in Latin America."

137. The United States allocated $103 million in assistance to Guatemala in fiscal year 1986; in October 1986, $300 million more was promised by Belgium, Spain, Germany, France, and Italy. Bureau of Inter-American Affairs, "Guatemala's Transition Toward Democracy," Public Information Series (Washington, DC: State Department Bureau of Public Affairs, November 1986).

138. According to Schirmer, the BROE was trained by two hundred Israeli military experts and armed with $750,000 worth of military equipment. Schirmer, *The Guatemalan Military Project*, 165.

139. Nairn and Simon, "Bureaucracy of Death," 14.

140. USE/G to DOS, "Rising Violence in Guatemala Again Causing Concern," 12 December 1987, DNSA, GU01139.

141. CERI-GUA, "Cerezo recibe ayuda para las fuerzas policiales," *Vistazo Mensual*, no. 8 (October 1986), CIRMA: Colección CIRMA, Serie Trudeau. As Nairn and Simon write, the abolition of the DIT "won the armed forces international praise, while G-2's assassinations continue[d] as before." Nairn and Simon, "Bureaucracy of Death," 17.

142. Representación Unitaria de Oposición Guatemalteca (RUOG), "La disolución del DIT," 1986, CIRMA: Colección Infostelle.

143. Hugo Arce, "La sombra del coronel," *Siglo Veintiuno* (26 July 1990).

144. Schirmer, *The Guatemalan Military Project*, 180.

145. Cited in Kobrak, *Organizing and Repression*, 100.

146. Glebbeek, *In the Crossfire of Democracy*, 107.

147. Elliott Abrams to USE/G, "Reply to the Interior Minister's Letter to the President Requesting Police Aid S/S No. 8619593," 8 July 1986; italics mine.

148. Elliott Abrams to USE/G, "Reply to the Interior Minister's Letter to the President." Kuzmarov discusses the U.S. transition from providing police counterinsurgency aid to providing police counternarcotics aid in his *Modernizing Repression*.

149. Schirmer, *The Guatemalan Military Project*, 197; United States Army Intelligence and Security Command, "Army Country Profile—Guatemala, Part II (U)," February 1994, DNSA, GU01793. Also see Department of Defense Joint Staff, "IIR (redacted) Intelligence Directorate (D-2) of the Guatemalan National Defense General Staff (U)," 16 February 1990, DNSA, GU01308.

150. Glebbeek, *In the Crossfire of Democracy*, 107; and Schirmer, *The Guatemalan Military Project*, 198–200.

151. "Ex-soldados serán empleados como agentes policíacos," *Prensa Libre* (17 March 1992).

152. Jonas, *The Battle for Guatemala*, 164.

153. Quoted in Schirmer, *The Guatemalan Military Project*, 198.

154. Kobrak, *Organizing and Repression*, 100–101; Washington Office on Latin America, "Cases Where the Guatemalan Military or Police Have Been Directly Implicated in

Human Rights Abuses," March 1988, CIRMA: Colección de Documentos. Also see CEH, *Guatemala: Memoria del silencio*.

155. Department of Defense, "IIR [redacted] Visit to National Police HQ—A Step Backward in Time," 6 May 1987, DNSA, GU01109.

156. CERI-GUA, "Otros dos asesinatos y un secuestro," and "Jefe policial justifica asesinatos" (10 March 1987).

157. CIA, untitled cable, February 1989, NSA/GDP.

158. Glebbeek, *In the Crossfire of Democracy*, 101; and McClintock, *The American Connection*, 160. Here the two systems overlapped: while the PN used its *rebajados* to carry out undesirable labors and the military did the same with its own *rebajados*, the PN was also encouraged to hire former military soldiers into the regular force as a means of "strengthening" the police. "Reforzarán Policía Nacional: Soldados de baja del ejército podrían ser contratados," *El Gráfico* (1 March 1992).

159. CIA, untitled cable, February 1989, courtesy NSA/GDP.

160. CIA, untitled cable, February 1989.

161. These materials include WOLA's series of publications on police training, *Temas y debates en la reforma de la seguridad pública*; also see UN High Commission on Human Rights, *Derechos humanos y aplicación de la ley*; IEPADES, *Manual de casos para el curso de derechos*; and the UNDP/ICCPG publication *La actuación policial y los derechos humanos en Guatemala*. Human rights training was also emphasized for the military: for example, as of 1993, army soldiers were required to carry a "code of conduct" document in their pockets detailing how they needed to "respect human rights." USE/G to DOS, "Human Rights Awareness for Guatemalan Army Troops," 23 March 1993, NSA/GDP, Box 13, Folder: 950114DIAO10.

162. Glebbeek, *In the Crossfire of Democracy*, 107.

163. Despite such strong words, it is worth remembering that functionaries like Stroock were often not permitted to comment on the full range of intelligence available. Before giving a press conference on Central American violence in September 1989, his preconference talking points indicated, "Mr. Stroock was advised . . . [to] avoid the words right and left. Use the word extremists or dissident elements. Don't use the term private sector as a source of the violence." Unlabeled, unpublished document, September 1989, NSA/GDP, Box: Guatemala Incoming FOIAS.

164. USE/G to DOS, "Ambassador Calls on New National Police Director Col. Julio Caballeros," 5 July 1990, DNSA, GU01347.

165. For "spies," see USE/G to DOS, "National Police Director on His Plans." On efforts to purge the PN, see "Cosas del lado oscuro de la Policía Nacional," *Prensa Libre* (8 September 1991); on civil society's calls for more police purges, see "Urge la depuración de la Policía Nacional," *La República* (30 September 1994); on cynicism about the possibility of police reform, see "FRG afirma que depuración en la Policía Nacional es 'show politico,'" *La República* (1 February 1996).

166. Interview, PRAHPN014, 31 October 2007. The anniversary of the 1944 revolution was 20 October.

167. Interview, PRAHPN014.

168. On the inadequacies of postwar security reform, see Arévalo de León, *Función militar*; Gutiérrez, *Hacia un paradigma democrático*; Peacock and Beltrán, *Poderes ocul-*

tos; Byrne, Stanley, and Garst, *Rescuing Police Reform*; Garst, *Military Intelligence and Human Rights*; Hernández, "A Long Road." On police reform in postconflict transitions, see Stanley and Holiday in Steadman et al., eds., *Ending Civil Wars*; on police reform in other settings, see Chevigny, *The Edge of the Knife*.

169. Gobierno de Guatemala, Unidad Revolucionaria Nacional Guatemalteca, and Naciones Unidas, *Acuerdo sobre el fortalecimiento del poder civil y función del Ejército en una sociedad democrática*.

170. Many details in this paragraph come from Jonas, *Of Centaurs and Doves*, 151.

171. ICITAP began assisting the PN in 1986, after the Reagan administration's reversal of the 1974 congressional ban on U.S. foreign police aid.

172. MINUGUA, "La Policía Nacional Civil," 2001; Stanley and Holiday, "Broad Participation, Diffuse Responsibility," 451.

173. Byrne, Stanley, and Garst, *Rescuing Police Reform*, 4; Pérez, "Iglesia, PDH y la Usac."

174. Seijo, "Nuevo jefe depurará el Dinc."

175. Bayley, *Patterns of Policing*, 189; Bittner, *Aspects of Police Work*, 22.

SIX. REVOLUTIONARY LIVES IN THE ARCHIVES

1. The murder of Bishop Juan Gerardi by army officers after the release of the REMHI report in April 1998 is the best-known, but by no means the only, such case.

2. Interview, Alberto Fuentes; italics mine.

3. For example, interview, PRAHPN006; interview, PRAHPN018; interview, PRAHPN014; interview, PRAHPN022.

4. Interview, PRAHPN022.

5. Interview, PRAHPN024.

6. Interview, PRAHPN022.

7. All names used, except for those of public figures like the Project's director and assistant director, are pseudonyms. Some workers' stories will be familiar to others within the Project, given the long histories some of them share; the goal, simply, is that they be untraceable beyond the Project. I do not obscure details of workers' past political involvement; scholars opposed to the "shock anthropology" of those who compile tales of abstracted horror deracinated from the political conditions of their production have exposed the reactionary politics of such an approach. See McAllister, *The Good Road*. The people interviewed for this chapter constitute a small minority of the Project staff, and some are no longer employed there, which muddies the waters of personal identification. Ultimately, the PNC already knows far more about the Project staff—down to their license plate numbers and home addresses—than I reveal here.

8. Interview, PRAHPN005.

9. Interview, PRAHPN002; Nelson, *A Finger in the Wound*.

10. Cohen, *States of Denial*, 84, 153; Feitlowitz, *A Lexicon of Terror*, 20.

11. Cohen, *States of Denial*, 130.

12. Garton Ash, *The File*, 108.

13. Schafer, *The Soundscape*.

14. Interview, PRAHPN014.

15. Interview, PRAHPN027.

16. Interview, PRAHPN027.

17. Interview, PRAHPNO18.

18. Interview, PRAHPNO17, 8 November 2007.

19. On *conciencia*, see McAllister, "Good People."

20. Interview, PRAHPNO22.

21. Kate Doyle mentions this in her article "The Atrocity Files," 63. See also interviews, PRAHPNO03, PRAHPNO05, PRAHPNO10, PRAHPNO22, PRAHPNO17, PRAHPNO06, and Alberto Fuentes.

22. Interview, PRAHPNO07.

23. Interview, PRAHPNO22.

24. Interview, Edeliberto Cifuentes.

25. Interview, PRAHPNO18.

26. See Derrida, *Archive Fever*; Mbembe, "The Power of the Archive," 25.

27. Mbembe, "The Power of the Archive," 25.

28. Interview, PRAHPNO06.

29. Interview, PRAHPNO06.

30. Interview, PRAHPNO27; Doyle, "The Atrocity Files."

31. Interview, PRAHPNO05.

32. Interview, PRAHPNO24. The need on the part of these survivors to have their claims recognized by the state, even while being constantly confronted with evidence of state violence, speaks to the magic and power of the state itself—as an interpellating enemy but also, potentially, an interpellating friend and legitimizer. Either way, and despite themselves, these memory workers remain archival subjects in ways not altogether empowering. For many a resolution to this tension is found, as Felman writes, in the form of criminal justice as both idea and practice—a tightly woven relationship between law and trauma that responds to "the great catastrophes and the collective traumas of the twentieth century." Felman, *The Juridical Unconscious*, 3.

33. Interview, PRAHPNO24.

34. Interview, PRAHPNO14.

35. Interview, PRAHPNO18.

36. Interview, PRAHPNO02.

37. Interview, PRAHPNO04.

38. Interview, PRAHPNO02.

39. Harris, "The Archival Sliver," 63–86.

40. Interview, PRAHPNO10.

41. Interview, PRAHPNO17.

42. Interview, PRAHPNO27.

43. Interview, PRAHPNO06.

44. Interview, Alberto Fuentes; and see ODHAG, *La memoria tiene la palabra*, an after-the-fact reflection by REMHI participants on the process of having worked on the REMHI report.

45. Interview, Fredy Peccerelli, 30 October 2007.

46. Interview, PRAHPNO17.

47. Interview, PRAHPNO14.

48. Interview, PRAHPNO06.

49. Interview, PRAHPNO07.

50. Interview, Alberto Fuentes.

51. Interview, PRAHPN014.

52. Interview, PRAHPN022.

53. Interview, PRAHPN007.

54. As such, the experiences of workers in the PN archives contradict interpretations of trauma as "unspeakable," "untranslatable," and therefore nonspecific and impossible to link to the political conditions of its production. See Scarry, *The Body in Pain*; for a more developed version of this critique, see Grandin, introduction to Grandin and Joseph, eds., *A Century of Revolution*.

55. On "traitors to the homeland," see interview, Carla Villagrán.

56. On the defamation of GAM, see Departamento de Información y Divulgación del Ejército, "El Ejército de Guatemala remite al GAM ante la opinion pública," 17 September 1986, CIRMA: Colección de Documentos, 2807.

57. Interview, PRAHPN006.

58. Interview, PRAHPN024.

59. Interview, PRAHPN028.

60. Interview, PRAHPN024.

61. Interview, PRAHPN022.

62. Interview, Carla Villagrán. Villagrán lost her first husband to state-sponsored terror, a case featured in the Diario Militar; see Doyle, "The Atrocity Files."

63. On *engaño*, see Nelson's *Reckoning*.

64. Interview, PRAHPN018.

65. Trace, "What Is Recorded Is Never Simply 'What Happened.'"

66. Interview, PRAHPN018.

67. Sometimes these mass raids were reported in the press, sometimes not. For an example, see "625 Capturados en redadas," *El Imparcial* (4 June 1984), in which more than ten thousand "security agents" were deployed over the course of a week in order to "control common delinquency," or else "Más de mil van capturados," *El Imparcial* (24 September 1984).

68. Interview, PRAHPN002.

69. Arendt, *Eichmann in Jerusalem*, 84–85.

70. Cohen draws on Taussig and Feitlowitz in his discussion of "talking terror." Cohen, *States of Denial*, 84.

71. Jelin, *State Repression*, 6–7.

72. Interview, PRAHPN010.

73. Interview, PRAHPN002.

74. Interview, PRAHPN028.

75. Interview, PRAHPN018.

76. "Instalaciones norteamericanas para el entrenamiento contrainsurgente," Document 266, Colección Payeras-Colom, CIRMA. Throughout the 1960s and early 1970s, the Guatemalan press regularly reported on groups of PN officers returning from Washington or Panamá after receiving training in, for example, "handling special weapons," "persecuting delinquency," and "reducing criminality and subversive activities."

77. Interview, PRAHPN027; interview, PRAHPN028.

78. Interview, PRAHPN022.

79. Interview, PRAHPN005.

80. Interview, Alberto Fuentes.

81. Interview, Ana Corado.

82. Interview, PRAHPN010.

83. Interview, PRAHPN027.

84. Interview, PRAHPN022.

85. Interview, PRAHPN018.

86. Interview, PRAHPN003.

87. Interview, PRAHPN007.

88. Interview, Ana Corado.

89. Interview, PRAHPN002.

90. Interview, PRAHPN028.

91. Interview, PRAHPN007.

92. Interview, Alberto Fuentes.

93. Browning, *Ordinary Men*.

94. Interview, PRAHPN007.

95. Interview, PRAHPN005.

96. Interview, PRAHPN003.

97. Interview, PRAHPN028.

98. See Arriaza and Roht-Arriaza, "Social Reconstruction"; Fletcher and Weinstein, "Violence and Social Repair," 573.

99. Interview, Alberto Fuentes.

100. Interview, PRAHPN007.

101. Interview, PRAHPN018.

102. A fascinating account of exiles in Mexico is found in Ludec, "Voces del exilio."

103. Interview, PRAHPN006; also, see Ludec, "Voces del exilio."

104. Interview, PRAHPN005.

105. Interview, PRAHPN022.

106. Interview, PRAHPN005.

107. Interview, PRAHPN007.

108. Interview, PRAHPN018.

109. Interview, PRAHPN024.

110. Interview, PRAHPN007.

111. Interview, Iduvina Hernández.

112. Interview, PRAHPN018.

113. Interview, PRAHPN022.

SEVEN. ARCHIVES AND THE NEXT GENERATION(S)

1. See editor Roque Dalton's essay, "Otto René Castillo," in Castillo, *Informe de una injusticia*, 208–12.

2. Translation is an amalgam of Margaret Randall's and Deborah Levenson's translations, found in Randall, trans., *Let's Go!*, and Fried et al., eds., *Guatemala in Rebellion*.

3. PRAHPN, "Informe de Avances—Agosto 2007."

4. Susana Kaiser refers to the post-terror generation in Argentina as "gray zoners." See Kaiser, *Postmemories of Terror*.

5. See, for example, Dillenburger, Fargas, and Akhonzada, "Long-Term Effects of Political Violence."

6. Interview, PRAHPNO23.

7. Hoffman, *Complex Histories, Contested Memories*, 5.

8. For example, Guatemala has nothing like the German phenomenon of *Vaterliteratur*, the literature produced by writers analyzing their fathers' roles as Holocaust perpetrators. See Schlant, *The Language of Silence*; Fuchs, *Phantoms of War*.

9. Hoffman, *Complex Histories, Contested Memories*, 19.

10. Interviews, PRAHPNO01, 9 August 2007; PRAHPNO09, 13 October 2007; PRAHPNO12; PRAHPNO13, 30 October 2007; PRAHPNO15; PRAHPNO16, 6 November 2007 and 17 January 2008; PRAHPNO21, 13 November 2007; PRAHPNO23.

11. Blouin and Rosenberg, "Preface and Acknowledgments," in their *Archives, Documentation, and Institutions*, ix.

12. Interview, PRAHPNO29, 23 January 2008.

13. Interview, PRAHPNO23; interview, PRAHPNO15; interview, PRAHPNO12.

14. On the Nicaraguan *colmena* experience, see Ramírez, dir., *Las colmenas*.

15. Interview, PRAHPNO29.

16. Interview, PRAHPNO23.

17. Children caught up in political conflicts have different ways of responding to their parents' involvement: some with acceptance, but others with resistance and hostility. A well-known case of the latter is that of Bettina Röhl, the daughter of Ulrike Meinhof—the German journalist who cofounded the Red Army Faction. As a condition of permitting the posthumous publication of her mother's journalistic work, Röhl required that the volume include an essay of her own in which she attacks Meinhof's political legacy. See Röhl, "Icon of the Left," in Bauer, ed., *Everybody Talks about the Weather . . . We Don't*, 257–63.

18. Interview, PRAHPNO19, 9 November 2007.

19. Interview, PRAHPNO29.

20. Interview, PRAHPNO19.

21. Interview, PRAHPNO12.

22. Interview, PRAHPNO13.

23. Interview, PRAHPNO01.

24. Interview, PRAHPNO09.

25. Interview, PRAHPNO21.

26. Interview, PRAHPNO16.

27. Stern, *Battling for Hearts and Minds*, 5.

28. Interview, PRAHPNO12.

29. Interview, PRAHPNO23.

30. Hoffman, *After Such Knowledge*, 66.

31. Hoffman, *After Such Knowledge*, 106.

32. Interview, PRAHPNO13.

33. Interview, Ana Corado.

34. Interview, PRAHPNO16.

35. Interview, PRAHPNO13.

36. Interview, PRAHPNO01.

37. Technology coordinator Jorge Villagrán pointed out that this was a particular challenge for the team of document codifiers that he oversaw, who were frustrated with a task that was "very monotonous in practice. So we've had problems, people have been unhappy in the work, because they get bored of doing the same thing, of interpreting the documents in the same way over and over again. . . . So that's been one of the most difficult aspects of this work: making sure that the staff are motivated, that they're eager to do the work, that they feel good about doing a job that is extremely repetitive." Interview, Jorge Villagrán.

38. For transition from "family" to "workplace," see interview, PRAHPNO29.

39. Interview, PRAHPNO23.

40. Interview, PRAHPNO29.

41. Interview, PRAHPNO01.

42. Interview, PRAHPNO19.

43. Interview, Alberto Fuentes.

44. Interview, Gustavo Meoño.

45. Interview, Gustavo Meoño.

46. Interview, Gustavo Meoño.

47. Interview, PRAHPNO21.

48. Interview, PRAHPNO05.

49. Interview, PRAHPNO05.

50. Interview, PRAHPNO21.

51. Interview, PRAHPNO13.

52. Interview, PRAHPNO05.

53. Interview, PRAHPNO13.

54. Interview, PRAHPNO21.

55. Interview, PRAHPNO16.

56. Interview, PRAHPNO21.

57. Interview, PRAHPNO06.

58. Interview, PRAHPNO23.

59. The small size of Guatemala's human rights sector was not necessarily an indication that no one else cared about justice; instead, it should be interpreted in the context of the relatively tiny size of the middle class. While most of the population had to focus on economic survival, this did not mean they were disinterested in efforts to recover the history of the armed conflict; one recent national survey found that 90 percent of the population "demands and expects" reparations for war victims. Only 24 percent of those interviewed wanted to "neither know about nor discuss the past." However, the study did find that youths were far less likely to be interested in learning about the past, or to have substantive knowledge about recent history. Marcela Gereda, "Juventud, historia, y memoria," *El Periódico* (10 August 2009).

60. Zone 10 is a wealthy area of Guatemala City. Interview, PRAHPNO29.

61. Interview, PRAHPNO01.

62. Interview, PRAHPNO01.

63. Interview, PRAHPNO05.

64. Interview, PRAHPNO05.

65. Winaq, a new political party led by Rigoberta Menchú, aimed to represent Gua-

temala's Maya majority. For the 2007 presidential elections, it allied with Encuentro por Guatemala, another new party led by Nineth Montenegro; their coalition was crushed at the ballot box.

66. Interview, PRAHPNO23.

67. Interview, PRAHPNO23.

68. Interview, PRAHPNO24.

69. Interview, PRAHPNO21.

70. Interview, PRAHPNO23.

71. Interview, Gustavo Meoño.

72. Interview, PRAHPNO19.

73. Interview, PRAHPNO18.

74. Interview, PRAHPNO03.

75. Interview, PRAHPNO17.

76. Interview, PRAHPNO18.

77. HIJOS, a name used throughout the hemisphere by groups of young activists who lost family members to Cold War dictatorships, was founded in Guatemala by the daughter of PGT activist Luz Haydee Méndez Calderón, whose case was among those in the Diario Militar. See Nolin, *Transnational Ruptures*, 72.

78. Interview, PRAHPNO17.

79. Interview, PRAHPNO27.

80. Interview, PRAHPNO01.

81. Interview, PRAHPNO23.

82. Interview, PRAHPNO23; interview, PRAHPNO21.

83. Interview, PRAHPNO21.

84. Interview, PRAHPNO23.

85. Interview, PRAHPNO23.

86. Interview, PRAHPNO23.

87. Interview, PRAHPNO16.

88. Interview, PRAHPNO13.

89. Interview, PRAHPNO23.

90. In 2006, Guatemala was ranked lowest in the Americas on the Human Development Index except for Haiti. See CIIDH, *Situación de los derechos económicos, sociales, y culturales en Guatemala, 2006*; State Department, Bureau of Democracy, Human Rights, and Labor, *2008 Country Reports on Human Rights Practices: Guatemala*.

91. Norma Stoltz Chinchilla details how Latin American feminists have linked authoritarianism in society to authoritarianism in the family. Stoltz Chinchilla, "Marxism, Feminism, and the Struggle for Democracy."

92. Cited in Claudia Méndez Arriaza, "Este archivo explica por qué somos callados, desconfiados y amishados," *El Periódico* (23 July 2006).

93. Cited in Méndez Arriaza, "Este archivo explica por qué somos callados, desconfiados y amishados."

94. Interview, PRAHPNO16.

95. Interview, PRAHPNO16.

96. Interview, PRAHPNO01.

97. Interview, PRAHPNO09.

98. Interview, Alberto Fuentes.

99. Interview, PRAHPNO29.

EIGHT. CHANGING THE LAW OF WHAT CAN BE SAID, AND DONE

1. On the AGCA, see interview, Anna Carla Ericastilla; on the Project's budget, see Leonardo Cereser, "Capturaban sin orden de juez," *Prensa Libre* (19 January 2008).

2. Lucía Escobar, "Uli Stelzner en la isla del horror," *El Periódico* (29 March 2009); also see Uli Stelzner, dir., *La isla*.

3. "Sale a luz tráfico de niños durante la guerra interna," *El Periódico* (24 March 2009); editorial, "Los huérfanos del conflicto," *Prensa Libre* (24 March 2009); Ligia Flores, "Archivo de SBS podría esclarecer adopciones ilegales durante guerra," *La Hora* (10 March 2009).

4. Interview, Ingrid Molina.

5. "Luchan por encontrar la identidad perdida," *Prensa Libre* (8 August 2009); interview, Fredy Peccerelli.

6. Interview, Gustavo Palma; interview, Alberto Fuentes.

7. Interview, Alberto Fuentes.

8. Leonardo Cereser, "Archivo histórico peligra por falta de mantenimiento," *Prensa Libre* (4 May 2009).

9. Guatemala lagged, regionally, in passing an access to information law—Honduras and Nicaragua passed theirs in 2006, Panamá in 2002, and Belize in 1994.

10. Hugo Alvarado, "Carlos Barreda: Queremos más y mejor acceso a información," *Prensa Libre* (15 September 2008); Leonardo Cereser, "Avanzan preparativos para verificar nueva Ley de Acceso a la Información," *Prensa Libre* (15 February 2009).

11. The law's main proponents were Acción Ciudadana, a watchdog outfit that monitored public administration; the local chapter of Transparency International; and the Association of Guatemalan Journalists. Luisa F. Rodríguez, "Diversos sectores urgen aprobación de ley de acceso a información," *Prensa Libre* (2 April 2008); "Guatemala muestra atrasos en lucha contra la corrupción," *El Periódico* (7 December 2007); Leslie Pérez, "Guatemaltecos, sin acceso a la información pública," *Prensa Libre* (20 January 2008).

12. Letter, Andrew Hudson et al. to General Abraham Valenzuela González, 3 February 2009, www.humanrightsfirst.org/pdf/090204-HRD-ltr-mil-arch-esp.pdf.

13. Audit culture operated here in full force. See Nelson, *Reckoning*, 27; Strathern, *Audit Cultures*; Power, *The Audit Society*; Hetherington, *Guerrilla Auditors*.

14. Anonymous intelligence official cited in Gramajo Valdés, *El derecho de acceso*, 99.

15. Lorena Seijo, "Plan Sofía confirma autoría de masacres," *Prensa Libre* (18 March 2007).

16. "Ejército dice que 'desaparecieron' dos informes militares," *Prensa Libre* (26 February 2009). In December 2009, human rights organizations presented Plan Sofía as evidence in Spain's genocide case against eight Guatemalan military and police officials. See Doyle, "Operation Sofía."

17. Carmen Esquivel Sarría, "Apertura de archivos militares," *Prensa Latina* (3 March 2008); "Aplausos y críticas por anuncio de apertura," *Prensa Libre* (25 February 2009).

18. See editorial, *La Hora* (27 February 2009); "Aplausos y críticas por anuncio de

apertura," *Prensa Libre* (25 February 2009); Miguel Angel Albízures, "El ofrecimiento de Colom," *El Periódico* (4 March 2009).

19. Javier Estrada Tobar, "PDH acompañará investigaciones en archivos militares," *La Hora* (4 March 2009).

20. Field notes, 2008.

21. Juan Luis Font, "Abrir archivos es poca cosa," *El Periódico* (29 February 2009).

22. Guy Adams, "The Lawyer Taking on Guatemala's Criminal Gangs," *Independent* (4 January 2012).

23. Hugo Alvarado, "Ejército se niega a entregar archivos," *Prensa Libre* (22 October 2008).

24. Linares and Pérez Molina are cited in "Aplausos y críticas por anuncio de apertura," *Prensa Libre* (25 February 2009). On Pérez Molina and the Gerardi killing, see Goldman, *The Art of Political Murder*.

25. "Gobierno abre más de 12 mil archivos militares," *Prensa Libre* (20 June 2011).

26. Danilo Valladares, "The Best-Kept Secrets: The Military's," *Inter Press Service News Agency* (9 March 2010).

27. This text was once available on the "Fundamentos" section of the Presidential Peace Secretariat's website, www.sepaz.gob.gt, but ceased to be available after president Otto Pérez Molina shut down the Peace Archives Directorate in 2012.

28. This included the push for a freedom of information law, which included political pressure and implementation suggestions from the UN and the Organization of American States. Gramajo Valdés, *El derecho de acceso*, 96.

29. See Memoria del Mundo, *Directrices para la salvaguardia del patrimonio documental*; *Manual técnico para la administración, manejo, y conservación del patrimonio documental*.

30. Interview, Michael Moerth.

31. Interview, Michael Moerth; interview, Agnes Bernzen; interview, Åsa Wallton.

32. Nelson highlights the "two-facedness" of international aid in Guatemala—neither wholly beneficent nor wholly counterinsurgent. Nelson, *Reckoning*, 310–11.

33. Interview, PRAHPN005.

34. See Hernández Pico, *Terminar la guerra*; Sandoval and Ríos, *La izquierda*; Sáenz de Tejada, *Revolucionarios*.

35. Interview, Mario Polanco; interview, Estuardo Galeano; interview, Iduvina Hernández.

36. Interview, Iduvina Hernández.

37. Interview, Estuardo Galeano.

38. R. Estrada and R. Quinto, "Piden acceso a archivos de la PN," *El Periódico* (26 February 2008).

39. For reactions to Chupina's death, see Leonardo Cereser and Julio Lara, "Murió Germán Chupina Barahona," *Prensa Libre* (18 February 2008); Miguel Angel Albizures, "Chupina no fue absuelto," *El Periódico* (19 February 2008); Ana Miza, "Críticas contra justicia por deceso en impunidad," *La Hora* (19 February 2008).

40. Interview, Alberto Fuentes.

41. The Spanish filed international arrest warrants for the accused in July 2006; surprisingly, the Guatemalan courts initially upheld the warrants and arrested both Guevara

and García Arredondo. But in 2007, Guatemala's highest court overturned that decision, ruling that Spain did not have jurisdiction in the case and releasing Guevara and García Arredondo back into civilian life. The Spanish, undeterred, began in 2008 to interview witnesses for the case. See Roht-Arriaza and Bernabeu, "The Guatemalan Genocide Case in Spain," 1–4; Roht-Arriaza, "Making the State Do Justice." In 2011 and 2012, Ríos Montt, Mejía Víctores, and Pedro García Arredondo were all indicted by the domestic court system for crimes against humanity.

42. As of the time of this writing, that is.

43. See, for example, Leonardo Cereser, "Revela estrategia represiva de PN," *Prensa Libre* (25 March 2009).

44. Tomuschat, "Clarification Commission in Guatemala"; Nelson, *A Finger in the Wound*; Grandin, "Chronicles."

45. See Sergio Fernando Alvarado Morales, *Informe Anual Circunstanciado: 2003* and the corresponding yearly reports for 2004, 2005, and 2006.

46. Interview, Alvarado Morales; "Harán museo," *El Periódico* (12 January 2008).

47. Reappointment required the support of two-thirds of the members of Congress.

48. Interview, Iduvina Hernández.

49. Miguel Angel Albizures, "A qué juega el Procurador," *El Periódico* (10 September 2009); on memory as a political commodity, see Bilbija and Payne, eds., *Accounting for Violence*.

50. Nelson, *Reckoning*.

51. Interview, PRAHPN027.

52. Field notes, February 2008; "Doctor Pablo Werner Ramírez," *El Defensor del Pueblo* (January 2008): 7.

53. Interview, PRAHPN028.

54. Interview, PRAHPN027.

55. Field notes, 2006–2008.

56. Interview, PRAHPN027.

57. Field notes, February 2008.

58. See PDH, Accord No. SG-003-2009, "Reglamento del Servicio de Referencia Sobre Violaciones a los Derechos Humanos," published in *Diario de Centroamérica* (27 February 2009). After the archives were transferred from PDH to AGCA custody, SEREVIDH was eliminated and replaced by the Unidad de Acceso a la Información.

59. Leonardo Cereser, "PDH señala agresiones, amenazas, y persecuciones en caso García," *Prensa Libre* (20 March 2009); Juan Manuel Castillo, "PDH denuncia amenazas contra su personal," *El Periódico* (20 March 2009).

601. "Día cruento deriva en caos vial en varias arterias de la capital," *Prensa Libre* (24 March 2009).

61. "Comercio cierra sus puertas antes de lo acostumbrado," *Prensa Libre* (24 March 2009).

62. "No es necesario un estado de Excepción, dice Colom," *Prensa Libre* (24 March 2009).

63. González Quintana, "La respuesta del terror."

64. I attended this ceremony; the following descriptions are taken from my notes.

65. Nothing more was heard from Luis de Lión (this was his nom de plume; his given name was José Luis de León Díaz) until his name appeared in the Diario Militar.

66. Quoted in Manuel Roig-Franzia, "Sending a Brutal Message about Human Rights," *Washington Post* (11 April 2009).

67. Leonardo Cereser, "Procurador repudia ataque contra su esposa," *Prensa Libre* (27 March 2009).

68. For Castresana's quote and "dead or alive," see Claudia Méndez Arriaza, "La historia detrás de la petición," *El Periódico* (4 August 2009).

69. Miguel Angel Sandoval, "La PDH está bajo la lupa" (23 June 2009), www.albedrio. org; Erwin Pérez, "Los aprietos del Procurador Sergio Morales" (26 June 2009), www .i-dem.org.

70. CICIG, Caso No. 01071-2009-00678, Juzgado Undécimo de Primera Instancia Penal, 2do Oficial, briefing available at www.cicig.org.

71. Alejandro Pérez, "PDH sin recursos para mantener archivos de la Policía Nacional," *El Periódico* (20 June 2009).

72. R. Sandoval and O. Herrera, "El Gobierno no puede financiar el trabajo de los archivos de la PN," *El Periódico* (27 June 2009).

73. Claudia Méndez Arriaza, "Exigen captura de ex-jefe de Cuarto Cuerpo de Policía," *El Periódico* (26 June 2009).

74. Various organizations, "ONGs exigen protección de Archivo Histórico de la Policía Nacional," www.albedrio.org (29 June 2009).

75. Ricardo Quinto, "Archivos de la extinta PN serán públicos," *Prensa Libre* (30 June 2009).

76. "Presidente oficializa traslado de archivos de la PN al Ministerio de Cultura," *Prensa Libre* (30 June 2009).

77. PRAHPN, "Se inicia nueva fase en el proyecto 'Archivo Histórico de la Policía Nacional.'"

78. Foucault, *The Archaeology of Knowledge*, 129.

79. Foucault, *The Archaeology of Knowledge*, 130.

80. Robertson, "Mechanisms of Exclusion."

81. On "thinkability," see Hacking, *Historical Ontology*.

82. Interview, PRAHPN007.

83. Combe, *Archives interdites*, 321.

NINE. CONCLUSION

1. Taussig, *Shamanism, Colonialism, and the Wild Man*.

2. Cook and Schwartz, "Archives, Records, and Power," 13.

3. Cited in Ketelaar, "Recordkeeping and Societal Power," 6.

4. Cited in Stephen Kinzer, "East Germans Face Their Accusers," *New York Times* (12 April 1992); the case is also discussed in Garton Ash, *The File*.

5. Garton Ash, *The File*, 231.

6. Guadamuz, "Habeas Data."

7. See www.un.org/en/events/righttotruthday/; see also the IACHR's Office of the Special Rapporteur for Freedom of Expression, "Right to the Truth," www.cidh.org/relatoria /showarticle.asp?artID=156&lID=1; and "Promotion and Protection of Human Rights: Report of the OHCHR," ECOSOC E/CN.4/2006/91, 8 February 2006.

8. See Open Society Justice Initiative et al., "*Amicus Curiae* Submission in the Case

of *Gomes Lund and Others v. Brazil*," June 2010; Inter-American Court on Human Rights, sentence, *Gomes Lund and Others v. Brazil*, November 24, 2010, both available at www .soros.org/initiatives/justice/litigation/brazil.

9. Sikkink, *The Justice Cascade*.

10. Roht-Arriaza, *The Pinochet Effect*; Rory Carroll, "Latin America Confronts State Atrocities of Bloody Past," *Guardian* (25 January 2012).

11. Two previous cases, those of Choatalúm and El Jute, were the first convictions for the crime of forced disappearance; both involved military perpetrators.

12. Doyle and Willard, "27 Years Later, Justice for Fernando García."

13. Statement by Alejandra García Montenegro, 1 November 2010, casofernando garcia.org.

14. Doyle, "'I Wanted Him Back Alive': An Account of Edgar Fernando García's Case from Inside 'Tribunals Tower,'" in *Unredacted: The National Security Archive, Unedited and Uncensored* (26 October 2010), http://nsarchive.wordpress.com.

15. "Guatemala Jails Former Police Chief over Student Kidnapping," *Telegraph* (22 August 2012). As of this writing, García Arredondo's lawyers were appealing the sentence.

16. Raúl Minondo Ayau, "Comentarios," *elPeriódico* (22 June 2011).

17. Emphasis in original. "La Asociación de Veteranos Militares de Guatemala AVEMILGUA Ante la opinión Nacional e Internacional MANIFIESTA," *Prensa Libre* (July 22, 2011).

18. Weld, "Dignifying the Guerrillero."

19. Oswaldo J. Hernández, "La marcha de los veteranos," *Plaza Pública* (15 November 2011); Julio Revolorio, "Exigen terminar con la persecución contra militares," *elPeriódico* (15 November 2011); "Militares rechazan que haya habido genocidio," *Prensa Libre* (14 November 2011).

20. Jose Andrés Ochoa, "Méndez Ruiz," *Plaza Pública* (27 January 2012).

21. "Sí, es contra Claudia Paz y Paz," *elPeriódico* (29 November 2011).

22. Ricardo Méndez Ruiz, "Y lo sostengo, por el amor de Dios!," *elPeriódico* (5 February 2012).

23. Daniela Castillo, "En Guatemala no hubo genocidio," *elPeriódico* (31 January 2012); Martín Rodríguez Pellecer, "Quiero que alguien me demuestre que hubo genocidio," *Plaza Pública* (25 July 2011).

24. CEH, *Guatemala: Memoria del silencio*, Conclusions, para. I:49.

25. Weld, "Dignifying the Guerrillero."

26. Hayner, *Unspeakable Truths*, 5.

27. Interview, PRAHPN018.

28. McAdams notes of the Stasi archives that "above and beyond the challenge of retrieving lost data from the archives, a more serious objection to the use of the MfS files to reconstruct the past was that they were factually unreliable." McAdams, *Judging the Past*, 67.

29. On history and memory, see Jelin, *State Repression*, chap. 4; Oglesby, "Educating Citizens in Postwar Guatemala."

30. Derrida, *Archive Fever*, 4.

31. This point echoes the argument that Guatemalan terror was not a function of state *decomposition* but rather was a component of state *formation*—the foundation of

the military's plan of national stabilization through a return to constitutional rule. See Grandin, "The Instruction of Great Catastrophe."

32. Gramajo Valdés writes that increased access to state information can "form the genesis of a modification in the established relations between government and governed." Gramajo Valdés, *El derecho de acceso*, 68.

33. Derrida, *Archive Fever*.

34. The permanent preservation of the digitized records was guaranteed by the Swiss Federal Archives; their accessibility online was made possible by the University of Texas at Austin.

35. Interview, PRAHPNO02.

36. The murder of Bishop Juan Gerardi in 1998 illustrated this all too well.

37. "Suciedad civil" is a pun on "sociedad civil," or "civil society," translating to something like "civil filth." Raúl Minondo Ayau, "Comentarios," *El Periódico* (1 July 2009).

38. For a detailed discussion of this process, see Grandin, "The Instruction of Great Catastrophe."

39. Interview, PRAHPNO29.

40. Arendt, *Eichmann in Jerusalem*, 232–33.

41. Interview, PRAHPNO05.

42. Stoler, *Along the Archival Grain*, 45.

43. Trouillot, *Silencing the Past*.

44. Castillo, "La Tumba de Dios," in Castillo, *Informe de una injusticia*, 222–23.

45. Zinn, "Secrecy, Archives, and the Public Interest."

46. I borrow "eternal tyranny" from Jean-Marie Simon.

47. Interview, PRAHPNO24.

BIBLIOGRAPHY

BIBLIOGRAPHIC NOTE

Research for this book was conducted at the Historical Archives of the National Police (AHPN), the Archivo General de Centroamérica (AGCA), the Centro de Investigaciones Regionales de Mesoamérica (CIRMA), the Hemeroteca Nacional (HN), the National Security Archive's Guatemala Documentation Project (NSA/CGP), the archives of the Tipografía Nacional (TN), and the U.S. National Archives at College Park (NACP). I also obtained digitized documents from the Declassified Documents Reference System (DDRS), the Digital National Security Archive (DNSA), and the Central Intelligence Agency FOIA Reading Room (CIA/F). Periodicals cited in the notes are listed below. Most can be found in the Hemeroteca Nacional, in CIRMA's press clippings archive, or in the AGCA's own *hemeroteca*. Interviews with workers at the Project for the Recovery of the National Police Historical Archives (PRAHPN) were conducted confidentially, except in the cases of a handful of leaders who had already identified themselves to the national or international press. I assigned an internal code number to each interview with a PRAHPN worker, and gave each worker a pseudonym in the text. Interviews with external figures were nonconfidential. All interviews were conducted in Guatemala City.

PERIODICALS

Agencia CERI-GUA. Centro de Reportes Informativos Sobre Guatemala. Guatemala. 1983–2010.

Boletín Internacional. Guatemalan Human Rights Commission. Mexico. 1983–1988.

Claridad. Partido Guatemalteco de Trabajo. Guatemala. 1982–1984.

Compañero. Ejército Guerrillero de los Pobres. Guatemala. 1976–1981.

Defensor del Pueblo, El. Procuraduría de los Derechos Humanos. Guatemala. 2005–2010.

Gaceta de la Policía. Policía Nacional. Guatemala. 1921–1940.

Gráfico, El. Guatemala. 1980–1985.

Imparcial, El. Guatemala. 1950–1984.

Informador Guerrillero. Ejército Guerrillero de los Pobres. Guatemala. 1982–1986.

Informador del Ministerio de Gobernación. Interior Ministry. Guatemala. 1964–1973.

Inforpress Centroamericana. Inforpress. Guatemala. 1975–1990.

New York Times. United States. 1954–2010.

No Nos Tientes. Guatemala. 1978–1990.

Orden: Organo de la Policía Nacional de la República de Guatemala. Guatemala. 1955–1963.

Periódico, el. Guatemala. 1995–2012.

Prensa Libre. Guatemala. 1980–present.

Revista de la Policía Nacional. Guatemala. 1969–1985.

Siete Días en la USAC. Guatemala. 1978–1982.
Siglo Veintiuno. Guatemala. 1990–2012.
Sucesos de la Semana. 1970–1982.
Verdad. Partido Guatemalteco de Trabajo. 1982–1985.

INTERVIEWS

PRAHPN001, 9 August 2007
PRAHPN002, 28 September 2007
PRAHPN003, 1 October 2007
PRAHPN004, 3 October 2007
PRAHPN005, 8 October 2007
PRAHPN006, 9 October 2007
PRAHPN007, 10 October 2007
PRAHPN008, 11 October 2007
PRAHPN009, 13 October 2007
PRAHPN010, 16 October 2007
PRAHPN011, 18 October 2007
PRAHPN012, 30 October 2007
PRAHPN013, 30 October 2007
PRAHPN014, 31 October 2007
PRAHPN015, 2 November 2007
PRAHPN016, 6 November 2007, 17 January 2008
PRAHPN017, 8 November 2007
PRAHPN018, 9 November 2007
PRAHPN019, 9 November 2007
PRAHPN020, 12 November 2007
PRAHPN021, 13 November 2007
PRAHPN022, 29 November 2007
PRAHPN023, 3 December 2007
PRAHPN024, 5 December 2007
PRAHPN025, 6 December 2007
PRAHPN026, 21 January 2008
PRAHPN027, 22 January 2008
PRAHPN028, 22 January 2008
PRAHPN029, 23 January 2008, 27 February 2008
PRAHPN030, 9 February 2008
Barrientos, Lizbeth, 29 January 2008
Bernzen, Agnes, 12 February 2008
Cifuentes, Edeliberto, 10 November 2007
Corado, Ana, 23 January 2008
Elich, Christina Maria, 4 December 2007
Ericastilla, Anna Carla, 29 November 2007
Fuentes, Alberto, 21 February 2008
Galeano, Estuardo, 6 February 2008
Guzmán Böckler, Carlos, 6 December 2007

Hedvall, Ulla-Britt, 18 January 2008
Hernández, Iduvina, 26 November 2007
La Rue, Frank, 7 February 2008
Meoño, Gustavo, 3 December 2007
Moerth, Michael, 8 February 2008
Molina, Ingrid, 11 November 2007
Morales, Sergio, 12 February 2008
Palma, Gustavo, 14 November 2007
Peccerelli, Fredy, 30 October 2007
Polanco, Mario, 20 February 2008
Salvadó, Rodrigo, 26 February 2008
Turner, Lucy, 15 November 2007
Velásquez Nimatuj, Irmalicia, 26 October 2007
Villagrán, Carla, 12 October 2007
Villagrán, Jorge, 21 February 2008
Villagrán, Marina de, 15 November 2007
Wallton, Åsa, 28 November 2007

WORKS CITED

Abrams, Elliott. "An End to Tyranny in Latin America." *Current Policy* 777 (January 1986): 1–4.

Agamben, Giorgio. *State of Exception*. Translated by Kevin Attell. Chicago: University of Chicago Press, 2005.

Aguilar, Paloma. "Transitional or Post-Transitional Justice? Recent Developments in the Spanish Case." *South European Society and Politics* 13, no. 4 (2008): 417–33.

Aguilera Peralta, Gabriel. "Estado militar y lucha revolucionaria en Guatemala." *Polémica* 6. San José, Costa Rica: ICADIS, 1982.

———. *Las propuestas para la paz*. Guatemala City: FLACSO, 1993.

———. *Seguridad, función militar y democracia*. Guatemala City: FLACSO, 1994.

Aguilera Peralta, Gabriel, and Jorge Romero Imery. *Dialéctica del terror en Guatemala*. San José, Costa Rica: EDUCA, 1981.

Alberti, Gloria. "Archives of Pain in Latin America." Paper presented at the XXXVIIe Conference Internationale de la Table Ronde des Archives, Cape Town, South Africa, 20–25 October, 2003.

Albizures, Miguel Angel. *El movimiento sindical: Lucha, represión, y reactivación 1973–1983*. Guatemala City: Dirección de los Archivos de la Paz, 2011.

———. *Tiempo de sudor y lucha*. Mexico City: Talleres de Praxis, 1987.

Alonso, Conrado. *15 fusilados al alba: Repaso histórico jurídico sobre los tribunales de fuero especial*. Guatemala City: Serviprensa Centroamericana, 1986.

Alvarado Morales, Sergio Fernando. *Informe Anual Circunstanciado: 2003*. Guatemala City: Procuraduría de los Derechos Humanos, 2003.

———. *Informe Anual Circunstanciado: 2004*. Guatemala City: Procuraduría de los Derechos Humanos, 2004.

———. *Informe Anual Circunstanciado: 2005*. Guatemala City: Procuraduría de los Derechos Humanos, 2005.

———. *Informe Anual Circunstanciado: 2006*. Guatemala City: Procuraduría de los Derechos Humanos, 2006.

———. *Informe Anual Circunstanciado: 2007*. Guatemala City: Procuraduría de los Derechos Humanos, 2007.

———. *Informe Anual Circunstanciado: 2008*. Guatemala City: Procuraduría de los Derechos Humanos, 2008.

———. *Informe Anual Circunstanciado: 2009*. Guatemala City: Procuraduría de los Derechos Humanos, 2009.

Amézquita, Carlos. *Guatemala: De Vicente Menchú a Juan Gerardi: 20 años de lucha por los derechos humanos*. Bilbao: Universidad de Deusto, 2000.

Amnesty International. *Persecution and Resistance: The Experience of Human Rights Defenders in Honduras and Guatemala*. London: Amnesty International, 2007.

Arana Osorio, Carlos. *Informe al Honorable Congreso de la República, Segundo Año de Gobierno*. Guatemala City: Tipografía Nacional, 1972.

Archivo Histórico de la Policía Nacional. *Del silencio a la memoria: Revelaciones del Archivo Histórico de la Policía Nacional*. Guatemala City: AHPN, 2011.

———. *El archivo en cifras*. Guatemala City: AHPN, 2011.

Arenas Bianchi, Clara, Charles R. Hale, and Gustavo Palma Murga, eds. *Racismo en Guatemala? Abriendo debate sobre un tema tabú*. Guatemala City: AVANCSO, 1999.

Arendt, Hannah. *Eichmann in Jerusalem: A Report on the Banality of Evil*. New York: Penguin, 1994.

Arévalo de León, Bernardo. *Función militar y control democrático*. Guatemala City: United Nations Office for Project Services, 2001.

Arias, Arturo. "After the Rigoberta Menchú Controversy: Lessons Learned about the Nature of Subalternity and the Specifics of the Indigenous Subject." *Modern Language Notes* 117 (2002): 481–505.

———, ed. *The Rigoberta Menchú Controversy*. Minneapolis: University of Minnesota Press, 2001.

Armon, Jeremy, Rachel Sieder, Richard Wilson, Gustavo Palma Murga, and Tania Palencia. *Guatemala 1983–1997: ¿Hacia dónde va la transición?* Guatemala City: FLACSO, 1997.

Arquivo Nacional de Brasil. "Memorias Reveladas." 2010. www.memoriasreveladas.arquivonacional.gov.br.

Arriaza, Gilberto, and Arturo Arias. "Claiming Collective Memory: Maya Languages and Civil Rights." *Social Justice* 25 (1998): 70–79.

Arriaza, Laura, and Naomi Roht-Arriaza. "Social Reconstruction as a Local Process." *International Journal of Transitional Justice* 2, no. 2 (2008): 152–72.

Asociación de Investigación y Estudios Sociales en Guatemala (ASIES). *Más de cien años del movimiento obrero urbano en Guatemala*. Vol. 2, *Reorganización, auge, y desarticulación del movimiento sindical 1954–1982*. Guatemala City: ASIES, 1991.

Ball, Patrick, Paul Kobrak, and Herbert Spirer. *State Violence in Guatemala, 1960–1996: A Quantitative Reflection*. Washington, DC: American Association for the Advancement of Science, 1999.

Balsells Tojo, Edgar Alfredo. *Olvido o Memoria: El dilema de la sociedad guatemalteca*. Guatemala City: F & G Editores, 2001.

Barrientos, Lizbeth. "Importancia de la conservación dentro de un programa de trata-miento documental en un archivo." *Boletín: Asociación de Conservadores de Archivos, Bibliotecas, y Museos de Guatemala* 12, nos. 1–3 (2004): 1–7.

Bastos, Santiago, and Manuela Camus. *El movimiento maya en perspectiva: Texto para reflexión y debate.* Guatemala City: FLACSO, 2003.

———. *Sombras de una batalla: Los desplazados por la violencia en la ciudad de Guatemala.* Guatemala City: FLACSO, 1994.

Bauer, Karin, ed. *Everybody Talks about the Weather . . . We Don't: The Writings of Ulrike Meinhof.* New York: Seven Stories Press, 2008.

Bayley, David. *Patterns of Policing: A Comparative International Analysis.* New Brunswick, NJ: Rutgers University Press, 1985.

Benjamin, Walter. *Illuminations: Essays and Reflections,* edited by Hannah Arendt. Trans-lated by Harry Zohn. New York: Schocken Books, 1969.

Bickford, Louis. "The Archival Imperative: Human Rights and Historical Memory in Latin America's Southern Cone." *Human Rights Quarterly* 21, no. 4 (1999): 1097–122.

———. "Human Rights Archives and Research on Historical Memory." *Latin American Research Review* 35, no. 2 (2000): 160–82.

Bilbija, Ksenija, and Leigh A. Payne, eds. *Accounting for Violence: Marketing Memory in Latin America.* Durham, NC: Duke University Press, 2011.

Bittner, Egon. *Aspects of Police Work.* Boston: Northeastern University Press, 1990.

Black, George. *Garrison Guatemala.* New York: Monthly Review Press, 1984.

Blanco-Rivera, Joel A. "Transitional Justice and the Role of Archives During Democratic Transitions in Latin America." *Memory: Newsletter of the Latin American and Caribbean Cultural Heritage Archives Roundtable, Society of American Archivists* 1, no. 2 (2009): 5–6.

Blanton, Thomas S. "Recovering the Memory of the Cold War: Forensic History and Latin America." In *In from the Cold: Latin America's New Encounter with the Cold War,* edited by Gilbert M. Joseph and Daniela Spenser, 47–73. Durham, NC: Duke University Press, 2009.

Blom Hansen, Thomas, and Finn Stepputat. *States of Imagination: Ethnographic Explora-tions of the Postcolonial State.* Durham, NC: Duke University Press, 2001.

Blouin, Francis X., Jr., and William G. Rosenberg, eds. *Archives, Documentation, and In-stitutions of Social Memory: Essays from the Sawyer Seminar.* Ann Arbor: University of Michigan Press, 2006.

Bobbio, Norberto. *The Future of Democracy: A Defence of the Rules of the Game.* Minneap-olis: University of Minnesota Press, 1987.

Bradley, Harriet. "The Seductions of the Archive: Voices Lost and Found." *History of the Human Sciences* 12, no. 2 (1999): 107–22.

Brown, Richard Harvey, and Beth Davis-Brown. "The Making of Memory: The Politics of Archives, Libraries, and Museums in the Construction of National Consciousness." *History of the Human Sciences* 11, no. 4 (1998): 17–32.

Browning, Christopher R. *Ordinary Men: Reserve Police Battalion 101 and the Final Solution in Poland.* New York: HarperCollins, 1992.

Buchenau, Jurgen, and Lyman Johnson, eds. *Aftershocks: Earthquakes and Popular Politics in Latin America.* Albuquerque: University of New Mexico Press, 2009.

Burns, Kathryn. *Into the Archive: Writing and Power in Colonial Peru.* Durham, NC: Duke University Press, 2010.

Burton, Antoinette M., ed. *Archive Stories: Facts, Fictions, and the Writing of History.* Durham, NC: Duke University Press, 2005.

———. *Dwelling in the Archive: Women Writing Home, House, and History in Late Colonial India.* New York: Oxford University Press, 2003.

Byrne, Hugh, William Stanley, and Rachel Garst. *Rescuing Police Reform: A Challenge for the New Guatemalan Government.* Washington, DC: Washington Office on Latin America, 2000.

Cajal, Máximo. *Saber quién puso fuego ahí! Masacre en la Embajada de España.* Madrid: Siddharth Mehta Ediciones, 2000.

Call, Charles T., and William D. Stanley. "Military and Police Reform after Civil Wars." In *Contemporary Peacemaking: Conflict, Violence and Peace Processes,* edited by John Darby and Roger MacGinty, 212–23. New York: Palgrave Macmillan, 2003.

———. "Protecting the People: Public Security Choices after Civil War." *Global Governance* 7, no. 2 (2001): 151–72.

Cardoza y Aragón, Luis. *La revolución guatemalteca.* Guatemala City: Editorial Pensativo, 2004.

Casaús Arzú, Marta Elena. *Guatemala: Linaje y racismo.* Guatemala City: F & G Editores, 2007.

Castañeda, Mario. "Historia del rock en Guatemala: La música rock como expresión social en la ciudad de Guatemala durante los años 1960 a 1976." Licenciatura diss., University of San Carlos, Guatemala, 2008.

Castillo, Otto René. *Informe de una injusticia,* edited by Roque Dalton. San José, Costa Rica: Editorial Universitaria Centroamericana, 1975.

Castillo Chacón, Margarita, Verónica Godoy Castillo, and Heidi Martínez Cardona. *Reforma policial y desmilitarización de la sociedad Guatemalteca.* Guatemala City: Programa Universitario de Investigación de Estudios para la Paz, 2001.

Catela, Ludmila da Silva, and Elizabeth Jelin, eds. *Los archivos de la represión: Documentos, memoria, y verdad.* Madrid: Siglo Veintiuno de España Editores, 2002.

Centro de Investigación y Documentación Centroamericana. *Violencia y contraviolencia: Desarrollo histórico de la violencia institucional en Guatemala.* Guatemala City: Editorial Universitaria, 1980.

Centro Internacional de Investigaciones en Derechos Humanos (CIIDH). *Situación de los derechos económicos, sociales, y culturales en Guatemala, 2006: A 10 años de la firma de los Acuerdos de Paz.* Guatemala City: CIIDH, 2006.

Chevigny, Paul. *The Edge of the Knife: Police Violence in the Americas.* New York: New Press, 1995.

Chinchilla Aguilar, Ernesto. "La clasificación del Archivo Nacional de Guatemala, obra del profesor J. Joaquín Pardo." *Boletín del Archivo General de la Nación,* vol. 1 no. 3 (1968): 55–61.

Chomsky, Aviva, and Steve Striffler. "Latin America Solidarity: The Colombian Coal Campaign." *Dialectical Anthropology* 32 (2008): 191–96.

Coalición para la Comisión de Investigación de Cuerpos Ilegales y Aparatos Clandestinos y de Seguridad. "El rostro del terror: Análisis de los ataques en contra de defensores de derechos humanos del 2000 al 2003." Guatemala City: Coalición para la CICIACS, 2004.

Cohen, Stanley. *States of Denial: Knowing about Atrocities and Suffering.* Cambridge: Polity Press, 2001.

Cojtí Cuxil, Demetrio. *El movimiento maya (en Guatemala).* Guatemala City: Cholsamaj, 1997.

———. "The Politics of Maya Revindication." In *Maya Cultural Activism in Guatemala,* edited by Edward Fischer and R. McKenna Brown, 19–50. Austin: University of Texas Press, 1996.

Collins, Cath. "The Moral Economy of Memory: Public and Private Commemorative Space in Post-Pinochet Chile." In *Accounting for Violence: Marketing Memory in Latin America,* edited by Ksenija Bilbija and Leigh A. Payne, 236–63. Durham, NC: Duke University Press, 2011.

Colom, Yolanda. *Mujeres en la alborada: Guerrilla y participación femenina en Guatemala, 1973–1978.* Guatemala City: Artemis & Edinter, 1998.

Combe, Sonia. *Archives interdites: Les peurs françaises face à l'histoire contemporaine.* Paris: A. Michel, 1994.

Comisión de Derechos Humanos de Guatemala (CDHG). *Desapariciones forzadas involuntarias.* Mexico: CDHG, 1982.

Comisión para el Esclarecimiento Histórico. *Guatemala: Memoria del silencio.* 12 vols. Guatemala City: United Nations Office of Project Services, 1999.

Compendio de leyes sobre la protección del patrimonio cultural guatemalteco. Guatemala City: UNESCO, 2006.

Contreras Cruz, Adolfina, and Francisco Fernando Sinay Álvarez. "Historia de la Policía Nacional de Guatemala, 1881–1997." Licenciatura diss., University of San Carlos, Guatemala, 2004.

Cook, Terry. "Archival Science and Postmodernism: New Formulations for Old Concepts." *Archival Science* 1 (2000): 3–24.

———. "Remembering the Future: Appraisal of Records and the Role of Archives in Constructing Social Memory." In *Archives, Documentation, and Institutions of Social Memory: Essays from the Sawyer Seminar,* edited by Francis X. Blouin Jr. and William G. Rosenberg, 169–81. Ann Arbor: University of Michigan Press, 2006.

———. "What Is Past Is Prologue: A History of Archival Ideas since 1898, and the Future Paradigm Shift." *Archivaria* 43 (Spring 1997): 17–63.

Cook, Terry, and Joan M. Schwartz. "Archives, Records, and Power: From (Postmodern) Theory to (Archival) Performance." *Archival Science* 2 (2002): 171–85.

Cullather, Nick. *Secret History: The CIA's Classified Account of Its Operations in Guatemala, 1952–1954.* Stanford, CA: Stanford University Press, 2006.

Dalton, Roque. "Otto René Castillo." In *Informe de una injusticia,* edited by Roque Dalton. San José, Costa Rica: Editorial Universitaria Centroamericana, 1975.

Davenport, Christian, and Patrick Ball. "Views to a Kill: Exploring the Implications of Source Selection in the Case of Guatemalan State Terror, 1977–1995." *Journal of Conflict Resolution* 46, no. 3 (2002): 427–50.

Davis, Mike. *Planet of Slums.* New York: Verso Books, 2007.

Delgado Duarte, Antonio. *Aproximación al secreto de estado.* Guatemala City: Fundación Myrna Mack, 2003.

Derrida, Jacques. *Archive Fever: A Freudian Impression.* Translated by Eric Prenowitz. Chicago: University of Chicago Press, 1995.

———. *Paper Machine.* Translated by Rachel Bowlby. Stanford, CA: Stanford University Press, 2005.

Dillenburger, Karola, Montserrat Fargas, and Rym Akhonzada. "Long-Term Effects of Political Violence: Narrative Inquiry across a 20-Year Period." *Quantitative Health Research* 18, no. 10 (2008): 1312–22.

Dirks, Nicholas. "Annals of the Archive: Ethnographic Notes on the Sources of History." In *From the Margins: Historical Anthropology and Its Futures,* edited by Brian Axel, 47–65. Durham, NC: Duke University Press, 2002.

"Discurso del Profesor Julio Alberto Martí." Reprinted in *Boletín del Archivo General de la Nación,* 53–54. Guatemala City: Ministerio de Gobernación, 1967.

Discursos del Presidente Arana Osorio y Palabras Pronunciadas en Varias Ocasiones, Octubre–Diciembre 1970. Guatemala City: Tipografía Nacional, 1971.

Douglas, Mary. *How Institutions Think.* New York: Routledge, 1986.

Doyle, Kate. "The Art of the Coup: A Paper Trail of Covert Actions in Guatemala." NACLA *Report on the Americas* 31, no. 2 (1997): 34–40.

———. "The Atrocity Files: Deciphering the Archives of Guatemala's Dirty War." *Harper's Magazine* (December 2007): 52–64.

———. "Death Squad Diary: Looking Into the Secret Archives of Guatemala's Bureaucracy of Murder." *Harper's Magazine* (June 1999): 52–53.

———. "Operation Sofía: Documenting Genocide in Guatemala." National Security Archive Electronic Briefing Book No. 297. Washington, DC: National Security Archive, 2009. http://www.gwu.edu/~nsarchiv/NASEBB/NSAEBB297/.

———. "Remains of Two of Guatemala's Death Squad Diary's Victims Found in Mass Grave," National Security Archive Briefing Book No. 363. Washington, DC: National Security Archive, 2011. http://www.gwu.edu/~nsarchiv/NASEBB/NASEBB363/.

Doyle, Kate, and Jesse Franzblau, eds. "Historical Archives Lead to Arrest of Police Officers in Guatemalan Disappearance." National Security Archive Electronic Briefing Book No. 273. Washington, DC: National Security Archive, 2009. www.gwu.edu/~nsarchiv/ NASEBB/NASEBB273/index.htm.

Doyle, Kate, Carlos Osorio, Michael Evans, Tamara Feinstein, Gretta Tovar Siebenstritt, and Sarah Heidema, eds. "The Guatemalan Military: What the US Files Reveal." National Security Archive Electronic Briefing Book No. 32. Washington, DC: National Security Archive, 2000. www.gwu.edu/~nsarchiv/NSAEBB/NSAEBB32/index.html.

Doyle, Kate, and Emily Willard. "Remains of Three Death Squad Diary Victims Identified," *Unredacted,* 22 March 2012. nsarchive.wordpress.com.

———. "27 Years Later, Justice for Fernando García." National Security Archive Electronic Briefing Book No. 337. Washington, DC: National Security Archive, 2011. http://www.gwu.edu/~nsarchiv/NSAEBB/NSAEBB337/.

Duchein, Michel. "The History of European Archives and the Development of the Archival Profession in Europe." *American Archivist* 55 (Winter 1992): 14–25.

Duff, Wendy M., and Verne Harris. "Stories and Names: Archival Description as Narrating Records and Constructing Meanings." *Archival Science* 2 (2002): 263–85.

Erickson Nepstad, Sharon. *Convictions of the Soul: Religion, Culture, and Agency in the Central America Solidarity Movement.* New York: Oxford University Press, 2004.

Escobar, Arturo, and Sonia E. Álvarez, eds. *The Making of Social Movements in Latin America: Identity, Strategy, and Democracy.* Boulder, CO: Westview Press, 1992.

Falla, Ricardo. *Masacres en la selva: Ixcán, Guatemala, 1975–1982.* Guatemala City: Editorial Universitaria, 1992.

———. *Quiché Rebelde.* Guatemala City: Editorial Universitaria, 1978.

Feitlowitz, Marguerite. *A Lexicon of Terror: Argentina and the Legacies of Torture.* New York: Oxford University Press, 1998.

Felman, Shoshana. *The Juridical Unconscious: Trials and Traumas in the Twentieth Century.* Cambridge, MA: Harvard University Press, 2002.

Ferreira-Buckley, Linda. "Rescuing the Archives from Foucault." *College English* 61, no. 5 (1999): 577–83.

Ferry, Elizabeth Emma. *Not Ours Alone: Patrimony, Value, and Collectivity in Contemporary Mexico.* New York: Columbia University Press, 2005.

Figueroa Ibarra, Carlos. *El recurso del miedo: Ensayo sobre el estado y el terror en Guatemala.* San José, Costa Rica: EDUCA, 1991.

———. *Los que siempre estarán en ninguna parte: La desaparición forzada en Guatemala.* Mexico City: CIIDH, 1999.

Filóchofo. *La otra historia de los Mayas al informe de la "Comisión de la Verdad."* Guatemala City: HIVOS, 1999.

Fischer, Edward F., and R. McKenna Brown, eds. *Maya Cultural Activism in Guatemala.* Austin: University of Texas Press, 1996.

Fletcher, Laurel, and Harvey Weinstein. "Violence and Social Repair: Rethinking the Contribution of Justice to Reconciliation." *Human Rights Quarterly* 24 (2002): 573–639.

Flores, Marco Antonio. *Fortuny: Un comunista guatemalteco.* Guatemala City: Editorial Oscar de León Palacios, 1994.

———. *Los compañeros.* Mexico City: Editorial Joaquín Mortiz, 1976.

Flores Alvarado, Humberto. *Comentarios críticos de interpretación sobre el significado politico-social de los acuerdos de paz.* Guatemala: Artgrafic de Guatemala, 1997.

Foucault, Michel. *The Archaeology of Knowledge and the Discourse on Language.* Translated by A. M. Sheridan Smith. New York: Pantheon, 1972.

———. *Discipline and Punish: The Birth of the Prison.* Translated by Alan Sheridan. New York: Pantheon, 1978.

———. "History, Discourse and Discontinuity." Translated by Anthony M. Nazzaro. *Salmagundi* 20 (Summer–Fall 1972): 225–48.

———. *The Order of Things: An Archaeology of the Human Sciences.* Translated by Anonymous. New York: Vintage, 1994.

Fredriksson, Berndt. "Postmodernistic Archival Science: Rethinking the Methodology of a Science." *Archival Science* 3 (2003): 177–97.

Fried, Jonathan L., Marvin E. Gettleman, Deborah T. Levenson, and Nancy Peckenham, eds. *Guatemala in Rebellion: Unfinished History.* New York: Grove Press, 1983.

Fuchs, Anne. *Phantoms of War in Contemporary German Literature, Films, and Discourse: The Politics of Memory.* New York: Palgrave Macmillan, 2008.

Fujino, Alison, ed. *Winds of Resistance: The Giant Kites of Guatemala*. Seattle: Drachen Foundation, forthcoming.

Galich, Manuel. *Del panico al ataque*. Guatemala City: Editorial Universitaria, 1977.

Gallardo Flores, Carlos. *La utopia de la rosa: Fragmentos de la lucha socialista en Guatemala*. Guatemala City: Tipografía Nacional, 2002.

García, Prudencio. *El genocidio de Guatemala a la luz de la Sociología Militar*. Madrid: SEPHA, 2005.

García Laguardia, Jorge Mario. *La revolución del 20 de octubre de 1944*. Guatemala City: Procuraduría de los Derechos Humanos, 1994.

García Márquez, Gabriel. *One Hundred Years of Solitude*. Translated by Gregory Rabassa. New York: Harper and Row, 1970.

Garrard-Burnett, Virginia. *Terror in the Land of the Holy Spirit: Guatemala under General Efraín Ríos Montt, 1982–1983*. New York: Oxford University Press, 2010.

Garrido, Ariel, ed. *Secreto de estado*. Guatemala City: Fundación Myrna Mack, 1999.

Garst, Rachel. *Military Intelligence and Human Rights: The Archivo and the Case for Intelligence Reform*. Washington, DC: Washington Office on Latin America, 1995.

Garton Ash, Timothy. *The File: A Personal History*. New York: Vintage, 1997.

Glebbeek, Marie-Louise. *In the Crossfire of Democracy: Police Reform and Police Practice in Post–Civil War Guatemala*. Amsterdam: Rozenberg Publishers, 2003.

———. "Police Reform and the Peace Process in Guatemala: The Fifth Promotion of the National Civilian Police." *Bulletin of Latin American Research* 20, no. 4 (2001): 431–53.

Gleijeses, Piero. *Shattered Hope: The Guatemalan Revolution and the United States, 1944–1954*. Princeton, NJ: Princeton University Press, 1992.

Gobierno de la República de Guatemala, Unidad Revolucionaria Nacional Guatemalteca, and Naciones Unidas. *Acuerdo Sobre el Fortalecimiento del Poder Civil y Función del Ejército en una Sociedad Democrática*. Guatemala City: Fundación Friedrich Ebert, 1996.

Goldman, Francisco. *The Art of Political Murder: Who Killed the Bishop?* New York: Grove Press, 2008.

———. *The Long Night of White Chickens*. New York: Atlantic Monthly Press, 1992.

Goldsmith, Andrew J., and Colleen Lewis, eds. *Civilian Oversight of Policing: Democracy, Governance, and Human Rights*. Portland, OR: Hart, 2000.

González Echevarría, Roberto. *Myth and Archive: A Theory of Latin American Narrative*. Durham, NC: Duke University Press, 1998.

González Quintana, Antonio. "Archives of the Security Services of Former Repressive Regimes." Report prepared for United Nations Economic and Social Council on behalf of the International Council of Archives. Paris: UNESCO, 1997.

———. "La respuesta del terror a la apertura a la consulta del archivo de la Policía Nacional de Guatemala." *Archiveros Españoles en la Función Pública* weblog, posted 31 March 2009. http://archiverosefp.blogspot.com/2009/03/la-respuesta-del-terror-la-apertura-la.html.

Gosse, Van. "Active Engagement: The Legacy of Central America Solidarity." NACLA *Report on the Americas* 28, no. 5 (1995): 22–29.

Gramajo Morales, Hector Alejandro. *De la Guerra . . . a la Guerra: La difícil transición política en Guatemala*. Guatemala: Fonda de Cultura Editorial, 1995.

Gramajo Valdés, Silvio René. *El derecho de acceso a la información: Análisis del proceso de discussion y gestión en Guatemala*. Guatemala City: Asociación DOSES, 2003.

Gramsci, Antonio. *Selections from the Prison Notebooks*. New York: International Publishers, 1971.

Grandin, Greg. *The Blood of Guatemala: A History of Race and Nation*. Durham, NC: Duke University Press, 2000.

———. "Chronicles of a Guatemalan Genocide Foretold: Violence, Trauma, and the Limits of Historical Inquiry." *Nepantla: Views from South* 1, no. 2 (2000): 391–412.

———. *Denegado en su totalidad: Documentos estadounidenses liberados*. Guatemala City: AVANCSO, 2001.

———. *Empire's Workshop: Latin America, the United States, and the Rise of the New Imperialism*. New York: Metropolitan Books, 2006.

———. "The Instruction of Great Catastrophe: Truth Commissions, National History, and State Formation in Argentina, Chile, and Guatemala." *American Historical Review* 110, no. 1 (2005): 46–67.

———. "History, Motive, Law, Intent: Combining Historical and Legal Methods in Understanding Guatemala's 1981–1983 Genocide." In *The Specter of Genocide: Mass Murder in Historical Perspective*, edited by Robert Gellately and Ben Kiernan, 339–52. Cambridge: Cambridge University Press, 2003.

———. *The Last Colonial Massacre: Latin America in the Cold War*. Chicago: University of Chicago Press, 2004.

Grandin, Greg, and Gilbert M. Joseph, eds. *A Century of Revolution: Insurgent and Counterinsurgent Violence during Latin America's Long Cold War*. Durham, NC: Duke University Press, 2010.

Guadamuz, Andrés. "Habeas Data: The Latin-American Response to Data Protection." *Journal of Information, Law and Technology* 2 (June 2002). http://elj.warwick.ac.uk /jilt/00–2/guadamuz.html.

Guha, Ranajit. "The Prose of Counter-insurgency." In *Selected Subaltern Studies*, edited by Ranajit Guha and Gayatri Chakravorty Spivak, 45–84. Oxford: Oxford University Press, 1988.

Guilhot, Nicolas. *The Democracy Makers: Human Rights and International Order*. New York: Columbia University Press, 2005.

Gutiérrez, Edgar. *Hacia un paradigma democrático del sistema de inteligencia en Guatemala*. Guatemala: Fundación Myrna Mack, 1999.

Hacking, Ian. *Historical Ontology*. Cambridge, MA: Harvard University Press, 2004.

Hale, Charles R. "Consciousness, Violence, and the Politics of Memory in Guatemala." *Current Anthropology* 38, no. 5 (1997): 817–35.

———. *Más Que Un Indio: Racial Ambivalence and Neoliberal Multiculturalism in Guatemala*. Santa Fe, NM: School of American Research Press, 2006.

Hamilton, Carolyn, Verne Harris, Michèle Pickover, Graeme Reid, Razia Saleh, and Jane Taylor, eds. *Refiguring the Archive*. Cape Town: David Philip, 2002.

Handy, Jim. "Democratizing What? Some Reflections on Nation, State, Ethnicity, Modernity, Community, and Democracy in Guatemala." *Canadian Journal of Latin American and Caribbean Studies* 27, no. 53 (2002): 35–71.

———. *Gift of the Devil: A History of Guatemala*. Boston: South End Press, 1984.

———. *Revolution in the Countryside: Rural Conflict and Agrarian Reform in Guatemala, 1944–1954.* Chapel Hill: University of North Carolina Press, 1994.

Harper, Charles, ed. *Impunity: An Ethical Perspective: Six Case Studies from Latin America.* Geneva: WCC Publications, 1996.

Harris, Brent. "The Archive, Public History, and the Essential Truth: The TRC Reading the Past." In *Refiguring the Archive*, edited by Carolyn Hamilton, Verne Harris, Michèle Pickover, Graeme Reid, Razia Saleh, and Jane Taylor, 161–178. Cape Town: David Philip, 2002.

Harris, Verne. "The Archival Sliver: Power, Memory, and Archives in South Africa." *Archival Science* 2 (2002): 63–86.

———. "A Shaft of Darkness: Derrida in the Archive." In *Refiguring the Archive*, edited by Carolyn Hamilton, Verne Harris, Michèle Pickover, Graeme Reid, Razia Saleh, and Jane Taylor, 61–82. Cape Town: David Philip, 2002.

Harrison, Ann. "Guatemalan National Police Archive Project: An Astonishing Discovery." Human Rights Data Analysis Group, 2007. www.hrdag.org/about/guatemala -police_arch_project.shtml.

Hayner, Priscilla. *Unspeakable Truths: Confronting State Terror and Atrocity.* New York: Routledge, 2001.

Head, Randolph C. "Historical Research on Archives and Knowledge Cultures: An Interdisciplinary Wave." *Archival Science* 2 (2002): 21–43.

Hedstrom, Margaret. "Archives, Memory, and Interfaces with the Past." *Archival Science* 2 (2002): 21–43.

Hernández, Iduvina. "A Long Road: Progress and Challenges in Guatemala's Intelligence Reform." Washington, DC: Washington Office on Latin America, 2005.

Hernández Pico, Juan. *Terminar la guerra, traicionar la paz: Guatemala en las dos presidencias de la paz: Arzú y Portillo, 1996–2004.* Guatemala City: FLACSO, 2005.

Hetherington, Kregg. *Guerrilla Auditors: The Politics of Transparency in Neoliberal Paraguay.* Durham, NC: Duke University Press, 2011.

Higonnet, Etelle, ed. *Quiet Genocide: Guatemala 1981–1983.* Piscataway, NJ: Transaction Publishers, 2009.

Hoffman, Eva. *After Such Knowledge: Memory, History, and the Legacy of the Holocaust.* New York: Public Affairs, 2004.

———. *Complex Histories, Contested Memories: Some Reflections on Remembering Difficult Pasts.* Berkeley: Doreen B. Townsend Center for the Humanities, 2000.

Huggins, Martha. *Political Policing: The United States and Latin America.* Durham, NC: Duke University Press, 1998.

———. "U.S.-Supported State Terror: A History of Police Training in Latin America." In *Vigilantism and the State in Modern Latin America: Essays on Extralegal Violence*, edited by Martha Huggins. 292–42. New York: Praeger, 1991.

Human Rights First. "Human Rights Defenders in Guatemala." 2009. www.human rightsfirst.org/defenders/hrd_guatemala/hrd_guatemala.aspx?c=g4.

Huskamp Peterson, Trudy. "Application of ISAD(G) for Human Rights Archives." International Council of Archives, May 2005. www.ica.org/en/node/30452.

———. "Archives in Service to the State." In *Political Pressure and the Archival Record*, edited by Margaret Procter, Michael Cook, and Caroline Williams, 259–76. Chicago: Society of American Archivists, 2005.

———. "The End of the Beginning: The Completion of Phase 1 of the Proyecto de Recuperación del Archivo Histórico de la Policía Nacional, Guatemala." Speech presented at the Procuraduría de los Derechos Humanos, Guatemala City, 18 January 2008. www.trudypeterson.com/publications.html.

———. *Final Acts: A Guide to Preserving the Records of Truth Commissions.* Washington, DC: Woodrow Wilson Center Press, 2005.

———. "The Nasty Truth about Nationalism and National Archives." Paper presented at the annual conference of the East Asian Regional Branch of the International Council on Archives (EASTICA), Seoul, Korea, 17–21 September 2001.

———. "Privacy Is Not a Rose." Paper presented to the Society of American Archivists, 23 September 2007. www.trudypeterson.com/publications.html.

———. "The Probative Value of Archival Documents in Judicial Processes." Paper presented to the Procuraduría de los Derechos Humanos, Guatemala City, 19 November 2008. www.trudypeterson.com/publications.html.

———. "Processing the Archives of the Policía Nacional de Guatemala: A Report with Recommendations, Visit of July 2006." Internal report prepared for the Procuraduría de los Derechos Humanos. 22 August 2006.

———. "Processing the Archives of the Policía Nacional de Guatemala: A Report with Recommendations, Visit of August 2006." Internal report prepared for the Procuraduría de los Derechos Humanos. 14 September 2006.

———. "Records of the Policía Nacional de Guatemala: Report and Recommendations." Internal report prepared for the National Security Archive. 15 October 2005.

———. "The Role of Archives in Strengthening Democracy." Paper presented to the Procuraduría de los Derechos Humanos, Guatemala City, Guatemala, 26 November 2008.

Immerman, Richard H. *The CIA in Guatemala: The Foreign Policy of Intervention.* Austin: University of Texas Press, 1983.

Impunity Watch. *Recognising the Past: Challenges for the Combat of Impunity in Guatemala.* Guatemala City: Impunity Watch, 2008.

Inter-American Court of Human Rights. *Molina Thiessen v. Guatemala.* Judgment reached 4 May 2004. San José, Costa Rica. www.corteidh.or.cr/docs/casos/articulos/seriec_106_esp.pdf.

International Crisis Group, "Learning to Walk without a Crutch: An Assessment of the International Commission against Impunity in Guatemala," Latin America Report No. 36, 31 May 2011.

Jelin, Elizabeth. *State Repression and the Labors of Memory.* Minneapolis: University of Minnesota Press, 2003.

Jelin, Elizabeth, and Eric Hershberg. *Constructing Democracy: Human Rights, Citizenship, and Society in Latin America.* Boulder, CO: Westview Press, 1996.

Jonas, Susanne. *The Battle for Guatemala: Rebels, Death Squads, and U.S. Power.* Boulder, CO: Westview Press, 1991.

———. "Dangerous Liaisons: The U.S. in Guatemala." *Foreign Policy* 103 (Summer 1996): 144–60.

———. *Of Centaurs and Doves: Guatemala's Peace Process.* Boulder, CO: Westview Press, 2000.

Joseph, Gilbert Michael, and Daniel Nugent, eds. *Everyday Forms of State Formation: Rev-*

olution and the Negotiation of Rule in Modern Mexico. Durham, NC: Duke University Press, 1994.

Joseph, Gilbert M., and Daniela Spenser, eds. *In from the Cold: Latin America's New Encounter with the Cold War.* Durham, NC: Duke University Press, 2009.

Kaiser, Susana. *Postmemories of Terror: A New Generation Copes with the Legacy of the "Dirty War."* New York: Palgrave Macmillan, 2005.

Ketelaar, Eric. "Archival Temples, Archival Prisons: Modes of Power and Protection," *Archival Science* 2 (2002): 221–38.

———. "Muniments and Monuments: The Dawn of Archives as Cultural Patrimony." *Archival Science* 7 (2007): 343–57.

———. "The Panoptical Archive." In *Archives, Documentation, and Institutions of Social Memory: Essays from the Sawyer Seminar*, edited by Francis X. Blouin Jr. and William G. Rosenberg, 144–50. Ann Arbor: University of Michigan Press, 2006.

———. "Recordkeeping and Societal Power." In *Archives: Recordkeeping in Society*, edited by Sue McKemmish, Michael Piggott, Barbara Reed, and Frank Upward, 277–98. Wagga Wagga, Australia: Charles Sturt University, 2005.

———. "Tacit Narratives: The Meanings of Archives." *Archival Science* 1 (2001): 131–41.

Kinzer, Stephen, and Stephen E. Schlesinger. *Bitter Fruit: The Story of the American Coup in Guatemala.* Cambridge, MA: Harvard University David Rockefeller Center for Latin American Studies, 1999.

Kobrak, Paul. *Organizing and Repression in the University of San Carlos, Guatemala, 1944 to 1996.* New York: American Association for the Advancement of Science, 1999.

Konefal, Betsy. *For Every Indio Who Falls: A History of Maya Activism in Guatemala, 1960–1990.* Albuquerque: University of New Mexico Press, 2010.

Krujit, Dirk. "Low-Intensity Democracies: Latin America in the Post-dictatorial Era." *Bulletin of Latin American Research* 20, no. 4 (2001): 409–30.

———. *Sociedades de terror: Guerrillas y contrainsurgencia en Guatemala y el Perú.* San José, Costa Rica: FLACSO, 1996.

Kuzmarov, Jeremy. *Modernizing Repression: Police Training and Nation Building in the Twentieth Century.* Amherst: University of Massachusetts Press, 2012.

———. "Modernizing Repression: Police Training, Political Violence, and Nation-Building in the 'American Century.'" *Diplomatic History* 33, no. 2 (2009): 191–222.

La isla: Archives of a Tragedy. Uli Stelzner, dir. Iskaciné, 2009.

Langguth, A. J. *Hidden Terrors: The Truth about U.S. Police Operations in Latin America.* New York: Pantheon, 1979.

Las colmenas. Alejandro Ramírez, dir. CANEK/Del Pensativo. 2007.

Levenson-Estrada, Deborah. "The Life That Makes Us Die/The Death That Makes Us Live: Facing Terrorism in Guatemala City." *Radical History Review* 85 (Winter 2003): 94–104.

———. *Trade Unionists against Terror: Guatemala City, 1954—1985.* Chapel Hill: University of North Carolina Press, 1994.

Lobe, Thomas. "The Rise and Demise of the Office of Public Safety." *Armed Forces and Society* 9, no. 2 (1983): 187–213.

Lovell, George. *A Beauty That Hurts: Life and Death in Guatemala.* Austin: University of Texas Press, 2001.

Lowenthal, David. "Archives, Heritage, and History." In *Archives, Documentation, and Institutions of Social Memory: Essays from the Sawyer Seminar*, edited by Francis X. Blouin Jr. and William G. Rosenberg, 193–204. Ann Arbor: University of Michigan Press, 2006.

———. *The Heritage Crusade and the Spoils of History*. Cambridge: Cambridge University Press, 1998.

———. *The Past Is a Foreign Country*. Cambridge: Cambridge University Press, 1999.

Ludec, Nathalie. "Voces del exilio guatemalteco desde la ciudad de México." *Amérique Latine Histoire et Mémoire*, no. 2 (2001). http://alhim.revues.org/document599.html.

Luján Muñoz, Jorge. *La tragedia de la Embajada de España en Guatemala, 31 de enero de 1980. Perspectivas, controversias y comentarios*. Guatemala City: Academia de Geografía e Historia de Guatemala, 2007.

Macías, Julio César. *La guerrilla fue mi camino: Epitafio por César Montes*. Guatemala City: Editorial Piedra Santa, 1997.

Maldonado, Mario. "Marzo y abril de 1962: El inicio de la guerra." *Diálogo* (FLACSO) 47 (February 2006): 1–6.

Manoff, Marlene. "Theories of the Archive from Across the Disciplines." *Libraries and the Academy* 4, no. 1 (2004): 9–25.

Manz, Beatriz. *De la memoria a la reconstrucción histórica*. Guatemala City: AVANCSO, 1999.

———. *Refugees of a Hidden War: The Aftermath of the Counterinsurgency in Guatemala*. Albany: State University of New York Press, 1988.

Martínez Peláez, Severo. *La patria del criollo*. Mexico City: Ediciones en Marcha, 1994.

Mbembe, Achille. "The Power of the Archive and Its Limits." In *Refiguring the Archive*, edited by Carolyn Hamilton, Verne Harris, Michèle Pickover, Graeme Reid, Razia Saleh, and Jane Taylor, 19–20. Cape Town: David Philip, 2002.

McAdams, A. James. *Judging the Past in Unified Germany*. Cambridge: Cambridge University Press, 2001.

McAllister, Carlota. "Good People: Revolution, Community, and *Conciencia* in a Maya-K'iche' Village in Guatemala." PhD diss., Johns Hopkins University, 2003.

———. *The Good Road: Conscience and Consciousness in a Postrevolutionary Guatemalan Village*. Durham, NC: Duke University Press, forthcoming.

———. "Rural Markets, Revolutionary Souls, and Rebellious Women in Cold War Guatemala." In *In from the Cold: Latin America's New Encounter with the Cold War*, edited by Gilbert M. Joseph and Daniela Spenser, 350–80. Durham, NC: Duke University Press, 2008.

McCleary, Rachel. *Dictating Democracy: Guatemala and the End of Violent Revolution*. Gainesville: University of Florida Press, 1999.

McClintock, Michael. *The American Connection: State Terror and Popular Resistance in Guatemala*. London: Zed Books, 1985.

McCoy, Alfred W. *Policing America's Empire: The United States, the Philippines, and the Rise of the Surveillance State*. Madison: University of Wisconsin Press, 2009.

McCreery, David. *Rural Guatemala 1760–1940*. Stanford, CA: Stanford University Press, 1996.

———. "Wage Labor, Free Labor, and Vagrancy Laws: The Transition to Capitalism in

Guatemala, 1920–1945." In *Coffee, Society, and Power in Latin America*, edited by William Roseberry, Lowell Gudmundson, and Mario Semper Kutschbach, 206–31. Baltimore: Johns Hopkins University Press, 1995.

Memoria del Mundo. *Directrices para la salvaguardia del patrimonio documental.* Guatemala City: UNESCO, 2002.

———. *Manual técnico para la administración, manejo, y conservación del patrimonio documental.* Guatemala City: UNESCO, 2006.

Menchú Tum, Rigoberta. *I, Rigoberta Menchú: An Indian Woman in Guatemala*, edited by Elisabeth Burgos-Debray. Translated by Ann Wright. London: Verso, 1984.

Menjívar, Cecilia, and Néstor Rodríguez, eds. *When States Kill: Latin America, the US, and Technologies of Terror.* Austin: University of Texas Press, 2005.

Military Intelligence and Human Rights in Guatemala: The Archivo and the Case for Intelligence Reform. Washington, DC: Washington Office on Latin America, 1995.

Millar, Laura. "Creating a National Information System in a Federal Environment: Some Thoughts on the Canadian Archival Information Network." In *Archives, Documentation, and Institutions of Social Memory: Essays from the Sawyer Seminar*, edited by Francis X. Blouin Jr. and William G. Rosenberg, 182–92. Ann Arbor: University of Michigan Press, 2006.

Ministerio de Cultura y Deportes. *Ley para la protección del patrimonio cultural de la nación, Decreto Número 26-97 y sus reformas.* Guatemala City: Dirección General del Patrimonio Cultural y Natural, Unidad de Comunicación Social, 2007.

———. *Políticas culturales y deportivas nacionales.* Guatemala City: Taller Nacional de Grabados en Acero, 2000.

Moller, Jonathan, and Rigoberta Menchú Tum. *Our Culture Is Our Resistance: Repression, Refuge, and Healing in Guatemala.* Brooklyn, NY: Powerhouse Books, 2004.

Montejo, Víctor. "Convention 169 and the Implementation of the Peace Accords in Guatemala." *Abya-Yala News: The Journal of the South and Mesoamerican Indian Rights Center* 10, no. 4 (1997).

———. *Maya Intellectual Renaissance: Identity, Representation, and Leadership.* Austin: University of Texas Press, 2005.

———. *Voices from Exile: Violence and Survival in Modern Maya History.* Norman: University of Oklahoma Press, 1999.

Morán, Enmy, and Claudia Virginia Samayoa. Evolución de las estructuras de la Policía Nacional: Resultado de la investigación exploratoria. Internal report prepared for the Procuraduría de los Derechos Humanos, Guatemala City, Guatemala, 13 January 2006.

Morán, Rolando (Ricardo Ramírez de León). *Saludos revolucionarios: La historia reciente de Guatemala desde la óptica de la lucha guerrillera, 1984–1996.* Guatemala City: Fundación Guillermo Toriello, 2002.

Nairn, Allan, and Jean-Marie Simon. "Bureaucracy of Death: Guatemala's Civilian Government Faces the Enemy Within." *New Republic* (30 June 1986): 13–17.

Nelson, Diane M. *Reckoning: The Ends of War in Guatemala.* Durham, NC: Duke University Press, 2009.

———. *A Finger in the Wound: Body Politics in Quincentennial Guatemala.* Durham, NC: Duke University Press, 1999.

————. "Maleficium Jingle, State Commodity Fetishism: Guatemala's Peace Process, the Piñata Effect, and the Global Security and Exchange Market." Paper presented at the annual conference of the American Anthropological Association, Washington, DC, 19–23 November 1997.

Nolin, Catherine. *Transnational Ruptures: Gender and Forced Migration.* London: Ashgate, 2006.

Obando Sánchez, Antonio. *Memorias: La historia del movimiento obrero.* Guatemala: Editorial Universitaria, 1978.

Oficina de Derechos Humanos del Arzobispado de Guatemala (ODHAG). *La memoria tiene la palabra: Sistematización del Proyecto Interdiocesano de Recuperación de la Memoria Histórica REMHI.* Guatemala City: ODHAG, 2007.

Oglesby, Elizabeth. "Educating Citizens in Postwar Guatemala: Historical Memory, Genocide, and the Culture of Peace." *Radical History Review* 97 (2007): 77–98.

Osorio, Carlos. "Argentina: Declassification of Military Records on Human Rights." Free dominfo.org, 14 January 2010. http://freedominfo.org/news/20100114.htm.

O'Toole, James M. "Between Veneration and Loathing: Loving and Hating Documents." In *Archives, Documentation, and Institutions of Social Memory: Essays from the Sawyer Seminar,* edited by Francis X. Blouin Jr. and William G. Rosenberg, 43–53. Ann Arbor: University of Michigan Press, 2006.

————. "Cortes's Notary: The Symbolic Power of Records." *Archival Science* 2 (2002): 45–61.

Payeras, Mario. *El trueno en la ciudad: Episodios de la lucha armada urbana de 1981 en Guatemala.* Mexico City: Editorial Juan Pablos, 1987.

————. *Los días de la selva.* Havana: La Casa de las Américas, 1981.

————. *Los fúsiles de octubre: Ensayos y artículos militares sobre la revolución guatemalteca.* Mexico City: Editorial Juan Pablos, 1991.

Peacock, Susan C., and Adriana Beltrán. *Poderes ocultos: Grupos ilegales armados en la Guatemala pos-conflicto y las fuerzas detrás de ellos.* Washington, DC: Washington Office on Latin America, 2006.

Perla, Hector. "Si Nicaragua Venció, El Salvador Vencerá: Central American Agency in the Creation of the U.S.–Central American Peace and Solidarity Movement." *Latin American Research Review* 43, no. 2 (2008): 136–58.

Policía Nacional de Guatemala. *Centenario de la Policía Nacional 1881–1981.* Guatemala City: Tipografía Nacional, 1981.

————. *Historia de la Policía Nacional 1881–1981.* Guatemala City: Tipografía Nacional, 1981.

Power, Michael. *The Audit Society: Rituals of Verification.* New York: Oxford University Press, 1999.

Procter, Margaret, Michael Cook, and Caroline Williams, eds. *Political Pressure and the Archival Record.* Chicago: Society of American Archivists, 2006.

Procuraduría de los Derechos Humanos. "Informe Archivo Histórico de la Policía Nacional—por el derecho a la verdad." Guatemala City: Procuraduría de los Derechos Humanos, 2 March 2006.

Programa de Seguridad Ciudadana y Prevención de la Violencia. *Informe estadístico de la violencia en Guatemala.* United Nations Development Program. Guatemala City: Magna Terra Editores, 2007.

Proyecto de Recuperación del Archivo Histórico de la Policía Nacional. *El derecho a saber: Informe especial del Archivo Histórico de la Policía Nacional.* Guatemala City: Procuraduría de los Derechos Humanos, 2009.

———. "Informe de Avances—Agosto 2007." Guatemala City: Procuraduría de los Derechos Humanos, August 2007.

———. "Informe de Avances—Diciembre 2006." Guatemala City: Procuraduría de los Derechos Humanos, December 2006.

———. "Informe de Avances—Marzo 2008." Guatemala City: Procuraduría de los Derechos Humanos, March 2008.

———. "Informe General de Avances al 31 de diciembre de 2007." Guatemala City: Procuraduría de los Derechos Humanos, January 2008.

———. "Se inicia nueva fase en el proyecto 'Archivo Histórico de la Policía Nacional.'" Guatemala City, July 2009. Available at http://www.arxivers.org/docs/noticiasarchivo Guatemala8jul09_b.pdf.

Proyecto Interdiocesano de Recuperación de la Memoria Histórica (REMHI). *Guatemala: Nunca Más!* Guatemala City: Oficina de Derechos Humanos del Arzobispado de Guatemala, 1998.

Rabe, Stephen. *The Most Dangerous Area in the World: John F. Kennedy Confronts Communist Revolution in Latin America.* Chapel Hill: University of North Carolina Press, 1999.

Rama, Angel. *La ciudad letrada.* Hanover, NH: Ediciones del Norte, 2002.

Ramírez, Chiqui. *La guerra de los 36 años: Vista con ojos de mujer de izquierda.* Guatemala City: Editorial Oscar de León Palacios, 2001.

Randall, Margaret, trans. *Let's Go!* Willimantic, CT: Curbstone Press, 1971.

Rey Rosa, Rodrigo. *El material humano.* Barcelona: Editorial Anagrama, 2009.

Richards, Thomas. *The Imperial Archive: Knowledge and the Fantasy of Empire.* New York: Verso, 1996.

Ridener, John. *From Polders to Postmodernism: A Concise History of Archival Theory.* Duluth, MN: Litwin Books, 2008.

Riles, Annelise, ed. *Documents: Artifacts of Modern Knowledge.* Ann Arbor: University of Michigan Press, 2006.

Ríos Montt, José Efraín. *Mensajes del Presidente de la República, General José Efraín Ríos Montt.* Guatemala City: Tipografía Nacional, 1982.

Robertson, Craig. "Mechanisms of Exclusion: Historicizing the Archive and the Passport." In *Archive Stories: Facts, Fictions, and the Writing of History*, edited by Antoinette Burton. 68–86. Durham, NC: Duke University Press, 2005.

Robinson, William I. *Promoting Polyarchy: Globalization, US Intervention, and Hegemony.* London: Cambridge University Press, 1996.

Robles Montoya, Jaime. *El poder oculto: Serie de ensayos sobre los poderes ocultos.* Guatemala: Fundación Myrna Mack, 2002.

Röhl, Bettina. "Icon of the Left." In *Everybody Talks about the Weather . . . We Don't: The Writings of Ulrike Meinhof*, edited by Karin Bauer. New York: Seven Stories Press, 2008.

Roht-Arriaza, Naomi. "Making the State Do Justice: Transnational Prosecutions and International Support for Criminal Investigations in Post-conflict Guatemala." *Chicago Journal of International Law* 9, no. 1 (2008): 79–106.

———. *The Pinochet Effect: Transnational Justice in the Age of Human Rights*. Philadelphia: University of Pennsylvania Press, 2005.

Roht-Arriaza, Naomi, and Almudena Bernabeu. "The Guatemalan Genocide Case in Spain." *UC Berkeley Review of Latin American Studies* (Fall 2008): 1–4.

Rosada Granados, Hector. *El lado oculto de las negociaciones de paz: Transición de la guerra a la paz en Guatemala*. Guatemala City: Fundación Friedrich Ebert, 1998.

———. *Soldados en el poder: Proyecto militar en Guatemala 1944–1980*. San José, Costa Rica: FUNPADEM, 1999.

Rzeplinski, Andrzej. "Habeas Data: Documentary Evidence of Repressive Regimes." Undated manuscript. Copy in author's files.

Sabino, Carlos. *Guatemala, la historia silenciada, 1944–1989*. Vol. 1, *Revolución y liberación*. Guatemala City: Fondo de Cultura Económica, 2007.

Sáenz de Tejada, Ricardo. *Revolucionarios en tiempos de paz: Rompimientos y recomposición en las izquierdas de Guatemala y El Salvador*. Guatemala City: Editorial de Ciencias Sociales, 2007.

Sánchez del Valle, Rosa, ed., *Por el delito de pensar*. Guatemala City: Magna Terra Editores, 1999.

Sandoval, Miguel Angel. *Los días de la resistencia*. Guatemala City: Editorial Oscar de León Palacios, 1998.

Sandoval, Miguel Angel, and Augusta Ríos. *La izquierda y la transición democrática: Notas para un debate necesario*. Guatemala City: Editorial Oscar de León Palacios, 1997.

Saramago, José. *All the Names*. Translated by Margaret Jull Costa. Orlando, FL: Harcourt, 1999.

Saxon, Dan. *To Save Her Life: Disappearance, Deliverance, and the United States in Guatemala*. Berkeley: University of California Press, 2007.

Scarry, Elaine. *The Body in Pain: The Making and Unmaking of the World*. New York: Oxford University Press, 1987.

Schafer, R. Murray. *The Soundscape: Our Sonic Environment and the Tuning of the World*. Destiny Books, 1993.

Schirmer, Jennifer. *The Guatemalan Military Project: A Violence Called Democracy*. Philadelphia: University of Pennsylvania Press, 1999.

———. "The Guatemalan Politico-Military Project: Legacies for a Violent Peace?" *Latin American Perspectives* 26, no. 2 (1999): 92–107.

Schlant, Ernestine. *The Language of Silence: West German Literature and the Holocaust*. New York: Routledge, 1999.

Scott, James C. *Seeing Like a State: How Certain Schemes to Improve the Human Condition Have Failed*. New Haven, CT: Yale University Press, 1998.

Sellers-García, Sylvia Marina. "Distant Guatemala: Reading Documents from the Periphery." PhD diss., University of California at Berkeley, 2009.

Shetty, Sandhya, and Elizabeth Jane Bellamy. "Postcolonialism's Archive Fever." *Diacritics* 30, no. 1 (2000): 25–48.

Sichar Moreno, Gonzalo. *Guatemala: Contrainsurgencia o contra el pueblo?* Madrid: H & H, 1998.

Sieder, Rachel. *Guatemala after the Peace Accords*. London: Institute of Latin American Studies, 1999.

———, ed. *Impunity in Latin America*. London: Institute of Latin American Studies, 1995.

Sieder, Rachel, Megan Thomas, George Vickers, and Jack Spence. *Who Governs: Guatemala Five Years after the Peace Accords*. Boston: Hemisphere Initiatives, 2002.

Siekmeier, James. *Aid, Nationalism, and Inter-American Relations: Guatemala, Bolivia, and the United States 1945–1961*. Lewiston, NY: Edwin Mellen Press, 1999.

Sikkink, Kathryn. *The Justice Cascade: How Human Rights Prosecutions Are Changing World Politics*. New York: Norton, 2011.

Simon, Jean-Marie. *Eternal Spring, Eternal Tyranny*. New York: Norton, 1988.

Smith, Carol A., ed. *Guatemalan Indians and the State, 1540–1988*. Austin: University of Texas Press, 1992.

Smith, Christian. *Resisting Reagan: The U.S. Central America Peace Movement*. Chicago: University of Chicago Press, 1996.

Spence, Jack, David Dye, Paula Worby, Carmen Rosa de León-Escribano, George Vickers, and Mike Lanchin, eds. *Promise and Reality: Implementation of the Guatemalan Peace Accords*. Cambridge, MA: Hemisphere Initiatives, 1998.

Spieker, Sven. *The Big Archive: Art from Bureaucracy*. Cambridge, MA: MIT Press, 2008.

Stanley, William. "Building New Police Forces in Guatemala and El Salvador: Learning and Counter-Learning." *International Peacekeeping* 6, no. 4 (1999): 113–34.

———. "Business as Usual? Justice and Policing Reform in Postwar Guatemala." In *Constructing Justice and Security after War*, edited by Charles T. Call, 113–55. Washington, DC: United States Institute of Peace Press, 2007.

Stanley, William, and David Holiday. "Broad Participation, Diffuse Responsibility: Peace Implementation in Guatemala." In *Ending Civil Wars: The Implementation of Peace Agreements*, edited by Stephen John Steadman, Donald Rothschild, and Elizabeth M. Cousens, 421–62. New York: Lynne Rienner, 2002.

State Department, Bureau of Democracy, Human Rights, and Labor. *2008 Country Reports on Human Rights Practices: Guatemala*. 25 February 2009. www.state.gov/g/drl/rls/hrrpt/2008/wha/119161.htm.

Steadman, Stephen John, Donald Rothschild, and Elizabeth M. Cousens, eds. *Ending Civil Wars: The Implementation of Peace Agreements*. New York: Lynne Rienner, 2002.

Steedman, Carolyn. *Dust: The Archive and Cultural History*. New Brunswick, NJ: Rutgers University Press, 2002.

Steinberg, Michael K., Carrie Height, Rosemary Mosher, and Mathew Bampton. "Mapping Massacres: GIS and State Terror in Guatemala." *Geoforum* 37, no. 1 (2006): 62–68.

Stern, Steve J. *Battling for Hearts and Minds: Memory Struggles in Pinochet's Chile, 1973–1988*. Durham, NC: Duke University Press, 2006.

———. *Peru's Indian Peoples and the Challenge of Spanish Conquest: Huamanga to 1640*. Madison: University of Wisconsin Press, 1993.

Stoler, Ann Laura. *Along the Archival Grain: Epistemic Anxieties and Colonial Common Sense*. Princeton, NJ: Princeton University Press, 2009.

———. "Colonial Archives and the Arts of Governance." *Archival Science* 2 (2002): 87–109.

Stoll, David. *Rigoberta Menchú and the Story of All Poor Guatemalans*. Boulder, CO: Westview Press, 1999.

Stoltz Chinchilla, Norma. "Marxism, Feminism, and the Struggle for Democracy in Latin America." *Gender and Society* 3 (September 1991): 291–310.

Strathern, Marilyn. *Audit Cultures: Anthropological Studies in Accountability, Ethics, and the Academy*. New York: Routledge Press, 2000.

Streeter, Stephen M. *Managing the Counterrevolution: The United States and Guatemala, 1954–1961*. Athens: Ohio University Press, 2000.

———. "Nation-Building in the Land of Eternal Counterinsurgency: Guatemala and the Contradictions of the Alliance for Progress," *Third World Quarterly* 27, no. 1 (2006): 57–68.

Strobel, Margaret. "Becoming a Historian, Being an Activist, and Thinking Archivally: Documents and Memory as Sources." *Journal of Women's History* 11, no. 1 (1999): 181–92.

Taussig, Michael. *Shamanism, Colonialism, and the Wild Man: A Study in Terror and Healing*. Chicago: University of Chicago Press, 1987.

Taylor, Diana. "You Are Here: The DNA of Performance." *Drama Review* 46, no. 1 (2002): 149–69.

Thompson, E. P. *The Poverty of Theory: Or an Orrery of Errors*. London: Merlin Press, 1978.

Tierney, Nancy Leigh. *Robbed of Humanity: Lives of Guatemalan Street Children*. New York: Pangaea, 1997.

Tomuschat, Christian. "Clarification Commission in Guatemala." *Human Rights Quarterly* 23 no. 2 (2001): 233–58.

Toriello Garrido, Guillermo. *Guatemala: Más de 20 años de traición, 1954–1979*. Guatemala City: Editorial Universitaria, 1979.

Torres, M. Gabriela. "Bloody Deeds/*Hechos Sangrientos*: Reading Guatemala's Record of Political Violence in Cadaver Reports." In *When States Kill: Latin America, the U.S., and Technologies of Terror*, edited by Cecilia Menjívar and Nestor Rodríguez, 143–67. Austin: University of Texas Press, 2005.

———. "The Paper Trails of Counterinsurgency Violence: The Documented Design and Implementation of Political Violence in Guatemala, 1976–1984." PhD diss., York University (Canada), 2004.

Trace, Ciaran B. "What Is Recorded Is Never Simply 'What Happened': Record Keeping in Modern Organizational Culture." *Archival Science* 2 (2002): 137–59.

Trouillot, Michel-Rolph. *Silencing the Past: Power and the Production of History*. Boston: Beacon Press, 1995.

Unidad Revolucionaria Nacional Guatemalteca. *Línea política de los revolucionarios guatemaltecos*. Mexico City: Editorial Nuestro Tiempo, 1988.

United Nations Development Program (UNDP). *El costo económico de la violencia en Guatemala*. Guatemala City: Magna Terra Editores, 2006.

United Nations Development Program and Instituto de Estudios Comparados en Ciencias Penales de Guatemala. *La actuación policial y los derechos humanos en Guatemala*. Guatemala: CromoGráfica, 2000.

United Nations Educational, Scientific, and Cultural Organization. "Memory of the World Program." 1995. www.unesco.org/webworld/en/mow.

United Nations High Commission on Human Rights. *Derechos humanos y aplicación de la ley: Guía para instructores en derechos humanos para la policía*. New York: United Nations, 2004.

United Nations Office of the High Commision for Human Rights. "Report of the High Commissioner for Human Rights on the Situation of Human Rights in Guatemala." ECOSOC E/CN.4/2006/10/Add.1 (1 February 2006): 1–21.

United Nations Commission on the Truth for El Salvador. *De La Locura a La Esperanza: La Guerra De 12 Años En El Salvador: Informe De La Comisión De La Verdad Para El Salvador 1992–1993*. San Salvador: Editorial Arcoiris, 1993.

Van Zyl, Susan. "Psychoanalysis and the Archive: Derrida's *Archive Fever*." In *Refiguring the Archive*, edited by Carolyn Hamilton, Verne Harris, Michèle Pickover, Graeme Reid, Razia Saleh, and Jane Taylor, 39–60. Cape Town: David Philip, 2002.

Walker, Louise E. "Economic Fault Lines and Middle-Class Fears: Tlatelolco, Mexico City, 1985." In *Aftershocks: Earthquakes and Popular Politics in Latin America*, edited by Jurgen Buchenau and Lyman Johnson, 184–221. Albuquerque: University of New Mexico Press, 2009.

Warren, Kay B. *Indigenous Movements and Their Critics: Pan-Mayan Activism in Guatemala*. Princeton, NJ: Princeton University Press, 1998.

———. "Interpreting *La Violencia* in Guatemala: Shapes of Mayan Silence and Resistance." In *The Violence Within: Cultural and Political Opposition in Divided Nations*, edited by Kay B. Warren, 25–56. Boulder, CO: Westview Press, 1993.

Washington Office on Latin America. *Temas y debates en la reforma de la seguridad pública: Una guía para la sociedad civil*. Washington, DC: WOLA, 1998.

Weber, Max. "Bureaucracy." In *Essays in Sociology*, translated and edited by H. H. Gerth and C. Wright Mills, 196–244. New York: Oxford University Press, 1946.

Weld, Kirsten. "Dignifying the Guerrillero, Not the Assassin: Rewriting a History of Criminal Subversion in Postwar Guatemala." *Radical History Review* 113 (2012): 35–54.

———. "Reading the Politics of History in Guatemala's National Police Archives." PhD dissertation, Yale University, 2010.

Wilson, Richard. *Maya Resurgence in Guatemala: Q'eqchi' Experiences*. Norman: University of Oklahoma Press, 1995.

Winks, Robin. *Cloak and Gown: Scholars in the Secret War, 1930–1961*. London: Harvill Press, 1978.

Winn, Peter. *Weavers of Revolution: The Yarur Workers and Chile's Road to Socialism*. New York: Oxford University Press, 1986.

Young, James E. *The Texture of Memory: Holocaust Memorials and Meaning*. New Haven, CT: Yale University Press, 1993.

Zemon Davis, Natalie. *Fiction in the Archives: Pardon Tales and Their Tellers in Sixteenth-Century France*. Stanford, CA: Stanford University Press, 1987.

Zinn, Howard. "Secrecy, Archives, and the Public Interest." Speech reprinted in *Midwestern Archivist* 2, no. 2 (1977): 14–26.

archive wars, 24, 49, 52, 53, 234–35, 248, 264n49; Diario Militar case, 60–65; Free Access law and Peace Archives Directorate, 215–21; GAM campaign, 58–59

Archivists without Borders, 214, 269n29(79)

Arena, Luis (Tiger of the Ixcán), 124

ARENA political party (El Salvador), 119

Arendt, Hannah, 170, 253

Arevalo, Juan José, 102

Argentina, 17, 42, 61, 214, 239–40, 267n48, 283n93

Argueta, Arnolfo, 112

Armas González, Julio César, 106

Army Day annual protest, 16, 205, 206

Arriaga Bosque, Rafael, 108, 275n71

Arzú Irigoyen, Alvaro, 4, 35–36, 62, 65, 148, 166, 263n20

Association for Justice and Reconciliation (AJR), 216

Association of Guatemalan Journalists, 294n11

Authenticity of the Military Logbook in Light of the Historical Documents of the National Police (Peace Archives), 218–19

AVANCSO (Asociación para el Avance de las Ciencias Sociales de Guatemala), 260n39(10)

AVEMILGUA (Association of Military Veterans), 7, 44–45, 243–45

Avenging Jaguar (Jaguar Justiciero), 146

Bachelet, Michelle, 17

Ball, Patrick, 76, 269n29(79)

Bámaca Velásquez, Efraín, 64

Barreno Juárez, Cayetano, 106

Barrientos, Lizbeth, 67, 72, 79–80, 83, 270n33

Barrios, Alberto, 104

Barrios, Justo Rufino, 10

Barrios Celada, Héctor Mario, 4, 62, 64

Barrios Klee, Hugo, 112

Basque Country, 40

Battalion of Death, 130

Bayley, David, 149

Belgium, 147, 285n137

Belize, 294n9

Benetech, 76, 269n21, 269n29(79)

Benjamin, Walter, 19, 83, 258n14

Berger, Oscar, 42, 121

Bickford, Louis, 16, 40, 58, 260n45, 264n50

Biermann, Wolf, 264n45

Bittner, Egon, 149

Blouin, Francis, 185

Bol de la Cruz, Héctor Rafael, 138, 241, 243, 245

Bomberos Voluntarios (Guatemala City), 214

Bravo Soto, Ivan Alfonso, 131

Brazil, 17, 61, 96, 114, 239, 261n63, 267n48

BROE (Special Operations Reaction Brigade), 21, 141, 143, 279n36

Browning, Christopher, 177

Buitre Justiciero (Avenging Vulture) death squad, 113

Caballeros Ramírez, Aníbal Leonel, 125–26

Caballeros Seigné, Julio Enrique, 144, 146–47

Cabrera y Cabrera, Julio César, 131

CACIF (Coordinating Committee of Agricultural, Commercial, Industrial, and Financial Associations), 142, 245

Cacopardo, Ana, 41, 269n29(79)

CADEG (Anti-Communist Council of Guatemala), 106, 108

CALDH (Center for Human Rights Legal Action), 66, 216

Call, Charles, 122

Cambodia, 17–18, 214, 240, 247

Camilo (Project worker), 187, 190, 194, 196, 200–201, 203, 206–8

Casariego, Mario, 105, 108

Castañeda, Mario, 16

Castañeda de León, Oliverio, 130, 170, 200–201, 233, 281n76

Castillo, Otto René, 183–85, 210, 254

Castillo Armas, Carlos, 8, 91, 96–97, 131

Castillo Flores, Leonardo, 104

Castresana, Carlos, 230, 258n18

Catalonia, 40

Catholic Action, 125

Daniel, Hugh, 79
d'Aubuisson, Roberto, 119
Davíd (Project worker), 189, 194
Davis, Nathaniel, 108
Day against Forced Disappearances, 133
Day of the Dead festival (Sumpango
Sacatepéquez), 7–8, 9
Death-Squad Diary. See Diario Militar
(Death-Squad Diary)
Declassified Documents Reference System
(DDRS), 301
Decree-Law 17-68 (1968), 38, 55–56, 215
de la Torre Morel, Enrique, 106
de León Carpio, Ramiro, 60
de Lión, Luis (José Luis de León Díaz),
228, 296n66
Del silencio a la memoria (Project for the
Recovery of the National Police Histor-
ical Archives), 12
Department of Defense (U.S.), 20
derecho a saber, El (Project for the Recov-
ery of the National Police Historical
Archives), 223, 225–32
Derrida, Jacques, 16, 159, 247, 260n44,
261n53
desaparecidos. See forced disappearance
Detective Corps (Cuerpo de Detectives):
forced disappearances, 112, 132–35,
141, 149, 241, 279n30, 281n67; formation, purges, and replacement, 108,
121, 129, 135–36, 280n43; orejas (spies),
128
de Torrebiarte, Adela, 215
DGSN (General Directorate for National
Security), 97
Diario Militar (Death-Squad Diary), 16,
63–65, 64, 132, 141, 242, 268n62
DIC (Department of Criminal Investigations), 121, 144, 146, 148–49
Dien Bien Phu, 95
Digital National Security Archive (DNSA),
301
DINA (National Intelligence Directorate,
Chile), 267n49
DINC (Criminal Investigations Division),
120–21, 149
disappeared. See forced disappearance

DIT (Department of Technical Investigations), 60, 121, 136–41, 143–44,
280n43, 284n125, 285n141
Documentation Center of Cambodia, 17, 214
Dolores (Project worker), 156, 163, 172–74,
205
Dominican Republic, 94, 114
double discourse, 126, 155, 170
Doyle, Kate, 41, 64, 269n29(79)

earthquake (1976), 124–25, 154, 159
economy and economic change: as motivation for Project workers, 184, 186–87,
191, 201, 203, 206–8; and Project,
207–8, 234, 247; trade policy and local
elites, 14, 142, 187, 221; U.S. interests
in, 94–95, 98, 112–13; weakness and
inequality, 5, 134, 240, 250–52, 293n90
Ecuador, 61, 267n48
EGP (Guerrilla Army of the Poor), 8–9,
63, 124–25, 127, 130, 133–34, 280n55,
282n91
Egypt, 18
El Archivo (Archives and Support Services
of the Presidential General Staff),
63–66, 103, 136–37, 144–45. See also
Diario Militar (Death-Squad Diary);
EMP (Presidential Staff); Regional Telecommunications Center (CRIO)
El Bizonte arms warehouse raid, 127
Elich, Christina, 40
El Jute case, 298n11
El Salvador, 119, 122, 214, 239
EMDN (National Defense General Staff),
67, 123
EMP (Presidential Staff): archives, 37, 63,
65–68, 186, 190, 220, 222; and police
violence, 128–29, 182
Engle, Byron, 106, 113
Ericastilla, Anna Carla, 36, 39, 70, 80–82,
263n32
escuadronados, 130
Escuadrón de la Muerte (Death Squad),
130
Espada, Rafael, 223, 228–29
Esperanza (Project worker), 159–60,
163–64, 167, 179, 200, 202

divisions, 172–73, 247, 259n36; exile during, 179–80, 186–88; internal human rights and democracy, 43–44, 143, 217, 247; women in, 198. *See also* Left and progressive forces today

INTA (National Institute for Agrarian Transformation) bombing, 127

Intelligence Directorate (Buenos Aires police), 42

Inter-American Commission on Human Rights, 65, 113

Inter-American Court on Human Rights (IACHR), 20, 239, 242

Inter-American Police Academy (Panama Canal Zone), 102

International Convention on Forced Disappearance, 229

International Day for the Right to the Truth Concerning Gross Human Rights Violations and for the Dignity of Victims (March 24), 239

International Development Agency (Sweden), 40

International Human Rights Law Clinic (UC-Berkeley), 65

International Police Academy (Washington, DC), 102, 111, 114–15, 136

International Railways of Central America, 113

International Standard Archival Authority Record (ISAAR), 269n31

International Standard Archival Description (General) [ISAD(G)], 79

Investigative Squad of Civil Police (Guatemala), 96

Iraq Memory Foundation, 17, 214

Isabel (Project worker), 192–94, 198–200, 203, 207

Israel, 173, 283n93, 285n138

Italy, 285n137

Ixil Triangle counterinsurgency campaigns, 182, 216, 219, 245

Ixtahuacán miners' strike and march (1977), 125

Jacinto (Project worker), 156–57, 161, 168–69, 172, 175, 179, 181, 204

Jaschek, Ingrid, 41

Jelin, Elizabeth, 5, 22, 170

Joinet, Louis, 17

Jonas, Susanne, 148

José Antonio (Project worker), 69, 162, 170–71

Joseph, Gustavo, 10

Juárez Villatoro, Abel, 112

Judicial Police (Judiciales), 99–104, 100, 109, 121, 149

Kaiser, Susana, 290n4

Kaltschmitt, Alfred, 44

Kennedy, John F., 95, 102, 273n35

Kennedy, Robert F., 102

Ketelaar, Eric, 18, 236–37, 262n6, 269n9

KGB archives, 18, 42, 237, 261n68

Khmer Rouge archives, 17–18, 214, 247. *See also* Cambodia

Kobrak, Paul, 130, 138

Konefal, Betsy, 11, 260n39(10)

Kundera, Milan, 237

Kuzmarov, Jeremy, 115, 277n124, 285n148

la isla (the island), 2

La Lechu, 75

La Regional, 100, 136. *See also* Regional Telecommunications Center (CRIO)

La Rue, Frank, 39

Las Jornadas de Marzo y Abril de 1962 (Days of March and April 1962), 101

La Tigrera police compound, 99

Latin American Studies Association, 113

Laugerud García, Kjell, 123–27, 129, 142, 279n17

Laughlin, David, 97

La Verbena mass graves, 249

Left and progressive forces today, 168, 202–8, 221

Leonora (Project worker), 161

Levenson-Estrada, Deborah, 124

Ligorría, Fernando, 60

Lima López, Juan Antonio (El Chino), 112, 129, 134

Linares, Fernando, 217

Lithuania, 42

Lobe, Thomas, 117

Longan, John P., 104, 107, 117, 133

Nairn, Allan, 285n141
narcotrafficking and U.S. counternarcotics aid to Guatemala, 111, 115, 144–45, 149, 285n148
Natareno Salazar, Miguel Angel, 134
National Archives at College Park (NACP), 301
National Archives of Remembrance (Uruguay), 17
National Commission on Historical Memory, 232
National Committee for Defense against Communism, 96–97
National Day of Dignity for the Victims of the Armed Conflict (February 25), 216
National Defense General Staff (EMDN), 67
National Historical Archives (Spain), 42
National Movement for Human Rights, 262n15
National Movement of Pobladores (MONAP), 124
National Police Historical Archives (AHPN), 233, 301. See also Project for the Recovery of the National Police Historical Archives (PRAHPN)
National Security Agency (NSA), 20, 113
National Security Archive (Washington, DC), 21, 41, 64, 66, 220, 238, 261n68, 267n60(63), 301
National Security Council (NSC), 20, 95, 113
Naurocki, Alfred, 103
Nazi activity and archives, 4, 18, 94, 170, 237, 291n8
Negreros, Liliana, 281n67
Nelson, Diane, 225, 260n39(10)
neoliberalism, 173, 187, 193, 251, 260n41
Netherlands, 40
network analysis, 283n93
New Detective Corps, 135. See also Detective Corps (Cuerpo de Detectives)
Nicaragua, 94, 130–31, 179, 186–87, 294n9
NOA (New Anti-Communist Organization), 106, 108
No Nos Tientes (USAC), 136
Nowak, Manfred, 269n29(79)

Oberholzer, Erwin, 265n68
October Revolution (1944), 103, 130. See also Revolutionary Spring (1944–1954)
ODHAG (Human Rights Office of the Archdiocese of Guatemala), 16, 66
Office of the Coordinator of Inter-American Affairs (OCIA), 94
Oglesby, Elizabeth, 260n39(10)
Ojo por Ojo death squad, 111–12
Operación Limpieza, 104–5, 275n71
OPS (Office of Public Safety), 20, 95, 101–18, 277n124. See also USAID (U.S. Agency for International Development)
orejas (spies), 128–29, 280n43
Orentlicher, Diane, 17
Organization of American States, 239
Organization Zero death squad, 130
original order (archival), 67, 70–71, 79, 81–83
ORPA (Revolutionary Organization of People in Arms), 8–9, 63–64
Oslo Accord (1994), 61. See also Peace Accords (1996)
Otto René Castillo Front (EGP), 127, 134

PACS (Civil Self-Defense Patrols), 145
Palma, Gustavo, 265n10
Panamá and Panama Canal Zone, 102, 294n9
Pan Am airline, 113
Panel Blanca (White Van) murders, 146
Panzós peasant massacre (1978), 127
paper cadavers, 2–3, 26, 168, 209, 256
Paraguay, 4, 17, 42, 61, 214, 267n48
Pardo, José Joaquín, 54
Parlacen (Central American Parliament) murders, 119–21, 146, 149
Payeras, Mario, 127
Paz Vergara, Maria, 269n29(79)
Paz y Paz, Claudia, 241, 244
PDH (Human Rights Ombudsman's Office), 203, 220, 263n32; EMP archives' recovery, 66–67; memory museum and rose garden, 224, 226; and Project, 2, 29, 32–41, 43, 67–69, 209, 222–32; Special Cases Unit, 33; Unified Register of Forced Disappearances, 186